Readings in
STRATEGIC
MANAGEMENT

Readings in STRATEGIC MANAGEMENT

Arthur A. Thompson, Jr.
A. J. Strickland III
both of The University of Alabama
and
William E. Fulmer
*Colgate Darden Graduate School of
Business Administration
University of Virginia*

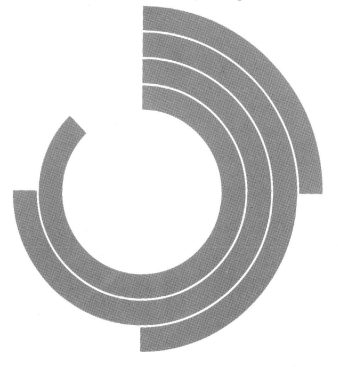

1987   Second Edition

BUSINESS PUBLICATIONS, INC.
Plano, Texas   75075

ISBN 0-256-03718-3

Library of Congress Catalog Card No. 86–72245

Printed in the United States of America

1 2 3 4 5 6 7 8 9 0 ML 4 3 2 1 0 9 8 7

Preface

During the past decade or so, business policy has expanded its status from being just an integrative course in the business curriculum to being a full-fledged discipline with a distinctive literature of its own. A large knowledge base is rapidly building on the concept of strategy, the tasks and process of strategy formulation and implementation, and all the ramifications of aligning the operations and culture of the enterprise to fit the requirements of strategy.

Important, insightful techniques for examining a company's competitive position, business strengths, industry attractiveness, and the makeup of multibusiness corporate portfolios have come to the fore. Formal strategy evaluations and annual strategy reviews are growing in use, having already risen to become a standard management practice in most large companies. There is heightened managerial application of such strategic concepts as driving forces, strategic groups, competitor analysis, key success factors, distinctive competence, strategic fit, switching costs, first-mover advantages, and strategic business units. Issues pertaining to strategy formulation and strategy implementation enjoy high priority on managerial action agendas. The whole strategic management cycle—from defining the business *to* strategy formulation *to* implementation and execution *to* evaluation of results *to* reformulation and fine-tuning of the game plan—is being intensively scrutinized by practitioners, consultants, and business school academics.

Although many instructors rely on text treatments and case analysis to teach their courses in strategic management, there is reason to supplement the "standard approach" with articles in the field of strategic management. For those instructors who see the value of incorporating samples of the strategic management literature into their course, *Readings in Strategic Management* attempts to provide a variety of current articles that reflect the thinking and research of academics and the state of the art as it is being practiced by consultants and managers.

This book contains 31 articles from a variety of up-to-date sources. Only one was published prior to 1980 and it appeared in 1979. Over half of the readings have been published in the last three years. More importantly, all are eminently readable and well matched to the level of most business policy/strategy texts.

The readings themselves are primarily of two types. One type, consisting of standard-length articles reprinted from first-tier journals, adds in-depth treatment to important topic areas covered in most business policy/strategy texts, thereby probing further into the details of particular techniques and exposing students to leading-edge research findings and conclusions. The second type includes shorter articles, drawn from practitioners' sources, that emphasize how strategic management concepts and tools relate directly to actual practice. In tandem, the two types of readings provide an effective and efficient vehicle for reinforcing and expanding text-case treatments and for giving students a flavor of both current literature and state-of-the-art strategic management applications.

Organization of the Readings

This book is divided into four sections. Each section is organized around one of the major building blocks of strategy management. At the beginning of each section is a brief overview of the topics covered and of how each article fits into the scheme and structure of strategy management as well as an introductory statement about the content of each article. Each of the two types of articles mentioned earlier are included in each section.

Section 1 addresses the role of the general manager as chief architect and chief implementer of strategy. The lead article emphasizes that "making it happen" is the real strategic challenge. James Brian Quinn then reports on his research findings on what the strategy formulation process is like in large corporations and how executives manage the process. Kenichi Ohmae's article gives a brief description of how Japanese managers manage. The next two articles, one by an academic and one by a consultant, report on some of the current criticisms of strategic planning. The last article is by the CEO of R. J. Reynolds Industries, Inc. (now RJR Nabisco) and reports on how strategic planning is used at his company.

Articles in Section 2 concern the formulation and analysis of business level strategy. Ian H. Wilson, the executive in charge of GE's highly regarded work in strategic planning, provides a very readable description of GE's pioneering efforts in environmental scanning and the role it plays in strategy formulation. The next six articles address strategies and their application to specific situations. First, there is Peter F. Drucker's discussion of entrepreneurial strategies. Pankaj Ghemawat discusses using the experience curve to pursue a low-cost strategy. Peter Wright examines three generic strategies—least-cost, differentation, and niche. Kevin P. Coyne explains the concept of "sustainable competitive advantage." Barrie G. James discusses the advantages of deterrence as a strategic thrust, and James Leontiades examines market share considerations in an international setting. The final article in this section is George S. Day's "Tough Questions for Developing Strategies."

Section 3 presents seven articles that address some of the issues facing strategic planners in diversified companies. Setting the stage for this section is a candid description of how Norton Company's strategic planning process works, written by Norton's president. This is followed by Richard A. Bettis and William K. Hall's article on the shortcomings of portfolio planning techniques. The next three articles deal with the timely subject of aquisitions.

Robert J. Terry offers "Ten Suggestions for Acquisition Success." David R. Willensky discusses "How to Execute an Acquisition," and Lionel L. Fray, David H. Gaylin, and James W. Down address "Successful Acquisition Planning." The last two articles in this section are by prominent names in the field of strategic management—William K. Hall and Ian C. MacMillan. In the first article, the strategies for surviving in a hostile environment are discussed. MacMillan and his coauthor Robin George discuss the challenge of corporate venturing as a strategic option.

The final section takes an in-depth look at the problems and tasks of strategy implementation. There are two articles on designing organizations to aid strategy implementation, one by Ian C. MacMillan and Patricia E. Jones and one by Thomas J. Peters. Also, there are articles on linking the reward structure to strategic performance, the McKinsey 7-S framework, and the attention that must be paid to corporate culture. These are followed by applications articles on the corporate culture at IBM, the introduction of a competitive-driven culture at AT&T, and the efforts to preserve the entrepreneurial culture at 3M. Next is a presentation by Barry Z. Posner and Warren H. Schmidt on their latest research findings concerning the values of American managers. The final article, by Ram Charan, gives an overview of the whole strategic management process and points to ways of avoiding some of the pitfalls of strategy review and strategic planning.

Acknowledgments

We wish to thank the various publishers and authors of the articles contained in this book. In addition, we wish to thank the staff of the library of the Colgate Darden Graduate School of Business for their assistance. Your comments regarding coverage and content will be most welcome. Please write us at Colgate Darden Graduate School of Business Administration, Box 6550, University of Virginia, Charlottesville, VA 22906 or PO Box J, Department of Management and Marketing, University of Alabama, University, AL 35486.

Arthur A. Thompson, Jr.
A. J. Strickland III
William E. Fulmer

Contents

1 The general manager and strategy

This section addresses the role of the general manager as chief architect and chief implementer of strategy. The lead article, by Robert D. Paulson of McKinsey & Co., emphasizes that "making it happen" is the real strategic challenge. James Brian Quinn then reports on his research findings on what the strategy formulation process is like in large corporations and how executives manage the process. Kenichi Ohmae's article gives a brief description of how Japanese managers manage. The next two articles, one by an academic and one by a consultant, report on some of the current criticisms of strategic planning. The last article is by the CEO of R. J. Reynolds (now RJR Nabisco) and reports on how strategic planning is used at his company.

What this article is about: Leadership is an essential factor when a major change in corporate strategy is planned. As a role model for managers, the CEO should be dynamic, open to suggestions, innovative, and expert in the fine art of delegating. This article discusses the whys and hows of the general manager's personal role in leading the task of strategy implementation.

1-1 The chief executive as change agent*

Robert D. Paulson

Robert D. Paulson is a director and manager of the Los Angeles office of McKinsey & Co.

"Weak leadership can wreck the soundest strategy; forceful execution of even a poor plan can often bring victory." So wrote the Chinese general and philosopher Sun Zi in 514 B.C. Today, 25 centuries later, that axiom still holds in business.

Much has been written recently about the need for effective business strategies. A new phase, "strategic management," has even been coined to describe the stage of management sophistication in which the principal role of line executives is to develop and implement effective strategies. Yet very few large companies have reached this level of sophistication.

New strategies inherently involve significant change for an organization. Productive change on a large scale is one of the most arduous and demanding assignments faced by any chief executive. The CEO's chances of leading a major change successfully are much better if he understands how to exploit the forces for change that are latent in his organization. Also, the CEO must determine precisely what role he should play and how to design a specific plan of action.

Assume that a company has developed a powerful new strategy, based on creative insights drawn from a thorough knowledge of its industry. Before this strategy can be converted into effective action, a number of things must happen. First and foremost, the CEO must be an active leader. But that is not

* Reprinted by permission of the publisher from *Management Review*, February 1982 © 1982 by AMACOM, a division of American Management Associations. All rights reserved.

enough. Constructive corporate staff work, a compatible organizational structure, appropriate management processes, and a supportive corporate environment will all be required to facilitate the needed change.

Chief Executive Leadership

There seems to be universal agreement among strategic planners that the key to strategic change is the chief executive. At a recent planning conference, a corporate planner complained that his CEO did not actively support the planning effort and asked the group what he should do. The candid and immediate advice was to find another job in a company with a CEO who wanted to make things happen.

Chief executives can inadvertently discourage strategic change in many ways. Some of the more dangerous of these traps are:

Seeking False Uniformity   It is unproductive for the CEO of a diversified company to impose artificial uniformity on business-unit goals, organization structure, management activities, rewards, and strategies. This ignores the essential differences among businesses, the importance of clear priorities, and the need to tailor approaches to specific competitive situations.

Trying to Eliminate Risk   In an uncertain world, risk cannot be eliminated, but it can be anticipated and effectively managed. Unfortunately, many chief executives stifle new initiatives by creating the impression that they prefer to avoid risk. This encourages people to assume the role of auditors and fault-finders rather than change catalysts.

Trusting Tradition   Faced with fundamental changes in his major markets, a CEO cannot safely assume that his own line experience still applies. Nor can the chief executive safely neglect to question the validity of the hidden assumptions that underlie the strategic plans he is asked to approve.

Dominating Discussions   As his organization grows in size and diversity, the chief executive is forced to delegate authority. As he does so, his firsthand contact and "feel" for the business fades, and he must largely depend on subordinates for vital information. If he is to maintain open communications with them, he must learn to be comfortable discussing uncertain issues and to encourage executives to pass on the bad news as well as the good.

Delegating Strategy   The CEO must not delude himself that the task of developing strategies can be delegated to his staff. It is true that managers can develop strategies for their individual businesses, but the chief executive still needs to provide a clear and cohesive corporate strategy or vision for the whole organization. While his staff can supply analysis and support, the CEO himself must be intimately involved in developing his overall corporate strategy. Otherwise, he becomes little more than a chief operating officer, leaving the company to face the future on the basis of the collective (and potentially conflicting) strategies of the various business units.

Just as there are dangerous traps for the chief executive, there are also powerful levers that he or she can use to bring about strategic change. First, he should realize that what the organization sees him *do* will carry far more conviction than what it hears him *say*. To awaken and redirect his organization, the CEO has many powerful signals at his disposal. They include guiding the activities of his staff, controlling the allocation of his time, defining a specific vision for the future of the company, and constantly reinforcing this theme in discussions, explanations, and public statements.

Staff Roles

The activities of the corporate and group staffs have a major impact on the organization and its attitude toward strategic change.

A staff whose perceived role is to prevent mistakes and point out short-comings can be a significant deterrent to real strategic management. One long-suffering division president dubbed the headquarters staff in his corporation "the seagulls": they flew in in the morning, he said, strutted around pecking at things, and flew away before sundown, leaving behind a small, distinctive, and unpleasant calling card. A much more positive, productive, and satisfying role for the corporate staff is to contribute substantively to the development of effective business-unit and corporate strategies, serving as direct support to both corporate and business-unit managers in areas of potential need, and focusing on important specific business issues rather than the routine operational matters. In some cases, staffs can serve as "centers of excellence," which contain the corporation's best thinkers on specialized issues of common concern.

Meeting behavior is an important indication of staff roles. Ceremonious, tightly controlled meetings resembling labor-management negotiations are a sure sign of unhealthy staff-line relationships. In some companies, staffs frankly regard it as their role to "make snowballs" for the boss to throw at proposals. Lively, action-oriented meetings, with discussion focused on a joint search for "unshakable facts," indicate that the staff is making a useful contribution.

Clear direction from the chief executive, rotation between line and staff duties, formal training, and clear agreement on the specific roles of the staff can all contribute to a constructive corporate staff environment.

Strategically Focused Organization

The important link between organization and strategy has long been recognized. Some authorities argue that organization should follow strategy; others, that strategy is inevitably shaped by organizational characteristics and boundaries. For the practical manager, however, the point is that they must be compatible. For example, there is often a strategic advantage in grouping similar businesses. Not only can shared resources frequently be better exploited, but line executives and staffs can be given a much broader field to search for strategic options.

Equally often, however, organizational constraints have discouraged or defeated strategic change. Organizations built on personalities or tradition tend to produce strategies that are parochial or extrapolations of the past. Frequently, organizational change is essential in the diversified company seeking to realize the potential synergies presented by new market or technological opportunities.

Tailored Management Processes

Line managers tend to take their cues from the way the company sets business objectives, monitors performance, and evaluates and rewards individuals. Failure by the CEO to take into account the motivational effects of these practical signals is likely to make down-the-line managers excessively short-term oriented and cautious in their relations with corporate management.

In setting objectives, the business-unit goals, required resources, and measurement standards should be openly negotiated between corporate management and the business-unit heads, so that business plans become, in effect, contracts between corporate and business-unit management. If top corporate management changes the business unit's performance targets, it must also be willing to revise the resources that will be provided. Likewise, both parties should continue to be concerned about whether the "contract" has been fulfilled.

In many companies, measurement and control systems put a premium on short-term financial performance, thus encouraging what many observers see as the unconscious "harvesting" of U.S. businesses. Equal attention should be given to the achievement of such nonfinancial business objectives as market-share growth, new product development, product quality and customer satisfaction. Measurement and control systems should measure progress in developing the most important competitive skills, and they should be tailored to fit the business plans and the natural time cycle of the business.

The basis of management evaluation also provides an important signal for strategic change. Middle-level managers in some companies feel that "corporate" evaluates them on their ability to exceed their forecasts, to mask any sign of competitive weakness, and to avoid risks. This naturally fosters a short-term orientation and an unwillingness to take initiatives. It also tends to result in unrealistically conservative financial plans.

Incentives can be a powerful lever for strategic change. A survey of more than 50 major corporations disclosed that inappropriate incentives are regarded as the most common weakness in the entire management system. Natural reluctance to engage in subjective evaluations or explain unpleasant news leads chief executives to rely on short-term-oriented, mathematically based incentives, which in turn lead to a standardized and shortsighted approach to strategy development. Some of the most effective incentive systems, designed around the concept of multiyear planning to achieve both financial and business objectives, clearly allow for differences among business units and their respective managers and different performance periods. Thus, incentives for the aggressive manager of a high-growth business should encourage building for the long term, while the manager of a mature or declining business should be rewarded primarily for maximizing and sustaining near-term performance.

Finally, the incentive system must be well understood by the recipients. Too many chief executives wrongly believe that "our people know where they stand." Unless recipients clearly understand how their individual rewards have been calculated, they will tend to focus on well-known, easily calculable financial criteria (that is, making budget).

Supportive Corporate Values

In virtually every large organization, there is a shared point of view about "who we are, where we are going, and how we will get there." These values, beliefs, or corporate philosophies constitute a set of subtle but powerful levers for strategic change.

Texas Instruments is one of many possible examples of an organization strongly shaped by a set of clearly articulated shared values. In the words of president Fred Bucy: "The image we want is of a high-technology innovator—it's the key to our strategy." In support of this overriding objective, reports *Business Week* (September 18, 1979), "TI stresses a strong spirit of belonging, strong work ethic, competitive zeal, company loyalty, and rational decision making." Working in teams, people are motivated by peer pressure and peer recognition. And top management, to make it clear that ideas are wanted from all TI employees, systematically encourages innovative thinking in a variety of ways.

Corporate values like these, which encourage risk taking, cooperation, substantive analysis, and competitive spirit, enhance the capacity and the readiness of an organization to undergo strategic change. Our research suggests that these shared values are an important factor distinguishing excellent companies from the also-rans.

In total, there are many ways to help an organization accept and successfully carry out strategic change. The challenge for chief executives and planners is to use these levers to bring about a coordinated and effective change program.

Achieving Strategic Change

In any large organization, new goals or a new strategy to achieve existing goals will create anxiety and tension. Managers will be expected to learn new skills, and individual businesses or staffs will gain or lose relative power. Familiar habits are challenged, and the uncertainty of the external world is highlighted.

Organizing and controlling a program of strategic change is a difficult task. However, a study of several successful programs reveals a number of effective basic ways to initiate and guide needed change.

Since early successes are critical to the continued effectiveness of a long-term change program, it is well to begin in areas that offer a high probability of success and relatively fast results. In this way, senior management can create positive reinforcement for the organization and build overall confidence.

Change should be seen as a gradual process. There are few examples of organizations gaining a new leader and immediately undergoing a successful strategic change. Unless there is a real threat to corporate survival, such upheavals should be avoided.

In the process of change, it is very useful to create "heroes" within the organization. An effective chief executive will often single out one or more promising line executives, provide encouragement and support, and highlight how effective their new approaches have been. Within this kind of public reinforcement, the organization will recognize a new role model.

A program of strategic change requires both top-down direction and bottom-up support. Senior management can point out the need for change and single out key issues, but the creative analysis, support, and implementation must come from the individual business units. Sometimes a vital stimulus can be provided by adding new people with a fresh perspective, through either promotion or outside recruitment.

Once a change program is launched, it is important that the chief executive and his staff members continue to probe deep into the organization to judge the effectiveness of the program and spot needed refinement. Another effective technique is to consciously describe the history of the organization to show that past practices were sensible once but that external conditions now require a new approach. Finally, competitive setbacks or market changes should be exploited to encourage and accelerate change. Under the guidance of senior managers and a staff that is effective at sensing the organization's mood, providing examples, and educating, a program of strategic change can be remarkably effective.

Essential Roles of CEO and CPO

One of the most important elements of an effective program of strategic change is a partnership between the chief executive officer and the chief planning officer (CPO). Their roles are complementary. It is the CEO's task to define the corporate vision and to provide personal leadership; in times of strategic change, the organization must be able to look to him as the "Moses" leading it through the wilderness toward a vision that is clear only to a few. Only if he involves himself in the early stages of strategy development will he be able to shape and redirect plans before they become rigid. Early involvement will also give him opportunities to motivate his subordinates to deepen their knowledge and understanding of their businesses.

For his part, the senior planning executive should support the CEO by continuously scanning the corporation and its environment with a view to generating or soliciting new options that can be evaluated and tested. To conserve the chief executive's time and to assure that it is applied to the areas of greatest strategic leverage, the chief planner must be an effective counselor to the CEO, advising him where and how to influence the organization and helping to shape the attitudes and practices of the organization. He has other, equally important roles: monitoring performance against plan and providing direct support to the various business units and the other staffs as they address strategic issues. In a sense, his staff serves as a resource pool for the entire corporation.

Although pace and effectiveness of strategic change cannot be judged in quantitative terms, there are useful criteria by which it may be assessed. Some of the more important hallmarks of progress include the following seven factors:

1. Strategies are principally developed by line managers with direct, constructive support by the staff.
2. Real strategic alternatives are openly discussed at all levels within the corporation.

3. Corporate priorities are relatively clear to senior management but permit flexible response to new opportunities and threats.
4. Corporate resources are allocated based on these priorities and in view of future potential as well as historical performance.
5. The strategic roles of business units are clearly differentiated; so are the performance measures applied to their managers.
6. Realistic responses to likely future events are worked out well in advance.
7. The corporate staff adds real value to the consideration of strategic issues and receives cooperation from most of the divisions.

A coordinated program of change in pursuit of a sound and relevant strategy, under the active direction of the chief executive and the chief planner, can lead to significant progress. While this may only begin a long-term program, it should yield benefits far out of proportion to the time and effort invested.

Effective strategic management will be an essential competitive skill in the 1980s. With limited resources to beat aggressive competitors in shrinking world markets, chief executives will need more effective strategies. Many new planning tools are being developed to encourage more creative and effective strategies; but to achieve the benefits they make possible, chief executives will still have to "make it happen."

What this article is about: Top managers in large organizations develop their major strategies through processes that formal approaches to planning inadequately explain. The dominant patterns in the successful management of strategic change in large organizations are incremental and evolutionary.

1–2 Managing strategic change*

James Brian Quinn

James Brian Quinn is the William and Josephine Buchanan Professor of Management at the Amos Tuck School of Business Administration, Dartmouth College.

Just as bad money has always driven out good, so the talented general manager—the person who makes a company go—is being overwhelmed by a flood of so-called professionals, textbook executives more interested in the form of management than the content, more concerned about defining and categorizing and quantifying the job, than in getting it done. . . . They have created false expectations and wasted untold man-hours by making a religion of formal long-range planning.[1]

H. E. Wrapp, New York Times

Two previous articles have tried to demonstrate why executives managing strategic change in large organizations should not—and do not—follow highly formalized textbook approaches in long-range planning, goal generation, and strategy formulation.[2] Instead, they artfully blend formal analysis, behavioral techniques, and power politics to bring about cohesive, step-by-step movement toward ends which initially are broadly conceived, but which

* Reprinted from "Managing Strategic Change," by James Brian Quinn, *Sloan Management Review 21,* no. 4, pp. 3–20, by permission of the publisher. Copyright © 1980 by the Sloan Management Review Association. All rights reserved.

[1] See H. E. Wrapp, "A Plague of Professional Managers," *New York Times,* April 8, 1979.

[2] This is the third in a series of articles based upon my study on 10 major corporations' processes for achieving significant strategic change. The other two articles in the series are: J. B. Quinn, "Strategic Goals: Processs and Politics," *Sloan Management Review,* Fall 1977, pp. 21–37; and J. B. Quinn, "Strategic Change: 'Logical Incrementalism'," *Sloan Management Review,* Fall 1978, pp. 7–21. The whole study was published as a book entitled *Strategies for Change: Logical Incrementalism* (Homewood, Ill.: Dow Jones-Irwin. 1981). All findings purposely deal only with strategic changes in large organizations.

are then constantly refined and reshaped as new information appears.[3] Their integrating methodology can best be described as "logical incrementalism."

But is this truly a process in itself, capable of being managed? Or does it simply amount to applied intuition? Are there some conceptual structures, principles, or paradigms that are generally useful? Wrapp, Normann, Braybrooke, Lindblom, and Bennis have provided some macrostructures incorporating many important elements they have observed in strategic change situations.[4] These studies and other contributions cited in this article offer important insights into the management of change in large organizations. But my data suggest that top managers in such enterprises develop their major strategies through processes which neither these studies nor more formal approaches to planning adequately explain. Managers *consciously* and *proactively* move forward *incrementally:*

- To improve the quality of information utilized in corporate strategic decisions.
- To cope with the varying lead times, pacing parameters, and sequencing needs of the "subsystems" through which such decisions tend to be made.
- To deal with the personal resistance and political pressures any important strategic change encounters.
- To build the organizational awareness, understanding, and psychological commitment needed for effective implementation.
- To decrease the uncertainty surrounding such decisions by allowing for interactive learning between the enterprise and its various impinging environments.
- To improve the quality of the strategic decisions themselves by (1) systematically involving those with most specific knowledge, (2) obtaining the participation of those who must carry out the decisions, and (3) avoiding premature momenta or closure which could lead the decision in improper directions.

How does one manage the complex incremental processes which can achieve these goals? The earlier articles structured certain key elements;[5] these will not be repeated here. The following is perhaps the most articulate short statement on how executives proactively manage incrementalism in the development of corporate strategies:

[3] See R. M. Cyert and J. G. March, *A Behavioral Theory of the Firm* (Englewood Cliffs, N.J.: Prentice-Hall, 1963), p. 123. Note this learning-feedback-adaptiveness of goals and feasible alternatives over time as organizational learning.

[4] See H. E. Wrapp, "Good Managers Don't Make Policy Decisions," *Harvard Business Review,* September–October 1967, pp. 91–99; R. Normann, *Management for Growth,* trans. N. Adler (New York: John Wiley & Sons, 1977); D. Braybrooke and C. E. Lindblom, *A Strategy of Decision: Policy Evaluation as a Social Process* (New York: Free Press, 1963); C. E. Lindblom, *The Policy-Making Process* (Englewood Cliffs, N.J.: Prentice-Hall, 1968); and W. G. Bennis, *Changing Organizations: Essays on the Development and Evolution of Human Organizations* (New York: McGraw-Hill, 1966).

[5] See, respectively, Quinn, "Strategic Goals," and Quinn, "Strategic Change."

Typically you start with general concerns, vaguely felt. Next you roll an issue around in your mind till you think you have a conclusion that makes sense for the company. You then go out and sort of post the idea without being too wedded to its details. You then start hearing the arguments pro and con, and some very good refinements of the idea usually emerge. Then you pull the idea in and put some resources together to study it so it can be put forward as more of a formal presentation. You wait for "stimuli occurrences" or "crises," and launch pieces of the idea to help in these situations. But they lead toward your ultimate aim. You know where you want to get. You'd like to get there in six months. But it may take three years, or you may not get there. And when you do get there, you don't know whether it was originally your own idea—or somebody else had reached the same conclusion before you and just got you on board for it. You never know. The president would follow the same basic process, but he could drive it much faster than an executive lower in the organization.[6]

Because of differences in organizational form, management style, or the content of individual decisions, no single paradigm can hold for all strategic decisions.[7] However, very complex strategic decisions in my sample of large organizations tended to evoke certain kinds of broad process steps. These are briefly outlined below. While these process steps occur generally in the order presented, stages are by no means orderly or discrete. Executives do consciously manage individual steps proactively, but it is doubtful that any one person guides a major strategic change sequentially through all the steps. Developing most strategies requires numerous loops back to earlier stages as unexpected issues or new data dictate. Or decision times can become compressed and require short-circuiting leaps forward as crises occur.[8] Nevertheless, certain patterns are clearly dominant in the successful management of strategic change in large organizations.

Creating Awareness and Commitment—Incrementally

Although many of the sample companies had elaborate formal environmental scanning procedures, most major strategic issues first emerged in vague or undefined terms, such as "organizational overlap," "product proliferation," "excessive exposure in one market," or "lack of focus and motivation."[9] Some appeared as "inconsistencies" in internal action patterns or "anomalies" between the enterprise's current posture and some

---

[6] See J. B. Quinn, *Xerox Corporation (B)* (copyrighted case, Amos Tuck School of Business Administration, Dartmouth College, Hanover, New Hampshire, 1979).

[7] See O. G. Brim, D. Class, et al., *Personality and Decision Processes: Studies in the Social Psychology of Thinking* (Stanford, Calif.: Stanford University Press, 1962).

[8] Crises did occur at some stage in almost all the strategies investigated. However, the study was concerned with the attempt to manage strategic change in an ordinary way. While executives had to deal with precipitating events in this process, crisis management was not—and should not be—the focus of effective strategic management.

[9] For some formal approaches and philosophies for environmental scanning, see W. D. Guth, "Formulating Organizational Objectives and Strategy: A Systematic Approach," *Journal of Business Policy,* Autumn 1971, pp. 24–31; and F. J. Aguilar, *Scanning the Business Environment* (New York: Macmillan, 1967). For confirmation of the early vagueness and ambiguity in problem form and identification, see H. Mintzberg, D. Raisinghani, and A. Theoret, "The Structure of 'Unstructured' Decision Processes," *Administrative Science Quarterly,* June 1976, pp. 246–75.

perception of its future environment.[10] Early signals may come from anywhere and may be difficult to distinguish from the background "noise" or ordinary communications. Crises, of course, announce themselves with strident urgency in operations control systems. But, if organizations wait until signals reach amplitudes high enough to be sensed by formal measurement systems, smooth, efficient transitions may be impossible.[11]

Need Sensing: Leading the Formal Information System

Effective change managers actively develop informal networks to get objective information—from other staff and line executives, workers, customers, board members, suppliers, politicians, technologists, educators, outside professionals, government groups, and so on—to sense possible needs for change. They purposely use these networks to short-circuit all the careful screens[12] their organizations build up to "tell the top only what it wants to hear." For example:

Peter McColough, chairman and CEO of Xerox, was active in many high-level political and charitable activities—from treasurer of the Democratic National Committee to chairman of the Urban League. In addition, he said, "I've tried to decentralize decision making. If something bothers me, I don't rely on reports or what other executives may want to tell me. I'll go down very deep into the organization, to certain issues and people, so I'll have a feeling for what they think." He refused to let his life be run by letters and memos. "Because I came up by that route, I know what a salesman can say. I also know that before I see [memos] they go through 15 hands, and I know what that can do to them."[13]

To avoid undercutting intermediate managers, such bypassing has to be limited to information gathering, with no implication that orders or approvals are given to lower levels. Properly handled, this practice actually improves formal communications and motivational systems as well. Line managers are less tempted to screen information and lower levels are flattered to be able "to talk about the very top." Since people sift signals about threats and opportunities through perceptual screens defined by their own values, careful executives make sure their sensing networks include people who look at the world very differently than do those in the enterprise's dominating culture. Effective executives consciously seek options and threat signals beyond the status quo. "If I'm not two to three years ahead of my organization, I'm not doing my job" was a common comment of such executives in the sample.

In some cases executives quickly perceive the broad dimensions of needed change. But they still may seek amplifying data, wider executive understand-

---

[10] For a discussion on various types of "misfits" between the organization and its environment as a basis for problem identification, see Normann, *Management for Growth,* p. 19.

[11] For suggestions on why organizations engage in "problem search" patterns, see R. M. Cyert, H. A. Simon, and D. B. Trow, "Observation of a Business Decision," *Journal of Business,* October 1956, pp. 237–48; for the problems of timing in transitions, see L. R. Sayles, *Managerial Behavior: Administration in Complex Organizations* (New York: McGraw-Hill, 1964).

[12] For a classic view of how these screens operate, see C. Argyris, "Double Loop Learning in Organizations," *Harvard Business Review,* September-October 1977, pp. 115–25.

[13] See Quinn, *Xerox Corporation (B).*

ing of issues, or greater organizational support before initiating action. Far from accepting the first satisfactory (satisficing) solution—as some have suggested they do—successful managers seem to consciously generate and consider a broad array of alternatives.[14] Why? They want to stimulate and choose from the most creative solutions offered by the best minds in their organizations. They wish to have colleagues knowledgeable enough about issues to help them think through all the ramifications. They seek data and arguments sufficiently strong to dislodge preconceived ideas or blindly followed past practices. They do not want to be the prime supporters of losing ideas or to have their organizations slavishly adopt "the boss's solution." Nor do they want—through announcing decisions too early—to prematurely threaten existing power centers which could kill any changes aborning.

Even when executives do not have in mind specific solutions to emerging problems, they can still proactively guide actions in intuitively desired directions—by defining what issues staffs should investigate, by selecting principal investigators, and by controlling reporting processes. They can selectively "tap the collective wit" of their organizations, generating more awareness of critical issues and forcing initial thinking down to lower levels to achieve greater involvement. Yet they can also avoid irreconcilable opposition, emotional overcommitment,[15] or organizational momenta beyond their control by regarding all proposals as "strictly advisory" at this early stage.

As issues are clarified and options are narrowed, executives may systematically alert ever wider audiences. They may first "shop" key ideas among trusted colleagues to test responses. Then they may commission a few studies to illuminate emerging alternatives, contingencies, or opportunities. But key players might still not be ready to change their past action patterns or even be able to investigate options creatively. Only when persuasive data are in hand and enough people are alerted and "on board" to make a particular solution work might key executives finally commit themselves to it. Building awareness, concern, and interest to attention-getting levels is often a vital—and slowly achieved—step in the process of managing basic changes. For example:

In the early 1970s there was still a glut in world oil supplies. Nevertheless, analysts in the General Motors Chief Economist's Office began to project a developing U.S. dependency on foreign oil and the likelihood of higher future oil prices. These concerns led the board in 1972 to create an ad hoc energy task force headed by David C. Collier, then treasurer, later head of GM of Canada and then of the Buick Division. Collier's group included people from manufacturing, research, design, finance, industry-government relations, and the economics staff. After six months of research, in May of 1973 the task force went to the board with three conclusions: (1)

---

[14] Cyert and March, *Behavioral Theory of the Firm,* suggest that executives choose from a number of satisfactory solutions; later observers suggest they choose the first truly satisfactory solution discovered.

[15] See F. F. Gilmore, "Overcoming the Perils of Advocacy in Corporate Planning," *California Management Review,* Spring 1973, pp. 127–37.

there was a developing energy problem; (2) the government had no particular plan to deal with it; (3) energy costs would have a profound effect on GM's business. Collier's report created a good deal of discussion around the company in the ensuing months. "We were trying to get other people to think about the issue," said Richard C. Gerstenberg, then chairman of GM.[16]

Changing Symbols: Building Credibility

As awareness of the need for change grows, managers often want to signal the organization that certain types of changes are coming, even if specific solutions are not in hand. Knowing they cannot communicate directly with the thousands who could carry out the strategy, some executives purposely undertake highly visible actions which wordlessly convey complex messages that could never be communicated as well—or as credibly—in verbal terms.[17] Some use symbolic moves to preview or verify intended changes in direction. At other times, such moves confirm the intention of top management to back a thrust already partially begun—as Mr. McColough's relocation of Xerox headquarters to Connecticut (away from the company's Rochester reprographics base) underscored that company's developing commitment to product diversification, organizational decentralization, and international operations. Organizations often need such symbolic moves—or decisions they regard as symbolic—to build credibility behind a new strategy. Without such actions even forceful verbiage might be interpreted as mere rhetoric. For example:

In GM's downsizing, engineers said that one of top management's early decisions affected the credibility of the whole weight-reduction program. "Initially, we proposed a program using a lot of aluminum and substitute materials to meet the new 'mass' targets. But this would have meant a very high cost, and would have strained the suppliers' aluminum capacity. However, when we presented this program to management, they said, 'OK, if necessary, we'll do it.' They didn't back down. We began to understand then that they were dead serious. Feeling that the company would spend the money was critical to the success of the entire mass-reduction effort."[18]

Legitimizing New Viewpoints

Often before reaching specific strategic decisions, it is necessary to legitimize new options which have been acknowledged as possibilities, but which still entail an undue aura of uncertainty or concern. Because of their familiarity, older options are usually perceived as having lower risks (or potential costs) than newer alternatives. Therefore, top managers seeking change often consciously create forums and allow slack time for their organizations to talk through threatening issues, work out the implications of new solutions, or gain an improved information base that will permit new options to be

---

[16] See J. B. Quinn, *General Motors Corporation: The Downsizing Decision* (copyrighted case, Amos Tuck School of Business Administration, Dartmouth College, Hanover, New Hampshire, 1978).

[17] See E. Rhenman, *Organization Theory for Long-Range Planning* (New York: John Wiley & Sons, 1973), p. 63. Here the author notes a similar phenomenon.

[18] See Quinn, *General Motors Corporation*.

evaluated objectively in comparison with more familiar alternatives.[19] In many cases, strategic concepts which are at first strongly resisted gain acceptance and support simply by the passage of time, if executives do not exacerbate hostility by pushing them too fast from the top. For example:

When Joe Wilson thought Haloid Corporation should change its name to include Xerox, he first submitted a memorandum asking colleagues what they thought of the idea. They rejected it. Wilson then explained his concerns more fully, and his executives rejected the idea again. Finally, Wilson formed a committee headed by Sol Linowitz, who had thought a separate Xerox subsidiary might be the best solution. As this committee deliberated, negotiations were under way with the Rank Organizations and the term Rank-Xerox was commonly heard and Haloid-Xerox no longer seemed so strange. "And so," according to John Dessauer, "a six-month delay having diluted most opposition, we of the committee agreed that the change to Haloid-Xerox might in the long run produce sound advantages."[20]

Many top executives consciously plan for such "gestation periods" and often find that the strategic concept itself is made more effective by the resulting feedback.

Tactical Shifts and Partial Solutions

At this stage in the process guiding executives might share a fairly clear vision of the general directions for movement. But rarely does a total new corporate posture emerge full grown—like Minerva from the brow of Jupiter—from any one source. Instead, early resolutions are likely to be partial, tentative, or experimental.[21] Beginning moves often appear as mere tactical adjustments in the enterprise's existing posture. As such, they encounter little opposition, yet each partial solution adds momentum in new directions. Guiding executives try carefully to maintain the enterprise's ongoing strengths while shifting its total posture incrementally—at the margin— toward new needs. Such executives themselves might not yet perceive the full nature of the strategic shifts they have begun. They can still experiment with partial new approaches and learn without risking the viability of the total enterprise. Their broad early steps can still legitimately lead to a variety of different success scenarios. Yet logic might dictate that they wait before committing themselves to a total new strategy.[22] As events unfurl, solutions to several interrelated problems might well flow together in a not-yet-perceived synthesis. For example:

---

[19] See R. M. Cyert, W. R. Dill, and J. G. March, "The Role of Expectations in Business Decision Making," *Administrative Science Quarterly,* December 1958, pp. 307–40. The authors point out the perils of top management advocacy because existing policies may unconsciously bias information to support views they value.

[20] See J. H. Dessauer, *My Years with Xerox: The Billions Nobody Wanted* (Garden City N.Y.: Doubleday, 1971).

[21] See H. Mintzberg, *The Nature of Managerial Work* (New York: Harper & Row, 1973). Note that this "vision" is not necessarily the beginning point of the process. Instead it emerges as new data and viewpoints interact; Normann, *Management for Growth.*

[22] See Mintzberg, Raisinghani, and Theoret, "Structure of Unstructured Decision Process." Here the authors liken the process to a decision tree where decisions at each node become more narrow, with failure at any node allowing recycling back to the broader tree trunk.

In the early 1970s at General Motors there was a distinct awareness of a developing fuel economy ethic. General Motors executives said, "Our conclusions were really at the conversational level—that the big car trend was at an end. But we were not at all sure sufficient numbers of large car buyers were ready to move to dramatically lighter cars." Nevertheless, GM did start concept studies that resulted in the Cadillac Seville.

When the oil crisis hit in fall 1973, the company responded in further increments, at first merely increasing production of its existing small car lines. Then as the crisis deepened, it added another partial solution, the subcompact "T car"—the Chevette—and accelerated the Seville's development cycle. Next, as fuel economy appeared more salable, executives set an initial target of removing 400 pounds from B–C bodies by 1977. As fuel economy pressures persisted and engineering feasibilities offered greater confidence, this target was increased to 800–1,000 pounds (three mpg). No step by itself shifted the company's total strategic posture until the full downsizing of all lines was announced. But each partial solution built confidence and commitment toward a new direction.

Broadening Political Support

Often these broad emerging strategic thrusts need expanded political support and understanding to achieve sufficient momentum to survive.[23] Committees, task forces, and retreats tend to be favored mechanisms for accomplishing this. If carefully managed, these do not become the "garbage cans" of emerging ideas, as some observers have noted.[24] By selecting the committee's chairman, membership, timing, and agenda, guiding executives can largely influence and predict a desired outcome, and can force other executives toward a consensus. Such groups can be balanced to educate, evaluate, neutralize, or overwhelm opponents. They can be used to legitimize new options or to generate broad cohesion among diverse thrusts, or they can be narrowly focused to build momentum. Guiding executives can constantly maintain complete control over these "advisory processes" through their various influences and veto potentials. For example:

IBM's Chairman Watson and Executive Vice President Larson had become concerned over what to do about: third-generation computer technology, a proliferation of designs from various divisions, increasing costs of developing software, internal competition among their lines, and the needed breadth of line for the new computer applications they began to foresee. Step by step, they oversaw the killing of the company's huge Stretch computer line (uneconomic), a proposed 8000 series of computers (incompatible software), and the prototype English Scamp computer (duplicative). They then initiated a series of "strategic dialogues" with divisional executives to define a new strategy. But none came into place because of the parochial nature of divisional viewpoints.

Larson, therefore, set up the SPREAD Committee, representing every major segment of the company. Its 12 members included the most likely opponent of an integrated line (Haanstra), the people who had earlier suggested the 8000 and Scamp

---

[23] Wrapp, "Good Managers Don't Make Policy Decisions," notes that a conditioning process that may stretch over months or years is necessary in order to prepare the organization for radical departures from what it is already striving to attain.

[24] See J. G. March, J. P. Olsen, S. Christensen, et al., *Ambiguity and Choice in Organizations* (Bergen, Norway: Universitetsforlaget, 1976).

designs, and Learson's handpicked lieutenant (Evans). When progress became "hellishly slow," Haanstra was removed as chairman and Evans took over. Eventually the committee came forth with an integrating proposal for a single compatible line of computers to blanket and open up the market for both scientific and business applications, with "standard interface" for peripheral equipment. At an all-day meeting of the 50 top executives of the company, the report was not received with enthusiasm, but there were no compelling objections. So Larson blessed the silence as consensus saying, "OK, we'll do it"—i.e., go ahead with a major development program.[25]

In addition to facilitating smooth implementation, many managers reported that interactive consensus building processes also improve the quality of the strategic decisions themselves and help achieve positive and innovative assistance when things otherwise could go wrong.

Overcoming Opposition: "Zones of Indifference" and "No Lose" Situations

Executives of basically healthy companies in the sample realized that any attempt to introduce a new strategy would have to deal with the support its predecessor had. Barring a major crisis, a frontal attack on an old strategy could be regarded as an attack on those who espoused it—perhaps properly—and brought the enterprise to its present levels of success. There often exists a variety of legitimate views on what could and should be done in the new circumstances that a company faces. And wise executives do not want to alienate people who would otherwise be supporters. Consequently, they try to get key people behind their concepts whenever possible, to co-opt or neutralize serious opposition if necessary, or to find "zones of indifference" where the proposition would not be disastrously opposed.[26] Most of all they seek "no lose" situations which will motivate all the important players toward a common goal. For example:

When James McFarland took over at General Mills from his power base in the Grocery Products Division, another serious contender for the top spot had been Louis B. "Bo" Polk, a very bright, aggressive young man who headed the corporation's acquisition-diversification program. Both traditional lines and acquisitions groups wanted support for their activities and had high-level supporters. McFarland's corporate-wide "goodness to greatness" conferences . . . first obtained broad agreement on growth goals and criteria for all areas.

Out of this and the related acquisition proposal process came two thrusts: (1) to expand—internally and through acquisitions—in food-related sectors and (2) to

---

[25] See T. A. Wise, "I.B.M.'s $5 Billion Gamble," *Fortune,* September 1966, pp. 118–24; and T. A. Wise, "The Rocky Road to the Marketplace" part 2: "I.B.M.'s $5 Billion Gamble," *Fortune,* October 1966, pp. 138–52.

[26] For an excellent overview of the process of co-optation and neutralization, see Sayles, *Managerial Behavior.* For perhaps the first reference to the concept of the "zone of indifference," see C. I. Barnard, *The Functions of the Executive* (Cambridge, Mass.: Harvard University Press, 1938). The following two sources note the need of executives for coalition behavior to reduce the organizational conflict resulting from differing interests and goal preferences in large organizations: Cyert and March, *Behavioral Theory of the Firm;* and J. G. March, "Business Decision Making," in *Readings in Managerial Psychology,* ed. H. J. Leavitt and L. R. Pondy (Chicago: University of Chicago Press, 1964).

acquire new growth centers based on General Mills' marketing skills. Although there was no formal statement, there was a strong feeling that the majority of resources should be used in food-related areas. But neither group was foreclosed, and no one could suggest the new management was vindictive. As it turned out, over the next five years about $450 million was invested in new businesses, and the majority were not closely related to foods.

But such tactics do not always work. Successful executives surveyed tended to honor legitimate differences in viewpoints and noted that initial opponents often shaped new strategies in more effective directions and became supporters as new information became available. But strong-minded executives sometimes disagreed to the point where they had to be moved or stimulated to leave; timing could dictate very firm top-level decisions at key junctions. Barring crises, however, disciplinary steps usually occurred incrementally as individual executives' attitudes and competencies emerged vis-à-vis a new strategy.

Structuring Flexibility: Buffers, Slacks, and Activists

Typically there are too many uncertainties in the total environment for managers to program or control all the events involved in effecting a major change in strategic direction. Logic dictates, therefore, that managers purposely design flexibility into their organizations and have resources ready to deploy incrementally as events demand. Planned flexibility requires: (1) proactive horizon scanning to identify the general nature and potential impact of opportunities and threats the firm is most likely to encounter, (2) creating sufficient resource buffers—or slacks—to respond effectively as events actually unfurl, (3) developing and positioning "credible activities" with a psychological commitment to move quickly and flexibly to exploit specific opportunities as they occur, and (4) shortening decision lines from such people (and key operating managers) to the top for the most rapid system response. These—rather than precapsuled (and shelved) programs to respond to stimuli which never quite occur as expected—are the keys to real contingency planning.

The concept of resource buffers requires special amplification. Quick access to resources is needed to cushion the impact of random events, to offset opponents' sudden attacks, or to build momentum for new strategic shifts. Some examples will indicate the form these buffers may take.

For critical purchased items, General Motors maintained at least three suppliers, each with sufficient capacity to expand production should one of the others encounter a catastrophe. Thus, the company had expandable capacity with no fixed investment. Exxon set up its Exploration Group to purposely undertake the higher risks and longer-term investments necessary to search for oil in new areas, and thus to reduce the potential impact on Exxon if there were sudden unpredictable changes in the availability of Middle East oil. Instead of hoarding cash, Pillsbury and General Mills sold off unprofitable businesses and cleaned up their financial statements to improve their access to external capital sources for acquisitions. Such access in essence provided the protection of a cash buffer without its investment. IBM's large R&D facility and its project team approach to development assured that it had a pool of people it could quickly shift among various projects to exploit interesting new technologies.

When such flexible response patterns are designed into the enterprise's strategy, it is proactively ready to move on those thrusts—acquisitions, innovations, or resource explorations—which require incrementalism.

Systematic Waiting and Trial Concepts

The prepared strategist may have to wait for events, as Roosevelt awaited a trauma like Pearl Harbor. The availability of desired acquisitions or real estate might depend on a death, divorce, fiscal crisis, management change, or an erratic stock market break.[27] Technological advances may have to await new knowledge, inventions, or lucky accidents. Despite otherwise complete preparations, a planned market entry might not be wise until new legislation, trade agreements, or competitive shakeouts occur. Organizational moves have to be timed to retirements, promotions, management failures, and so on. Very often the specific strategy adopted depends on the timing or sequence of such random events.[28] For example:

Although Continental Group's top executives had thoroughly discussed and investigated energy, natural resources, and insurance as possible "fourth legs" for the company, the major acquisition possibilities were so different that the strategic choice depended on the fit of particular candidates—e.g., Peabody Coal or Richmond Insurance—within these possible industries. The choice of one industry would have precluded the others. The sequence in which firms became available affected the final choice, and that choice itself greatly influenced the whole strategic posture of the company.

In many of the cases studied, strategists proactively launched trial concepts—Mr. McColough's "architecture of information" (Xerox), Mr. Spoor's "Super Box" (Pillsbury)—in order to generate options and concrete proposals. Usually these "trial balloons" were phrases in very broad terms. Without making a commitment to any specific solution, the executive can activate the organization's creative abilities. This approach keeps the manager's own options open until substantive alternatives can be evaluated against each other and against concrete current realities. It prevents practical line managers from rejecting a strategic shift, as they might if forced to compare a "paper option" against well-defined current needs. Such trial concepts give cohesion to the new strategy while enabling the company to take maximum advantage of the psychological and informational benefits of incrementalism.

Solidifying Progress—Incrementally

As events move forward, executives can more clearly perceive the specific directions in which their organizations should—and realistically can—move. They can seek more aggressive movement and commitment to their new perceptions, without undermining important ongoing activities or creating unnecessary reactions to their purposes. Until this point, new strategic

---

[27] Cyert and March, *Behavioral Theory of the Firm,* also note that not only do organizations seek alternatives but that "alternatives seek organizations" (as when finders, scientists, bankers, etc., bring in new solutions).

[28] See March, Olsen, Christensen, et al., *Ambiguity and Choice in Organizations.*

goals might remain broad, relatively unrefined, or even unstated except as philosophic concepts. More specific dimensions might be incrementally announced as key pieces of information fall into place, specific unanswered issues approach resolution, or significant resources have to be formally committed.

Creating Pockets of Commitment

Early in this stage, guiding executives may need to actively implant support in the organization for new thrusts. They may encourage an array of exploratory projects for each of several possible options. Initial projects can be kept small, partial, or ad hoc, neither forming a comprehensive program nor seeming to be integrated into a cohesive strategy. Executives often provide stimulating goals, a proper climate for imaginative proposals, and flexible resource support, rather than being personally identified with specific projects. In this way they can achieve organizational involvement and early commitment without focusing attention on any one solution too soon or losing personal credibility if it fails.

Once under way, project teams on the more successful programs in the sample became ever more committed to their particular areas of exploration. They became pockets of support for new strategies deep within the organization. Yet, if necessary, top managers could delay until the last moment their final decisions blending individual projects into a total strategy. Thus, they were able to obtain the best possible match among the company's technical abilities, its psychological commitments, and its changing market needs. By making final choices more effectively—as late as possible with better data, more conscientiously investigated options, and the expert critiques competitive projects allowed—these executives actually increased technical and market efficiencies of their enterprises, despite the apparent added costs of parallel efforts.[29]

In order to maintain their own objectivity and future flexibility, some executives choose to keep their own political profiles low as they build a new consensus. If they seem committed to a strategy too soon, they might discourage others from pursuing key issues which should be raised.[30] By stimulating detailed investigations several levels down, top executives can seem detached yet still shape both progress and ultimate outcomes—by reviewing interim results and specifying the timing, format, and forums for the release of data. When reports come forward, these executives can stand above the battle and review proposals objectively, without being personally on the defensive for having committed themselves to a particular solution too soon. From this position they can more easily orchestrate a high-level consensus on a new strategic thrust. As an added benefit, negative decisions

---

[29] Much of the rationale for this approach is contained in J. B. Quinn, "Technological Innovation, Entrepreneurship, and Strategy," *Sloan Management Review,* Spring 1979, pp. 19–30.

[30] See C. Argyris, "Interpersonal Barriers to Decision Making," *Harvard Business Review,* March–April 1966, pp. 84–97. The author notes that when the president introduced major decisions from the top, discussion was "less than open" and commitment was "less than complete," although executives might assure the president to the contrary.

on proposals often come from a group consensus that top executives can simply confirm to lower levels, thereby preserving their personal veto for more crucial moments. In many well-made decisions people at all levels contribute to the generation, amplification, and interpretation of options and information to the extent that it is often difficult to say who really makes the decision.[31]

Focusing the Organization

In spite of their apparent detachment, top executives do focus their organizations on developing strategies at critical points in the process. While adhering to the rhetoric of specific goal setting, most executives are careful *not* to state new goals in concrete terms before they have built a consensus among key players. They fear that they will prematurely centralize the organization, preempt interesting options, provide a common focus for otherwise fragmented opposition, or cause the organization to act prematurely to carry out a specified commitment. Guiding executives may quietly shape the many alternatives flowing upward by using what Wrapp refers to as "a hidden hand." Through their information networks they can encourage concepts they favor, let weakly supported options die through inaction, and establish hurdles or tests for strongly supported ideas with which they do not agree but which they do not wish to oppose openly.

Since opportunities for such focusing generally develop unexpectedly, the timing of key moves is often unpredictable. A crisis, a rash of reassignments, a reorganization, or a key appointment may allow an executive to focus attention on particular thrusts, add momentum to some, and perhaps quietly phase out others.[32] Most managers surveyed seemed well aware of the notion that "if there are no other options, mine wins." Without being Machiavellian, they did not want misdirected options to gain strong political momentum and later have to be terminated in an open bloodbath. They also did not want to send false signals that stimulated other segments of their organizations to make proposals in undesirable directions. They sensed very clearly that the patterns in which proposals are approved or denied will inevitably be perceived by lower echelons as precedents for developing future goals or policies.

Managing Coalitions

Power interactions among key players are important at this stage of solidifying progress. Each player has a different level of power determined by his or her information base, organizational position, and personal credibility.[33] Executives legitimately perceive problems or opportunities differ-

---

[31] See March, "Business Decision Making."

[32] The process tends to be one of eliminating the less feasible rather than of determining a target or objectives. The process typically reduces the number of alternatives through successive limited comparisons to a point where understood analytical techniques can apply and the organization structure can function to make a choice. See Cyert and March, *Behavioral Theory of the Firm.*

[33] For more detailed relationships between authority and power, see H. C. Metcalf and L. Urwick, eds., *Dynamic Administration: The Collected Papers of Mary Parker Follett* (New York: Harper & Row, 1941); and A. Zaleznik, "Power and Politics in Organizational Life," *Harvard Business Review,* May–June 1970, pp. 47–60.

ently because of their particular values, experiences, and vantage points. They will promote the solutions they perceive as the best compromise for the total enterprise, for themselves, and for their particular units. In an organization with dispersed power, the key figure is the one who can manage coalitions.[34] Since no one player has all the power, regardless of that individual's skill or position, the action that occurs over time might differ greatly from the intentions of any of the players.[35] Top executives try to sense whether support exists among important parties for specific aspects of an issue and try to get partial decisions and momenta going for those aspects. As "comfort levels" or political pressures within the top group rise in favor of specific decisions, the guiding executive might, within his or her concept of a more complete solution, seek—among the various features of different proposals—a balance that the most influential and credible parties can actively support. The result tends to be a stream of partial decisions on limited strategic issues made by constantly changing coalitions of the critical power centers.[36] These decisions steadily evolve toward a broader consensus, acceptable to both the top executive and some "dominant coalition" among these centers.

As a partial consensus emerges, top executives might crystallize issues by stating some broad goals in more specific terms for internal consumption. Finally, when sufficient general acceptance exists and the timing is right, the goals may begin to appear in more public announcements. For example:

> As General Mills divested several of its major divisions in the early 1960s, its annual reports began to refer to these as deliberate moves "to concentrate on the company's strengths" and "to intensify General Mills' efforts in the convenience foods field." Such statements could not have been made until many of the actual divestitures were completed and a sufficient consensus existed among the top executives to support the new corporate concept.

Formalizing Commitment by Empowering Champions

As each major strategic thrust comes into focus, top executives try to ensure that some individual or group feels responsible for its goals. If the thrust will project the enterprise in entirely new directions, executives often want more than mere accountability for its success—they want real commitment.[37] A significantly new major thrust, concept, product, or problem solution frequently needs the nurturing hand of someone who genuinely identifies with it and whose future depends on its success. For example:

---

[34] See J. D. Thompson, "The Control of Complex Organizations," in *Organizations in Action* (New York: McGraw-Hill, 1967).

[35] See G. T. Allison, *Essence of Decision: Explaining the Cuban Missile Crisis* (Boston: Little, Brown, 1971).

[36] See C. E. Lindblom, "The Science of 'Muddling Through,'" *Public Administration Review,* Spring 1959, pp. 79–88. The author notes that the relative weights individuals give to values and the intensity of their feelings will vary sequentially from decision to decision; hence the dominant coalition itself varies with each decision somewhat.

[37] Zaleznik, "Power and Politics in Organizational Life," notes that confusing compliance with commitment is one of the most common and difficult problems of strategic implementation. He notes that often organizational commitment may override personal interest if the former is developed carefully.

Once the divestiture program at General Mills was sufficiently under way, General Rawlings selected young "Bo" Polk to head up an acquisition program to use the cash generated. In this role Polk had nothing to lose. With strong senior management in the remaining consumer products divisions, the ambitious Polk would have had a long road to the top there. In acquisitions, he provided a small political target, only a $50,000 budget in a $500 million company. Yet he had high visibility and could build his own power base, if he were successful. With direct access to and the support of Rawlings, he would be protected through his early ventures. All he had to do was make sure his first few acquisitions were successful. As subsequent acquisitions succeeded, his power base could feed on itself—satisfying both Polk's ego needs and the company's strategic goals.

In some cases, top executives have to wait for champions to appear before committing resources to risky new strategies. They may immediately assign accountability for less dramatic plans by converting them into new missions for ongoing groups.

From this point on, the strategy process is familiar. The organization's formal structure has to be adjusted to support the strategy.[38] Commitment to the most important new thrusts has to be confirmed in formal plans. Detailed budgets, programs, controls, and reward systems have to reflect all planned strategic thrusts. Finally, the guiding executive has to see that recruiting and staffing plans are aligned with the new goals and that—when the situation permits—supporters and persistent opponents of intended new thrusts are assigned to appropriate positions.

Continuing the Dynamics by Eroding Consensus

The major strategic changes studied tended to take many years to accomplish. The process was continuous, often without any clear beginning or end.[39] The decision process constantly molded and modified management's concerns and concepts. Radical crusades became the new conventional wisdom, and over time totally new issues emerged. Participants or observers were often not aware of exactly when a particular decision had been made[40] or when a subsequent consensus was created to supersede or modify it; the process of strategic change was continuous and dynamic. Several GM executives described the frequently imperceptible[41] way in which many strategic decisions evolved:

We use an iterative process to make a series of tentative decisions on the way we think the market will go. As we get more data we modify these continuously. It is often difficult to say who decided something and when—or even who originated a decision. . . . Strategy really evolves as a series of incremental steps. . . . I frequently don't know when a decision is made in General Motors. I don't remember

---

[38] See A. D. Chandler, *Strategy and Structure: Chapters in the History of the Industrial Enterprise* (Cambridge, Mass.: MIT Press, 1962).

[39] See K. J. Cohen and R. M. Cyert, "Strategy: Formulation, Implementation, and Monitoring," *Journal of Business,* July 1973, pp. 349–67.

[40] March, "Business Decision Making," notes that major decisions are "processes of gradual commitment."

[41] Sayles, *Managerial Behavior,* notes that such decisions are a "flow process" with no one person ever really making the decisions.

being in a committee meeting when things came to a vote. Usually someone will simply summarize a developing position. Everyone else either nods or states his particular terms of consensus.

A major strategic change in Xerox was characterized this way:

> How was the overall organization decision made? I've often heard it said that after talking with a lot of people and having trouble with a number of decisions which were pending, Archie McCardell really reached his own conclusion and got Peter McColough's backing on it. But it really didn't happen quite that way. It was an absolutely evolutionary approach. It was a growing feeling. A number of people felt we ought to be moving toward some kind of matrix organization. We have always been a pretty democratic type of organization. In our culture you can't come down with mandates or ultimatums from the top on major changes like this. You almost have to work these things through and let them grow and evolve, keep them on the table so people are thinking about them and talking about them.

Once the organization arrives at its new consensus, the guiding executive has to move immediately to ensure that this new position does not become inflexible. In trying to build commitment to a new concept, individual executives often surround themselves with people who see the world in the same way. Such people can rapidly become systematic screens against other views. Effective executives therefore purposely continue the change process, constantly introducing new faces and stimuli at the top. They consciously begin to erode the very strategic thrusts they may have just created—a very difficult, but essential, psychological task.

Integration of Processes and of Interests

In the large enterprises observed, strategy formulation was a continuously evolving analytical-political consensus process with neither a finite beginning nor a definite end. It generally followed the sequence described above. Yet the total process was anything but linear. It was a grouping, cyclical process that often circled back on itself, with frequent interruptions and delays. Pfiffner aptly describes the process of strategy formation as being "like fermentation in biochemistry, rather than an industrial assembly line."[42]

Such incremental management processes are not abrogations of good management practice. Nor are they Machiavellian or consciously manipulative maneuvers. Instead, they represent an adaptation to the practical psychological and informational problems of getting a constantly changing group of people with diverse talents and interests to move together effectively in a continually dynamic environment. Much of the impelling force behind logical incrementalism comes from a desire to tap the talents and psychological drives of the whole organization, to create cohesion, and to generate identity with the emerging strategy. The remainder of that force results from the interactive nature of the random factors and lead times affecting the independent subsystems that compose any total strategy.

---

[42] See J. M. Pfiffner, "Administrative Rationality," *Public Administration Review*, Summer 1960, pp. 125–32.

An Incremental—Not Piecemeal—Process

The total pattern of action, though highly incremental, is not piecemeal in well-managed organizations. It requires constant, conscious reassessment of the total organization, its capacities, and its needs as related to surrounding environments. It requires continual attempts by top managers to integrate these actions into an understandable, cohesive whole. How do top managers themselves describe the process? Mr. Estes, president of General Motors, said:

> We try to give them the broad concepts we are trying to achieve. We operate through questioning and fact gathering. Strategy is a state of mind you go through. When you think about a little problem, your mind begins to think how it will affect all the different elements in the total situation. Once you have had all the jobs you need to qualify for this position, you can see the problem from a variety of viewpoints. But you don't try to ram your conclusions down people's throats. You try to persuade people what has to be done and provide confidence and leadership for them.

Formal-Analytical Techniques   At each stage of strategy development, effective executives constantly try to visualize the new patterns that might exist among the emerging strategies of various subsystems. As each subsystem strategy becomes more apparent, both its executive team and top-level groups try to project its implications for the total enterprise and to stimulate queries, support, and feedback from those involved in related strategies. Perceptive top executives see that the various teams generating subsystem strategies have overlapping members. They require periodic updates and reviews before higher-echelon groups that can bring a total corporate view to bear. They use formal planning processes to interrelate and evaluate the resources required, benefits sought, and risks undertaken vis-à-vis other elements of the enterprise's overall strategy. Some use scenario techniques to help visualize potential impacts and relationships. Others utilize complex forecasting models to better understand the basic interactions among subsystems, the total enterprise, and the environment. Still others use specialized staffs, "devil's advocates," or "contention teams" to make sure that all important aspects of their strategies receive a thorough evaluation.

Power-Behavioral Aspects: Coalition Management   All of the formal methodologies help, but the real integration of all the components in an enterprise's total strategy eventually takes place only in the minds of high-level executives. Each executive may legitimately perceive the intended balance of goals and thrusts differently. Some of these differences may be openly expressed as issues to be resolved when new information becomes available. Some differences may remain unstated—hidden agendas to emerge at later dates. Others may be masked by accepting so broad a statement of intention that many different views are included in a seeming consensus, when a more specific statement might be divisive. Nevertheless, effective strategies do achieve a level of understanding and consensus sufficient to focus action.

Top executives deliberately manage the incremental processes within each subsystem to create the basis for consensus. They also manage the coalitions that lie at the heart of most controlled strategy developments.[43] They recognize that they are at the confluence of innumerable pressures—from stockholders, environmentalists, government bodies, customers, suppliers, distributors, producing units, marketing groups, technologists, unions, special issue activists, individual employees, ambitious executives, and so on—and that knowledgeable people of goodwill can easily disagree on proper actions. In response to changing pressures and coalitions among these groups, the top management team constantly forms and reforms its own coalitions on various decisions.[44]

Most major strategic moves tend to assist some interests—and executives' careers—at the expense of others. Consequently, each set of interests serves as a check on the others and thus helps maintain the breadth and balance of strategy.[45] To avoid significant errors, some managers try to ensure that all important groups have representation at or access to the top.[46] The guiding executive group may continuously adjust the number, power, or proximity of such access points in order to maintain a desired balance and focus.[47] These delicate adjustments require constant negotiations and implied bargains within the leadership group. Balancing the focuses that different interests exert on key decisions is perhaps the ultimate control top executives have in guiding and coordinating the formulation of their companies' strategies.[48]

Establishing, Measuring, and Rewarding Key Thrusts

Few executives or management teams can keep all the dimensions of a complex evolving strategy in mind as they deal with the continuous flux of urgent issues. Consequently, effective strategic managers seek to identify a few central themes that can help to draw diverse efforts together in a common cause.[49] Once identified, these themes help to maintain focus and consistency in the strategy. They make it easier to discuss and monitor proposed strategic thrusts. Ideally, these themes can be developed into a matrix of programs and goals, cutting across formal divisional lines and dominating the selection and ranking of projects within divisions. This matrix can, in turn, serve as the basis for performance measurement, control, and reward systems that ensure the intended strategy is properly implemented.

---

[43] See R. James, "Corporate Strategy and Change—The Management of People" (monograph, University of Chicago, 1978). The author does an excellent job of pulling together the threads of coalition management at top organizational levels.

[44] See Cyert and March, *Behavioral Theory of the Firm*, p. 115.

[45] Lindblom, "The Science of 'Muddling Through,'" notes that every interest has a "watchdog" and that purposely allowing these watchdogs to participate in and influence decisions creates consensus decisions that all can live with. Similar conscious access to the top for different interests can now be found in corporate structures.

[46] See Zaleznik, "Power and Politics in Organizational Life."

[47] For an excellent view of the bargaining processes involved in coalition management, see Sayles, *Managerial Behavior*, pp. 207–17.

[48] For suggestions on why the central power figure in decentralized organizations must be the person who manages its dominant coalition, the size of which will depend on the issues involved, and the number of areas in which the organizations must rely on judgmental decisions, see Thompson, "Control of Complex Organizations."

[49] Wrapp, "Good Managers Don't Make Policy Decisions," notes the futility of a top manager trying to push a full package of goals.

Unfortunately, few companies in the sample were able to implement such a complex planning and control system without creating undue rigidities. But all did utilize logical incrementalism to bring cohesion to the formal-analytical and power-behavioral processes needed to create effective strategies. Most used some approximation of the process sequence described above to form their strategies at both subsystem and overall corporate levels. A final summary example demonstrates how deliberate incrementalism can integrate the key elements in more traditional approaches to strategy formulation.

In the late 1970s a major nation's largest bank named as its new president and CEO a man with a long and successful career, largely in domestic operating positions. The bank's chairman had been a familiar figure on the international stage and was due to retire in three to five years. The new CEO, with the help of a few trusted colleagues, his chief planner, and a consultant, first tried to answer these questions: "If I look ahead seven to eight years to my retirement as CEO, what should I like to leave behind as the hallmarks of my leadership? What accomplishments would define my era as having been successful? He chose the following as goals:

1. To be the country's number one bank in profitability and size without sacrificing the quality of its assets or liabilities.
2. To be recognized as a major international bank.
3. To improve substantially the public image and employee perceptions of the bank.
4. To maintain progressive policies that prevent unionization.
5. To be viewed as a professional, well-managed bank with strong, planned management continuity.
6. To be clearly identified as the country's most professional corporate finance bank, with a strong base within the country but with foreign and domestic operations growing in balance.
7. To have women in top management and to achieve full utilization of the bank's female employees.
8. To have a tighter, smaller headquarters and a more rationalized, decentralized corporate structure.

The CEO brought back to the corporate offices the head of his overseas divisions to be COO and to be a member of the Executive Committee, which ran the company's affairs. The CEO discussed his personal views concerning the bank's future with this committee and also with several of his group VPs. Then, to arrive at a cohesive set of corporate goals, the Executive Committee investigated the bank's existing strengths and weaknesses (again with the assistance of consultants) and extrapolated its existing growth trends seven to eight years into the future. According to the results of this exercise, the bank's forseeable growth would require that:

1. The bank's whole structure be reoriented to make it a much stronger force in international banking.
2. The bank decentralize operations much more than it ever had.
3. The bank find or develop at least 100 new top-level specialists and general managers within a few years.

4. The bank reorganize around a "four bank" principle (international, commercial, investment, and retail banks) with entirely new linkages forged among these units.

5. These linkages and much of the bank's new international thrust be built on its expertise in certain industries, which were the primary basis of its parent country's international trade.

6. The bank's profitability be improved across the board, especially in its diverse retail banking units.

To develop more detailed data for specific actions and to further develop consensus around needed moves, the CEO commissioned two consulting studies: one on the future of the bank's home country and the other on changing trade patterns and relationships worldwide. As these studies became available, the CEO allowed an ever wider circle of top executives to critique the studies' findings and to share their insights. Finally, the CEO and the Executive Committee were willing to draw up and agree to a statement of 10 broad goals (parallel to the CEO's original goals but enriched in flavor and detail). By then, some steps were already under way to implement specific goals (e.g., the four-bank concept). But the CEO wanted further participation of his line officers in the formulation of the goals and in the strategic thrusts they represented across the whole bank. By now 18 months had gone by, but there was widespread consensus within the top management group on major goals and directions.

The CEO then organized an international conference of some 40 top officers of the bank and had a background document prepared for this meeting containing: (1) the broad goals agreed upon, (2) the 10 major thrusts that the Executive Committee thought were necessary to meet these goals, (3) the key elements needed to back up each thrust, and (4) a summary of the national and economic analyses the thrusts were based upon. The 40 executives had two full days to critique, question, improve, and clarify the ideas in this document. Small work groups of line executives reported their findings and concerns directly to the Executive Committee. At the end of the meeting, the Executive Committee tabled one of the major thrusts for further study, agreed to refined wording for some of the bank's broad goals, and modified details of the major thrusts in line with expressed concerns.

The CEO announced that within three months each line officer would be expected to submit his own statement of how his unit would contribute to the major goals and thrusts agreed upon. Once these unit goals were discussed and negotiated with the appropriate top executive group, the line officers would develop specific budgetary and nonbudgetary programs showing precisely how their units would carry out each of the major thrusts in the strategy. The CEO was asked to develop measures both for all key elements of each unit's fiscal performance and for performance against each agreed-upon strategic thrust within each unit. As these plans came into place, it became clear that the old organization had to be aligned behind these new thrusts. The CEO had to substantially redefine the CEO's job, deal with some crucial internal political pressures, and place the next generation of top managers in the line positions supporting each major thrust. The total process from concept formulation to implementation of the control system was to span three to four years, with new goals and thrusts emerging flexibly as external events and opportunities developed.

Conclusions

In recent years, there has been an increasingly loud chorus of discontent about corporate strategic planning. Many managers are concerned that despite elaborate strategic planning systems, costly staffs for planning, and major commitments of their own time, their most elaborately analyzed strategies never get implemented. These executives and their companies generally have fallen into the trap of thinking about strategy formulation and implementation as separate, sequential processes. They rely on the awesome rationality of their formally derived strategies and the inherent power of their positions to cause their organizations to respond. When this does not occur, they become bewildered, if not frustrated and angry. Instead, successful managers in the companies observed acted logically and incrementally to improve the quality of information used in key decisions; to overcome the personal and political pressures resisting change; to deal with the varying lead times and sequencing problems in critical decisions; and to build the organizational awareness, understanding, and psychological commitment essential to effective strategies. By the time the strategies began to crystallize, pieces of them were already being implemented. Through the very processes they used to formulate their strategies, these executives had built sufficient organizational momentum and identity with the strategies to make them flow toward flexible and successful implementation.

What this article is about: Many of the major Japanese companies are highly centralized, run by one individual or by a small group of very senior executives. This article provides some important insights into the much talked about Japanese style of management—it challenges some of the popular views.

1–3 How Japanese managers manage*

Kenichi Ohmae

Kenichi Ohmae is a director of McKinsey & Co. and manages the firm's offices in Tokyo and Osaka.

Many observers of management think that Japanese corporations make major decisions from the bottom up. They are wrong. All the most dynamic Japanese manufacturers that compete in the world market—Honda, Sony, Seiko, Nissan—are tightly run by one individual or by a small and close-knit group of very senior executives.

In many of Japan's giant trading companies, which were established long ago and are now firmly entrenched in the domestic marketplace, decisions are decentralized. The sheer size of these companies and the diversity of their enterprises demand it. How could the CEO of a $50 billion company that sells everything from instant noodles to tools for energy exploration make all critical decisions himself?

On the other hand, Matsushita Electric Industrial, one of Japan's stunning postwar successes, the company behind the brand names Panasonic, Quasar, National, Technics, and JVC, offers a prime example of a chief executive's dominance. Eighty-seven-year-old Konosuke Matsushita, whose history recalls Thomas Edison's role with General Electric, founded the company and has been almost sole architect of its growth.

In 1933, Konosuke Matsushita and his long-term deputy, Arataro Takahashi, began to create a company with many divisions but a unified managerial style. Since then the corporation has acquired more than 20 ailing

---

* Kenneth Ohmae, "How Japanese Managers Manage," *The Wall Street Journal*, April 26, 1982. Reprinted by permission of the author.

companies and turned them around. Though Mr. Matsushita developed many talented entrepreneurs to head up these semiautonomous subsidiaries, he continued to make all the major decisions until he stepped down in 1973 to an honorary counselor role.

Mr. Matsushita was succeeded first by his son-in-law and then by Toshihiko Yamashita, who had ranked next to last on the company's 26-man board of directors and was clearly the founder's choice. Mr. Yamashita perpetuated the company's bold executive style. His decision to adopt the video cassette system developed by a subsidiary, JVC, was particularly tough, because it meant giving up the competing system developed by Matsushita Electric's own scientists and engineers. Hard choices of that kind are seldom made by consensus or recommended by rank-and-file employees.

Sony was run until 1971 by Masaru Ibuka, who started the company in 1946. Akio Morita, the current chairman and CEO, built up Sony's U.S. operations. His recent decision to buck the rest of the company's top management and manufacture the Walkman is already legendary. Though Mr. Morita and his staff encourage worker participation, these activities are so carefully orchestrated that the end result is to disseminate Mr. Morita's own ideas throughout the corporation.

Honda's flamboyant founder, Sokhiro Honda, took personal charge of his company's engineering and production capabilities, while Takeo Fujisawa, executive vice president for many years, developed and implemented financial and marketing strategies. YKK, the world's largest zipper manufacturer, is primarily the creation of Tadao Yoshida. And Yamaha's prominence in the music and sporting goods field is the work of a peppery tycoon named Gerrshchi Kawakami, who retired in 1977 after 25 years as CEO. "While my steps are firm, I'll say goodby," Mr. Kawakami proclaimed. Three years later he caused a furor by removing his successor and reclaiming his former position. Though Yamaha has many talented managers, Mr. Kawakami continues to make the crucial decisions.

Casio is run by four brothers, Tadao, Toshio, Kazuo, and Yukio Kashio. The founder of Omron, an 81-year-old inventor named Kazuma Tateishi, is still chairman, though in 1979 he gave up the presidency to his son Takao. Sanyo owes its success to the managerial skill of the three Iue brothers and the production engineering genius of Sefichi Gotoh.

Shizo Ohya, president of Teijin textiles for 26 years, was proud of his reputation as a tyrant. He once said: "The distance between the president and the executive vice president is greater than the distance between EVP and a company chauffeur."

Why have Japanese CEOs attained such tremendous power? International economist Keitaro Hasegawa believes the explanation lies in the legal definition of the job: The Japanese CEO must personally endorse all the liabilities of his company. He is held legally responsible, for instance, for any law suit or bankruptcy.

Since company presidency is not a well-paid position—Japanese CEOs today make only 7.8 times more than the average college graduate—few accept the position for money. Some may take the job for its prestige value; others do it by order from their predecessor. For many it is a form of self-sacrifice (''If I don't take the job, who will?'') that creates sympathy among their subordinates and thus encourages consensus.

The Japanese CEO has one important weapon: the authority to make personnel decisions. By using this power cleverly, the president can exercise his influence over critical decisions. He can also position his subordinates so that they will make decisions just as he would.

Japanese managers place great emphasis on *Jyoi-Katatsu,* the concept that the will and mind of the boss should be understood implicitly by his subordinates. Employees spend a great deal of time trying to divine their chief's real intentions and find strategies and recommendations that will mirror his style. That is why Japanese decision making may seem to be a bottom-up process at first glance. One executive who has to play this ulcer-provoking guessing game every day explained, ''I am *led* by my superior to make a decision, rather than making it myself.''

The emphasis on the critical role of the leader in a business enterprise also explains why so many CEOs read stories about old Chinese heroes, Japanese feudal lords of the 16th century, Meiji Restoration leaders from the late 19th century, and postwar entrepreneurs like Konosuki Matsushita, who is a modern culture hero. All are examples of leaders who mobilized their subordinates or followers at will, through the subtle manipulation of human behavior. Contrary to the prevailing rhetoric, most Japanese CEOs do indeed make the critical decisions for their companies, probably as forcefully as their U.S. counterparts.

What this article is about: Several reasons are briefly explored for why companies practicing strategic planning are falling behind competitors, largely of foreign origin, who place much less emphasis on strategic planning. Of particular concern to the author is the emphasis on "grandiose strategic leaps" rather than step-by-step improvements and ignoring the capabilities of the organization.

1-4 Why strategic planning goes awry*

Robert H. Hayes

Robert H. Hayes is professor of management and technology at Harvard Business School.

Let's face it. Strategic planning, as practiced by most American companies, is not working very well. This is embarrassing, because we essentially invented the idea, and have poured more resources into it than any other country in the world.

The whole purpose of strategic planning is to help a company get from where it is to where it wants to be, and in the process to develop a *sustainable* advantage over its competitors. Yet a growing number of industries and companies find themselves today more vulnerable strategically than when they started. Not only have they fallen short of the goals they set for themselves, they find themselves falling behind competitors, largely of foreign origin, who place much less emphasis on strategic planning.

How can we explain this?

One or more of three reasons are usually cited: most companies do not really engage in planning but simply play out an annual ritual; planning is carried out largely by outside consultants and corporate staff personnel, and therefore is becoming increasingly divorced from the realities of the business; and plans, once developed, tend to be too inflexible and constraining in rapidly evolving competitive environments. Cummins Engine, for example, was led to diversify by the expectations that its core business was dying. Instead, diversification siphoned off resources that were needed to exploit the continued vitality of the old one.

I would add two other reasons: planning's top-down orientation has emphasized the development of grandiose strategic leaps, rather than the patient step-by-step improvements that are difficult for competitors to copy;

---

* Reprinted from *The New York Times*, April 20, 1986.

and planning has led companies into competitive positions opposite to those desired because they were, in effect, doing it backwards.

The traditional strategic planning process is based on an "ends-ways-means" model. First, one is supposed to establish corporate objectives (ends). Given those objectives, one develops a strategy (ways) for attaining them. Then one marshals the necessary resources (means).

Most companies, unfortunately, base these plans on 5- to 10-year time frames. This makes it almost impossible for them to create a truly strategic difference—one that leads to a competitive advantage that is difficult to copy and, therefore, sustainable. Goals that can be achieved within five years are usually either too easy or are based on buying and selling something. Anything that a company can buy is probably available for purchase by its competitors.

Focusing on major milestones also induces a top-down, "strategic leap" mentality in an organization. Such "leaps" might take a variety of forms: a product redesign, a factory modernization or expansion, a relocation, acquiring a supplier of a critical material or component, or adopting a new manufacturing technology.

Such big steps are highly visible and usually require a major expenditure of funds. Therefore, much staff development is required, and the expertise of many highly specialized people—financial analysts, strategic planners, legal experts and outside consultants—must be tapped. In such companies, the corporate staff is regarded as the elite, and assignments of line managers to staff positions are typically felt to be promotions. This strategy does not require outstanding, highly trained people at lower levels in the organization. Their job is simply to operate the structure that top management and its staff of experts have created.

Increasingly, though, companies are succeeding by eschewing such strategic leaps and seeking competitive advantage through continual incremental improvements. This requires a very different kind of organization. Small improvements seldom involve major capital authorization requests, so there is little need for staff assistance or the advice of outside experts. Rather than putting huge resources into developing elaborate plans and projects, these companies expect most improvements to bubble up, in entrepreneurial fashion, from the lower ranks.

This approach requires a great deal of "low-level expertise" (not expertise *of* a low level, but expertise at low levels). Developing such expertise is a long process. Great effort must be spent on recruiting workers and managers who are both loyal and trainable. Once hired, the capabilities of these people must be continually improved and expanded, both through formal education and through job assignments that provide a broad understanding of the company's products, production systems, and competitive environment.

Such companies do not believe that many of the problems they face can be solved by top management, either because the information and expertise needed for dealing with them is lower in the organization or because the problems are continually evolving over time. Therefore, the role of top management is not to spot and solve problems as much as to create an organization that can spot and solve its own problems.

Most companies fall somewhere between these extremes. But our companies tend to favor "strategic leaps," while those of our two most powerful competitors, West Germany and Japan, tend to seek "incremental improvements" within an existing structure and technology. They are the tortoise, we are the hare.

In the fable, of course, the tortoise won the race. When this happens in business it is usually because a new breakthrough is not available exactly when it is needed. That is, we often see major competitive advantages nibbled away by competitors that gradually adapt themselves to the new technology and then push it beyond the limits we were able to achieve (as is happening in the semiconductor industry today). When this happens, we would like to make another leap. But what if our labs and strategists reach into their hats and find nothing there?

This is essentially the trap that our home electronics producers fell into. While they frantically sought to develop flat-screen television and set up labor-intensive factories in low-wage countries, their Japanese competitors were learning—step-by-step—how to automate production in Japan. Over a period of more than 15 years, Japanese companies patiently reduced the cost of Ampex's pioneering videotape recorder to one hundredth of its original cost, so they could introduce the first consumer VCR.

An obvious response would be to adopt an incremental approach, but this is hard for a company that has configured itself around the expectation of major breakthroughs. Entrepreneurship at the bottom cannot be "ordered" from the top—particularly when, as usually happens, top-down, staff-dominated planning and control systems have caused most of the entrepreneurs to leave.

The traditional approach to strategic planning also errs in its treatment of the third element: means—the resources necessary to implement the chosen strategy. Although many different types of resources will generally be required, most strategic planning focuses primarily on financial wherewithal, ignoring the capabilities of the organization.

A-M International, for example, developed an exciting strategic plan: It would turn to high technology to revitalize its aging office equipment product line. This led it to buy high-technology companies and hire new managers to run them. But it neglected to insure that its factories could make reliable, high-precision products and that its field organizations could sell and service the new products. The new strategy led to disaster because such capabilities cannot be bought. They must be grown from within.

The problems with strategic planning may run even deeper, to the underlying assumption that responsibility for organizational success lies primarily on the shoulders of top management. We need to realize that other approaches can be equally, if not more, effective.

One such approach is to turn the ends-ways-means logic on its head: means-ways-ends. A road map is useful if one is lost in a highway system, but not in a swamp whose topography is constantly changing. A simple compass—that indicates the general direction and allows you to use your own ingenuity in overcoming difficulties—is far more valuable.

Let's think about how such a logic might work.

First, it suggests that a company begin by investing in developing its capabilities along a broad front (means). New technologies and techniques are acquired and experimented with. Small, information-gathering subsidiaries are set up in strategic locations like Japan and Korea. R&D activity is spread more widely throughout the organization. Workers and managers are given cross-functional assignments so that they develop a broad understanding of the company's markets, technologies, and factories.

If American electronics companies had followed this approach 15 years ago, they wouldn't have discontinued the internal production of integrated circuits—because chip design is becoming interchangeable with systems design. Nor would American semiconductor companies have stopped producing much of their own manufacturing equipment—even though every advance in their product requires equal advance in the production process.

Second, as these capabilities develop and as technological and market opportunities appear, managers well down in the organization are encouraged to exploit matches wherever they occur (ways). Top management's job is to facilitate this kind of entrepreneurial activity, provide it with resources from other parts of the company and, where feasible, encourage cooperative activities.

In short, the company doesn't first develop plans and then seek capabilities; it builds capabilities and then encourages the development of plans for exploiting them. Rather than trying to develop optimal strategies that assume a static environment, it seeks opportunistic improvements in a dynamic environment.

Such a "reverse" logic tends to be most effective in rapidly changing competitive environments. Fixed objectives are likely to lose their attractiveness over time as the company and its competitive environment evolve. A common vision, however, will keep people moving ahead, around unforeseen obstacles and beyond the stated (largely because they were visible) immediate objectives.

In such organizations *everybody* is assumed to be responsible for the organization's prosperity. Its success rests on its ability to exploit opportunities as they arise, its ingenuity, its capacity to learn, its determination and its persistence. The obvious analogy is with guerrilla warfare.

Sometimes, of course, companies must change their objectives, decide to enter a new business or abandon an old one. Such decisions seldom bubble up from the bottom; they must flow from the top. The trick is to manage such discontinuities without undermining lower level managers. When a guerrilla army decides that the only person with any real authority is the supreme leader, its field commanders lose their credibility. And as the balance of power begins to shift, more and more is likely to be drained from lower levels. As the "counters" gain ascendancy over the "doers," the best doers are likely to become counters. Or they go elsewhere, where they can do it their way.

The struggle between American companies and their foreign competitors can be likened to a battle between a bunch of hares trained in conventional warfare and equipped with road maps, and a bunch of tortoises that are expert in guerrilla tactics and armed with compasses. Unfortunately, the battle is taking place in a swamp, and the ends-ways-means logic that got the hares into such a situation is unlikely to get them out.

They may have to replace it—or at least supplement it—with a reverse logic. Rather than building elaborate strategic plans around forecasts of an unworkable future, they might ask themselves why they were so successful when planning occupied little of their time, but their industrial capabilities were the envy of the world.

What this article is about: In spite of recent criticisms of formal strategic planning, most corporate executives and business-unit managers continue to practice—and value—strategic planning. The concept itself isn't the problem, according to the executives surveyed and interviewed. Rather, planning systems often break down because of faulty preparation and implementation. Well-managed companies can overcome these problems by involving line managers in the planning process, defining business units correctly, outlining action steps in detail, and integrating the strategic plan with other organizational controls.

1-5 Uses and misuses of strategic planning*

Daniel H. Gray

Daniel H. Gray is president and chief executive officer of Gray-Judson, Inc., a consulting firm based in Boston that specializes in strategic management.

There's nothing wrong with formal strategic planning—if you do it right.

Some writers on management today claim that strategic planning is on the wane—or at least on the defensive. Is yet another management fad about to fade away? Are we seeing still another example that shows the folly of trying to manage in "too rational" a way? Consider all those companies that have spent so much money on strategic planning yet still have problems. And look at all those impressive plans that fall apart during implementation.

Though it seems as if strategic planning is on the way out in some companies because of faulty diagnosis of its defects, I would say, on the basis of my research and experience, that reports of its demise are exaggerated and premature.

Strategic planning as many textbooks describe it may not be around much longer but not for the reasons most critics give. If formal strategic planning vanishes in a few years, it will be because wherever it is undertaken it either gets better or it gets worse, depending on how well it's done: if you do it poorly, either you drop out or you rattle around in its mechanics; if you do it well, you evolve beyond strategic planning to strategic management.

Strategic planning is usually seen, on adoption, as a separate discipline or a management function. It involves the allocation of resources to programmed activities calculated to achieve a set of business goals in a dynamic, competitive environment. Strategic management, on the other hand, treats strategic thinking as a pervasive aspect of running a business and regards strategic planning as an instrument around which all other control systems—budgeting, information, compensation, organization—can be integrated. This interdependency usually comes to light when a business has trouble implementing the results of a freestanding strategic planning process.

These distinctions and definitions emerged from a year-long research project that focused on where things most often go wrong in "good" strategic planning systems and what has been learned about shoring up these weak spots. In this research my colleagues and I have contacted a broad sample of business unit heads, corporate planning directors, and chief executive officers engaged in strategic planning in American multibusiness corporations. We used a questionnaire to pinpoint where things have gone wrong and conducted 14 executive seminars to search for remedies (see Figure 1 and Figure 2). To date there have been 300 respondents to the questionnaire and 216 participants in the day-and-a-half seminars.

Figure 1
Topics and responses in the evaluation of strategic planning systems in U.S. multibusiness companies

Topic	Response
Source of greatest frustration or disappointment	Implementation difficulties
Other areas of major concern	Skills of line managers Adequacy of information
Rating of current planning system on a scale of 1 to 10, from worst to best	56% in 6-7-8 range Mode: 7 Mean: 5.5
Nature of planning output	General direction or thrust for strategic action
Locus of planning responsibility	Line managers: 78%
Relation to budget process	Planning first, budgeting afterward: 55%
Sources of market information	In-house: 80%
Number of strategic business units (SBUs)	Range from 6 to 48
Basis of unit definition	Product lines: 57%
Relation of SBUs to profit centers	Coincide: 51%
How unit goals and objectives are set	Top-down: 33% Bottom-up: 67%
Who owns an SBU's cash flow	Corporation: 83%
Unit strategy development process	Interdepartmental group give-and-take: 34%
Linkage of planning to other controls	More to budgets than anything else: 42%
Impact of strategic planning on organizational structure	Structure often adapted to support strategy: 70%
Relationship of executive bonuses to strategic performance	Financial results only: 60% Financial and strategic mix: 22%
Authority of groups or divisions over SBU planning	Not significant: 68% Controlling: 32%
Corporate resource allocation process when resource requests exceed resources available	Perceived as unfair: 49% Perceived as fair: 37%

Figure 2
Executive seminar participants

Management Level			Industry Type		
Corporate executives	91	42%	Service businesses	89	41%
Corporate planning directors and staff	85	39	Manufacturing businesses	111	52
Business-unit managers	40	19	Government agencies	16	7
Total	216	100%	Total	216	100%

At this point we can report the following findings:

- First, most companies in our sample remain firmly committed to strategic planning, even though 87 percent report feelings of disappointment and frustration with their systems.
- Second, 59 percent attribute their discontent mainly to difficulties encountered in the implementation of plans.
- Third, when multibusiness executives compare their experiences, 67 percent trace their implementation problems to the design of their systems and the way they manage them.

While implementation failures have for some been the cause of frustration and withdrawal, such experiences have helped others learn to run their planning systems better. Consider the ''Gamma Corporation,'' a provider of upscale women's garments, jewelry, luggage, and cosmetics whose growth curve had flattened out. To recover, it acquired a related but embryonic service business with apparel and cosmetic appendages. The service business became a new Gamma profit center, while its appendages were assimilated into kindred profit centers of the parent. The corporate requirement that the new service business match the profit and cost control performance of the established business made rapid sales growth an imperative.

The hotshot, upscale marketer who was given the entrepreneurial opportunity to make something of the service unit tried to accomplish this through dress pattern and cosmetic giveaways. When sister profit centers blocked this move, he missed his targets and quit. The Gamma strategy to rejuvenate a low-growth company with a vigorous new synergistic service acquisition was the company's maiden voyage into strategic planning. The verdict at corporate headquarters was that the plan ''fell apart through poor implementation.''

After an extensive audit of this implementation failure, Gamma executives perceived that their strategy had been deeply flawed well before implementation: the company had made only a financial evaluation of the acquisition candidate. The new retail service unit was a poorly designed strategy center. It was lodged in the same organization with mature wholesale product businesses. Its best strategic options were preempted by an inappropriate financial strategy. There was no portfolio strategy to reconcile the new unit with others. The new unit head was not allowed to behave entrepreneurially. The company had no detailed action plan to mesh the new and old business strategies.

The Gamma Corporation and many other companies have stuck to their strategic plans in spite of their frustrations. Their persistence is rooted in the needs that led them to adopt strategic planning in the first place. They have come to realize that steering a business by financial controls alone is not enough. However vital the bottom line, balance sheet feedback is too lumpy, too stripped of connotative information, and often too late. Financial plans must be augmented and supplemented by strategic plans if managers are to make more timely and accurate midcourse corrections in response to external change. The competitive penalty for inabilty to adapt along the way is too great for most companies to do without strategic planning.

Another reason that companies persist in planning despite disappointment is evident in the way many respondents to our questionnaire rated their planning systems. On a scale of 1 to 10 (1 meaning worst and 10 meaning best), the modal rating (7) accounted for 27 percent of all responses. This rating was assigned to any system considered to be excellent for clarification of where one wants to go but not very good in execution. This finding suggests a view of planning as a two-part process—a strategy development part and a strategy execution part. One can then look with approval on strategy development and with disapproval on strategy execution. This allows strategy developers to view themselves as the victims of the poor work of implementers lower down in the organization and to overlook the crucial role that strategy development plays in determining whether a plan can be implemented.

Common Problems and Workable Solutions

When chief executives, corporate planning directors, and business-unit heads in our sample got together to discuss common problems, we observed that they tended to have second thoughts about how good their planning systems are, what is wrong with them, and where and how to put things right. (For a sample of what they said, see the ruled insert.) Two thirds of what these managers called implementation difficulties were, on closer scrutiny, attributed to these six preimplementation factors:

1. Poor preparation of line managers.
2. Faulty definition of business units.
3. Vaguely formulated goals.
4. Inadequate information bases for action planning.
5. Badly handled reviews of business-unit plans.
6. Inadequate linkage of strategic planning with other control systems.

The uncovering of these design and management errors can lead to new insights about how to avoid many implementation problems. In this article, we examine several of them. There are undoubtedly more to be uncovered in the ongoing search for the most effective principles of strategic planning. (see Figure 3 for some suggestions.)

Involve Line Managers

It does little good to allocate planning responsibility to line managers if they receive no preparation or poor preparation for this keyrole.

Figure 3
Some principles for strategic planning

Strategic planning is a line management function for which training in strategic analysis and participative skills is usually necessary.

Strategic business units need to be defined so that one executive can control the key variables essential to the execution of his or her strategic business plan.

A unit's concept of the business it is in must above all be formulated from the outside in so that it can most effectively engage the dynamics of its strategic environment.

Action plans for achieving business objectives are the key to implementing and monitoring strategy. They require extensive lower-level participation and special leadership skills. Action plans are complete when underlying assumptions, allocation of responsibilities, time and resource requirements, risks, and likely responses have been made explicit.

Participative strategy development, a prerequisite for successful strategy execution, often requires cultural change at the upper levels of corporations and their business units.

The strategic planning system and other control systems designed to guide managerial and organizational behavior must be integrated in a consistent whole if business strategies are to be executed well.

Productivity improvement programs are best treated as aspects of strategic business plans since productivity takes on significantly different meanings as the strategic balance between marketing and production shifts.

Well-managed organizations must be both centralized and decentralized—centralized so that strategies and control systems can be integrated and decentralized so that units in each strategic environment can act and be treated with appropriate differentiation.

Over time, good strategic planning, once considered a separate activity, becomes a mind-set, a style and a set of techniques for running a business—not something more to do but a better way of doing what has always had to be done.

At a major aerospace and automotive supplier, for example, managers complained that a sophisticated planning system had failed to "come alive" and that formal business-unit plans were lying "unused in bottom drawers." Recently, four years into their system and just after making a major acquisition, the company convened more than 40 heads of strategic business units (SBUs) to teach them the skills that strategic planning requires. Picture a week-long conference in posh surroundings: visiting management gurus doing star turns; reprints of landmark cases describing classic acquisition assimilation problems; workshops where messages from the participants to the corporate hierarchy could be hammered out; and, at the end of the week, a flying visit from the CEO to talk about his vision of the future. Total cost: more than $250,000. Result: last-minute watering-down of the messages, a 60-day fade-out of the experience, and no significant change in behavior.

It is now widely accepted that strategic planning is a line management function in which staff specialists play a supporting role. Yet many companies have done little to prepare line managers for this kind of leadership. When they are left to grope for the operational meaning of concepts like "strategic mind-set," "issue formulation," "conflict management," and "portfolio role," they feel ill at ease. Strategic planning seems more like a burden imposed from above than a better way of running their units. Not surprisingly, some of these line managers adopt a modest, mechanical approach to their planning duties. Then staff planners may creep back in to lend a hand and help fill the void.

Line managers in charge of business units say they want coaching in the skills required to guide strategy debates. They want to know how to draw department heads out of their specialized frames of reference and into a general management view of trade-offs between functions. They want to know what questions will be asked and what challenges to expect when they send their business plans up for approval.

Some companies have tried to help their unit heads by offering them quick-fix management development courses—often with disappointing results. A great deal of management development training is still carried on with generic or hypothetical case materials and with packages of received wisdom presented to groups of peers. Such training may be valuable, but it usually does not replicate the real conditions facing the line management strategist.

A better practice is to focus on real problems in managers' own companies so as to see the trouble in its current strategic context. This opportunity to learn how to be more flexible and adaptive (and to learn about learning) should be offered not as a gift but as part of a transaction—this assistance in exchange for that change in behavior. It should be offered to groups representing the various functions and levels whose cooperation is needed to solve tough problems.

An example of a company that successfully involved line managers in planning is a manufacturer of electronic components in the Sunbelt. Facing an urgent need to offset price declines with cost reductions, the company assembled a 25-person training squad of managers ranging from the level of superintendent to that of divisional chief operating officer. With the help of a process facilitator and with engineering, marketing, and personnel staff on call, the training squad was charged to explore the rationale, the feasibility and cost, the potential savings, and the cultural consequences of four options—asset reduction, productivity gain sharing, plant rationalization, and operator training—and then to recommend a remedial action program. Four of the 12 lowest ranking members of the team would be chosen for promotion and training roles in their own or other plants. In the end, the squad's plan was accepted, three men were promoted, and divisional operating costs dropped 17 percent in the ensuing six months.

Define the Business Unit

Even when its boundaries are strategically correct, a business unit is vulnerable to an outmoded conceptualization of the business it is in. Consider the difference between being a brewer of beer and being a seller of beer in English pubs. Under either category, the assets, products, markets, people, and functions are the same; but there is a world of difference in the kind of strategy developed, the direction of people's energies, the priorities of action, the indicators to be monitored, and the places where profit is taken. In one case, beer production is all-important; in the other, beer is fourth or fifth in importance in the customer's purchase decision. In an aging, oligopolistic industry with excess capacity, Courage Breweries' shift from a supply-side mind-set to a consumer lifestyle mind-set helped break open a stalemated industry's market share equilibrium and improve profits.

How a strategy center or an SBU conceives of its business can have a significant bearing on its strategic behavior and its competitive clout. Management's attitude toward a business is as important as its boundaries. For example, a manufacturer of rubber and plastic control devices and assemblies saw its business flatten out under a definition of itself as a company that supplies "these specific products to these specific industries." While continuing to make large batches of flow valves and gaskets for automobile and appliance makers, the manufacturer began to diagnose and treat the precision-molding process control problems of manufacturers in general. To its single-tier, high-volume, production-driven product line the company added an R&D and marketing-driven premium-price line.

If a multibusiness fails to define its strategy centers or its strategic business units correctly, the best planning techniques available can't undo the damage. When strategic planning is newly installed, it is often assumed that the organizational units already in place should handle the planning. These units, however, may owe their boundaries to many factors that make them inappropriate to use as a basis for planning: geography, administrative convenience, the terms of old acquisition deals, product lines, traditional profit centers, a belief in healthy internal competition, or old ideas about centralization and decentralization.

Frequently these familiar rationales for unit boundaries make for poor strategy centers. That they could be wrong may not occur to executives who take organizational structure as a given before planning begins. But strategic planning teaches its more successful practitioners that the main purpose of organization (including both structure and process) is to support the development and execution of strategy. Thus organization should come after strategic planning.

The following principles should guide the definition of business units:

- Include within the jurisdiction of the strategy center all variables the unit head needs for executing the strategy. For example it may not be wise to require a manager charged with opening up new markets for a cluster of products to buy manufacturing and distribution services from sister profit centers.
- Leave the unit head free to take profits where strategy dictates. Hence nothing smaller than a strategy center should be a profit center.
- Let external rather than internal forces shape unit boundaries. If competitive forces require a larger unit than normal spans of control would dictate, go with the larger unit.
- When separate units are strategically appropriate for external reasons but must, for economies of scale, share central facilities and services, let them share, but keep them as separate units. A Texas chemical company, for example, decided against combining the planning processes of its generic and specialized businesses. Although they share a common infrastructure, their customers and competitors are so different that the managers of these businesses could never agree on a common strategy.

While the application of these principles of unit definition is crucial to

WE'VE COME TO PRAISE STRATEGIC PLANNING, NOT TO BURY IT

Quotes from postseminar self-evaluation sheets

We expected too much of strategic planning and were disappointed. Now we know that planning is part of a larger process, and mastering *that* is fulfilling our expectations.

—*Corporate planning officer, insurance company*

I can't conceive of doing business without a strategy and a plan. Every company has to do it. Either you get to be good at it, or you do it poorly and suffer the consequences.

—*Chief executive officer, diversified manufacturer*

What we had was a kind of strategic rain dance—war cries, smoke signals, sacrificial offerings. We're much more thorough and disciplined now—more analytical and more demanding of ourselves.

—*President, retail division, clothing business*

We actually used to tell ourselves our planning system was OK, even though we admitted it fell apart in implementation. That was our way of telling ourselves that the trouble was not at the top.

Head of a strategic business unit in a 17-unit corporation

The way to get into a planning bind is to go at everything piecemeal. . . . First the organization chart—that's done. . . . Then the plan—that's done. . . . Then the budget—that's done. . . . The bonus system—that's done. . . . All that hard work and then nothing fits.

—*Executive vice president, health care holding company*

When you have two rival plans—a strategic business plan and a financial plan—either you dovetail them or before long the strategic plan and the will to do it are dead.

—*Financial director, department store chain*

good strategy development and execution, they can conflict with one another. As a practical matter, therefore, these principles cannot serve as absolutes. In the end, boundary setting is an executive judgment call but not a purely subjective one. The final judgment can be either adaptive, in which case the boundaries line up with the realities of the prevailing strategic game, or willful, in which case the company accepts the risks of trying to change the way the external game is played.

Failure to address the unit definition question at all or to address it without giving due weight to the external environment can lead to serious problems. Looking first at the environment, however, is by itself no guarantee of success. A rule often used in unit boundary setting is one product, one manager. This is meant to ensure direct accountability and single-minded strategic concentration on the fate of the product. The penalty for this approach, however, can be the loss of opportunities for discretionary profit taking, synergistic manipulation of related products, marketing cooperation, and economies of scale. The result is often the creation of too many business units too narrow to compete effectively.

Move beyond General Goals

Implementation is bound to go awry if strategy formulation goes no further than defining general thrusts and end-point goals. Consider a public utility that adopted a strategy of "energy conservation, high earnings, diversification, and excellence." These four goals were so general that the person in charge of managing each one could unwittingly be at cross-purposes with the others. Field personnel cuts made to improve earnings eliminated the very people needed to run a new diversification venture aimed at saving energy through home and factory audits and retrofits. At the same time, the pursuit of engineering "excellence" led to the purchase of materials that were too durable to mesh with the utility's plan for capacity replacement.

Approximately 7 out of 10 companies in our sample do not carry the formulation of strategy much beyond some general statement of thrust such as market penetration or internal efficiency and some generalized goal such as excellence. Having only generalizations to work with makes implementation very difficult. Targets don't mean much if no one maps out the pathways leading to them. After this kind of half-baked strategy is handed over for execution, subordinates who have not been in on the formulation of the strategy are left to deal with its cross-impacts and trade-offs when they bump into them. If told only that the name of the strategic game is high quality and prompt delivery, various people in an organization—designers, inspectors, schedulers, piece workers, and salespeople—may each reconcile these two factors differently. Subordinates' efforts are often parochial and improvisational; the way they carry out an undefined strategy is often unsatisfactory— if they elect to complete it at all.

Make More Detailed Action Plans

The cure for half-baked strategy is action detailing, but this task often baffles and irritates many executives. Only one in three of the companies in our study has a process or a forum for the interfunctional debate and testing of unit strategies. Their procedures for action detailing and other kinds of reality testing are often nonexistent or merely rudimentary. Action detailing of a sort is carried on in some places as a part of operational planning, but it usually follows strategic planning and takes the strategy as given. Planning in detail should be used as a further test of a strategy's feasibility.

One way to combine operational and strategic planning is to begin an advocacy process as soon as agreement on strategic thrusts has been reached. An interfunctional task force is set up for each thrust—with strong representation from middle management. Each team can identify and analyze the options for reaching a particular objective and then rough out the major action steps necessary to accomplish the option that it will advocate to the unit strategy team.

The team's job is to explain and defend what it considers the best way of bringing this option to life. Each team must deal with time frame, risk analysis, allocation of responsibility, resource requirements, organization obstacles, and monitoring devices. In mapping out and testing strategic options, managers begin to think explicitly about assumptions, alternatives, contingencies, and what competitive reactions to expect. Failure to come to grips with these details can undermine the execution of the strategy.

When senior executives are invited to try their hands at action detailing, they often find it an uncomfortable exercise. They tend to offer as action steps what are really no more than wishes or desired results—such as "upgrading front-line supervision," "introducing services that appeal to the customer," or "eliminating wasteful practices." Good action detailing however, requires the participation of middle and lower management and the work force. Top management knows the direction; those below know the terrain. Not only is lower level participation essential to working out practical steps, but it is also highly desirable. Through such participation, managers generate the kind of understanding, ownership, commitment, and motivation necessary for successful implementation. The alternative, which is to try to push strategic planning out into the organization and down through the ranks by exhortation and other forms of one-way "communication," has only minimal effect.

Companies trapped in half thought-out planning may lack the information and motivation necessary to good strategy execution. These companies may avoid the front-end costs of participation, discussion, and explicit detailing, but they pay the cost of not seeing their options, not reaching their goals, and spending days bogged down in implementation.

Manage the Face-Off

Even when all the steps in the strategy development process are taken according to the principles of best practice, strategic plans can be ruined and the whole system undermined at the final review stage. The issue is how good the design and management of the planning cycle is when the business units' proposed plans hit the corporate screen. We call this crucial encounter managing the face-off.

The face-off is a moment of inevitable, healthy conflict. Not only do all the units' resource requests frequently exceed what headquarters is prepared to provide, but their aggregate performance promises are often less than the corporation as a whole requires. Since performance requirements come from an analysis of capital markets while performance promises arise from strategies for dealing with each business unit's particular environment, this conflict is not surprising.

What should happen at the face-off is reconciliation, which often involves queuing, downsizing, redirection, and recycling. What actually does happen is often rather primitive: exhortation, backdoor dealing, across-the-board cuts, moving the goalposts, and mandated performance promises. In other words, the units' plans are force-fit in various ways into the corporate plan. At this stage of the game, companies normally focus their attention more on the numbers in the business plan than on the strategies. For example, one general manager responsible for an aging product described scaling down his profit projections after a rival company had captured a 4 percent market share in five months with a generic commodity substitute. This manager's boss, however, ordered the higher profit figures restored and asked him how he expected to win the marketing wars with "negative thinking." Unfortunately, this example is typical. Numbers are often altered at the face-off so as to close the gap without any discussion of the need to revise the risk assessments, competitive reactions, probability estimates, and other problems lying beneath the numbers.

Even if all the units have done their strategic planning very well up to the time of final review, think of the consequences for the next round of planning if they tack new financial projections arbitrarily onto strategies whose predicted effects in a particular competitive environment have already been calculated to be lower. The obligatory promise that headquarters extracts from a subunit may close the gap for a while, but it will undercut and degrade the next round of planning and budgeting. The force-fit at the face-off is an invitation to play games and a clear signal that scrupulous planning is considered a waste of valuable time.

Only a small minority of the companies we studied (13 percent) say they have a satisfactory process for managing the face-off. A little over one third report some attempt at "rigorous trade-off analysis among business units." Among corporate controls, strategic planning is often the new kid on the block. Some executives see strategic planning as challenging financial controls and think of the face-off as the place where financial management supersedes strategic management. In these companies, financial strategy is not reconciled with other strategies but preempts them as the final arbiters of corporate resource allocation.

Integrate Plans and Controls

A strategic planning system can't achieve its full potential until it is integrated with other control systems such as budgets, information systems, and reward systems. The badly designed, poorly managed face-off is a manifestation of a deeper problem—the "compartmentalization syndrome," which treats various control systems as freestanding and strategically neutral.

While most executives who have adopted strategic planning see it as an indispensable tool, they tend to treat it at first as just another addition to an array of control devices. Before long they may discover that one control is at odds with another. Then the notion of linking these different controls arises, and that is as close as most companies in our study have come to a concept of integrated control. The three linkage problems they frequently identified have to do with plans and budgets, plans and information systems, and plans and reward systems.

Plans and Budgets   The conflict between strategic plans and budgets is the most commonly perceived area of dissonance. Managers tend to view the annual planning and budgeting sequence as logically connected but not integrated in fact. While the best strategic planning starts from an environmental analysis and then works in the unit's ability to respond, budgeting usually proceeds by making incremental adjustments to the previous year's internal departmental budgets. This practice allows the momentum of last year's (possibly obsolete) business strategy and this year's functional strategies to determine the funding of this year's business-unit plan.

The absence of strategic action planning often thwarts those who want to integrate plans and budgets. Not until a company has formulated explicit action steps can it cast fixed capital, working capital, operating expense, and revenue and head-count implications in the form of strategy-based budgets. Most CEOs yearn for such budgets so that they can see how their strategies, not just their departments, are doing. But the same CEOs often report that they are told such budgets are not possible without disrupting the whole accounting system.

Plans and Information Systems   Many strategic planners in the units and at the top of multibusiness corporations express concern about the adequacy of their planning information bases and decision support systems. They worry about linking poor information bases with sophisticated computers. Even accurate, timely, and accessible information will not help the planner if it leads to an inappropriate strategy.

For example, a manufacturer of components for automobiles, appliances, medical equipment, and the like once developed a sophisticated data base for manpower planning that it can no longer use. The company's well-stocked management information system displays on demand how many machinists—white and black, male and female, high school educated and not—live within 30 minutes' commuting distance of its plant in New Jersey. The trouble is, the competition has changed, so that the company cannot be globally cost competitive unless it bases its production in Europe or Asia.

Like many businesses, this company based its strategy on data that had accumulated in response to questions raised by its financial managers and its technical and professional specialists, whose expertise was too narrow. The information system drove the strategy instead of the other way around. Strategy is what makes a fact relevant or irrelevant, and a relevant fact significant or insignificant.

Corporate CEOs and their business-unit heads are the ones who must raise the issues, ask the questions, and formulate the business definitions, missions, objectives, and strategies that will drive their decision support systems. With today's information technology, it is possible to move in the right or the wrong strategic direction with great speed.

Plans and Reward Systems   When companies design reward systems as separate, freestanding controls, they may overlook the fact that such controls are not strategically neutral. For example, a strategy for competitive survival required a Tennessee manufacturer of temperature control devices to put expensive new assets in place to bring out a new version of a fading product. Its management had less than a year to realize the six-figure bonuses they would receive under a three-year average ROI payout formula. The head-on collision of a strategy that increased the asset base at the expense of reducing executive bonuses delayed the strategy's implementation for five months.

Many companies have witnessed the quiet destruction of a two- or a three-year strategy while their executives protected their first-year profit-sharing bonuses. It is folly to appeal to managers' self-interest with rewards for behavior other than the kind the strategic business plan calls for, and it is naive to expect them to override the powerful incentives that reward systems evoke.

The Primacy of Strategic Planning

No organizational arrangement, control system, or productivity program is strategically neutral. Strategic planning becomes the device for consistently lining up such factors.

Among companies exploring the problem of integrated control systems, the idea is taking shape that strategic planning can serve as the core control instrument of a business enterprise, with other controls adjusted and adapted to facilitate the execution of strategy. Why this emphasis on strategic planning? Because of all control devices, it is the one that is driven by the business environment. Strategic planning comes before the final results are known, determines whether profit will be taken now or later, and decides which facts are relevant. While financial controls are obviously indispensable, the feedback they give is often too aggregated, too homogenized, and too late—not to mention too conservative of past business practices.

With strategic planning, the concept of integrated, or fused, controls goes further than the reconciliation of budgets, rewards, and decision support systems. As the unifying role of strategy in running a business becomes clear, we see that getting control over the productivity of a business is not strategically neutral either. It is apparent that in embryonic and growth industries productivity should refer to such things as market response time and market penetration, even if the price of these achievements is some internal inefficiency or postponed profit.

A leading paint manufacturer once lost volume by holding a price umbrella over its competitors and then seeking to restore falling margins through a productivity drive in every department of every plant. The company learned that the price cuts it made to restore volume and raise plant utilization above the break-even point did eight times as much for productivity as a $3 million waste elimination campaign had done earlier.

Seen as part of strategy, productivity is not exclusively concerned with physical input and output ratios or even with current net revenue. Productivity is keyed to the intended outcome of a business plan. Sometimes the intended outcome is profit today, in which case productivity may mean moving down the experience curve. Sometimes the goal is profit tomorrow, in which case productivity may mean preempting rivals and buying shares for future payback. Traditional corporate productivity czars presiding over programs that treat all business units alike can kill growth units before they ever get to the mature stage, when low-cost strategies are appropriate.

Finally, effective strategic planning that reflects the importance of integrated controls also takes organizational structure into account. For example, their strategic planning experience is enabling some executives to rethink the age-old problem of whether to centralize or decentralize management. Everyone knows that centralization inhibits the motivation of decision makers on the periphery of large organizations. In a multibusiness setup, centralization can lead to passive or reactive unit leadership. It is also widely understood that decentralization frequently leads to highly energetic policies and behaviors that may be suboptimal from the corporate viewpoint. Many companies trying to escape this apparent dilemma have swung back and forth between centralization and decentralization.

Now there appears to be a way out: multibusiness strategic planning clearly calls for both centralization and decentralization. No strategic corporate portfolio management and resource allocation rationale can exist without bringing the family of unit heads together at the center. Similarly, differentiated unit strategies cannot be executed in varying business environments without a process for local advocacy and local discretion in execution. In short, the planning process demands both integration and differentiation. These terms may be more useful and revealing than centralization and decentralization because they leave strategic planners free to decide what needs to be integrated at the center as well as what needs to be differentiated on the periphery and free to set up whatever organizational arrangements best facilitate strategy development, reconciliation, execution, and adaptation.

From this line of reasoning it is a short step to the conclusion that strategic planning, at its leading edge, is really just an aspect of strategic management. From this perspective it no longer makes sense to question people about the merits of their planning systems. What matters is whether their mind-sets, their plans, their practices, and their overall controls are coordinated and fit together harmoniously. In the most effective companies I've observed, strategic planning is no longer an added managerial duty. It is a way of thinking about a business and how to run it.

What this article is about: R. J. Reynolds is one successful company that attributes its substantial profits to careful planning. With the merger of Nabisco into RJR, the company will become the largest consumer products company in the United States. The chairman and CEO of the company discusses the planning function at RJR and the role it played in charting a new strategic direction for the company that has focused on consumer goods and services.

1–6 Strategic planning at R. J. Reynolds industries*

J. Tylee Wilson

J. Tylee Wilson is chairman and chief executive officer of R. J. Reynolds Industries, Inc.

Consider the situation of American business in 1985. *Business Week,*[1] and other critical observers, are saying that there are too many planners. The conventional wisdom is that in the 1970s, American business went directly from no planning at all to a sort of fixation on the science of strategic planning. And because of this, some companies badly neglected practical operations.

So the pendulum for strategic planning has swung. One reads about Company *A* slashing its planning group in half and Company *B* marching all its planners off the plank of corporate headquarters and into the briny deep of operating units. But many planners are now moving into key jobs in operating units because of the experience they gained in the planning function.

Yet looking back on what has been accomplished at R. J. Reynolds Industries, and looking forward to what the company expects to accomplish in the future, it is difficult to accept *Business Week*'s premise that there are too many planners in business. Without planning that was both practical and visionary, RJR would not have been able to create significant profits for its shareholders.

For example, look at the period from June 30, 1983, just prior to RJR's announcement of a possible spin-off of its subsidiary called Sea-Land Service, to year-end 1984. An investor holding stock during this period would have had a total return on investment, including dividends and Sea-Land stock, of nearly 57 percent. The absolute price of the RJR stock increased nearly 42 percent. By way of comparison, the S&P 400 industrial stocks over this same period decreased in value by 1.9 percent. This is firm confirmation of the market's positive assessment of RJR's strategic development plan.

* Reprinted from *The Journal of Business Strategy* 6, No. 2, Fall 1985, pp. 22–28.
[1] "The New Breed of Strategic Planner," Sept. 17, 1984.

During the same time period, RJR's market value increased from \$5.7 billion to \$7.5 billion. Its multiple increased from 7 times to 10 times earnings and pulled even with the S&P 400. And in 1985 RJR's momentum has not stopped. The company is continuing to outperform the market.

Successful Planning

What business requires is a plan that is pertinent, practical, actionable, and evolutionary—not revolutionary. Such plans do not come from ivory towers but develop out of the operation of the business. In other words, the planning function must not be isolated, but must be woven into the fabric of the company. The person charged with the planning responsibility must be a recognized member of the senior management team. And the plans must be implemented with the participation of senior management at the corporate level and at the operating unit or subsidiary level. To be effective, the planning function must be part of the daily operations of management at all levels of the company.

That, at any rate, is how the planning function is viewed at RJR. The planning officer reports directly to me and is present at all meetings of key people. And every so often, I take the time to meet with the planning officer and a handful of other senior executives in a retreat atmosphere, where we fine-tune our existing plans and often take another look at the overall question of where we want to go, and how we expect to get there.

Planning and Growth at RJR

Of course, planning was not always such a major consideration at RJR. About 10 years ago, RJR, like most companies, had very little formal planning. The company had grown dramatically from the small tobacco business that was started in 1875 and had become a somewhat curious assortment of related and unrelated businesses.

Tobacco had remained its most important line. But tobacco was approaching mature status in the United States. The major growth opportunities for tobacco were overseas, and 10 years ago RJR's interests beyond the borders of the United States were still quite limited. In addition to tobacco, the company had a small foods business that included brands such as Hawaiian Punch and Chun King, which completed its consumer portfolio.

RJR had gone into two nonconsumer fields in a big way. It owned Sea-Land Service, which had revolutionized the shipping industry with its containerized freight concept. See-Land had been acquired in 1969 as an attractive investment for the cash flow from RJR's tobacco operations. And RJR owned Aminoil Inc., the nation's second largest independent petroleum exploration and production company.

Although a good case could be made for RJR's investments in transportation and energy at the time, it became evident by the middle 1970s that the company had diversified away from its strength. The company's long suit, from its earliest days, had been as a producer and marketer of consumer goods. By late 1977, RJR had considerable difficulty saying in a few words just what it was. What the company settled on was that RJR was "a premier consumer goods company with strategic investments in transportation and

energy.'' We were often asked the definition of a ''strategic investment''—
and sometimes we weren't sure ourselves. We found this was confusing to
shareholders and the financial community.

A New Strategic Direction

It was at this juncture that a new strategic direction was charted for the
company. Henceforth, it was decided that RJR would concentrate its strategic focus on *consumer* goods and services. Since then it has made some bold
strides. RJR is now, in many ways, a very different company.

The transformation was no simple matter. RJR went into some totally new
ventures involving billions of dollars of investments, and it divested other
assets also running into the billions. All this was done through a great deal of
hard work and attention to detail, but it was all based on planning.

Of course, in 1977 we did not have the clear vision to see what circumstances would be in 1985. The fact was that the direction was set, but the
process itself was evolutionary. There were certain things that simply had to
happen in sequence. There were other factors and opportunities that could
not be foreseen. Nevertheless, RJR did have overall direction, and the
company also had a pretty clear idea of what it wanted to do in each of its
lines of business.

First, RJR knew that there were growth opportunities for tobacco overseas, so it stepped up its worldwide expansion through a series of acquisitions and joint ventures. It formed a new subsidiary company, R. J. Reynolds
Tobacco International, to manage these interests. It is now the fourth largest
tobacco company in the world outside the United States.

As for the domestic tobacco industry, RJR knew it was not growing in the
aggregate. But there were opportunities for segmented growth in selected
categories. The company had proved that earlier by taking a leadership
position in the low ''tar'' segment with Vantage. More recently, RJR has
introduced Century and a reformulated Doral in the ''value'' segment and
Sterling and Ritz in the prestige, upscale segment.

Some Critical Planning

Some of RJR's most critical planning, however, dealt with the area of
foods and beverages. In the late 1970s, it could look back on about a decade
of experience with its small, entrepreneurial brands—the Chun Kings and
the Patios. They were good in their way, but not nearly big enough to give
RJR any real presence in the marketplace.

The choice was simple: expand RJR's presence in foods or retire from the
field. But in a way, the company had already made that decision when it
determined that the future lay in consumer products. It followed that the
decision regarding foods would be not to get out, but to get big.

RJR's acquisition of Del Monte in 1979 was a major milestone for RJR. At
the time, RJR was severely criticized for it. Del Monte was known as a
somewhat stodgy, production-driven company with a low return on assets.
But the Del Monte name was recognized and respected all over the world. To
consumers everywhere, Del Monte was synonymous with quality, and deser-

vedly so. RJR's strategy for Del Monte was to transform it into an innovative, marketing-driven company. In the process, RJR sought to make full use of Del Monte's worldwide franchise, its distribution strength, and its reputation for quality. The transformation of Del Monte was essentially completed in 1984.

RJR built a stronger presence in the frozen food business. By acquiring Morton Frozen Foods for Del Monte, it got greater manufacturing capacity that laid the groundwork for more cost-effective manufacturing of existing lines. RJR also gained the capacity to introduce new products as well.

RJR also saw an inviting opportunity in the fresh fruit market in the eastern United States. The only way to get high-quality fresh pineapple to the East Coast and Midwest was by air. If RJR could ship to those markets by surface transportation, it would have a significant advantage. Accordingly, the company invested in a $35 million pineapple plantation in Costa Rica. When it is fully on line in 1989, RJR will ship some 120,000 tons of fresh pineapple a year.

Another part of the Del Monte plan was to broaden RJR's base in beverages. The company had just about hit the wall with Hawaiian Punch and Del Monte's juices. To expand its beverage distribution network, RJR acquired Canada Dry. And to further add to that base, RJR acquired the number-one-selling orange-flavored soft drink, Sunkist. Now RJR has a viable share of market in each of the beverage segments it competes in, and the company has a greatly expanded bottler network in the United States and abroad. This is expected to be one of RJR's best growth areas in the years ahead.

How Planning Evolved in Other Segments of the Company

In 1982, an opportunity presented itself for RJR to further enlarge its food and beverage business by making another major acquisition. Heublein Inc. had a variety of leading spirits and wines such as Smirnoff Vodka and Inglenook Wines, a line of specialty food products led by A.1. Steak Sauce, and the worldwide Kentucky Fried Chicken quick-service restaurant system.

RJR had not singled out Heublein in advance. Nor did RJR's plan necessarily call for entering another mature business, such as spirits, to go with tobacco. But when Heublein was subjected to an unfriendly takeover attempt and sought a white knight, RJR saw immediately that it would make a perfect fit. Had RJR not been deep into strategic thinking, it would not have seen the possibilities and so would have overlooked a major opportunity.

Analysis showed that spirits and wines would dovetail beautifully with RJR's tobacco business because of the similarity in distribution methods and the demographics of the consumers. RJR could see that Heublein's grocery products were much like RJR's original food brands—too small on their own to have much clout in the marketplace. But they would be valuable additions to Del Monte.

Heublein also brought RJR the big, vibrant Kentucky Fried Chicken system, which was just waiting for the infusion of substantial funds to expand rapidly in the United States and many other parts of the world. And

WHY SOME STRATEGIC PLANS HAVE FAILED

While planning can be responsible for much financial success, it's worth asking why so many corporate strategic plans of recent years, carefully crafted by the best available planning professionals, apparently went awry. The guilty party is usually not so much the planning officer as the CEO. Here are some typical examples:

First, Planning, with a capital P, has too often been confused with lowercase planning. The CEO will take a horrified look at inventory and say, "We've got to get those widgets out the door. Plan that for me," which means, "Come up with some kind of discount."

But that's not planning; that's expediting. The professional, upper-case Planner is concerned with longer-range questions, such as whether one should be targeting widgets to that particular market or whether one should be making widgets at all.

The second reason that plans sometimes fail is that planning may become so exalted that it loses all credibility. Again, it's partly the fault of the CEO. Say the chairman recognizes the need to plan, and brings in the best guru his headhunter can bag. The guru then heads for the ivory tower—located a few doors down from the chairman's office—and starts crunching numbers. What results is an impressive volume or volumes, complete with charts, appendixes, and cross-references.

This plan is accepted with reverence. Everybody takes it home to read on the weekend—and the next weekend and the next. But it's never implemented because it's never really studied.

The third reason for the misuse of the planning function is that very often the CEO, despite his willingness to establish a top-notch planning function, can't seem to give planning enough personal attention. He doesn't want to take time away from the daily realities of his job.

Obviously, anyone charged with responsibility for a corporate enterprise must deal with the needs of his principal constituents—the shareholders, the financial community, the media—not to mention daily consultation with direct reports. Most of these demands involve pressing, immediate matters. But in giving them the time they require, the CEO may fall victim to myopia and fail to attend to the longer-term future.

The time may come, however, when the CEO does set aside the time, takes that plan home and actually reads it and sets out to implement it. He decides to get this thing moving and to follow the plan down to the last detail, thus falling victim to the fourth cause of failure of some plans.

A strategic plan is often referred to as a road map. And so it is. But let us remember that even the best road map from Rand McNally doesn't list all the temporary detours. And what appears to be a direct route often turns out to be a twisting, turning drive through unknown territory with no warning signs.

It's always a mistake to follow any plan slavishly, with no room for

(concluded)

adjustment. In fact, this is the most common cause of all for planning failures, and not just in business. The Soviets have provided us with the classic example: their endless five-year plans. Because of the forbidding bureaucracy that was in charge, these plans could never be changed, so they never worked. In planning, flexibility is absolutely vital. Any plan that can't be changed will surely turn out to be a bad plan.

that's exactly what Kentucky Fried Chicken is doing now. It is opening a new store somewhere in the world roughly every 21 hours, and it will continue to do so through 1987.

Again, RJR did not *plan* to buy Heublein. But because RJR had planned the overall direction of the company, management jumped at the chance when Heublein became available.

Meanwhile, RJR had moved on another front with its growth plan. In 1981, before the Heublein acquisition, the company realized that it needed a way to gain windows on new technologies and development concepts. But RJR wanted to be able to do this without taking major positions in entirely new businesses until they could be properly evaluated. So a separate company, R. J. Reynolds Development Corporation, was formed to evaluate new business concepts with growth potential. It also nurtures and develops businesses that might have the potential to become one of RJR's core businesses.

In effect, Development Corporation became the entrepreneurial arm of RJR. It is currently directing a variety of companies engaged in packaging, mail-order retailing, the management of dental services, and other emerging businesses. But Development Corporation is not just an experimental and testing unit. Last year, its sales of more than $700 million would have placed it comfortably within the Fortune 500 listing of top industrials.

By 1983, RJR could truly describe itself as "a premier, globally oriented consumer products and services company," but it still had to add the modifier "with major investments in transportation and energy."

The basic direction of its diversification had been established in the late 1970s. But the time had come to further refine the company's strategic focus.

Planning When Businesses Are Diverse

In a portfolio of businesses as diverse and complex as those within RJR, there has to be a two-way flow to the strategic planning process. From the bottom up it is quite regular and formal. Planning is highly decentralized at the early stages with subsidiary company strategies devised at the operating levels. Operating company management rather than headquarters planners are best equipped to make the plans at the early stages. At later stages, subsidiary company plans are consolidated, reviewed, and measured against corporate standards and goals.

The other part of the two-way flow is from the top down. It's much less formal and structured. It's where the CEO sits down with a few knowledgeable and forward thinkers, closes the door and puts the butcher paper on the wall and opens up the blackboard. It's a time to question everything and put it to the test.

In the fall of 1983, we held one of those small meetings of key officers of RJR to look at strategic direction. Out of this meeting came a significant refinement of that direction. We examined and restated the corporate mission. We defined what we wanted to be, established corporate goals for each of the businesses, and defined the measures by which we would chart progress. What emerged was a detailed strategy for growth and a vision of RJR's future. The following is a summary:

- RJR's mission is the achievement of acceptable, orderly growth of shareholder value over time. And to accomplish this mission of increasing shareholder value, RJR must maintain predictable and sustainable quality earnings growth.
- Clear numerical goals were set in terms of earnings growth, dividend payout, and return on equity. Expectations from each subsidiary company were quantified so that their progress could be charted.
- The keys to achieving the goals were determined. First, we systematically examined the value of everything RJR is doing. Resource management became the corporation's number one short-term priority.
- Value analysis programs were established in each business and in corporate staff departments. *Value analysis* is the term used at RJR to describe the commitment to reducing costs while maintaining or improving quality of the product or service provided.
- Another aspect of resource management RJR is focusing on is a stronger emphasis on achieving "lowest cost" producer status in all of RJR's major lines of business—again, without compromising product quality.

Another goal is the achievement of operational and marketing spending effectiveness. Still another goal is closer coordination of the common applications among RJR's products, markets, distribution systems, and administrative functions. Other key aspects of resource management are ongoing review and disposal of low-return assets or businesses, and the effective management of financial resources.

Strategies for Internal and External Growth

Internal business development is based on attention to the key elements that ensure the growth of existing businesses. These elements are:

- Selective attention to share of market and unit volumes.
- Margins.
- Product and service quality.
- Advertising and promotion spending effectiveness.
- Intangibles such as reputation.

Another priority for attention where internal growth is concerned is an increased investment in research and development. Consumer tastes are developing and changing more rapidly than ever. RJR is using increased resources to keep itself at the leading edge in product technology and innovation. RJR is also maintaining a continued focus on marketing innovation exemplified by new products, new markets, product improvement, and product differentiation. Still another aspect of RJR's internal development strategy is the continued testing and probing by Development Corporation for consumer products and service developmental concepts that offer significant potential for future growth.

RJR's external business development strategy has three components. First, there are smaller-scale "add on" or "fill in" acquisitions for spirits, wines, foods and beverages, as well as the acquisition of franchisee territories. An example of what is meant by "add on" acquisitions is RJR's recent acquisition of Canada Dry and Sunkist, which added on to an already significant Del Monte position in nonalcoholic beverages. Examples of "fill ins" were the addition of a Wild Turkey bourbon and Finlandia vodka to Heublein's mix of premium spirits.

The second external business development component is to make acquisitions that establish sufficient size or enhance distribution capabilities for consumer products or services with development potential. This is the responsibility of R. J. Reynolds Development Corp.

The third external development component is large-scale acquisitions. By the fall of 1984, RJR was in position to consider such a move. The company had divested itself of its major nonconsumer operations. The transportation unit had been spun off to shareholders, and RJR had sold its energy interests for $1.7 billion. RJR stated publicly several times that it was maintaining the financial flexibility to make a major acquisition on an opportunistic basis. And the company defined "opportunistic" as at the right time, at the right price, and with the right fit with its existing businesses and strategic plans.

RJR noted that because two of its four core businesses were in essentially mature markets, it had an obligation to be constantly on the watch for opportunities to add long-range growth potential to the portfolio. But it said that any merger candidate would have to be in a business it understands, with distribution channels similar to those where RJR already operates—primarily the supermarket. RJR would be interested in a candidate whose marketing orientation was like its own, and one whose financial position was stable. Certainly, any merger would have to enhance shareholder value to be considered.

The opportunity for such a merger arose sooner than had been anticipated. Because RJR had done its planning homework, the company was able to hold meaningful discussions in the spring of 1985 with Nabisco Brands, Inc. The merger agreement took shape in due course, and will result in formation of the largest consumer products company in the United States, and the second largest in the world.

Nabisco's brands, such as Ritz Crackers, Oreo Cookies, Planters Nuts and Snacks, Royal Desserts, Life Savers, and Fleischmann's and Blue Bonnet

Margarines, are some of the best-known in the country. And Nabisco also has a strong international presence, adding to RJR's existing international franchises in tobacco, foods, spirits, fresh fruit, and quick-service restaurants.

Earnings Results

For 1984, RJR reported all-time record results with net earnings from continuing operations up 20 percent and earnings per share up 24 percent. Obviously, the ultimate test of any planning effort is the result achieved. Today, RJR can accurately describe itself as one of the world's premier consumer goods and services companies. Its direction for the future is clear. An investor wanting a pure play in consumer goods can invest in RJR without having to take on energy and transportation as well.

Planning is no panacea. Nor is it necessary to overcomplicate the process, making up those elaborate flow charts with circles and squares and arrows going in every direction, which was so evident in the 1970s. But good planning is something that we simply cannot do without. Planning in business is not a virtue: it is a necessity. As such, it's the real mother of invention.

2 Business strategy formulation

The focus of this section is the formulation and analysis of business level strategy. Ian Wilson, the executive in charge of GE's highly regarded work in strategic planning, provides a very readable description of GE's pioneering efforts in environmental scanning and the role it plays in strategy formulation in "Environmental Scanning and Strategic Planning." The next six articles address strategies and their application to specific situations. First, there is Peter Drucker's discussion of entrepreneurial strategies. Pankaj Ghemawat discusses using the experience curve to pursue a low-cost strategy. Peter Wright examines three generic strategies—least-cost, differentiation, and niche. Kevin Coyne explains the concept of "sustainable competitive advantage." Barrie James discusses the advantages of deterrence as a strategic thrust, and James Leontiades examines market share considerations in an international setting. The final article in this section is George Day's "Tough Questions for Developing Strategies."

What this article is about: The primary purpose of strategic planning is to optimize the fit between the business and its current and future environment and environmental scanning is an important element in such planning. General Electric's approach to environmental scanning is described.

2-1 Environmental scanning and strategic planning*

Ian H. Wilson

Ian H. Wilson is an executive with the General Electric Company.

At the outset I should make clear my own conviction about the basic linkage between environmental scanning and strategic planning. The primary purpose of strategic planning, as I see it, is to optimize the "fit" between the business and its current and future environment—to enable the business to operate with maximum congruence, and minimum friction, with the changing expectations and conditions of an uncertain world. By the term *environmental scanning* I mean to encompass both the monitoring of current events in the business environment *and* the forecasting of future trends. And by *environment* I mean the *totality* of the external conditions and trends in which the business lives and moves and has its being—the market and competitive situation, economic and technological trends, and (increasingly) social and political developments.

From the above assertion about the purpose of strategic planning, two further statements derive:

1. Environmental scanning of the total business environment becomes an essential and integral part of strategic planning. It sets up the contextual framework within which planning can then logically proceed.
2. A business strategy that is adequate to meet the totality of these changing conditions must, in truth, be a strategy for the *total* business. That is,

* This article is reprinted from *Business Environment/Public Policy: 1979 Conference Papers* (St. Louis: American Assembly of Collegiate Schools of Business, 1980), pp. 159–63.

it should encompass not merely a market strategy, but also a technology strategy, a human resources strategy, a financial strategy, a public policy/government relations strategy, and so on.

If we put these two statements together, we can see the emergence of a holistic/systemic approach to planning, i.e., viewing the environment as a whole and as integral to planning, and planning for the business as a total system.

With this as preface, we can now look a little more closely at the nature and role of environmental scanning. For all practical purposes, most corporate "long-term" planning currently focuses on a "window in time" three to five years from the present. This is not true for all businesses; nor does it mean that some exploratory thinking and planning does not extend to a more distant time horizon. However, when assessing the actionable implications and strategic options for the corporation, most attention tends to get focused on a time horizon about five years out.

Both conceptually and practically, there are two different approaches to this "window in time." On the one hand, it is possible, by analyzing the macro sweep of long-term trends, to take a leap into the future, developing alternative scenarios for the future 10–15 years hence, and then, calculating backward by a process of deductive reasoning, to develop hypotheses as to corporate implications for the intermediate period. On the other hand, one can focus attention on the micro picture, monitoring events as they occur, assembling the jigsaw of evidence into a coherent picture, and then projecting forward by a process of inductive reasoning to create a picture of the future five years out.

These two approaches, it should be noted, are more appropriately viewed as complements than as alternatives. Environmental scanning can make its soundest contributions to planning when it provides perspectives from both macro/long-term and micro/short-term analyses. For one thing, the longer term scenarios are, at best, hypotheses as to plausible futures. The trajectory of these scenarios must be constantly compared with the trajectory of actual events to determine what revision to the planning assumptions may be required.

To the extent that environmental scanning involves a forecasting element, it can be said to constitute an early warning system whose purpose is to buy lead time, to identify emerging issues in sufficient time for adaptive, "noncrisis" action to be taken by the corporation. So, while the system may be absorbing and analyzing current data, it should never lose its future focus.

In 1967 General Electric established a Business Environment Studies component to analyze long-term social and political trends in the United States and their implications for the corporation. Four years later, in 1971, we commenced the first cycle of our new strategic planning system, a key element of which—in fact, the starting point for the cycle—was the long-term environmental forecast. In looking over our experience with these ventures, I derive the following characteristics for a successful environmental scanning system.

1. It must be *holistic* in its approach to the business environment, i.e., it should view trends—social, economic, political, technical—as a piece,

not piecemeal. Ecology and general systems theory both point to the maxim that "everything is related to everything else"; and Jay Forrester has demonstrated the dangers of applying linear, segmented thinking to analysis of any closed, complex system—a corporation, a city, or a society—with its dynamic, interacting parts and constantly operating feedback loops. The scanning system should, therefore, be comprehensive in its scope and integrative in its approach (cross-impact analyses and scenarios are remarkably useful techniques in this regard).

2.   It must also be continuous, *iterative* in its operation. In a fast-changing world, it makes little sense to rely on one-shot, or even periodic, analyses of the environment. Only constant monitoring, feedback and modification of forecasts can be truly useful. Carrying on the radar analogy, I call this a "cybernetic pulsing through the future." The system must be designed to deal with *alternative futures*. In an uncertain environment we can never truly know the future, no matter how much we may perfect our forecasting techniques. It is highly misleading, therefore, to claim (or believe) that an early warning system can predict *the* future. What it can do—and do effectively, if well designed—is to help us clarify our assumptions about the future, speculate systematically about alternative outcomes, assess probabilities, and make more rational choices.

3.   It should lay heavy stress on the need for *contingency planning*. This is a necessary corollary to the preceding point. In fact, there is (or should be) a strong logical connection in our thinking among uncertainty, alternatives, and contingencies: the three concepts are strongly bound together. In the final analysis, of course, after considering alternatives, we have to commit to a plan of action based on our assessment of the most probable future. But those lesser probabilities—even the "wild card" scenarios—should not be neglected, for they represent the contingencies for which we should also, in some degree, plan. A commitment to contingency planning is, it seems to me, the essence of a flexible strategy.

4.   Most important, the environmental scanning system should be an *integral part of the decision-making system* of the corporation. Speculation about alternative futures makes no real contribution to corporate success if it results merely in interesting studies. To contribute, it must be issue-oriented and help make today's decisions with a better sense of futurity; but it can do this *only* if the planning and decision-making system is designed to include the requirement of such monitoring and early warning.

The positioning of environmental scanning/analysis with respect to other planning and analysis activities is shown in Figure 1. This schematic diagram serves to demonstrate the fact that analysis of current and future environmental trends is, at least conceptually, the starting point for the strategic planning process. Within that process, issues analysis is central. Strategic planning should have as its focus identification of the key strategic issues[1] confronting

---

[1] A "strategic issue" can be defined as a major opportunity or threat which could critically affect the long-term future of the business. An issue may be immediate or emerging, internal or external in origin, concerned with any facet of the business—competitive, marketing, technological, human resources, financial, etc.

Figure 1

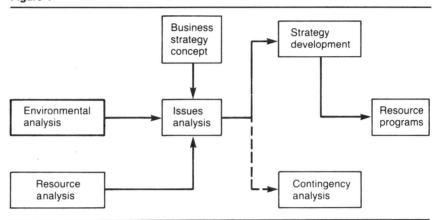

the business (issues that arise from the interaction of the business with environmental forces) and the development of strategies to deal with these issues. Contingency planning and analysis is also important for strategic positioning in an uncertain environment.

Over the past 10 years the techniques of environmental monitoring and forecasting have grown in scope and sophistication. By 1976 General Electric and The Futures Group had developed the FUTURSCAN system, which is a state-of-the-art combination of:

- Futurcasts data bases (potential future events).
- Delphi technique.
- Trend-impact analysis—how events move trends.
- Cross-impact analysis—how events move one another.
- Probabilistic system dynamics—how events and trends shape alternative futures.
- Scenarios.

Essentially the system operates in six stages:

1. Prepare background.
   Assess overall environmental factors for the industry (or market, society, etc.) under investigation.
   Demographic and lifestyle.
   General business and economic.
   Legislative and regulatory.
   Scientific and technological.
   Develop crude "systems" model of the industry.
2. Select critical indicators.
   Identify the industry's key indicators (trends).
   Undertake literature search to identify potential future events impacting the key trends.
   Nominate Delphi panel participants whose expert opinion is credible in evaluating the industry's future.

3. Establish past behavior for each indicator.
    Establish the historical performance for each indicator.
    Enter data into the data base of the Trend Impact Analysis program.
    Analyze reasons for past behavior of each trend.
       Demographic and social.
       Economic.
       Political and legislative.
       Technological.
    Construct Delphi panel interview.
4. Verify potential future events.
    Interrogate Delphi panel.
       Evaluate past trends.
       Assess the potential impact of future events.
       Assess the probability of future events.
       Forecast future values.
    Specify and document assumptions for forecasts.
    Specify and document rationale for projected values.
5. Forecast each indicator.
    Operate the Trend Impact Analysis and Cross Impact Analysis pro-
    grams on the literature search and Delphi output to establish the
    range of future values.
    Analyze forecast results.

The detailed operation of the FUTURSCAN system is a topic for another paper.[2] Here it is simply worth noting that the value of utilizing such a multidimensional analysis of the future environment lies in the fact that:

• It makes explicit *all* the environmental assumptions on which corporate planning and policymaking should be based.
• It integrates the "social" factors and the "business" factors into the planning framework.
• It confronts future corporate problems as a system of interrelated issues and pressures, with all their attendant complexities and "trade-offs."
• It identifies the spectrum of probable future constraints *and opportunities* for corporate performance.
• It provides an opportunity, early in the planning cycle, for determining needed corporate responses to changing conditions.

---

[2] See, for instance, the article on this topic by L. H. Cullum in *Business Tomorrow* 1, no. 3 (World Future Society, 1978).

What this article is about: Although strategy has become an "in" word, there has been little if any discussion on entrepreneurial strategies. In this excerpt from his book *Innovation and Entrepreneurship,* Peter Drucker examines two major entrepreneurial strategies, how they work, how they have been successfully used in the past, and how they can be applied in today's business environment.

2-2 Entrepreneurial strategies*

Peter F. Drucker

Peter F. Drucker is Clarke Professor of Social Sciences and Management at the Claremont Graduate School, Claremont, California.

We only began quite recently to talk of "strategies" in connection with a business.[1] Of late, of course, strategy has become the "in" word with any number of books written on it.[2] However, I have not come across any discussion of entrepreneurial strategies. Yet they are important, they are distinct, and they are different.

Fustest with the Mostest

Being "Fustest with the Mostest" was how a Confederate Cavalry General in America's Civil War explained his consistently winning his battles. When applying this strategy to the contemporary business, the entrepreneur aims at leadership, if not dominance, in a new market or new industry. Being "Fustest with the Mostest" does not necessarily imply creating a big business right away—though often this is indeed the aim. However, it does from the start aim at achieving a permanent leadership position.

Being "Fustest with the Mostest" is the approach which many people

---

* This article consists of two chapters from *Innovation and Entrepreneurship* by Peter F. Drucker, published in 1985 by Harper & Row. Copyright © 1985 by Peter F. Drucker.

[1] The 1952 edition of the *Oxford Concise Dictionary* still defined "strategy" as: "Generalship; the art of war: management of an army or armies in a campaign." Alfred D. Chandler, Jr., first applied the term in 1962 to the conduct of a business in his pioneering *Strategy and Structure* (Cambridge, Mass.: MIT Press, 1962) which studied the evolution of management in the big corporation. But when I, shortly thereafter in 1963, wrote the first analysis of business strategy, the publisher and I found that the word could not be used in the title without risk of serious misunderstanding. Booksellers, magazine editors, and senior business executives all assured us that "strategy" for them meant the conduct of military or election campaigns. The book discussed much that is now considered "strategy"—it uses the word in the text. But the title we chose was *Managing for Results* (New York: Harper & Row, 1962).

[2] Of the books on the subject of strategy, the one I have found most useful is Michael Porter's *Competitive Strategies* (New York: The Free Press, 1980).

consider the entrepreneurial strategy *par excellence*. Indeed, if one were to go by the popular books on entrepreneurship[3] one would conclude that "Fustest with the Mostest" is the *only* entrepreneurial strategy. A good many entrepreneurs, especially the high-tech ones, seem to be of the same opinion.

They are wrong, however. To be sure, a good many entrepreneurs have indeed chosen this strategy. Yet "Fustest with the Mostest" is not even the dominant entrepreneurial strategy, let alone the one with the lowest risk or the highest success ratio. On the contrary, of all entrepreneurial strategies, it is the greatest gamble. And it is unforgiving, making no allowances for mistakes and allowing no second chance.

But, if successful, being "Fustest with the Mostest" is highly rewarding.

Following are some examples which show what this strategy consists of and what it requires.

- Hofmann-LaRoche of Basel has for many years been the world's largest and, in all probability, its most profitable pharmaceutical company. But its origins were quite humble. Until the mid-1920s, Hofmann-LaRoche was a small and struggling manufacturing chemist which made a few textile dyes and was totally overshadowed by the huge German dye-stuff makers and three much bigger chemical firms in its own Switzerland. Then it gambled on the newly-discovered vitamins—at a time when the scientific world still could not quite get itself to accept that such substances could exist. It acquired the vitamin patents—which nobody else wanted. It hired the discoverers away from Zürich University at several times the salary they could ever hope to get as professors—salaries that even industry had never before paid. It invested all the money it had and could borrow in manufacturing and marketing these new substances. Sixty years later—long after all vitamin patents have expired—it still controls nearly half the world's vitamin market, which amounts to billions of dollars a year. Hofmann-LaRoche followed the same strategy twice more: in the 1930s, it went into the new sulfa drugs—even though most scientists of the time "knew" that systemic drugs could not be effective against infections; and then, twenty years later, it went into the muscle-relaxing tranquilizers Librium and Valium—which at that time were equally "heretical" and incompatible with what "every scientist knew."

- Du Pont followed the same strategy when developing Nylon. In the mid-1920s, it was already the leading American chemical company (though still confined almost completely to explosives). Du Pont hired a chemist named Wallace H. Carothers and provided him with funds and facilities to do research in polymer chemistry—something which most chemists had either discounted or given up on. For a dozen years, Carothers produced no results. But when he finally came up with the first truly synthetic fiber, Nylon, Du Pont at once mounted massive efforts. It

[3] Perhaps the most readable recent examples of books on entrepreneurship is George Gilder's *The Spirit of Enterprise* (New York: Simon & Schuster, 1984).

built huge plants, went into mass advertising (Du Pont had never before had consumer products to advertise), and created the industry we now call ''plastics.''

These are ''big-company'' stories, it will be said. But when it started in vitamins, Hofmann-LaRoche was but an ailing dwarf. Following are some more recent examples of companies that started from nothing with a strategy of ''Getting there Fustest with the Mostest.''

- The ''Word Processor'' is not much of a ''scientific'' invention. It does not do much more than hook up three existing instruments: a typewriter, a display screen, and a fairly elementary computer. But this combination resulted in a genuine innovation which has radically changed office work. Dr. An Wang was a lone entrepreneur when he conceived of this combination some time in the mid-1950s. He had no track record as an entrepreneur and had a minimum of financial backing. Yet from the beginning he clearly aimed at creating a new industry that would revolutionize office work—and Wang Laboratories has, of course, become a very big company.
- Similarly, the two young engineers who started the Apple computer—in the proverbial garage and without financial backers or previous business experience—aimed from the beginning at creating an industry and dominating it.

Not every ''Fustest with the Mostest'' strategy needs to aim at creating a big business—though it must always aim at creating a business that dominates its market. The 3M Company in St. Paul, Minnesota, does not—as a matter of deliberate policy, it seems—attempt an innovation that might result in a big business by itself. Nor does Johnson & Johnson, the health care and hygiene producer. Both companies are among the most fertile and most successful innovators. Both look for innovations that will lead to medium-sized rather than to giant enterprises which are, however, dominant in their markets.

Being ''Fustest with the Mostest'' is not confined to businesses. It is also available to public-service institutions.

- When Wilhelm von Humboldt founded the University of Berlin in 1809, he clearly aimed at being ''Fustest with the Mostest.'' Prussia had just been defeated by Napoleon and had barely escaped total dismemberment. It was bankrupt—politically, militarily, and above all financially. It looked very much the way Germany looked after Hitler's defeat in 1945. Yet Humboldt set out to build the largest university the Western world had ever seen or heard of—three to four times as large as anything then in existence. He set out to hire the leading scholars in every single discipline, beginning with the foremost philosopher of the time, Georg W.F. Hegel. He paid his professors up to 10 times as much as professors had ever been paid before at a time when first-class scholars were going begging (the Napoleonic Wars had forced many old and famous universities to disband).

• A hundred years later, in the early years of this century, two surgeons in Rochester (an obscure Minnesota town far from population centers or medical schools) decided to establish a medical center based on totally new—and totally heretical—concepts of medical practice. They focussed on building teams in which outstanding specialists would work together under a coordinating team leader. Frederick William Taylor, the father of "Scientific Management," had never met the Mayo Brothers. But in his well-known testimony before the Congress in 1911, he called the Mayo Clinic the "only complete and successful scientific management" he knew. These unknown provincial surgeons aimed from the beginning at dominance of the field, at attracting outstanding practitioners in every branch of medicine, and at attracting patients able and willing to pay what were then outrageous fees.

• Twenty-five years later, the strategy of being "Fustest with the Mostest" was used by the "March of Dimes" to organize research on infantile paralysis (polio). Instead of gathering new knowledge step by step—as all earlier medical research had done—the "March of Dimes" aimed from the beginning at total victory over a completely mysterious disease. No one before had ever organized a "research lab without walls" in which a large number of scientists in a multitude of research institutions were commissioned to work on specific stages of a planned and managed research program. The "March of Dimes" established the pattern on which the U.S., a little later, organized the first great research projects of World War II: the atom bomb, the Radar Lab, the Proximity Fuse, and then another 15 years later, "Putting a Man on the Moon"—all innovative efforts using the "Fustest with the Mostest" strategy.

These cases show first that being "Fustest with the Mostest" requires an ambitious aim; it is bound to fail otherwise. It always aims at creating a new industry or a new market. At the least, as at the Mayo Clinic or the March of Dimes, being "Fustest with the Mostest" aims at creating a new and quite different—and highly unconventional—process. The du Ponts surely did not say to themselves in the mid-1920s, when they brought in Carothers: "We will establish the plastics industry" (indeed, the term was not in wide use until the 1950s). But enough of the internal Du Pont documents of the time have been published to show that the top management people did aim at creating a new industry. They were far from convinced that Carothers and his research would succeed. But they knew that they would have founded something big and brand-new in the event of success, and something that would go far beyond a single product or even beyond a single major product line. Dr. Wang did not coin the term "the Office of the Future," as far as I know. But in his first advertisements, he announced a new office environment and new concepts of office work. From the beginning, both the du Ponts and Wang clearly aimed at dominating the industry they hoped they could succeed in creating.

Because being "Fustest with the Mostest" must aim at creating something truly new and different, nonexperts and outsiders seem to do as well as "experts," in fact, often better. Hofmann-LaRoche, for instance, did not owe its strategy to chemists, but to a musician who had married the grand-daughter of the company's founder and needed more money to support his orchestra than the company then provided through its meager dividends. To this day the company has never been managed by chemists, but always by financial men. Wilhelm Von Humboldt was a diplomat with no earlier ties to academia or experience in it. Du Pont's top management people were businessmen rather than chemists and researchers. And while the Brothers Mayo were well-trained surgeons, they were totally outside the medical establishment of the time and were isolated from it.

Of course, there are also the true "insiders": a Dr. Wang, or the people at 3M, or the young computer engineers who designed the Apple computer. But when it comes to being "Fustest with the Mostest" the outsider may have an advantage. He does not know what everybody within the field knows, and therefore does not know what cannot be done.

Continued Efforts

Being "Fustest with the Mostest" has to hit the bull's eye or it misses the target altogether. Or, to vary the metaphor, being "Fustest with the Mostest" is very much like a moon shot: a deviation of a fraction of a minute of the arc and the missile disappears into outer space. Once launched, the "Fustest with the Mostest" strategy is difficult to adjust or to correct.

For this strategy to succeed requires thought and careful analysis of the opportunities for innovation. Even then, it requires extreme concentration of effort. There has to be *one* goal and all efforts have to be focused on it. And when this effort begins to produce results, the innovator has to be ready to mobilize resources massively. As soon as Du Pont had a usable synthetic fiber—long before the market had begun to respond to it—Du Pont built large factories and bombarded both textile manufacturers and the general public with advertisements, trial presentations, speeches, and so on.

After the innovation has become a successful business, the work really begins. Then the strategy of "Fustest with the Mostest" demands substantial and continuing efforts to retain leadership position. Otherwise, all one has done is to create a market for a competitor. The innovator has to run even harder than ever once he has the position of leadership. He has to continue innovative efforts, and on a very large scale. The research budget has to be higher *after* the innovation has successfully been accomplished. New uses have to be found and new customers have to be supplied, identified, and persuaded to try the new product. Above all, the entrepreneur who has succeeded in being "Fustest with the Mostest" has to be able to make his product or process obsolete before a competitor can. Work on the successor to the successful product or process has to start immediately, with the same concentration of effort and the same investment of resources that led to the initial success.

The Du Pont Company went much further. It systematically sought out and helped bring competitors into the Nylon business by granting them a license. This way it kept control of the market to a large extent. By doing this they put people into business who then, on their own part, found new markets, new uses, and new customers. This helped expand and develop the market much faster than Du Pont, despite patent protection, could possibly have hoped to do alone as the sole supplier.

Finally, the entrepreneur who has attained leadership by being "Fustest with the Mostest" has to be the one who systematically cuts the price of the product or process. To keep prices high simply encourages potential competitors.

The longest-lived private monopoly in economic history is the Dynamite Cartel founded by Alfred Nobel after his invention of dynamite. The Dynamite Cartel maintained a worldwide monopoly until World War I and even beyond—long after the Nobel patents had expired. It did this by cutting prices every time demand rose by 10 to 20 percent. By that time, the companies in the Cartel had fully depreciated the investment they had had to make to get the additional production. This made it unattractive for any potential competitor to build new dynamite factories, while the Cartel itself maintained its profitability. It is no accident that Du Pont has consistently followed this same policy in the United States; the Du Pont company was the American member of the Dynamite Cartel. Wang has done the same with respect to the word processor, Apple with its computers, and 3M with all of its products.

The Risk of Failure

These are all success stories. They do not show how risky the strategy of being "Fustest with the Mostest" actually is. The failures disappeared. Yet we know that for every one who succeeds with this strategy, many more fail. There is only one chance with the "Fustest with the Mostest" strategy. If it does not work right away, it is total failure.

Everyone knows the old Swiss story of Wilhelm Tell the archer, whom the tyrant promised to pardon if he succeeded in shooting an apple off his son's head on the first try. If he failed, he would either kill the child or be killed himself. This is exactly the situation of the entrepreneur in the "Fustest with the Mostest" strategy. There is no "almost success" and no "near-miss." There is only success or failure.

Even the success stories may be successes only by hindsight. At least we know that in several of the examples, failure was very close; only luck and chance saved them.

Du Pont only succeeded in Nylon because of a fluke. Carothers' final result was a fiber. But there was no market for a Nylon fiber. It was far too expensive to compete with cotton and rayon, the cheap fibers of the time. It was actually even more expensive than silk, the luxury fiber which the Japanese, in the severe depression of the late 1930s, had to sell for whatever price they could get. What saved Du Pont was the outbreak of World War II, which stopped Japanese silk exports. By the time the Japanese could start up their silk industry again (around 1950), Nylon was firmly entrenched, with its cost and price down to a fraction of what both had been in the late 1930s.

The strategy of being "Fustest with the Mostest" is risky because it is based on the assumption that it will fail far more often than it can possibly succeed. It will fail because the will is lacking. It will fail because efforts are inadequate. It will fail because, despite successful innovation, not enough resources are deployed, are available, or are being put to work to exploit success. While "Fustest with the Mostest" is indeed highly rewarding if successful, it is much too risky and much too difficult to be used for anything but major innovations. It requires profound analysis and a genuine understanding of the sources of innovation and of their dynamics. It requires extreme concentration of efforts and substantial resources. In most cases there are alternative strategies that are available and preferable—not because they carry less risk, but because for most innovations the opportunity is not great enough to justify the costs, the efforts, and the investment of resources required for the "Fustest with the Mostest" strategy.

Hit Them Where They Ain't

Two completely different entrepreneurial strategies can be derived from a saying of another battle-winning Confederate general, "Hit Them Where They Ain't." They are called "Creative Imitation" and "Entrepreneurial Judo."

Creative Imitation

Creative imitation is a contradiction in terms. What is "creative" must surely be "original." If there is one thing imitation is not, it is being "original." Yet the term fits. It describes a strategy which is "imitation" in its substance. Here, the entrepreneur does something somebody else has already done. It is "creative" because the entrepreneur who applies this strategy understands what the innovation *represents* better than the people who made the innovation.

The foremost practitioner of this strategy, and the most brilliant one, is IBM. It is also the strategy which the Procter & Gamble Co. has been using to obtain and maintain leadership in the soap, detergent, and toiletries markets. The Hattori Company in Japan, whose Seiko watches have become the world's leader, also owes its domination of the market to "creative imitation."

- IBM built a high-speed calculating machine in the early 1930s to do calculations for the astronomers at New York's Columbia University. A few years later, it built a machine that was designed as a computer— again, to do astronomical calculations (this time at Harvard). By the end of World War II, IBM had built a real computer—the first one that had the features of the true computer: a "memory" and the capacity to be "programmed." And yet there are good reasons why the history books pay scant attention to IBM as a computer innovator. For as soon as it had finished its advanced 1945 computer—the first computer to be shown to the lay public—IBM abandoned its own design and switched to the design of its rival, the ENIAC developed at the University of Pennsylvania. The ENIAC was far better suited to business applications such as payroll—however, its designers did not see this. IBM then restructured the ENIAC so that it could be manufactured and serviced and could do mundane "numbers crunching." When IBM's version of the ENIAC came out in 1953, it immediately set the standard for commercial, multipurpose mainframe computers.

This is "creative imitation." It waits until somebody else has introduced the new, but only in a limited way. Then it goes to work—and within a short time it comes out with what the new really should be to be useful, to satisfy the customer, to do the work customers want and pay for. Then, the "creative imitation" sets the standard and takes over the market.

- IBM practiced "creative imitation" again with the personal computer. The original idea was Apple's. Everybody at IBM "knew" that a small, free-standing computer was a mistake—uneconomical, far from optimal, and expensive. Yet the personal computer was a success. IBM immediately went to work to design a machine that would become the standard in the personal computer field and dominate, or at least lead, the entire field. The result was the PC—and within two years it had taken the leadership position away from Apple, became the fastest-selling brand, and became the standard in the field.

- When semiconductors became available, everyone in the watch industry knew that they could be used to power a watch much more accurately, much more reliably, and much more cheaply than traditional watch movements. The Swiss were the first to introduce a quartz-powered digital watch. But they had so much invested in traditional watchmaking that they decided on a gradual introduction of quartz-powered digital watches over a long period of time, during which these new timepieces would remain expensive luxuries. The Hattori Company in Japan had long been making conventional watches for the Japanese market. It saw the opportunity and went in for "creative imitation." It developed and marketed the quartz-powered digital watch as a *standard* timepiece. By the time the Swiss had woken up, it was too late. Seiko watches had become the world's best sellers, with the Swiss almost pushed out of the market.

Like being "Fustest with the Mostest," creative imitation is a strategy aimed at market or industry leadership, if not at market or industry dominance. It is less risky than being "Fustest with the Mostest." By the time the creative imitator moves, the market has been established and the new has been accepted. Indeed there is usually more demand for it than the original innovator can easily supply. The market segmentations are known or at least knowable. Most of the uncertainties that abound when the first innovator appears have been dispelled or at least analyzed and studied. No one has to explain anymore what a "personal computer" or a "digital watch" are and what they do.

Of course, there is the risk that the original innovator may do it right the first time, thus closing the door to "creative imitation"—as Hofmann-LaRoche did with vitamins, Du Pont did with nylon, and Wang did with the word processor. But the number of entrepreneurs engaging in "creative imitation"—and their substantial success—indicates that perhaps the risk of the first innovator's preempting the market by doing it right is not an overwhelming one.

Another example of creative innovation is Tylenol, "the non-aspirin aspirin." This case shows more clearly than any other I know what "creative imitation" consists of, what its requirements are, and how it works.

- Acetaminophen (the substance in Tylenol) had been used for many years as a painkiller. Until relatively recently, it was available in the U.S. only by prescription. Also until not too long ago, aspirin, the much older painkiller, was considered perfectly safe and had the pain-relief market to itself. Acetaminophen is a less potent drug than aspirin. It is effective as a painkiller but has no anti-inflammatory effect and also no effect on blood coagulation. Because of this, it is free from the side effects (especially gastric upset and stomach bleeding) which aspirin can cause, especially if used in large doses and over long periods of time (e.g., for arthritis).

   When acetaminophen became available without prescription, the first brand on the market was presented and promoted as a drug for those who suffered side effects from aspirin. It was eminently successful, indeed, far more successful than its makers had anticipated. But it was this very success that created the opportunity for "creative imitation." Johnson & Johnson realized that there was a market for a drug that *replaced* aspirin as the painkiller of choice, with aspirin confined to the fairly small market where anti-inflammatory and blood coagulation effects were needed. From the start, Tylenol was promoted as the safe, *universal* painkiller. Within a year or two, it had taken over the market.

Creative imitation, these cases show, does not exploit the failure of the pioneers as "failure" is commonly understood. On the contrary, the pioneer must be successful. The Apple computer was a great success story, and so was the acetaminophen brand which Tylenol ultimately pushed out of market leadership. But the original innovators failed to understand their success. The makers of the Apple were product-focused rather than user-focused, and therefore offered additional hardware where the user needed programs and software. In the Tylenol case, the original innovators failed to realize what their own success meant.

The creative innovator exploits the *success* of others. Creative imitation is not "innovation" in the sense in which the term is most commonly understood. The creative imitator does not invent a product or service, he perfects and positions it. The way it has been introduced lacks something. It may lack additional product features. It may lack segmentation so that slightly different versions fit slightly different markets. It may lack proper positioning of the product in the market.

The creative imitator looks at products or services from the point of view of the customer. IBM's personal computer is practically indistinguishable from the Apple in its technical features. But from the beginning, IBM offered the customer programs and software. Apple maintained traditional computer distribution through specialty stores. IBM developed—in a radical break with its own traditions—all kinds of distribution channels, specialty stores, major retailers like Sears Roebuck, its own retail stores, and so on. It made it easy for the consumer to buy and it made it easy for the consumer to use the product. This, rather than hardware features, were the "innovations" which gave IBM the personal computer market.

Altogether, "creative imitation" starts out with markets rather than with products, with customers rather than with producers. It is market-focused and market-driven.

Creative imitation requires a rapidly growing market. Creative imitators do not succeed by taking away customers from the pioneers, rather they serve markets the pioneers have created but do not adequately service. Creative imitation does not create demand, rather it satisfies demand that already exists.

Creative imitation has its own risks—and they are considerable. Creative imitators are easily tempted to splinter their efforts in the attempt to hedge their bets. Another danger is to misread the trend and imitate creatively what then turns out not to be the winning development in the marketplace.

IBM—the world's foremost and, in many ways, its most successful creative imitator—exemplifies these dangers in its approaches to office automation. It successfully imitated every major development. As a result it has the leading product in every single area. But its products are so diverse and so incompatible with one another that it is all but impossible to build an integrated, automated office out of IBM building blocks. Being designed to imitate creatively the developments of half a dozen different pioneers, the IBM products outdo them, but they do not, by themselves, constitute a unified approach—each having different architecture, different logic, and different software. It is thus still doubtful that IBM can assume leadership in the automated office and provide it with the integrated system that will be the main market of the future. The *risk of being too clever* is inherent in the creative-imitation strategy.

Creative imitation is likely to work most effectively in "high tech" areas for one simple reason: "high tech" innovators are least likely to be market-focused, and most likely to be technology- and product-focused. The innovators therefore tend to misunderstand their own success and to fail to exploit and supply the demand they have created. However, they are by no means the only ones to do so.

Because creative imitation aims at market dominance, it is best suited to a major product, process, or service. By the time "creative imitators" go to work, the market has already been identified and the demand has already been created. But what it lacks in risk, creative imitation makes up for in its requirements for alertness, flexibility, and willingness to accept the verdict of the market. Above all, it requires hard work and massive efforts.

Entrepreneurial Judo

- In 1947, Bell Laboratories invented the transistor. It was at once realized that the transistor was going to replace the vacuum tube, especially in consumer electronics such as the radio and the then-brand-new television set. Everybody knew this, but nobody did anything about it. The leading manufacturers—at that time they were all Americans—began to "study" the transistor and to make plans for conversion to the transistor "sometime around 1970." Till then, they proclaimed, the transistor "would not be ready." In Japan, Sony read about the transistor in the newspapers. At that time, Sony was practically unknown outside of Japan and was not even in consumer electronics. But Akio Morita, Sony's president, went to the United States and bought from Bell Labs a license for the new transistor for a ridiculous sum (all of $25,000). Two years later, Sony brought out the first portable transistor radio, which weighed less than one fifth of comparable vacuum-tube radios on the market and cost less than one third. Three years later, Sony had the market for cheap radios in the United States. Five years later, the Japanese had the radio market all over the world.

Sony's success is not the real story. What explains the fact that the Japanese repeated this same strategy again and again and again? And always with success, always surprising the Americans? They repeated it with television sets and digital watches and hand-held calculators. And they repeated it with copiers when they moved in and took a large share of the market away from the original inventor, the Xerox Corporation. The Japanese, in other words, have been successful again and again in practicing "entrepreneurial judo" against the Americans.

Americans have also been successful in practicing this strategy. MCI and Sprint used the Bell Telephone System's (AT&T) own pricing to take away from the Bell System a very large part of the long-distance business. ROLM was also successful when it used Bell System's policies against it to take a large part of the private branch exchange (PBX) market. Similarly, Citibank met with success when it started a consumer bank in Germany, the *Familienbank* (Family bank), which within a few short years came to dominate German consumer finance.

• The German banks knew that consumers had obtained purchasing power and had become a desirable bank customer. They went through the motions of offering banking services to consumers, but they really did not want them. Consumers, they felt, were beneath the dignity of a major bank with its business customers and its rich investment clients. If consumers needed an account at all, they should have it with the postal savings bank. Whatever their advertisements said to the contrary, the banks made it abundantly clear that when consumers came into the august offices of the local branch, the bank had little use for them. This was the opening Citibank exploited when it founded its *Familienbank* and catered to no one but consumers, designed the services consumers needed, and made it easy for consumers to do business with a bank. Despite the tremendous strength of the German banks and their pervasive presence in a country where there is a branch of a major bank on the corner of every downtown street corner, Citibank's *Familienbank* attained dominance in the German consumer banking business within five years.

All these newcomers—the Japanese, MCI, ROLM, Citibank—practiced "entrepreneurial judo." Of all entrepreneurial strategies, especially the strategies aiming at obtaining leadership and dominance in an industry or a market, "entrepreneurial judo" is by all odds the least risky and the most likely to succeed.

Every policeman knows that a habitual criminal will always commit his crime the same way. He will, for instance, crack a safe the same way or enter a building he wants to loot the same way. He leaves behind a "signature" which is as individual and as distinct as a fingerprint. And he will not change his "signature" even though it leads to his being caught again and again.

It is not only the criminal who is set in his habits. All of us are. And so are businesses and industries. The habit will be persisted in even though it leads again and again to loss of leadership and loss of market. American manufacturers persisted in habits that enabled the Japanese to take over their market again and again.

If the criminal is caught, he rarely accepts that his habit has betrayed him. On the contrary, he will find all kinds of excuses—and will continue the habit that led to his being captured. Similarly, businesses that are being betrayed by their habits will not admit it and will find all kinds of excuses. The American electronic manufacturers, for instance, blame the Japanese successes on "low labor costs" in Japan. Yet the few American manufacturers that have faced up to reality (e.g., RCA and Magnavox in television sets) are able to turn out products in the United States that are competitive in both price and quality with those of the Japanese—all this despite their paying American wages and union benefits. The German banks uniformly explain the success of Citibank's *Familienbank* with its taking risks they themselves would not touch. But *Familienbank* has lower credit losses with consumer loans than the German banks, and its lending requirements are as strict as those of the Germans. The German banks know this, of course, yet they keep on explaining away their failure and *Familienbank's* success. This is typical and is the reason why the same strategy—the same "entrepreneurial judo"—can be used over and over again.

There are five fairly common bad habits which enable newcomers to use "entrepreneurial judo" and catapult themselves into a leadership position against established companies.

1. The first bad habit is what American slang calls *NIH* (Not Invented Here), the arrogance that leads a company or an industry to believe that something new cannot be any good unless they themselves thought of it. Thus, the new invention is spurned, as was the transistor by the American electronics manufacturers.

2. The second bad habit is the tendency to *cream* a market, that is, to get the high-profit part of it.

    This is basically what Xerox did and what made it an easy target for the Japanese imitators of its copying machines. Xerox focused its strategy on the big users, the buyers of large numbers of machines or of expensive high-performance machines. It did not reject the others; but it did not go after them. In particular, it did not see fit to give them service. In the end it was dissatisfaction with the service—or rather with the nonservice—which Xerox provided for its smaller customers which made them receptive to competitors' machines.

Creaming is a violation of elementary managerial and economic precepts. It is always punished by loss of market.

Xerox was resting on its laurels. They were indeed substantial and well-earned, but no business ever gets paid for what it did in the past. Creaming is an attempt to try to get paid for past contributions. Once a business gets into that habit, it is likely to continue in it and thus continue to be vulnerable to "entrepreneurial judo."

3. Even more debilitating is the third bad habit: the belief in *quality*. Quality in a product or service is not what the supplier puts in. It is what the customer gets out and is willing to pay for. Contrary to what most manufacturers believe, a product is not quality because it is hard to make and costs a lot of money. That is incompetence. Customers pay only for what is of use to them and gives them value. Nothing else is quality.

The American electronics manufacturers in the 1950s believed that their products with all those wonderful vacuum tubes were quality because they had put 30 years of effort making radio sets bigger, more complicated, and more expensive. They considered the product to be quality because it needed a great deal of skill to turn out, whereas a transistor radio was simple and could be made by unskilled labor on an assembly line. But in consumer terms, the transistor radio was clearly of far superior quality. It weighed much less so that it could be easily taken to the beach, on a trip, or to a picnic. It rarely had something go wrong; there were no tubes to replace. It cost a great deal less. In range and fidelity it very soon surpassed even the most magnificent Super Heterodyne with 16 vacuum tubes (one of which always burned out when needed).

4. Closely related to both creaming and quality is the fourth bad habit, the delusion of the *premium* price. A premium price is always an invitation to the competitor.

Since the days of J.B. Say in France and David Ricardo in England in the early years of the 19th century, economists have known that the only way to get a higher profit margin, except through a monopoly, is through lower costs. The attempt to achieve a higher profit margin through a higher price is always self-defeating. It holds an umbrella over the competitor. What looks like higher profits for the established leader is in effect a subsidy to the newcomer who, in a very few years, will unseat the leader and claim the throne for himself. Premium prices should always be considered a threat and a dangerous vulnerability.

Yet the delusion of higher profits to be achieved through premium prices is almost universal, even though it always opens the door to "entrepreneurial judo."

5. Finally, there is a fifth bad habit which is typical of established businesses and leads to their downfall. Again, Xerox is a good example. They *maximize rather than optimize*. As the market grows and develops, they try to satisfy every single user through the same product or service.

As a hypothetical example, let's say a new analytical instrument to test chemical reaction is being introduced. At first its market is quite limited, let's say to industrial laboratories. Then, university laboratories, research institutes, and hospitals all begin to buy the instrument.

But each wants something slightly different. And so, the manufacturer puts in one feature to satisfy this customer, then another one to satisfy that customer, and so on, until what started out as a simple instrument has become complicated. The manufacturer has maximized what the instrument can do. As a result, the instrument no longer satisfies anyone; for by trying to satisfy everybody, one always ends up satisfying nobody. The instrument has also become expensive. It has also become hard to use and hard to maintain. However, the manufacturer is proud of the instrument—his full-page advertisement lists 64 different things the instrument can do. This manufacturer will almost certainly become the victim of "entrepreneurial judo." What he thinks is his very strength will be turned against him. The newcomer will come in with an instrument designed to satisfy one of the markets, the hospital, for instance. It will not contain a single feature the hospital people do not need, but it will have a higher performance capacity than the multipurpose instrument can possibly offer. The same manufacturer will then bring out a model for the research laboratory, for the government laboratory, for industry. In no time at all, the newcomer will have taken away the markets with instruments that are designed for the users, instruments that optimize rather than maximize.

Similarly, when the Japanese came in with their copiers in competition with Xerox, they designed machines that fitted specific groups of users—the small office, for instance, whether that of the dentist, the doctor, or the school principal. They did not try to match the features of which the Xerox people themselves were the proudest—e.g., the speed of the machine or the clarity of the copy. They gave the small office what the small office needed the most, a simple machine at a low cost. Once they had established themselves in that market, they then moved in on the other markets, with products designed to optimally serve a specific market segment.

Similarly, Sony first moved into the low end of the market, the market for cheap portables with limited range. Once it had established itself there, it moved in on the other market segments.

"Entrepreneurial judo" first aims at securing a beachhead, one which the established leaders either do not defend at all or defend only half-heartedly (as was the case when the Germans did not counterattack when Citibank established *Familienbank*). Once that beachhead has been secured, that is, once the newcomers have an adequate market and adequate revenue, they then move in on the rest of the territory. In each case, they repeat the strategy. They design a product or a service which is specific to a given market segment and optimal for it. Almost never do the established leaders beat them to this game. Almost never do the established leaders change their own behavior before the newcomers have taken over the leadership and have acquired dominance.

There are three situations in which the "entrepreneurial judo" strategy is likely to be particularly successful.

1.   The first is the common situation in which the established leaders refuse

to act on the unexpected, whether success or failure, and either overlook it altogether or try to brush it aside. This is what Sony exploited.

2. The second is the Xerox situation. A new technology emerges and grows fast. But the innovators who introduced the new technology—or the new service—behave like the classical monopolists: they use their leadership position to cream the market and to get premium prices. They either do not know or refuse to know what has been amply proven: a leadership position, let alone any kind of monopoly, can only be maintained if the leader behaves as a "benevolent monopolist" (a term coined by Joseph Schumpeter). A benevolent monopolist cuts his prices before a competitor can cut them. He makes his product obsolete and introduces a new product before a competitor can do so. There are enough examples of this around to prove the validity of the thesis. It is the way, for instance, in which the Du Pont Company has acted for many years and in which the American Bell Telephone System (AT&T) used to act before it was overcome by the inflationary problems of the 1970s.

3. Finally, "entrepreneurial judo" works when market or industry structure undergoes rapid change—e.g., the *Familienbank* story. As Germany became prosperous in the 1950s and 1960s, ordinary people became customers for financial services beyond the traditional savings account or the traditional mortgage. The German banks stuck to their old markets at the sacrifice of the new ones.

"Entrepreneurial judo" is always market-focused and market-driven. To use the "entrepreneurial judo" strategy one starts out with an analysis of the industry: the producers and the suppliers, their habits (especially their bad habits), and their policies. Then one looks at the markets and looks for the place where an alternative strategy would meet with the greatest success and the least resistance.

"Entrepreneurial judo" requires some degree of genuine innovation. It is, as a rule, not good enough to simply offer the same product or the same service at lower cost. There has to be something that distinguishes it from what already exists. When the ROLM Company offered a private-branch exchange (a switchboard for business and office users) in competition with AT&T, it built in additional features designed around a small computer. These were not "high tech," let alone new inventions. Indeed, AT&T itself had designed similar features. But AT&T did not push them—and ROLM did. Similarly, when Citibank went into Germany with the *Familienbank* it put in some innovative services which German banks as a rule did not offer to small depositors (e.g., travelers checks and tax advice).

It is not enough, in other words, for the newcomer to do as good a job as the established leader and at a lower cost or with better service. The newcomers have to make themselves distinct.

Like being "Fustest with the Mostest" and "creative imitation," entrepreneurial judo aims at obtaining a leadership position and eventual dominance. But it does not do so by competing with the leaders—or at least does not do it where the leaders are aware of competitive challenge or are worried about it. Entrepreneurial judo "Hits Them Where They Ain't."

What this article is about: Many managers see the experience curve as out of date. They base their assessment on simplistic promises of success in every business and the curve's failure to deliver. Debunking has gone too far, says this author. Experience curve strategies can improve competitive performance in some clearly defined situations. Successful use of the curve requires understanding why and how it works and when to apply it.

2-3 Building strategy on the experience curve*

Pankaj Ghemawat

Pankaj Ghemawat is assistant professor of business administration at the Harvard Business School, where he teaches courses on industry and competitor analysis and business policy. His current research focuses on the dynamics of competitive advantage.

A venerable management tool remains valuable—in the right circumstances.

In 1972 Du Pont decided to exploit the experience curve to preempt competitors in the titanium dioxide industry by investing $410 million over the following seven years. By 1979 capacity use in the industry had plummeted from 88 to 64 percent and Du Pont's return on sales dropped to half its initial level of 7.5 percent.

Du Pont's misadventure is not unique. The most notorious example is Ford's blind progress down the Model T experience curve. Between 1910 and 1921, Ford cut Model T costs by three quarters by modernizing plants, integrating vertically to reduce the cost of purchased inputs, increasing the division of labor, and eliminating model changes. (The Model T came only in black because black paint dried the quickest, which helped speed up the car's assembly.) Market share soared from 10 to 55 percent, and Ford was enormously profitable.

But by its single-minded focus on cost reduction, Ford had sown the seeds of its own downfall. As consumer demand shifted to a heavier, closed body and to a greater emphasis on comfort and styling, Ford responded by tacking on features to the Model T rather than changing models, as GM did. Worried about having to replace its massive investment in facilities dedicated to the Model T, Ford continued to build the car until 1927, when customer preferences forced it to close down its plants for nearly a year while it retooled the

Figure 1
Seventy percent experience curve for dynamic RAMs

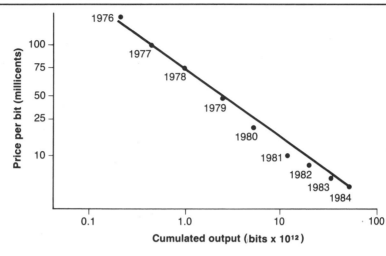

SOURCE: Integrated Circuit Engineering Corporation.

Model A. In the process Ford lost $200 million and suffered an irreversible decline in market share.[1]

Despite these gloomy stories, some companies have built strategies successfully on the experience curve. Since 1980, for example, Bausch & Lomb has consolidated its position in soft contact lenses by automating, using computerized lens design, and continuing to expand its one Soflens plant. As a result, its market share climbed from 55 percent in 1980 to 65 percent in 1983 and it now earns gross margins 20 to 30 percentage points higher than its competitors. Lincoln Electric's continued cost leadership in electric arc welding supplies derives in large part from personnel policies designed to encourage experience-based cost reductions.

What distinguishes the winners from the losers in the experience curve game is their grasp of both the logic of the experience curve and the characteristics of the competitive arena that determine its suitability as a strategic weapon.

How It Works

Use of the experience curve concept began over three decades ago to describe the mathematical relation between the cumulated output of a product and its costs. Literally thousands of studies have shown that production costs usually decline by 10 to 30 percent with each doubling of cumulated output. For example, if the thousandth unit of a product costs $100, the two-thousandth unit will normally cost $70 to $90. (Experience curve slopes generally fall in the 70 to 90 percent range.) Figure 1 illustrates the 70 percent experience curve encountered in chip production.

---

[1] William J. Abernathy and Kenneth Wayne, "Limits of the Learning Curve," *Harvard Business Review*, September–October 1974, p. 109.

Figure 2
Experience curve variation by product

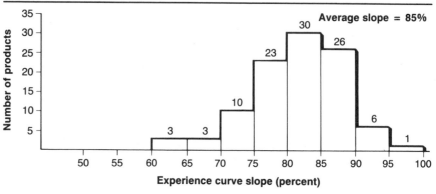

SOURCE: Ninety-seven academic studies, compiled by the author.

To a strategist, the experience curve suggests that the company with the highest share of an industry's cumulated output will also be the low-cost producer. Some consulting firms have argued that a business unit's route to a cost advantage lies through cutting price in order to buy share. The increased share of current output is supposed to propel the aggressive business unit's costs down the experience curve more rapidly than its rivals', thus improving its relative position.

But the Du Pont and Ford examples show that such a strategy can be a recipe for failure. The experience curve is too complex to be encapsulated in simple prescriptions. Successful strategy formulation requires a closer analysis of why and how the curve works.

Various Shapes   Many companies routinely assume 75 to 85 percent experience curves for their products, but this can lead to serious financial problems. For example, Douglas Aircraft fixed prices for the DC-9 on the basis of an 85 percent experience curve. When the estimated cost reductions failed to materialize, its losses forced Douglas into acquisition by the McDonnell Company.

Big surprises like this happen because experience curve slopes vary widely from product to product (Figure 2). In some industries the slope may be as steep as 60 percent; in others it may not occur at all.

Such variations take place for two reasons. First, cost reductions are almost never automatic; companies must work for them. Incentive programs should reward people for cost-reducing ideas and companies must encourage managers to implement them. Otherwise, costs may stagnate or even increase as time passes.

Second, some products and processes have greater potential for improvement over time than others do. Statistical studies show that manufacturing activities encounter steeper experience curves than raw materials purchasing, marketing, sales, or distribution. Manufacturing costs decline particularly steeply in industries with standardized product ranges and complex, labor-intensive production processes such as the airframe assembly or machine tool businesses.

Figure 3
Direct manufacturing costs for diodes*

Activity	Initial Cost Index	Experience Curve Percent	Cost after Cumulated Output Doubled
Photolithography	$ .06	80%	$ .05
Diffusion	.17	85%	.14
Contact plating	.11	70%	.08
Scribing	.42	80%	.34
Furnace sealing	2.00	85%	1.70
Total	**$2.76**		**$2.31**

* Excludes raw materials costs.
SOURCE: Adapted from Louis E. Yelle, "Estimating Learning Curves for Potential Products," *Industrial Marketing Management,* June 1976, p. 147.

A useful forecasting practice is to identify all the discrete activities that a business unit performs and estimate, on the basis of historical records, the experience curve slope for each of them. Figure 3 shows how such analysis can predict the behavior of an electronic component's manufacturing costs. Of course, estimators must analyze the costs of raw materials and other inputs in order to understand the component's total cost behavior.

Shared Inputs and Processes In many industries, the "platform" or base for experience includes more than just one product. In the case of the diode (Figure 3), all activities except furnace sealing were shared with other products the same company manufactured. This is not unusual; many companies use the same components, production facilities, or delivery system for their products. When such interrelationships exist, the strategist must consider them.

The dire fate of the British motorcycle industry exemplifies the perils of ignoring these interrelationships among cost factors.[2] Different bike classes share many parts and manufacturing processes. Manufacturers did not realize that achieving and maintaining a variable cost position for one product might require retaining market positions (and experience bases) in others. When threatened by Japanese competition in small bikes, the British withdrew from that market. This boosted short-run profits but in the long run destroyed most of their remaining motorcycle business. The Japanese used the cost advantage from their dominance in small bikes to push the British out of larger bikes, and left them with a small niche in superbikes. The British share of their own home market plunged from 34 percent in 1968 to 3 percent in 1974.

Nippon Electric Company (NEC) is another example of a Japanese company that successfully exploits interrelationships for its telecommunications and computer products. Forced to compete globally with much larger companies such as AT&T and IBM, NEC has used common components and technology, and shared systems and plants throughout its business units.

[2] Boston Consulting Group, *Strategy Alternatives for the British Motorcycle Industry* (London: Her Majesty's Stationery Office, 1975).

Cost Reduction Sources   Most experience curve applications confuse three cost reduction sources: exogenous progress (improvements in general technical knowledge and inputs plus feedback from customers), exploiting scale economies, and basic improvements learned from cumulated output (better product design, factory and labor efficiencies). These factors have critically different implications for strategy.

In businesses where exogenous progress is the primary source of cost reduction, the strategic imperative is to maximize bargaining power with suppliers and buyers. Ways to do this include adroit supplier and buyer selection, threats of vertical integration, and attempts to increase upstream and downstream switching costs. Before the recent auto industry crisis, GM and Ford had achieved these objectives by insisting on multiple sources, integrating partially backward into key components, analyzing in detail suppliers' costs, and avoiding long-term contracts.

If scale economies drive costs, then sustaining competitive advantage requires aggressive pursuit of market share. However, this strategy will succeed only to the extent that competitors are unwilling or unable to match investment in large, efficient facilities. Otherwise competitive gridlock, not competitive advantage, will resut as the whole industry gets mired in over-capacity. U.S. paper companies discovered this costly truth when they tried to leapfrog each other by building increasingly larger mills.

Basic improvements learned from cumulated output offer the most sustainable route to a cost advantage. The only cost-competitive method for producing titanium dioxide in the 1970s, for example, was through Du Pont's ilmenite chloride process, reportedly one of the most difficult the company had ever mastered. Scaling up from pilot plants materially affected operating characteristics and product quality. Competitors' only hope of approaching Du Pont's costs, therefore, was to shake down an efficiently scaled factory over a number of years. Because Du Pont kept expanding capacity ahead of demand, none of them attempted to do this.

Separating these three cost reduction sources usually requires expert estimates or regression analysis. In a dozen cases I compiled where businesses have tried this, they've experienced cost reductions as high as 90 percent from the basic improvement component. But extreme variations—with a critical impact on strategy formulation—occur by industry. In acrylonitrile manufacturing, for instance, the 87 percent experience curve is due mainly to improvements in catalyst technology (exogenous progress). Monsanto, which tried to rush down the experience curve by investing aggressively in large facilities such as the U.K. Seal Sands complex, lost money because the expected cost advantage did not materialize.

Leaks   Companies cannot keep all cost reductions secret from competitors. In nuclear power plant construction, for example, it appears that observant competitors have picked up roughly a third of each builder's experience-related cost reductions (stemming primarily from better design). Leakages are likely to be especially high when exogenous progress is producing cost reductions, when basic improvements are in reverse-engineered products, or when learning is vested in a small number of employees (such as design teams) whom competitors can lure away.

Figure 4
Experience curve strategy payoffs

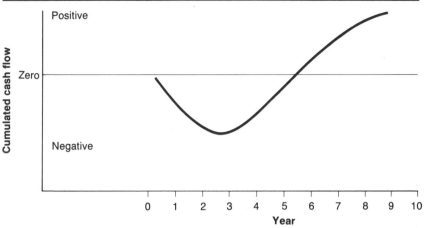

Sometimes leaks can be blocked. Japanese motorcycle manufacturers make most of their machine tools, a practice that tends to protect specialized machining techniques. Stung by a long succession of imitators, IBM has begun to omit key component details from its technical manuals and to sue vigorously people who give away or exploit what it considers its trade secrets.

Despite such measures, leakage will remain high in some environments. In such circumstances, companies gain little strategic advantage through aggressive output expansion because followers can simply imitate and attain cost proximity without making comparable investments.

Inflexibility Energetic pursuit of the experience curve usually requires such measures as lage investments in automation or penetration pricing in the hope of future profits (Figure 4). Given this expected cash-flow profile, managers should be wary of anything that might make the rainbow's pot of gold disappear. Du Pont's experience in the cellophane industry highlights how such disruptions may occur.[3]

In the early years of the U.S. cellophane industry, Du Pont had a monopoly. Sylvania's entry in 1930 with a new product, heat-sealable coatings, shattered it. This Sylvania innovation reduced Du Pont's experience base value, but the companies prevented matters from getting out of hand by cross licensing. Du Pont encountered trouble again between 1947 and 1953 as a result of an antitrust suit. The settlement required Du Pont to license a new competitor, Olin. Over the next few years, Du Pont had to keep prices higher than it would have liked (moderating its pursuit of an experience curve strategy), because lower prices might have driven Olin out of the market and

---

[3] P. R. Cowley, "The Experience Curve and the History of the Cellophane Business," Cranfield School of Management, Cranfield Institute of Technology, 1982, forthcoming in *Long Range Planning*.

prompted another antitrust investigation. Higher prices encouraged all competitors to expand their business and overcapacity became a serious problem. Since 1960, moreover, plastic film has become a substitute for cellophane, eroding even further the value of Du Pont's experience base.

The range of potential disruptions to experience curve strategies is even greater than the cellophane story suggests. Unexpected surges in demand, for example, can also sometimes raise costs because production systems canot handle them efficiently. In the case of the unlucky Lockheed Tristar, the need to increase output sharply to 25 planes a year in 1980 and 1981 meant that the company had to hire 11,000 extra workers. Later, labor efficiency plummeted by 50 percent.

When It Works

Industry structure, the relative positions of key competitors, and government impact are the critical variables that define the competitive arena. Careful analysis of each of these factors exposes both the opportunities and the traps in putting the experience curve to work for your company.

Industry Life Stages Experience curve strategies usually gain greatest leverage early in a product's life cycle because cumulated output doubles very rapidly at this stage. Compare, for instance, optical fibers and vacuum cleaners. Both follow experience curves of 60 to 65 percent, but it currently takes less than 2 years to double fiber optics' cumulated output whereas the vacuum cleaner industry requires nearly 20. Exploiting the experience curve can chop costs by a quarter each year in optical fibers, therefore, but it achieves only a 2 to 3 percent cost savings in vacuum cleaners.

The experience curve came into widespread use after the mid-1960s when it proved an important analytical tool for the burgeoning chemical and electronics industries. For mature or declining industries such as beer and cement, however, experience curve strategies caused trouble. The reason for this is simple: since cumulated output is doubling so slowly in the later product life-cycle phases, nearly all practicable, experience-related cost reductions have already been squeezed out of the production process; success now requires finding other competitive advantage sources. The cost leaders—Inland Steel in integrated steel production, for example—frequently do not have the most experience, but have smaller, focused, more modern facilities than competitors.[4]

Technological Risk The earliest product life-cycle stage, despite its opportunities for experience curve strategies, harbors traps for the unwary. One of the most important of these becomes evident when a company invests early to build up its experience base and discovers that it bet on the wrong technology.

The case of RCA, which failed to get its videodisc technology adopted by the industry, demonstrates how costly such blunders can be. Companies that face technological uncertainty have to make a basic choice. The lower risk (and lower return) strategy is to forgo a head start (and also an experience-

---

[4] William K. Hall, "Survival Strategies in a Hostile Environment," *Harvard Business Review,* September–October 1980, p. 75.

related cost advantage) by waiting until the technological uncertainty is resolved. For example, despite public commotion, no biotechnology company was willing to preempt the interferon market. As a result, six companies are now trying to get FDA approval for their interferon products.

The higher risk, higher return alternative is to invest heavily and try to make a technology or design dominant in an industry. For example, after some initial fence-sitting, Corning decided to promote optical fiber standardization by offering a very high-quality product, even though quality may have been excessively high in some end uses.

Price Sensitivity Experience curve strategies are particularly appropriate when a company's product is very sensitive to price changes. Cutting prices in such industries leads to huge jumps in demand. This additional demand accelerates the company's progress down the experience curve by permitting rapid increases in cumulated output. The lower costs that result provide leeway for the next round of price cuts and the process repeats itself.

The classic example of such a product is the handheld calculator. Advances in C-MOS (complementary metal-oxide semiconductor) technology and enormous price-sensitive demand provided fertile ground for the calculator market. When Texas Instruments Incorporated decided to enter it with an experience curve strategy in 1972, unit costs tumbled from thousands of dollars to single figures in less than a decade, while sales skyrocketed. Since prices were going to come down anyway because of the steep experience curve and the price sensitivity of the demand, TI did well in this market by choosing the role of an experience-based cost leader rather than a follower.

TI's experience in another market with a steep experience curve and price-sensitive demand, home computers, provides an ironic illustration of the same lesson. TI should not have let Commodore get ahead in the price-cutting and cost-reducing game.

Competitor Analysis Studying competitors is crucial before deciding whether to exploit the experience curve. Weak competitors tend to be undercapitalized business units, handicapped by both high-cost positions and corporate parents that do not understand experience curve logic, especially the need for large, up-front investments. The British motorcycle manufacturers discussed earlier are good examples.

On the other hand, competitors to watch out for have good cost positions, substantial financial resources, and a history of following aggressive experience curve strategies. A price war with one or more such competitors usually helps only the customer.

The U.S. brewing industry before the 1970s is a notorious illustration of how cutthroat competition can dissipate profits. The industry's subsequent success in breaking out of this stalemate through product differentiation suggests that when rivals are determined and able to ride down the experience curve, companies should explore other sources of competitive advantage. In the calculator business, Hewlett-Packard Company realized this and decided to focus on the premium end of the market rather than battling with TI in the high-volume segments. In semiconductors, Intel decided to rely on innovation to escape the cross fire between TI and National Semiconductor.

Government Intervention   Government affects the viability of experience curve strategies through its competition policy and the cost of capital. The latter is critical because experience curve strategies' early phases swallow up large amounts of cash. Governments influence this cost in a number of ways: subsidies, tax rates, depreciation policies, and interest rates. The net impact on U.S. companies relative to many of their foreign competitors is generally unfavorable. According to one estimate, for example, the real costs of capital in 1981 were 19 percent for American corporations but only 5½ percent for their Japanese counterparts.[5] These figures might not be exact, but the difference between them suggests that American companies will find it unprofitable to compete head-to-head down the experience curve against Japanese businesses, unless they already have an advantageous start.

Government competition policies may also block success for experience curve strategies. The U.S. government, for example, has sometimes attacked experience curve pricing on the grounds that it is a predatory attempt to monopolize the market. Although the courts overturned the FTC's most important recent challenge along these lines—an attempt to force Du Pont to share its cost reductions in the titanium dioxide industry with all its competitors—definitive precedents have yet to be set. In the meantime, American companies should be careful to document cost efficiencies due to the experience curve.

Will It Work for Me?

In sum, branding the experience curve as either a panacea or a Pandora's box is neither accurate nor useful. If you are considering an experience curve strategy in your business, ask yourself the following questions:

> Does my industry exhibit a significant experience curve?
>
> Have I defined the industry broadly enough to take into account interrelated experience?
>
> What is the precise source of cost reduction?
>
> Can my company keep cost reductions proprietary?
>
> Is demand sufficiently stable to justify using the experience curve?
>
> Is cumulated output doubling fast enough for the experience curve to provide much strategic leverage?
>
> Do the returns from an experience curve strategy warrant the risks of technological obsolescence?
>
> Is demand price-sensitive?
>
> Are there well-financed competitors who are already following an experience curve strategy or are likely to adopt one if my company does?
>
> Is there a significant antitrust risk?

---

[5] George N. Hatsopoulos, "High Cost of Capital: Handicap of American Industry" (Report prepared for the American Business Conference, Boston, 1983).

THE MODEL T AND THE EXPERIENCE CUR⌐

The price of the touring car on October 1, 1908, was $850, and ⸳ was increased to $950 on October 1, 1909. From that date there was a progressive reduction of the price of this car until it reached a low of $360 on August 1, 1916. During the period of rising wage rates and prices of materials in the latter part of the war period and the immediate post-war period, the prices were increased from time to time to a maximum of $575 on March 4, 1920. After that date, prices were again reduced progressively and reached a new low of $290 on December 2, 1924. There was an increase of $20 on February 11, 1926. Commencing with a price of $590 on October 1, 1911, the prices of the runabout followed a course paralleling that of the prices of the touring car. A minimum of $345 was reached on August 1, 1916, after which the prices were increased progressively to $550 on March 4, 1920, and again were progressively decreased thereafter to a new low of $260 on December 2, 1924. The price of the runabout was increased $30 on February 11, 1926.

With these progressively diminishing prices, the sales of Model T cars increased by leaps and bounds. The aggregate sales during the calendar year 1908 amounted to 5,986 cars. The sales during the succeeding calendar years up to 1919 were as follows: 1909, 12,292 cars; 1910, 19,293 cars; 1911, 40,402 cars; 1912, 78,611 cars; 1913, 182,809 cars; 1914, 260,720 cars; 1915, 355,276 cars; 1916, 577,036 cars; 1917, 802,771 cars; 1918, 402,908 cars; and 1919, 777,694 cars.

SOURCE: Alfred D. Chandler, Jr., *Giant Enterprise: Ford, General Motors, and the Automobile Industry* (New York: Harcourt Brace Jovanovich) © 1964 by Harcourt Brace Jovanovich. Reprinted with the permission of the publisher.

Answers to these questions, rather than simple past prescriptions, will help you decide whether experience curve strategies could pay off for you.

out: Three different firms pursue three different but
chose the least-cost option, Coca-Cola opted for differ-
rd Headed Products, Inc. found a niche in its market. All
cause they adjusted their strategy and repositioned their
product-markets changed.

16

2–4   strategic options of least-
cost, differentiation, and niche*

Peter Wright

*Peter Wright is a professor of management at Southeastern
Louisiana University, Hammond.*

- RCA's television division commanded market leadership in America from
  the 1940s to the 1960s. With the decade of the 60s, however, foreign
  competition for the U.S. market began to exert a negative effect on RCA
  and other American television producers.
- Over the years Coca-Cola, the world's largest soft drink producer,
  witnessed its competitors making inroads into its customer base.
  Competitors such as Royal Crown, Pepsico, and 7UP jumped the gun on
  Coca-Cola and offered new products in innovative containers. These
  moves resulted in Coke's temporarily losing market share.
- For decades Rockford Headed Products, Inc., produced standard fasteners
  for general wholesalers. This small manufacturer chose local general
  distributors as its customers. The crucial weapon in this industry became
  price competition. And over the years Rockford's profitability turned
  into losses.

RCA, Coca-Cola, and Rockford, though to different degrees, all faced
difficulties because of the changing competitive environment. By responding
strategically to the environmental changes, all three firms have done well. By
continuously examining and reexamining their product-market scopes, these
enterprises have made competitive forces work in their favor. Yet each
company responded in quite a different way.

RCA's corporate managers realized that the competitive forces of cheaper
imports had transformed the television industry into one with fairly standard-

---

* This article is reprinted from *Business Horizons*, March–April 1986.

ized product-market dimensions. RCA considered two options. First, the firm could switch its product-market option away from mass merchandising, and toward high-quality television units, as Curtis Mathes had done successfully. Second—and this was RCA's choice—the firm could become price competitive by expanding its TV production capacity to a world scale in order to capitalize on cheaper resources in various countries. RCA also has capitalized on the innovation capabilities of its world business units to improve its output technologically.

Coca-Cola's competitive response has been to broaden its product lines and to compete head-on with rival soft drink companies. Because of its huge resources, Coca-Cola has been able to support its competitive moves successfully through massive advertising.

Rockford's financial losses resulted in a change of top management. At that point, most sales were of standardized fasteners. The new management switched the plant capacity away from standard fasteners and toward the production of technologically new, custom-made self-threading screws, which permitted faster assembly. The change resulted in a return to profitability. Specialized fasteners are normally sold directly to the end users, who purchase on the basis of customized specifications, on-time delivery, superior performance, and—last of all—price.

What Strategic Options Are Available?

These three cases point to the need for a periodic appraisal of the strategic options available to an enterprise. By viewing the firm from the perspective of strategic options, top management can structure a viable fit between an enterprise and its external environment.

A business unit's decision to compete with specific product-market dimensions links the business unit to one of three strategic options: least-cost, differentiation, and niche.

Least-Cost: The RCA Picture   When a firm chooses to compete with uniform, standardized products, it is choosing the strategic option of least-cost. RCA chose this option, which emphasizes producing at very low per unit costs. The competitive environment for businesses producing uniform products rewards primarily those firms that are able to offer low prices.

Differentiation: The Case of Coca-Cola   When a business unit prefers to compete by offering unique products, it chooses the strategic option of differentiation. Its outputs must be considered exceptional. The competitive environment for unique products rewards enterprises that create demand for their products, even at relatively high prices, by convincing the consumer that the products are of superior value. Coca-Cola adopted this strategy.

Niche: The Rockford File   Finally, when a business unit decides to fill a limited need, to offer a product that only a few buyers will purchase, it is selecting a special niche as its strategic option. The competitive environment for need-fulfilling outputs rewards those businesses that are willing to satisfy, at premium prices, the particular desires of small clusters of buyers. Rockford made this choice.

Each of these strategic options has distinct ramifications for a firm's international involvement. Each has implications for profitability and innovation.

Least-Cost

When a firm decides to provide uniform, standardized outputs that have substantial demand, it chooses the **least-cost** strategic option.[1] This option emphasizes producing a standardized product at very low per unit costs. Ideally, firms that decide in favor of the least-cost option should be the larger ones in the industry or be willing to become so; they also should have greater access to resources than do their competitors. Such firms need functional support from finance, manufacturing, and at times R&D.[2] Their overriding objective should be to seek a high level of "experience" or cumulative volume of production.

The experience curve that conceptualizes cumulative volume of production allows lower per unit costs through a combination of:

1. Substantial economies of scale.
2. Capital-labor substitution possibilities.
3. An incrementally increasing learning curve.[3]

Equally important for the least-cost strategic option is gaining access to low cost inputs such as labor, energy, and freight. Firms that choose the least-cost option must be willing to strive for larger production capacities and market shares in their industries.

Firms that compete with least-cost strategies are confronted with a relatively elastic market demand that is likely to promote price concession policies.[4] Because the business entity and its competitors produce uniform goods, the firm ordinarily expects competitive price pressures as buyers everywhere are drawn to those enterprises offering lower prices.

Industries subject to the least-cost option progressively have become global in order to achieve cumulative volume of production and gain access to low-cost inputs. Vernon mentions several examples of outputs that lend themselves to the least-cost strategy and are becoming "world products":

The manufactured products that appear in the stalls and markets of Accra or Dar es Salaam are no longer very different from those in Djakarta or Cartagena or Recife . . . Electric batteries and electric bulbs are taking over the function of kerosene, wood, vegetable oils . . . the portable radio and the aspirin tablet are joining the list of life's universal necessities . . . middle-income automobiles, when judged

---

[1] See J. S. Bain, *Essays on Price Theory and Industrial Organization* (Boston: Little Brown, 1972), pp. 1–127; T. Flaherty, "Industry Structure and Cost Reducing Investment: A Dynamic Equilibrium Analysis" (Ph.D. diss., Carnegie-Mellon University, 1976), pp. 1–184.

[2] This point is made by J. S. Bain, *Industrial Organization* (New York: John Wiley & Sons, 1968), pp. 1–7.

[3] M. Porter, "How Competitive Forces Shape Strategy," *Harvard Business Review*, March–April 1979, pp. 137–44.

[4] See F. M. Scherer, *Industrial Market Structure and Economic Performance* (Chicago: Rand McNally, 1970); W. F. Mueller and L. G. Hamm, "Trends in Industrial Market Concentration, 1947–1970," *Review of Economics and Statistics*, 56 (November 1974), pp. 511–20.

by appearance and performance, are losing their last traces of national distinction, bicycles and ski equipment are universal commodities tailored to a global market.[5]

International Involvement

Like RCA, firms that produce standardized outputs which subject them to the least-cost option are forced in many instances to place business units strategically across the globe, in order to minimize costs. RCA, for example, located business units in such countries as Taiwan, Japan, Mexico, and Canada. These business units are managed interdependently with RCA units located in the U.S. Each business unit performs complementary production or support functions. One may be a mass producer of components or parts. Other business units may assume support functions such as subassembly work, warehousing, or distribution on a massive scale. Each business unit is a link in the overall input-output strategy of RCA's world operations.

Enterprises that choose to compete through the least-cost strategy should strive for the efficiency of the firm's global system. Because coordination is crucial in such a system, the international involvement of the enterprise requires structuring multilateral relationships among its various global business units.

Ramifications for Profitability and Innovation

According to numerous studies conducted by various groups, per unit costs typically fall by about one third with every doubling in the number of outputs produced.[6] Because costs per unit decrease with greater production, then the firm that produces the most should have the lowest marginal cost.

Hence, the key to profitability when producing uniform products is to become a global market share leader. Since the name of the game is price competition, higher profitability requires larger volumes of production and sales worldwide.

Such an assessment assumes a constant level of technology. Given this assumption, a firm's obvious course of action would be to add to production capacity and to gain market share at all costs. But business enterprises do not face a stable level of technology forever. Fortunately for RCA, its Japanese business units continually have developed innovative products (wide screens, thin picture tubes, recording capabilities) that then have been globally manufactured and distributed by RCA.

But firms in other industries have not always been so fortunate. For example, the largest producer of glass bottles for milk had developed the most stable and efficient technology for glass bottles. This firm had the most to lose, therefore, when technology shifted and waxed cartons replaced glass bottles as containers for milk. When demand for glass bottles was no longer

---

[5] R. Vernon, *Storm Over The Multinationals* (Cambridge, Mass.: Harvard University Press, 1977), pp. 20.

[6] See, for example, G. Allan and J. Hammond, *Note on the Use of Experience Curves in Competitive Decision-Making* (Cambridge, Mass.: Harvard Intercollegiate Clearing House of Cases, 1975), pp. 1–42; Boston Consulting Group, "Perspectives on Experience" (Boston, 1976), pp. 1–82.

there, the substantial investments made in plant and equipment for making glass bottles had to be written off.

For decades American car manufacturers emphasized reducing costs through cumulative production volume. Management continuously attempted to stabilize technology and to reduce further the marginal cost of production. U.S. car makers did not consider technological innovations that dealt with variables other than reducing the manufacturing cost. Technological developments outside of America—in Japan and Germany—finally made Detroit realize that consumers preferred innovative cars. When American auto firms adopted aerodynamically efficient car bodies, transaxle and transverse mounted engines, and such fuel-saving parts as advanced plastic, graphite fibers, and dual-phased steel, the result was a car that was more reliable and less expensive to operate.

If a firm with standardized product-market scope, competing through the least-cost strategy, is to remain viable in the long run, it must also be willing to be a leader in technology. To be simultaneously a leader in technology *and* a least-cost producer is quite a challenge. Least-cost producers depend on a stable technology over time in order to cut manufacturing costs through cumulative volume of production. Reliance on a stable technology contradicts in many ways actively seeking innovations that might lead to the replacement of the present technology. The question is, **How do corporate managers balance the needs of a stable technology—and substantial investments in plant and equipment geared to that technology—against those needs to actively seek innovations that might replace present technology?**

History provides partial answers to this question. Any technology can be improved over time. But a point will be reached when further improvements in that technology will require prohibitively expensive inputs that will not improve product performance significantly. Exactly at such times, more emphasis should be placed on actively seeking innovations, at the cost of rendering obsolete the present stable technology. If one enterprise does not emphasize innovations at such critical times, others will. Instances abound in many industries.

For years NCR had the best and the cheapest mechanical cash register, which was the number one choice of the marketplace. Then Burroughs developed a fully integrated electronic cash register that was superior in performance. The demand shifted away from mechanical cash registers and toward electric cash registers.

The typewriter is another illustration of product improvements taking place throughout the years through shifts in technology. The mechanical typewriter was improved in many ways: it was made more sensitive to the touch, the keys were arranged for faster operator performance and less operator fatigue, and its size and weight were reduced. Underwood, the leading maker of mechanical typewriters, did not realize, however, that further improvements to the typewriter required a different technology—activating the keyboard electrically instead of mechanically. It was IBM that pioneered the electric typewriter, which essentially has replaced the mechanical typewriter.

Still a diffe
Because of its
puter-assisted
did not pionee
marketplace fo
made IBM wor

This brings
onslaught of a n
and sometimes
for years have
dedicated to tha
developing and
technologically

market-by-market basis.
diverse product requi
risks. As long as
allow local man
And where
have mult
produc
busi

Differentiation

A firm that de   98
industry chooses
functional suppor
of their corporati
manufacturing ef   ....ations in existing products and
quick responses to changes in the nature or volume of demand. With unique
outputs, low costs are not of crucial importance. For products to maintain
their distinguishable identities, the firms must bear the costs of their modification, packaging, distribution, and advertising. Because lower costs are not
vital, smaller as well as larger firms may compete effectively with unique
products.

Functional support from the manufacturing and marketing sectors helps a
firm to position its unique products favorably so that it can make the most of
the relatively inelastic market demand.[9] The relatively inelastic market
demand for its outputs allows the firm, in turn, to set higher pricing policies
and profit margins. Depending on the size of the business unit and the
preference of its top managers, firms that compete through differentiation
may choose smaller or larger market shares for their outputs.

International Involvement

When product-market choices yield unique outputs, as with Coca-Cola,
then planning for the firm's international involvement necessitates structuring independent relationships among its various world business units. That
is, business units are created that function independently of each other on a

[7] See W. S. Comanor and T. A. Wilson, *Advertising and Market Power* (Cambridge, Mass.:
Harvard University Press, 1974); M. Porter, *Competitive Strategy: Techniques for Analyzing
Industries and Companies* (New York: Free Press, 1980), pp. 1–396.

[8] Robert Stobaugh and Piero Telesio, "Match Manufacturing Policies and Product Strategy," *Harvard Business Review,* March–April 1983, p. 118.

[9] See P. Wright, "Competitive Strategies for Small Businesses" in *Readings in Strategic
Management,* ed. William Fulmer (Plano, Tex.: Business Publications, 1984), pp. 86–91;
P. Wright, "Systematic Approach in Finding Export Opportunities," in *Managing Effectively
in the World Marketplace,* ed. Harvard Graduate School of Business (New York: John Wiley &
Sons, 1983), pp. 331–42.

ach independent business unit's market may have
ements, competitive forces, and economic/political
eturn on investment remains acceptable, top managers
agers great autonomy in making decisions.

as corporate entities with standardized product-market options
lateral relationships among corporate groups, firms with unique
-market options tend to have bilateral relationships only between each
ess unit and company headquarters. The international involvement of
rms competing through the strategy of differentiation may include exporting, licensing, joint ventures, and manufacturing. With this strategy, the
world marketplace may be viewed as a potential area of activity.

Ramifications for Profitability and Innovation

Products that are considered unique are normally priced well above production costs. And their sales potential is relatively insensitive to price.
Consequently, modifications in existing products and quick responses to
changes in the nature of volume of demand by far supersede considerations
that would lower manufacturing costs.

Some centralized planning and implementation efforts are likely to boost
profitability and innovation potentials of enterprises with unique products.
For example, a degree of centralized engineering and R&D activities may
provide useful inputs into the future product planning of any one business
unit of the corporate entity. And some centralized efforts in advertising may
save each business unit substantial sums. For instance, Coca-Cola is bottled
in 115 countries. Part of its massive advertising is done by films, films made
for use in many of the international markets. This centralized approach in
film advertising alone saves Coca-Cola's world bottlers millions of dollars
per year.[10]

For enterprises that compete through differentiation, innovations tend to
arise from the local market demand and product development, as well as
from unique market characteristics that may require offering special credit
terms, packaging, promotion, and distribution services. Local market forces
do not always influence all innovative aspects of a firm. For example, Coca-
Cola provides the same product to all world markets. But though Coca-
Cola's top managers do not allow various consumer tastes and preferences to
affect the taste of the product, they do let local market forces influence credit
terms, distribution, and promotion policies.

Manufacturers of home appliances, on the other hand, allow local market
forces to influence their product-market scope heavily. Their rice cookers, as
one instance, cook rice in substantially different form and quality, depending
on local consumer tastes. Sometimes particular local preferences provide
product ideas that can be implemented successfully in other regions. Originally intended for the Asian market, rice cookers that develop separate and
fluffy grains of rice are now marketed in America as well.

With the least-cost strategic option, higher profitability correlated

---

[10] Jay Leviton, ''Coke's Big Market Blitz,'' *Business Week,* May 30, 1983, p. 61.

positively with greater production capacity and market share. With the differentiation option, however, according to a number of studies, higher profitability may correlate with either smaller or greater production capacity and market share.[11] In the mainframe computer manufacturing industry, for example, Burroughs, with less than 7 percent of market share, has had a high ROI (14 percent) with its unique products. IBM, also competing through differentiation, has also had a high ROI (20 percent), with a whopping 59 percent of market share.[12]

Niche

When a business unit decides to offer existing products or technologically new or improved products that fulfill the needs of particular buyers in an industry, it has chosen the strategic option of niche.[13] Products of both the differentiation and niche options normally have well-known brands to distinguish them from the products of competitors. But though the unique products of the differentiation option are aimed at the whole industry, the need-fulfilling products of the niche option address specific clusters of buyers within an industry.

Firms using the niche strategic option need functional support primarily from their research and development, manufacturing, and marketing sectors.[14] While established products that have been in the marketplace for some time tend to rely primarily on marketing, technologically new or improved products depend primarily on R&D and manufacturing.

Low costs are less important with the niche option than with the differentiation option. Because, under the niche option, the firm will produce fewer units than under the differentiation option, per unit costs tend to be higher. Technologically oriented product-market choices also require rapid product modifications and frequent and costly new-product introductions. These requirements make unfeasible lower manufacturing costs through larger volumes of production, particularly since accurate sales projections for innovative products are difficult to make.

Hence, business units competing through the niche option should be prepared to face and cultivate a highly inelastic market demand for their products.[15] Market demand for its outputs allows the firm to set higher pricing policies and profit margins than with the differentiation option. Under the niche option, larger and smaller firms with varying amounts of resources may compete effectively with need-fulfilling products.

---

[11] See Carolyn Y. Woo and Arnold C. Cooper, "Strategies of Effective Low Share Businesses," *Strategic Management Journal,* July–Sept. 1981, pp. 301–18; Carolyn Y. Woo, "Market Share Leadership—Not Always So Good," *Harvard Business Review,* January–February 1984, pp. 50–54.

[12] R. G. Hamermesh, M. J. Anderson, and J. E. Harris, "Strategies for Low Market Share Businesses," *Harvard Business Review,* May–June 1978, pp. 95–102.

[13] P. Wright, "MNC-Third World Business Unit Performance: Application of Strategic Elements," *Strategic Management Journal,* August 1984, pp. 231–40.

[14] P. Wright, "Strategic Management Within A World Parameter," *Managerial Planning,* ed. Henry C. Doofe (Oxford: Planning Executive Institute, 1985), pp. 33–37.

[15] Wright (note 13), pp. 231–40.

International Involvement

Business units subject to the niche option have only limited opportunities for international involvement. Their markets are often restricted to advanced, high-income countries, though some exporting may be done to the developing nations. For example, Rockford's specialized fasteners are particularly appropriate for capital-intensive manufacturers that produce substantial volumes and implement high value addition in their production process. Such manufacturers are usually found in the advanced countries.

International involvement may begin with exporting. It may culminate in establishing production units in select advanced, high-income countries, such as Canada, Germany, Sweden, Switzerland, England, and Japan. Because low costs are not of paramount importance, there is little incentive to adapt product technology to local factor costs.[16] Hence, the corporate headquarters of firms competing through the niche option would tend particularly to influence product technology in all markets.

Ramifications for Profitability and Innovation

The niche strategic option emphasizes product outputs that fulfill the special needs of few buyers. Because need-fulfilling products present very high values to their consumers and are produced in lower numbers, the route to profitability is through very high profit margins and pricing policies. Higher profitability for need-fulfilling outputs tends to correlate negatively with production capacity and market share.[17] An executive of a toothpaste firm that specializes in treating gum diseases provides an example:

We used to produce and sell $20 million per year and our return on investment was around 20 percent. Now we sell twice as much since we began expanding our market share. But we are lucky to have our return on investment break the single-digit range. The more customers we gain, it seems, the more we have to give price concessions.[18]

Innovative prospects of the niche strategic option tend to be brightest when R&D and manufacturing are emphasized. Although innovations may occur under any one of the options, the niche strategy, which revolves around smaller and more flexible production and R&D sectors, is best suited for making and responding to rapid technological advances. The task of R&D is to explore opportunities for superior outputs, and the mission of manufacturing is to remain flexible enough to accommodate specific demands for the products. For example, R&D provided the impetus for Rockford's technologically new, self-threading screw that permits faster assembly. And flexible manufacturing at Rockford has allowed the innovative fastener to be custom-made in size, strength, and coating for each customer.

Specific product-market choices tend to link an enterprise to the strategic options of least-cost, differentiation, or niche. But strategies are subject to change.

Select need-fulfilling products over time may be repositioned to compete

[16] Stobaugh and Telesio, "Match Manufacturing," p. 20.
[17] M. Porter, *Competitive Strategy*, pp. 1–34.
[18] Quoted in Wright, "Competitive Strategies for," p. 88.

as unique and subsequently standardized outputs. For example, the innovative, need-fulfilling computer of today, which is addressed to fewer buyers, eventually may be directed to larger portions of the market as a unique product. As its functions are superseded by more advanced technology, the same computer may carry a lower price tag and may be mass-produced for the price-sensitive consumer. The successful firm not only chooses a strategic option but also, as the product-market changes, adjusts its strategy and repositions its product.

What this article is about: Sustainable competitive advantage is the goal of every competitive strategy. This article describes a number of established strategic concepts and builds on them to develop a clear and explicit concept of sustainable competitive advantage. In doing so, it identifies some of the conditions for it and the implications for business strategy.

2-5 Sustainable competitive advantage—what it is, what it isn't*

Kevin P. Coyne

Kevin P. Coyne is an associate in McKinsey & Company's Washington, D.C., office. Formerly he was executive assistant to the deputy secretary of the treasury.

I shall not today attempt to define the kinds of material to be embraced within that shorthand description; and perhaps I could never succeed in intelligibly doing so. But I know it when I see it.

Supreme Court Justice Potter Stewart
(Jacobellis v. *State of Ohio)*

Although it was pornography, not sustainable competitive advantage, that the late Justice Stewart doubted his ability to define, his remark neatly characterizes the current state of thinking about the latter subject as well. Explicitly or implicitly, sustainable competitive advantage (SCA) has long occupied a central place in strategic thinking. Witness the widely accepted definition of competitive strategy as "an integrated set of actions that produce a sustainable advantage over competitors."[1] But exactly what constitutes sustainable competitive advantage is a question rarely asked. Most corporate strategists are content to apply Justice Stewart's test; they know an SCA when they see it—or so they assume.

But perhaps an SCA is not always so easy to identify. In developing its liquid hand soap, Minnetonka, Inc., focused its efforts on building an advantage that was easily copied later. In the wristwatch market, Texas Instruments attempted to exploit an advantage over its competitors that turned out to be unimportant to target consumers. RCA built barriers to competition in the vacuum tube market in the 1950s only to find these barriers irrelevant when transistors and semiconductors were born. CB radio

---

* This article is reprinted from *Business Horizons,* January–February 1986, pp. 54–61.
[1] *Competitive strategy,* as the term is used in this article, is exclusively concerned with defeating competitors and achieving dominance in a product/market segment. It is thus—in concept, and usually in practice—a subset of business strategy, which addresses the broader goal of maximizing the wealth of shareholders.

producers built capacity to fill a demand that later evaporated. In each case, the companies failed to see in advance that, for one reason or another, they lacked a sustainable competitive advantage.

Perhaps it is because the meaning of sustainable competitive advantage is superficially self-evident that virtually no effort has been made to define it explicitly. After all, it can be argued that the dictionary's definitions of the three words bring forth the heart of the concept. But every strategist needs to discover whether an SCA is actually or potentially present, and if so, what its implications are for competitive and business strategy.

Therefore, this article will describe a number of established strategic concepts and build on them to develop a clear and explicit concept of SCA.

Specifically, we will examine:

1. *The conditions for SCA.* When does a producer have a competitive advantage? How can the strategist test whether such an advantage is sustainable?
2. *Some implications of SCA for strategy.* Does having SCA guarantee success? Can a producer succeed without an SCA? Should a producer always pursue an SCA?

Conditions for SCA

Any producer who sells his goods or services at a profit undeniably enjoys a competitive advantage with those customers who choose to buy from him instead of his competitors, though these competitors may be superior in size, strength, product quality, or distribution power. Some advantages, however, are obviously worth more than others. A competitive advantage is meaningful in strategy only when three distinct conditions are met:

1. Customers perceive a consistent difference in important attributes between the producer's product or service and those of his competitors.
2. That difference is the direct consequence of a capability gap between the producer and his competitors.
3. Both the difference in important attributes and the capability gap can be expected to endure over time.

In earlier strategy work, these conditions have been jointly embedded in the concepts of "key factors for success" (KFS), "degrees of freedom," and "lower costs or higher value to the customer." In the interest of clarity, however, they deserve separate consideration.

Differentiation in Important Attributes

Obviously, competitive advantage results from differentiation among competitors—but not just any differentiation. For a producer to enjoy a competitive advantage in a product/market segment, the difference or differences between him and his competitors must be felt in the marketplace: that is, they must be reflected in some *product/delivery attribute* that is a *key buying criterion* for the market. And the product must be differentiated enough to win the loyalty of a significant set of buyers; it must have a *footprint in the market.*

Product/Delivery Attribute

Customers rarely base their choice of a product or service on internal characteristics of the producer that are not reflected in a perceived product or delivery difference. Indeed, they usually neither know nor care about those characteristics. Almost invariably, the most important contact between the customer and the producer is the marketplace—the "strategic triangle" where the producer meets his customers and competitors. It is here that the competitive contest for the scarce resource, the sales dollar, is directly engaged.

Just as differences among animal species that are unrelated to scarce resources do not contribute to the survival of the fittest, so producer differences that do not affect the market do not influence the competitive process. Differences among competitors in plant locations, raw material choices, labor policies, and the like matter only when and if those differences translate into product/delivery attributes that influence the customers' choice of where to spend their sales dollars.

"Product/delivery attributes" include not only such familiar elements as price, quality, aesthetics, and functionality, but also broader attributes such as availability, consumer awareness, visibility, and after-sales service. Anything that affects customers' perceptions of the product or service, its usefulness to them, and their access to it is a product/delivery attribute. Anything that does not affect these perceptions is not.

Having lower costs, for example, may well result in significantly higher margins. But this *business* advantage will become a *competitive* advantage only if and when the producer directly or indirectly recycles the additional profits into product/delivery attributes such as price, product quality, advertising, or additional capacity that increases availability. Only then is the producer's competitive position enhanced. Two examples illustrate this point.

- For years, the "excess" profits of a major packaged goods company—the low-cost producer in its industry—have been siphoned off by its corporate parent for reinvestment in other subsidiaries. The packaged goods subsidiary has therefore been no more able to take initiatives or respond to competitive threats than if it did not produce those excess profits. Thus, business advantage may exist, but competitive advantage is lacking. If risk-adjusted returns available from investments in other business exceed those of additional investment in the packaged goods subsidiary, the corporate parent may be making the best business decisions. However, the packaged goods subsidiary has gained no competitive advantage from its superior position.

- The corporate parent of a newly acquired, relatively high-cost producer in an industrial products market has decided to aggressively expand its subsidiary. This expansion is potentially at the expense of the current market leader, an independent company occupying the low-cost position in the industry. The resources that the new parent is willing to invest are far larger than the incremental profits generated by the market leader's lower costs. Because the new subsidiary can invest more than the market leader in product design, product quality, distribution, and so forth, it is the subsidiary that has, or soon will have, the competitive advantage.

In short, it is the application, not just the generation, of greater resources that is required for *competitive* advantage.

Key Buying Criterion

Every product has numerous attributes that competitors can use to differentiate themselves to gain some degree of advantage. To be strategically significant, however, an advantage must be based on positive differentiation of an attribute that is a *key buying criterion* for a particular market segment and is not offset by a negative differentiation in any other key buying criterion. In the end, competitive advantage is the result of all net differences in important product/delivery attributes, not just one factor such as price or quality. Differences in other, less important attributes may be helpful at the margin, but they are not strategically significant.

Key buying criteria vary, of course, by industry and even by market segment. In fact, because market segments differ in their choice of key buying criteria, a particular product may have a competitive advantage in some segments while being at a disadvantage in others. Price aside, the elaborate technical features that professional photographers prize in Hasselblad cameras would baffle and discourage most of the casual users who make up the mass market.

In any one product/market segment, however, only a very few criteria are likely to be important enough to serve as the basis for a meaningful competitive advantage. These criteria are likely to be basic—that is, central to the concept of the product or service itself, as opposed to "add-ons" or "features." For example, in the tubular steel industry, there are just two key product/delivery attributes: a single measure of quality (third-party testing reject rate), and local availability on the day required by the customer's drilling schedule.

Texas Instruments (TI) apparently did not fully understand the importance of differentiation along key buying criteria when it entered the wristwatch market. Its strategy was to build upon its ability to drive down costs—and therefore prices (the product attribute)—beyond the point where competitors could respond. But this competitive strategy, which had worked in electronic components, failed in wristwatches because price, past a certain point, was no longer a key buying criterion: customers cared more about aesthetics. TI had surpassed all of its competitors in an attribute that did not matter in the marketplace.

Footprint in the Market

To contribute to an SCA, the differences in product/delivery attributes must command the attention and loyalty of a substantial customer base: in other words, they must produce a "footprint in the market" of significant breadth and depth.

Breadth How many customers are attracted to the product above all others by the difference in product attributes? What volume do these customers purchase?

Depth How strong a preference has this difference generated? Would minor changes in the balance of attributes cause the customers to switch?

Breadth and depth are usually associated in marketing circles with the concept of "branding." Branding can indeed be a source of competitive advantage, as shown by Perrier's spectacular advantage in a commodity as prosaic as bottled mineral water.

But the importance of breadth and depth are not limited to branding strategies. Even a producer who is pursuing a low-price strategy must ensure that his lower price will cause customers to choose his product and that changes in nonprice attributes by competitors would be unlikely to lure them away.

Durable Differentiation

Positive differentiation in key product/delivery attributes is essential to competitive advantage. However, a differentiation that can be readily erased does not by itself confer a meaningful advantage. Competitive advantages described in such terms as "faster delivery" or "superior product quality" are illusory if competitors can erase the differentiation at will.

For example, Minnetonka, Inc., created a new market niche with "Softsoap." As a result, its stock price more than doubled. Before long, however, 50 different brands of liquid soap, some selling for a fifth of Softsoap's price, appeared on the market. As a result, Minnetonka saw its earnings fall to zero and its stock price decline by 75 percent.

An advantage is durable only if competitors cannot readily imitate the producer's superior product/delivery attributes. In other words, a gap in the *capability* underlying the differentiation must separate the producer from his competitors; otherwise no meaningful competitive advantage exists. (Conversely, of course, no meaningful advantage can arise from a capability gap that does not produce an important difference in product/delivery attributes.)

Understanding the capability gap, then, is basic to determining whether a competitive advantage actually exists. For example, an attribute such as faster delivery does not constitute a real competitive advantage unless it is based on a capability gap such as may exist if the company has a much bigger truck fleet than its competitors can afford to maintain. Higher product quality does not in itself constitute a competitive advantage. But unique access to intrinsically superior raw materials that enable the producer to deliver a better-quality product may well do so.

A capability gap exists when the function responsible for the differentiated product/delivery attribute is one that only the producer in question can perform, or one that competitors (given their particular limitations) could do only with maximum effort. So defined, capability gaps fall into four categories.

1. *Business system gaps* result from the ability to perform individual functions more effectively than competitors and from the inability of competitors to easily follow suit. For example, differences in labor-union work rules can constitute a capability gap resulting in superior

production capability. Superior engineering or technical skills may create a capability gap leading to greater precision or reliability in the finished product.

2. *Position gaps* result from prior decisions, actions, and circumstances. Reputation, consumer awareness and trust, and order backlogs, which can represent important capability gaps, are often the legacy of an earlier management generation. Thus, current competitive advantage may be the consequence of a past facilities location decision. BHP, the large Australian steel maker, enjoys important production efficiencies because it is the only producer to have located its smelter adjacent to its iron ore source, eliminating expensive iron ore transportation costs.

3. *Regulatory/legal gaps* result from government's limiting the competitors who can perform certain activities, or the degree to which they can perform those activities. Patents, operating licenses, import quotas, and consumer safety laws can all open important capability gaps among competitors. For example, Ciba-Giegy's patent on a low-cost herbicide allowed it to dominate certain segments of the agricultural chemical market for years.

4. *Organization or managerial quality gaps* result from an organization's ability consistently to innovate and adapt more quickly and effectively than its competitors. For example, in industries like computers or financial services, where the competitive environment is shifting rapidly, this flexibility may be the single most important capability gap. In other industries, the key capability gap may be an ability to out-innovate competitors, keeping them always on the defensive.

Note that only the first category, business system gaps, covers actions that are currently under the control of the producer. Frustrating as it may be to the strategist, competitive advantage or disadvantage is often the result of factors he or she is in no position to alter in the short term.

The broad concept of a capability gap becomes useful only when we succeed in closely specifying a producer's *actual* capability gap over competitors in a *particular* situation. Analysts can detect the existence of a capability gap by examining broad functions in the business system, but they must then go further and determine the root cause of superior performance in that function.

Individual capability gaps between competitors are very specific. There must be a precise reason why one producer can outperform another, or there is no competitive advantage. The capability gap consists of specific, often physical, differences. It is likely to be prosaic and measurable, not intangible. Abstract terms, such as "higher labor productivity" or "technological leadership," often serve as useful shorthand, but they are too general for precise analysis. Moreover, they implicitly equate capability gaps with marginal performance superiority, rather than with discrete differences—such as specific work rule differences or technical resources capacity—that are not easily imitated.

For example, if marginal performance superiority constituted competitive advantage, one would expect "focus" competitors—those who have no capability advantage but excel in serving a particular niche through sheer concentration of effort—to win out over more general competitors who decide to invade that niche. But as American Motors learned when Detroit's "Big Three" began producing small cars, and as some regional banks are learning as money center banks enter their markets, "trying harder" is no substitute for the possession of unique capabilities.

Only by understanding specific differences in capability can the strategist accurately determine and measure the actions that competitors must take to eliminate the gap and the obstacles and costs to them of doing so.

Lasting Advantage (Sustainability)

If a meaningful advantage is a function of a positive difference in important attributes based on an underlying capability gap, then the sustainability of the competitive advantage is simply a function of the durability of both the attributes and the gap.

There is not much value in an advantage in product/delivery attributes that do not retain their importance over time. Manufacturers of CB radios, video games, and designer jeans saw their revenues decline and their financial losses mount not because their competitors did anything to erode their capability advantages, but because most of their customers simply no longer valued those products enough to pay the price. In each case, industry participants believed that they had benefited from a permanent shift in consumer preferences and began to invest accordingly. In each case they were wrong.

Whether consumers will continue to demand a product over time, and how they can be influenced to prefer certain product attributes over time, are essentially marketing issues, subject to normal marketing analytical techniques. How basic is the customer need that the product meets? How central to its function or availability is the attribute in each question? These may be the key questions to ask in this connection.

The sustainability of competitive advantage is also a function of the durability of the capability gap that created the attractive attribute. In fact, the most important condition for sustainability is that existing and potential competitors either cannot or will not take the actions required to close the gap. If competitors can and will fill the gap, the advantage is by definition not sustainable.

Obviously, a capability gap that competitors are unable to close is preferable to one that relies on some restraint. Unfortunately, a producer cannot choose whether a particular capability gap meets the former or the latter condition.

Consider the two cases more closely.

* *Case I: Competitors cannot fill the gap.* This situation occurs when the capability itself is protected by specific entry and mobility barriers such as an important product patent or unique access to a key raw material (for example, DeBeer's Consolidated Mines). In a Case 1 situation, sustainability is assured at least until the barrier is eroded or eliminated

(converting the situation to Case 2). Barriers can erode or be eliminated over time, unless they are inherent in the nature of the business.[2]

A more significant danger to Case 1 advantages, however, probably lies not in the gradual erosion of barriers, but in the possibility that competitors may leapfrog the barriers by a new game strategy.

For example, the introduction of the transistor in 1955 did nothing to erode the barriers that RCA had created in vacuum tubes; it simply made RCA's leadership irrelevant. Therefore, although sustainability can be estimated by (1) considering all the changes (environmental forces or competitor actions) that could erode the barriers, and (2) assessing the probabilities of their occurrence over a specified time horizon, there will, of course, always be uncertainty in the estimate.

- *Case 2: Competitors could close the capability gap but refrain from doing so.* This situation might occur for any one of four reasons.

    1. *Inadequate potential.* A simple calculation may show competitors that the costs of closing the gap would exceed the benefits, even if the possessor of the advantage did not retaliate.

    For example, the danger of cannibalizing existing products may preclude effective response: MCI, Sprint, and others were able to create the low-price segment of the U.S. long-distance telephone market largely because AT&T did not choose to respond directly for some time. Most likely it considered that the cost of cutting prices for 100 percent of its customers in order to retain the 1 to 2 percent in the low-price segment was simply too high, and that only when the segment grew to sufficient size would a response become worthwhile.

    Other examples of situations where a payoff is not worth the required investment include investing in capacity to achieve "economies of scale" when the capacity required to achieve the required economy exceeds the likely additional demand in the industry; and labor work rules, where the additional compensation demanded by the union in return for such changes would more than offset the potential savings.

    The inadequate-potential situation represents a sustainable advantage because the "end game" has already been reached: there are no rational strategic countermoves for competitors to take until conditions change.

    2. *Corresponding disadvantage.* Competitors may believe that acting to close the capability gap will open gaps elsewhere (in this or other market segments) that will more than offset the value of closing this one.

    For example, a "niche" competitor often relies on this factor to protect him against larger competitors, who (or so he hopes) will reckon that an

---

[2] For example, if the business is a "natural monopoly." A natural monopoly exists where either (1) economies of scale cause marginal costs to decline past the point where production volume equals market demand (that is, where the most efficient economic system is to have only one producer); or (2) the social costs of installing duplicate production/distribution systems outweigh the benefits, a situation usually leading to the establishment of a legal monopoly by government fiat.

effective attack on his niche advantage would divert resources (including management time) needed elsewhere, destroy the integrity of their own broader product lines (opening gaps in other segments), or create some other gap.

A "corresponding disadvantage" situation constitutes at least a temporarily sustainable advantage, because for the moment an "end game" has been reached. However, as the attractiveness of competitors' other markets changes, so does their estimate of whether a corresponding disadvantage is present in the niche (as American Motors learned to its cost). In addition, competitors will always be searching for ways to fill the capability gap without creating offsetting gaps. Only if the creation of offsetting gaps is an automatic and inevitable consequence of any such action will the producer's advantage be assured of sustainability in the long run.

3. *Fear of reprisal.* Even though it initially would appear worth doing so, competitors may refrain from filling the capability gap for fear of retaliatory action by the producer. The sustainability of the producer's existing advantage depends, in this case, on the competitors' continuing to exercise voluntary restraint, accepting in effect the producer's position in this market segment.

For example, Japanese steel makers voluntarily refrain from increasing their U.S. market share for fear that American producers can and will persuade the U.S. government to take harsh protectionist measures.

"Fear of reprisal" is probably among the most common strategic situations in business, but it must be considered unstable over time, as competitors' situations and managements shift.

4. *Management inertia.* Finally, there are cases where competitors would benefit from closing the capability gap but fail to do so, either because management has incorrectly assessed the situation or because it lacks the will, the ability, or the energy to take the required action.

For example, Honda's success in dominating the British motorcycle industry is generally attributed to Norton Villiers Triumph's failure to respond to a clear competitive threat until too late.

Psychologists tell us that managers will implement real change only when their discomfort with the status quo exceeds the perceived personal cost of taking the indicated action. This may well explain why competitors often tolerate a performance gap that they could profitably act to close. But it is risky for a producer to rely for long on the weakness or inertia of competitors' management to protect a competitive advantage; by definition the end game has not been reached.

In all four cases, how long competitors will tolerate capability gaps they are capable of closing depends largely on the relationship between the value of the advantage created by the gap and the cost (to each competitor) of closing it. The worse the cost-to-benefit ratio, the longer the advantage is likely to be sustainable, because greater changes in the environment are required before value would exceed cost. Coupled with an informed view of the rate of environmental change in the industry, this ratio thus allows the analyst to estimate sustainability.

SCA and Strategy

The classic definition of competitive strategy as "an integrated set of actions designed to create a sustainable advantage over competitors" might suggest that possessing an SCA is synonymous with business success—that those producers who have an SCA are guaranteed winners, and that those competitors who lack one should simply exit the business to avoid financial disaster.

This apparently reasonable conclusion is, however, incorrect. Although an SCA is a powerful tool in creating a successful business strategy, it is not the only key ingredient. In fact:

1. Possessing an SCA does not guarantee financial success.
2. Producers can succeed even when competitors possess an SCA.
3. Pursuing an SCA can sometimes conflict with sound business strategy.

Losing with an SCA

Although an SCA will help a producer to achieve, over time, higher returns than his competitors, there are at least three circumstances where its possessor can fail financially:

1. *If the market sector is not viable.* In many cases (including most new-product introductions), the minimum achieveable cost of producing and selling a particular product or service exceeds its value to the customer. In this situation, an SCA will not guarantee the survival of its possessor; it will tend merely to ensure that his competitors will fare even worse.

2. *If the producer has severe operational problems.* An SCA can allow management the luxury of focusing more fully on achieving operational excellence, but thousands of companies have failed for operational, rather than strategic, reasons.

3. *If competitors inflict tactical damage.* An SCA rarely puts a producer completely beyond the reach of competitor actions such as price cuts and "buying" market share, which may be unrelated to the SCA itself. A producer will be particulary vulnerable to such competitive tactics if the SCA is not very important, either because the depth of the "footprint" described earlier is shallow or because the gap in capability is minor.

In these cases, producers must select their actions very carefully. Actions that can and will be imitated may result only in intensified competitive rivalry. And, where the producer's advantage is unimportant, he will have little cushion against the competitive repercussions. For example, recent airline pricing policies and "frequent flyer" programs have done nothing to contribute to the long-term profitability or competitive positions of their originators. Unimaginative direct cost-reduction efforts (cutting overhead or staffs, for example) may improve profitability in the short term. But if competitors can and will imitate these efforts, the only long-run effect may be to raise the general level of misery throughout the industry.

Competing against an SCA

By definition, not all producers can possess an SCA in a given product market segment. Other competitors face the prospects of competing (at least for some time) from a handicapped position. Under certain circumstances, however, it is still possible for some to succeed.

Rapidly growing markets constitute one such situation. As long as real market growth over a given period exceeds the additional capacity advantaged competitors can bring on line during that time (due to organizational constraints, risk aversion, and so forth), even weak competitors can thrive. For example, the booming market for microcomputer software over the past five years has enabled many weak competitors to grow rich. Only when market growth slows or the advantaged competitors increase the rate at which they can grow will true competition begin and the impact of an SCA make itself felt.

In markets where true competition for scarce sales dollars is taking place, the number of disadvantaged competitors who can succeed, the degree to which they can prosper, and the conditions under which they can prosper will vary, depending on the value of the advantage held by the "number one" competitor.

If the number one competitor has only a shallow or unimportant advantage, many disadvantaged competitors can prosper for long periods. As noted earlier, each competitor is unique. When all attributes are considered, each will have a competitive advantage in serving some customers. The disadvantaged competitors are more likely to receive lower returns than the number one producer, but they certainly may be viable.

If the number one competitor has an important advantage in a given product/market segment, some theorists assert that over the long run there will be only one viable competitor. Others may remain in the segment, but they will be plagued by losses and/or very inadequate returns. If there are six different ways to achieve a major advantage, this reasoning runs, then the market will split into six segments, each ruled by a different competitor, who uniquely excels in the attribute most valued by the customers in that segment.

Be that as it may, in practice other strong competitors may also profitably exist alongside Number One under two conditions:

1. *If the number one producer's advantage is limited by a finite capacity* that is significantly less than the size of the market; that is, he may expand further, but will not retain his advantage on the incremental capacity. Obstacles to continued advantaged expansion are common: limited access to superior raw materials, finite capacity in low-cost plants, prohibitive transportation costs beyond certain distances. Antitrust laws also tend to act as barriers to expansion beyond a certain level by number one competitors.

2. *If the size of the individual competitors is small* relative to the size of the market. In this case, a number of strong competitors can expand for many years without directly competing with each other, by taking share from weak competitors rather than each other.

Weak competitors, of course, are likely to fare badly when competition is intense and the depth of the advantage enjoyed by others is great. Their choices are:

1. To leave the business.
2. To endure the situation until the advantage is eroded.
3. To seek to create a new advantage.

If a weak competitor chooses to pursue a new advantage, then he must ensure that it will be preemptive, or that competitors will not notice his move and will fail to respond until he has consolidated his position. Otherwise, his action is virtually certain to be copied and the intended advantage erased.

Pursuing the Wrong SCA

Although its attainment is the goal of *competitive* strategy, sustainable competitive advantage is not an end in itself but a means to an end. The corporation is not in business to beat its competitors, but to create wealth for its shareholders. Thus, actions that contribute to SCA but detract from creating shareholder wealth may be good strategy in the competitive sense but bad strategy for the corporation. Consider two examples.

- *Low-cost capacity additions in the absence of increased industry demand.* Adding low-cost capacity and recycling the additional profits into product/delivery attributes that attract enough customers to fill that capacity is usually a sound business strategy. However, as industry cost curve analysis has demonstrated, if the capacity addition is not accompanied by increases in industry demand, the effect may well be to displace the high-cost, but previously viable, marginal producer. When this happens, prices in the industry will fall to the level of the costs of the new marginal producer, costs which by definition are lower than the costs of the former marginal producer. Thus, the profit per unit sold of all participants will be reduced.

  Depending on the cost structure of the industry, the declines in the profit per unit sold can be dramatic (for example, if all the remaining producers have similar costs). In this case, even the producer who added the new capacity will face declining profitability on his preexisting capacity; in extreme cases his total profit on new and old capacity may fall below the profit he had previously earned on the old capacity alone. While gaining share and eliminating a competitor (good competitive strategy), he has invested *more* to profit *less* (bad business strategy).

- *Aggressive learning-curve pricing strategies that sacrifice too much current profit.* Under these strategies, prices are reduced at least as fast as costs in order to buy market share and drive out competitors. The assumption is that the future payoff from market dominance will more than offset the costs of acquiring it. The value of new business, however, is likely to be very sensitive to the precise relationship between prices and costs. This is true particularly in the early stages of the learning curve, when the absolute levels of prices, costs, and margins are relatively high and the profit consequences are therefore greater for any given volume. Especially in high-tech industries such as electronics, where the lifetime of technologies is short, the long-term value of the market share bought by overly aggressive learning-curve strategies can be less than the profit eliminated in the early stages by pricing too close to costs.

The framework for SCA proposed in this article is far from complete. Its treatment of product/delivery attributes and capability gaps (notably organizational strength) is impressionistic rather than detailed. It leaves other aspects of the topic (for example, the sustainability of competitive advantage at the corporate level) unexplored.

But a major concern of the business-unit strategist is to determine whether the enterprise (or a competitor's) possesses or is in a position to capture an SCA, and, if so, to examine is strategic implications. The conditions for SCA and the implications of SCA for strategy that have been proposed provide an initial framework for these tasks.

What this article is about: Military strategy is directly relevant to current business conditions. Although business always has used attack strategies to acquire market share and defense strategies to protect market territory, deterrence—the indirect approach—has been largely ignored. Deterrence is presented as the ultimate business strategy. It offers companies the opportunity to win conflicts in the marketplace without resorting to fratricidal battles with competitors.

2-6 Deterrence—A strategy that pays*

Barrie G. James

Barrie G. James is head of marketing development in the pharmaceutical division of CIBA-GEIGY AG, Basel, Switzerland.

The supreme excellence of war is not to win a hundred victories in a hundred battles, but to subdue the armies of your enemies without even having to fight them.

Sun Tzu, circa 500 B.C.

Military strategy is attracting growing management attention because of its relevance to current market conditions. Probably at no time in the recent past has business been so competitive, placing so much emphasis on survival and growth under adversity. In fact, business is now on a war footing. In declining markets, business success rests either on timing disengagement and withdrawing in good order or on finding a new way to win. In static or low-growth markets, success depends on taking share away from competitors and protecting existing share from competitive aggression. In high-growth markets, companies are confronted with the need to carve out and hold a share in the market in the face of strong opposition from a myriad of competitors all eager to obtain the spoils of growth.

While the attack-defense strategies are widely practiced in business, one military strategy—*deterrence*, the indirect approach—is largely ignored by management and strategists. However, if properly devised and executed, deterrent strategies offer the highest return. They can circumvent costly resource battles with competitors in the marketplace and preserve intact the company's security, sovereignty, and power.

* This article is adapted from a chapter in *Business Wargames*, by permission of Abacus Press, London. Reprinted from *Business Horizons*, Nov.–Dec. 1985, pp. 60–64.

An excellent example from recent military history is Israel's deterrent strategy with Jordan. Following the 1967 Arab-Israeli war, the Israelis have been successful in persuading the Jordanians to avoid military confrontation. By building up their sophisticated air and ground capability, the Israelis have made certain that the risks of military action outweigh the benefits.

What Is Deterrence?

Deterrence is a strategy to prevent conflict by persuading a rational competitor that you are willing and able to punish noncompliance with your clearly expressed and understood wishes. Deterrence is a strategy for an acceptable peace rather than for war. It depends more on intuition and emotion than on logic. Because it means inducing a competitor to cooperate through voluntary restraint, deterrence is a battle won in the mind of the competitor through psychological pressure rather than physical combat.

Market conflict occurs when a company anticipates that the risk is low in relation to the gains from a planned aggressive move or from an impulsive act. An effective deterrent strategy must discourage combat in either form. It must deal effectively with direct attacks, extremely provocative acts, and aggressive adventures by competitors.

Direct Attacks Chesebrough-Ponds Inc. correctly anticipated that, by launching a new product into a market of small importance to a major manufacturer, it could achieve spectacular results. Chesebrough launched Rave into the then $40 million U.S. market for home permanents, a market dominated in the mid-1970s by Gillette's Toni. Rave, a superior product with no ammonia and no smell, was backed by a small but skillful marketing program. The market increased to $100 million by 1981, and Rave took brand leadership away from Toni.

Extremely Provocative Acts An extremely provocative act was Duracell's entrance into the battery market in the United Kingdom, a market dominated by Eveready with an 85 percent share.

Duracell gambled correctly that Eveready would emphasize its traditional strength in the declining zinc-carbon battery segment rather than in the growing alkaline segment and would maintain its traditional distribution through specialist retailers rather than open up mass merchandising through supermarkets. Within two years Eveready's market share had fallen to 65 percent. By using new technology and mass distribution techniques, Duracell, the newcomer, had reached 22 percent.

Aggressive Adventurism Starting in the early 1960s, Japanese car manufacturers correctly anticipated that their cumulative strategy for enveloping the European car market country by country would not be deterred by either competitors or European governments until the aggressive adventure was essentially complete.

Elements of Effective Deterrence Strategies

Four key elements are present in all effective deterrent strategies in both war and business: credibility, capability, communication, and rationality.

Credibility

Credibility means one company's convincing its competitor that, to further its aims or to maintain its market position, it is willing to inflict unacceptable losses on that firm. The competitor is also persuaded that it has something to gain from restraint. If the second firm is willing to accept the risk of punishment, it obviously does not regard the threat as credible.

Texas Instruments successfully used its credibility to win a battle for future supply. In 1981 TI announced a price for random access memory (RAM) chips to be marketed in 1983. Within a week Bowmar offered a lower price for RAM chips with the same characteristics. Three weeks later Motorola followed with an even lower price. Two weeks after Motorola's offer, TI announced a new price one half of that offered by Motorola. Because of its proven credibility as the lowest cost producer of RAM chips, TI won the battle even before the product was manufactured.

In contrast, in the mid-1970s Fokker, the Dutch airframe manufacturer, signaled British Aerospace that it would not tolerate BAe's projected HS-146 aircraft competing directly with Fokker's existing F-28 short-haul jet airliner. Fokker indicated that more than 40 percent of the total cost of both its F-27 and F-28 aircraft was supplied by British companies and that both contracts were at risk if the HS-146 project went ahead. BAe correctly gauged that the threat was not credible. Fokker's costs for redesigning, retooling, and recertifying both aircraft, using non-British equipment, would have been prohibitive. The HS-146 project went ahead. In mid-1985 Fokker announced the end of the production run for the F-28 and started development of the larger F-100 aircraft. BAe began quantity deliveries of the HS-146 to major customers, including Air Wisconsin, Aspen, and PSA.

Capability

A company uses capability when it convinces a competitor that, in addition to being willing, it has the means and the resources to carry out the threat of punishment.

Because of high start-up costs and a limited customer base, IMS has been able to deter competitors from entering the pharmacy and hospital audit markets for drug products on virtually a worldwide basis. On the other hand, A. C. Nielsen, with its dominant position in the U.S. grocery sales and television audience measurement markets, was unable to deter competition. Despite Nielsen's imposing technological prowess, innovative use of sophisticated data handling and analysis, and formidable legacy of historical data, AGB of the United Kingdom, Times' Sales Area Marketing, McGraw-Hill's Data Resources, and Control Data's Arbitron subsidiaries were not deterred by its capabilities. All successfully penetrated Nielsen's markets.

Communication

A company uses communication to clearly signal a competitor of its intention to further its aims or maintain its position, and it makes the competitor fully aware of the benefits of cooperation and the punishments that may be meted out for noncompliance.

Boeing successfully used deterrent communications to avoid a physical contest with other airframe manufacturers over its 747 aircraft. The development cost of the 747, some two billion dollars, was then the largest private funding of a civilian jet airliner. In the late 1960s there was a limited demand for routes for an intercontinental airliner with 350 or 400 seats. Developing a large, expensive aircraft with such a limited sales volume would have been economic suicide for another aircraft manufacturer. From its introduction into airline service in 1970, Boeing's 747 has remained without a direct competitor.

In contrast, U.S. truck manufacturers in the period from 1979 to 1981 were unsuccessful in communicating the poor operating economics and low margins of the medium-sized truck market in the United States. Therefore, they were unable to deter market entrance by Daimler-Benz, IMAC, Renault, and Volvo. The economic situation in Europe meant that these companies were facing problems in their home markets and looked to the United States as a way of reviving depressed demand. Because of ineffective communication, the U.S. manufacturers were forced to fight additional new competitors in a weak truck market.

Rationality

A company, although acting arbitrarily and unreasonably, uses rationality to avoid arousing emotion on the part of a competitor. It puts the competitor at a disadvantage because, to avoid forgoing the benefits of cooperation, the competitor has been persuaded to act rationally, reasonably, and objectively. Although rationality is the key to an effective deterrence strategy, actual potential competitors do not always act rationally.

IBM's introduction of its advanced Displaywriter line of word processors in mid-1980 did not force all its twenty-odd competitors to act rationally when faced with a superior product and the power of IBM's sales and service organization. Some firms counterattacked by introducing new, better, and less expensive models as a direct response. Other firms, faced with shrinking profit margins and volumes, acted rationally and looked for mergers or left the market.

Designing Deterrent Strategies

Deterrent strategies in business consist of a number of marketing, production, financial, technological, and managerial substrategies designed to prevent competitors from upsetting market equilibrium. These strategies create significant entry barriers to the market and erect profit-taking hurdles.

Marketing Deterrents

Distribution   Japanese companies have successfully used the complexity of the distribution system in Japan to deter potential competitors from doing their own distributing. Instead, competitors use the local system or a Japanese partner. This strategy produces another layer of costs for the foreign competitor to absorb and removes the new company from direct contact with the customer. Therefore, foreign firms are less competitive than their Japanese counterparts.

Promotion   A hallmark of The Procter & Gamble Co. in the United States is its massive advertising and promotion budget. In 1981 it spent more than $500 million or media alone. Its use of its budget to buy and maintain market share acts as a strong deterrent to many companies seeking to enter or increase share in markets dominated by P&G products.

Franchise   Over the years Hewlett-Packard (HP) has built a strong reputation with such major manufacturing companies as Boeing and GM by supplying high-quality electronic test and measurement instruments. HP's reputation among such companies was sufficient to deter them from purchasing rival mini-computers; instead, they bought HP models from a firm they knew and trusted.

Customer Relations   In the late 1960s IBM announced its 370 series computer far and wide. Two to three years before the 370 series was commercially available, IBM promised that it would have a level of performance far exceeding current competitors. This product announcement deterred customers from purchasing an existing competitive computer and enticed them to wait for the new advanced 370 series.

Service   Pitney-Bowes' 92 percent share of the postage meter market in the United States is due in part to the 7,500-person sales and service force that calls on thousands of small firms. Despite encouragement from the U.S. Justice Department, few firms want to enter a market so dominated by one company's product and its sales and service force.

Quality   Following TWA's withdrawal in the mid-1970s, Swissair successfully deterred U.S.-based carriers from competing profitably on scheduled Swiss-U.S. air routes. Swissair discouraged potential competitors by skillfully maintaining prices, matching demand closely with capacity, and offering exemplary in-flight cabin service.

Pricing   In the soft contact lens market in the United States, Bausch & Lomb deterred competitors by drastically reducing prices and pushing for wider distribution. It changed the product from a specialty to a price-sensitive, mass-market item. The majority of competitors were small firms who were financially unable to match the changed economics of the market and the new distribution system; therefore, they sought buyers for their companies.

Production Deterrents

Capacity   By building production capacity to meet world demand, Hoffmann-La Roche successfully deterred existing and potential competitors in the bulk vitamin C market. By creating the specter of the lowest cost supplier who was able to meet and win any price war, it so intimidated competitors that many withdrew from the market. By 1980 Roche had cornered some 60 percent of the world market for vitamin C.

Utilization   In the free-for-all following airline deregulation in the United States, a few regional carriers such as Piedmont, Southwest, and U.S. Air increased capacity, with more frequent services at lower costs on existing routes, to deter competition. Because the airline with the most flights on a route gets a disproportionate share of traffic and the load factor determines profitability, many new airlines were deterred from competing on routes dominated by Piedmont, Southwest, and U.S. Air.

Equipment   Eastman Kodak Company's monopoly on film for its new Disc camera forced film processing companies either to purchase special, relatively expensive processing equipment from Kodak or to hand over their Disc film processing business to Kodak's own facilities. Either way, by deterring direct competition, Kodak could maintain a strong profit position in the Disc film processing business.

Financial Deterrents

Costs   Because of the high costs of participation, existing semiconductor firms have successfully deterred new competitors from entering the industry. In the early 1970s new manufacturing facilities cost up to $5 million. By 1982 a single new plant for building advanced VLSI 64K RAM chips cost between $60–120 million, exacting a high entrance fee for new competitors.

Economics   Federal Express Corp. is the leading low-cost air courier service in the United States. Federal Express's overnight letter service was introduced in 1981 at a low price with the aim of becoming profitable on volume in a 12 month period. Because it was difficult to make money when pitted against the lowest cost competitor, who was using marginal costing and penetration pricing, competitors were deterred from entering the overnight letter market.

Technological Deterrents

Innovation   All but the largest new companies have been deterred from entering the pharmaceutical industry. Risks are high—the number of products reaching the market is small. The business cycle is long-run—the discovery to marketing time averages 12 years. Costs are high—development costs range between $50–100 million per product. In fact, with the exceptions of Janssen and Syntex, no company totally new to the drug market has succeeded in becoming a medium-sized pharmaceutical firm in the last 30 years.

Information   To provide itself with lead time over competitors who wish to supply compatible equipment to plug into new IBM computers, IBM is believed to delay the release of new product specifications. This policy deters an immediate response from plug-compatible competitors.

Managerial Deterrents

Acquisitions   Firms use both vertical and horizontal integration as a deterrent. By integrating backward, a firm can secure control over production and supply sources. Tube Investments in the United Kingdom integrated backwards by buying into steel making when the industry was first denationalized in 1953. Tube Investments deterred its competitors by obtaining security of raw materials and the profits made by its previous suppliers. By integrating forward, a firm can secure control of distribution or other benefits. Genentech, a leading biotechnology company, is integrating forward from research into production. By limiting the transfer of critical purification know-how, it will deter current clients from becoming future competitors.

In horizontal integration, firms seek to corner the market to deter competitors. In the United States, fast-food market firms seek the first franchise in new shopping malls to deter other fast-food companies from opening up competitive outlets. All integration strategies have the potential to deny competitive access to raw materials, know-how, and customers. Therefore, they can be powerful deterrents.

Mergers   In 1983 Thomson-Brandt of France acquired 75 percent of AEG-Telefunken's television and videotape recorder subsidiary. The merged entity held 25 percent of the West German and 20 percent of the European color TV markets and 10 percent of the West German video recorder market. Brandt's strategy was designed to build a large European consumer electronics group with 1982 sales of $2.6 billion, a force capable of competing with and deterring further Japanese penetration into the European consumer electronics market.

Alliances   None of the three leading jet aero-engine manufacturers—General Electric (GE), Pratt & Whitney (P&W), and Rolls Royce—were willing to fund alone the development of a new fuel-efficient engine to power a 150-seat airliner. The estimated development cost was $1.5 billion. But none could face the prospects of competing against the two other manufacturers for the same market. Each of the firms attempted to form alliances with smaller firms (GE with Snecma; P&W with MTU and Fiat; and Rolls Royce with Kawaski, Mitsubishi, and IHI) in an effort to deter the others from entering the market.

In early 1983 Pratt & Whitney formed a consortium with Rolls Royce. Together with MTU and Fiat, Pratt & Whitney would design and build the gearbox and turbines. Rolls Royce and its Japanese partners would in turn build the fan and compressors for the new engine.

The Value of Deterrence

Deterrent strategies in business attempt to induce stability by encouraging prudence on the part of competitors. Rather than signifying that the combatants can inflict *equal* damage on each other, this stability reflects their ability to inflict unacceptable losses on one another in the worst case and, under less violent circumstances, a greater loss for the challenger. To deter a competitive thrust effectively, a firm must present a credible and visible case. It must convince competitors that challenges to the market equilibrium will be met and that, beyond a certain point, the challenge is not in the long-term best interests of the aggressor. If a company is not prepared to fight a war in the marketplace, it cannot rationally or credibly threaten another company, and its own survival will be threatened if it adopts a deterrent strategy.

The most critical factor in a deterrent strategy is gauging the capabilities and intentions of a challenger. Because full information can never be obtained, this process must be imprecise. Capabilities in terms of management, products, and resources constantly change and are not entirely tangible. Nevertheless, they can be determined with some degree of objectivity.

Intentions are a state of mind and can be gauged only subjectively. Measuring intention means judging the interests and objectives of a competitor and the temperament and will of its management.

Companies frequently appear to be unaware that, in addition to a physical component, market conflict has psychological dimensions. Being able to predict and effectively counter competitive moves is a major strategic task. Business, unlike the military, has conducted little research to identify the intentions of a competing management and its psychological behavior. Yet such study would enable a firm to use its capabilities fully in order to deter a challenge.

As the examples suggest, deterrent strategies are highly successful in avoiding fratricidal battles in the market. They enable companies to win without resorting to the debilitating physical contest of resources in the market.

Most military practitioners and theorists, from Sun Tzu around 500 B.C. to the present day, have believed implicitly in the strategic value of deterrence. Napoleon said that all his ''care will be to gain victory with the least shedding of blood.'' Most deterrent strategies in business appear to be adopted unconsciously as part of an overall strategic response rather than as a conscious competitive policy. Unfortunately, business appears to be wedded to the attack-defense syndrome of market conflict, thereby forgoing the considerable benefits of deterrence.

Because current market conditions require innovative strategic approaches to combat competition, companies that actively pursue deterrent strategies have an opportunity to gain a high payoff at the expense of companies adopting more traditional approaches to market conflict.

What this article is about: A study of companies in three different industries—auto, computers, and semiconductors—shows that growing internationalization of business brings about major changes in the positioning of competitors and the appropriate competitive strategies. Only after going through a financial crisis did the companies studied emerge from national to international status.

2-7 Market share and corporate strategy in international industries*

James Leontiades

James Leontiades is senior lecturer in international management, Manchester Business School, University of Manchester, England.

Corporate strategy, with its emphasis on the adjustment of the firm to its environment, has obvious application for the study of international business. However, care must be taken that the concepts and principles forwarded under this heading are suited to the special situation of the firm operating in an international environment.

For example, evidence has been assembled to show that there is a positive correlation between market share and profitability—a relationship that has considerable significance for strategic planning. This poses two problems for international firms which do not generally trouble the managers of domestic companies.

- *What is the geographic area encompassed by the market?* Should it be calculated nationally or is the *relevant* market (i.e., relevant for strategy formulation) international in scope? While the domestic national market may be assumed as the basis for calculating market share for some firms in certain industries, there are clearly others, e.g., jet planes, microcircuits, computers, and so on, where this assumption cannot be made.
- *Is the present geographic basis for calculating market share changing?* For some companies, the relevant geographic market is changing, that is, expanding from national to international. This entails questions of strategy related to the new situation posed by an enlarged market.

Purpose

The main thesis to be developed here is that the geographic scope of what is meant by the industry and its competitive environment cannot be assumed to be either stable over time or readily ascertainable. This implies that a

---

* This article is reprinted with permission from *The Journal of Business Strategy* 5, no. 1 (Summer 1984), pp. 30–37.

national definition of market share/ROI (return on investment) can be dangerously misleading.

Some of the present evidence linking market share and ROI tends to be obscure on these points since (1) the precise geographic definition of the market is unstated and (2) the evidence showing a positive relationship between ROI and market share, as in Figure 1, is based on comparisons among U.S. companies. These may be unrepresentative. The exceptional size of the North American market may dominate the market share/ROI relationship to the point where it may swamp international effects.

A broader aim is to investigate the changing nature of competition and strategy formulation in the more international industries. It is a priori evident that a significant number of industries are becoming increasingly international. We may postulate that industries are going through progressive developmental stages. We recognize that at one time industries that were subnational in terms of geographic coverage changed. National industries emerged with consequent implications for strategy. In more recent times industries that are more international than national have emerged.

The questions and strategic decisions posed by the internationalization of an industry and its competitive sphere are quite different from those posed by the internationalization of a firm. In the case of the latter, the focus is on management decisions associated with company moves into new national environments. The internationalization of industry brings about basic changes in the firm's environment which pose questions for both domestic as well as international companies.

Some firms will adjust to the new situation better than others. We may speculate that the more international firms positioned to take maximum advantage of economies and efficiencies of the wider international market would do best in such industries. We may also hypothesize that, for this sort of firm, performance within any given national market (e.g., in terms of the market share/ROI relationship) would have less meaning.

Figure 1
Relationship of market share to profitability

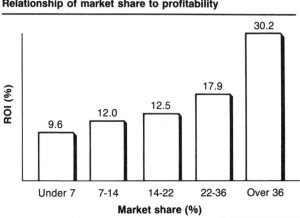

SOURCE: Schoeffler, Buzzell, and Heany, "Impact of Strategic Planning on Profitability," *Harvard Business Review*, March–April 1974.

We will now examine the market share/ROI performance of three pairs of firms. Each pair includes one of the following:

- *A major national competitor.* This refers to a company whose production and marketing operations are focused on a particular national territory. Its dominant strength in terms of production and marketing facilities lies within that national market, although this does not preclude the presence of some facilities, exports, or other operations in other countries.

- *A major international competitor.* This refers to a company with major involvement in multiple national markets. The firm's national facilities and sales are only a part (often a small part), of an internationally integrated network of facilities and operations.

The Automotive Industry: Ford versus BL

Since 1967, the Ford Motor Company has operated its European facilities on a highly integrated pan-European basis. The firm's regional headquarters exercises control over a network of major manufacturing and assembly facilities located in Britain, Germany, France, Belgium, and Spain. Market research is coordinated across the major national markets to arrive at a standardized product line. Production is rationalized on a European basis, with the various national plants tending to specialize in high-volume production of components and products which are then shipped cross-nationally to be assembled and finally sold through the firm's various national distribution systems.

More than half of Ford's European and passenger car sales are outside the United Kingdom. The market share figures and profitability reported in Figures 2 and 3 refer to Ford's national subsidiary in Britain.

BL (formerly BLMC Ltd. and before that the British Leyland Motor Corporation) has a predominantly national orientation. The great majority of its car sales are within its British home market. Passenger car sales in the

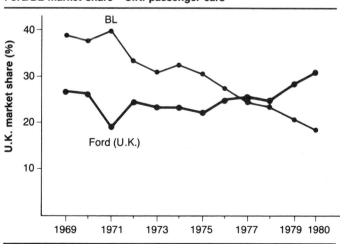

Figure 2
Ford/BL market share—U.K. passenger cars

SOURCE: SMMT.

Figure 3
Return on investment

	BL	Ford (U.K.)
1969	16%	18%
1970	6	11
1971	13	(loss)
1972	12	19
1973	16	28
1974	8	7
1975	(loss)	9
1976	20	31
1977	9	55
1978	8	35
1979	(loss)	49
1980	(loss)	24

SOURCE: The Times 1000.

United Kingdom as measured by new car registrations now comprise about 80 percent of its total Western European sales. Throughout the past 12 years, the British national market has dominated its sales performance. Figure 2 shows that BL had the highest national market share in Britain from 1969 through 1975. However, Figure 3 indicates that Ford has the higher ROI for six of these eight years. Subsequently, Ford's market share exceeded that of BL and its ROI advantage improved still further over the national competitor. BL has received extensive government assistance in recent years. Financial crises have brought about a change in strategy, including a partnership with Honda, the Japanese automobile producer.

Computers: ICL versus IBM

Historically, ICL has had the advantage over IBM in terms of national market performance. Figure 4 employs national (U.K.) market sales of ICL and IBM as a proxy for the relative market share of these two companies within the British market. Despite its smaller national market share, IBM's ROI performance averaged over 1978–1980 has been significantly better than ICL's. However, ICL's sales, both globally and within Western Europe, are much below those of IBM.

As with BL, the government has been forced to come to the assistance of the national competitor. ICL incurred a net loss of £50 million during 1981. The government provided credit guarantees in the amount of £200 million which were used to implement a fundamental change in ICL strategy. This included a major shift in the firm's competitive positioning toward the rapidly growing market for small computers and telecommunications and away from mainframe computers, the traditional IBM strength.

Semiconductors: Texas Instruments versus Ferranti

In the semiconductor industry, Texas Instruments' British subsidiary enjoys a higher ROI than its national competitor, Ferranti Ltd., despite the higher national market share of the latter. (See Figure 5.) Ferranti has also had to resort to government help (in early 1974) to survive against international competition. Though it has recently improved its profitability and ceased to rely on government assistance, its ROI position relative to Texas

Figure 4
IBM/ICL—ROI and relative market share position
(Average 1978–1980)

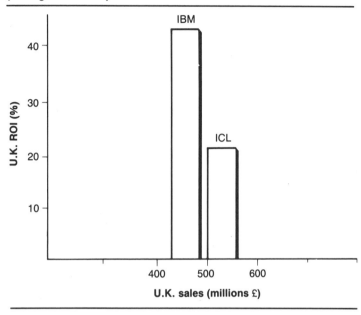

SOURCE: Annual Reports, The Times 1000.

Figure 5
Texas Instruments/Ferranti—ROI and relative market share position
(Average 1978–1980)

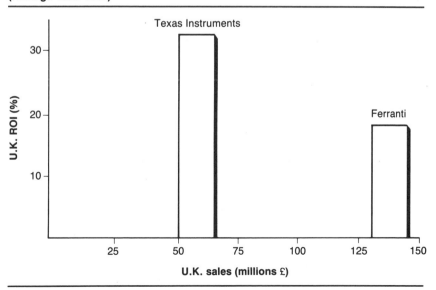

SOURCE: Annual Company Reports, The Times 1000.

Instruments-U.K. continues to deteriorate. (Texas Instruments-U.K. ROI during 1981 was over 90 percent.)

Competition for the mass markets in this fast-moving industry is based on high volume, technological leadership, and experience curve pricing. The national British market represents only a small fraction of world sales. The entire Western European market represents less than 15 percent of the total world market for semiconductors, still too small to provide economies of large-scale production [2, p. 110]. Ferranti's total world sales in 1980 were approximately 10 percent of Texas Instruments' world total. Ferranti's present strategy concentrates on a specialized segment of this market, the so-called custom-built devices as opposed to the standardized, high-volume, mass-produced circuits.

Common Features

While a sample of this size cannot "prove" anything, it is interesting that the above three comparisons have the following features in common:

1. The position of all three national competitors (BL, ICL, Ferranti) has been gradually eroded over the years. Each of these companies were at one time the leader in their respective national industries.
2. In all three situations, the U.K. industry viewed on a national basis has become increasingly less significant. Both markets and competition have become international in scope.
3. National market share does not appear to be positively correlated with national ROI, as per the relationship in Figure 1.
4. In all three situations, the international competitors, while smaller nationally, enjoyed the larger market share internationally (in terms of Western Europe or globally). Hence, any attempt to explain ROI as positively related to market share would have to rely on an international definition of the market.
5. All three international competitors operated on a supranational basis. That is, production, marketing, and research were rationalized across national boundaries as part of an international system aimed at securing maximum efficiencies of international scale and volume.
6. The national competitors have all encountered severe financial crises in recent years while their international competitors have prospered, the latter enjoying both higher national ROI and a growing national market share.
7. Subsequent to their financial crises, all three national competitors have undergone a fundamental reassessment and realignment of their competitive strategy.
8. All three of the national companies were at one time strong national firms considered to be leaders in their industry. The erosion of their position over time seems to be due to a basic change in the geographic scope of their industry and its marketplace, from national to international.

The last two points merit further elaboration. In terms of strategy formulation, the reality to which the national competitors have had to adjust following their financial crises is, first, that their industry and competitive environment are now of international proportions. National barriers are no longer effective in segmenting the industry along national boundaries. Not only have trade barriers been reduced between countries, but international firms have now developed an improved ability to operate internationally in a way that enables them to make use of their larger size to gain efficiencies of scale and their attendant advantages, especially in the high-volume markets.

Second, the national competitors find that in this wider competitive environment, their strategic posture vis-à-vis the larger international companies has significantly altered. The national firms now find themselves in a different competitive league. In regional (Western Europe) or global terms they are now "small" rather than "large" and their strategy has had to adjust accordingly.

Ferranti's Experience

In his study of British electronics firms, Edmond Sciberras [5] finds that these firms now fall into two distinct competitive leagues. The big-league firms are those major international companies (Texas Instruments, Phillips, Motorola, and others) that have the resources and sufficient capital and technological resources to compete in the high-volume mass markets for semiconductors. Small-league firms develop strategies based on avoidance of head-on competition with big-league companies, indicating strategies based on some form of specialization.

For example, Ferranti is now seen as belonging to the small league, representing a fundamental change in its strategic positioning vis-à-vis its competitors. Sciberras noted, "The answer to the problem of avoiding the competitive pressures of which Ferranti's experiences have made it so aware has been to opt out of the mass established competitive markets . . . and to specialize" [5, p. 182]. He also observed, "The Company is very much aware of the competitive pressure upon it in the industry and seeks to avoid this pressure as far as possible. Its competitive awareness leads it to a policy of competitive avoidance through technology hive off and application of its specialized technology to custom markets" [5, p. 187].

ICL's Experience

ICL underwent a closely analogous transformation in its strategy after its 1981 financial crisis. Major elements of the new ICL strategy include:

1. A partnership agreement with Fujitsu, the large Japanese electronics firm, to supply ICL with microcircuits and related technology.
2. An agreement to market Fujitsu mainframe computers under an ICL brand name (Atlas) to compensate in some part for ICL's more limited effort in this area.
3. An agreement with the U.S. firm Three Rivers to produce its new small computer. This is part of the new strategy reflected in the managing director's statement: "We will make ICL big in small systems" [6].
4. A change in policy to make the firm's new products plug-compatible with those of IBM.

The general strategy has been to use the firm's nationally based strengths, and particularly its U.K. and European marketing system, to forge links with foreign producers. These links have enabled ICL to shift the focus of its own efforts away from direct competition with the larger international firms, and to make more intensive use of its own resources in specialized areas. The latter will be in the high-growth small computer and telecommunications segments. The emphasis has moved away from direct "head to head" competition with IBM and other big-league firms.

The year 1982 saw a return to profitability. The overall change in strategy seems to be working, although it is still too early to say with any degree of certainty.

BL's Experience

BL has also changed its strategy. The partnership with Honda to develop new motor vehicles is a significant departure from past practice for a firm that prides itself on its Britishness. In other respects, however, BL has not followed the specialization strategies of ICL and Ferranti. Although a number of industry analysts have concluded that the firm's commercial future would be improved by concentration on its specialty products (e.g., Jaguar, Rover, Triumph), national policy considerations have constrained management's freedom in this direction.[1] BL still competes directly against the major international firms in its industry. Of the three national competitors, BL continues to operate at a loss.

Competitive Strategy in International Industries

The gist of the above analysis is that there has been a change in the definition of industry which has had a major impact on corporate strategy. Over time, industry has become progressively internationalized, to the point where the demarcation of markets and environment is now international rather than national. This internationalization has brought about changes in the competitive leagues or groupings within industry.

The strategic significance of these competitive leagues has also been identified in a domestic context in research carried out by Hatten, Schendel, and Cooper [1]. In an analysis of the U.S. brewing industry, it was concluded that identification of homogeneous groups of companies (similar strategies within groups but differing between groups) was necessary for an understanding of industry strategy. For example, the authors found that "plant expansion was associated with increased profitability for the national brewers . . . though it is negative for other groups." The authors underlined the fact that strategies for the small firms do not apply to the large firms.

---

[1] Volume cars and specialist cars: Having accepted that BL should remain a major producer of cars, we considered whether it should continue as at present to cover the full range of the market from the "small/light" sector (represented by the Mini) to the luxury sector (represented by the Jaguar). In the past the more expensive models produced by BL (not only Jaguars, but also Rovers and Triumphs) have proved more profitable, and a less satisfactory return has been earned on volume cars, particularly the Mini. We therefore examined whether BL should adopt a strategy of abandoning the bottom end of the volume car market. This would mean in effect that no replacement would be brought forward for the Mini. We are strongly of the view that this would be the wrong strategy [7, pp. 15–16].

Michael Porter [3] sounds a similar theme when he points out that identifying the "strategic groups" within an industry is an important part of industry analysis and strategy formulation.

In an international context, our study supports the importance of "leagues" or "strategy groups." The question of what league the firm belongs to is an important one for the strategist. However, it also brings out the fact that the firm's league is subject to change over time as the industry becomes more international. Identifying what league a firm is in requires a perception of the geographic scope of the industry. One must determine whether it is national or international. This may not be readily apparent. Internationalization of the industry is a gradual process. Such recognition, with its implication for some firms that they have now become members of the "little league," may be resisted. In the three cases reviewed here, this perception of the changed nature of the industry came about only after financial crises for the three national competitors.

The story is a familiar one. The same theme is detectable in the development of the European industry for major household appliances such as washing machines and refrigerators. During the 1960s, a number of Italian producers of these goods expanded to achieve international scale. With the lowering of trade barriers, the industry became international on a regional basis. Firms that remained predominantly national producers found themselves relegated to the small league, as compared to the big-league Italian firms. A number were driven to financial collapse. Many were amalgamated and merged into other companies. National competitors that survived were forced to realign their strategies with the competition of the large Italian firms.

The same phenomenon overtook the U.S. television manufacturers. The orientation of Zenith, Motorola, and other U.S. producers was predominantly toward the national market. The United States accounted for the bulk of their business. In 1960, Japanese exports of television (monochrome) sets to the United States accounted for only 2 percent of total Japanese production. By 1970, the Japanese were exporting more sets abroad (66 percent of production) than they were selling at home. Two thirds of such exports went to the United States [4]. Eventually, the Japanese achieved economies of volume that enabled them to undercut the U.S. competitors. Those U.S. firms that survived clearly became little-league firms in a more international industry.

Switching Leagues

Figure 6 employs Porter's U-shaped interpretation of the market share/ROI relationship to describe the switch of leagues discussed above. Porter argues that if the relationship between market share and ROI were extended to cover the smaller firms, one would find that it was U-shaped. This reflects the fact that many of the smaller firms and not just the giants enjoy high ROIs. It is the firms in between, neither large enough to enjoy the advantages of large size nor small enough to make use of advantages associated with small size that are in trouble [3, p. 43].

In terms of the national competitors, their relative size would vary with the

Figure 6
Change in market share/ROI position of national firms
(At national and international stages of industry)

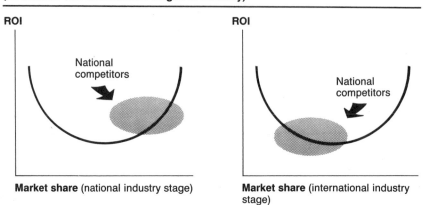

Market share (national industry stage)   **Market share** (international industry stage)

scope of the industry. As illustrated in Figure 6, within a national industry, the national competitors (such as those previously discussed) would find that they were large enough to qualify as big-league competitors.

However, if the market, for whatever reason, became international, many of these same firms would find their position changed. The successful ones would adjust their strategies and size to the new international environment, and gain a return to profitability. The less successful ones would (like BL) fall in between—enjoying neither the advantages of being small nor the advantages of being large.

The changeover of an industry from national to international scope is characterized by a major shakeout and industry realignment of company strategies. National competitors that do not adapt to the new competitive environment with its international competition are likely to go under. Two major options are open to them:

1. Attain the size and international organization necessary to join the big league. A good number of European national industries have taken this course, often with the assistance and blessings of government, to attain the larger size required in light of international competition. Many firms are presently engaged in such increases in size. The recipe here usually involves extensive mergers and amalgamations to attain the larger size required by changing industry conditions. The German firms Grundig and AEG are examples of firms currently caught up in this process.
2. Realign the firm's national strategy, based as it is on national competition in the national big league, to the new reality of international competition in the international little league.

Big-League and Little-League Strategies in International Industries

While it is not possible to outline the strategy appropriate to a group of firms in any detail, it is possible to point to a few common attributes that appear to be associated with strategies appropriate to big- and little-league competitors in industries that have become international.

The Big-League Firms

Strategies for the big-league firms in international industries are characterized by the following:

1. Pricing, production, and marketing aimed at high-volume mass markets defined on a multinational basis.
2. Design, research, and production aimed at making maximum use of economies of scale and accumulated volume.
3. Facilities of multinational firms engaged in these operations are operated as part of a single system, irrespective of national boundaries. This calls for an internationally integrated approach to production, marketing, and research.
4. The firm's environmental opportunities and competition are interpreted on a regional and/or global basis.
5. The firm cultivates an international image and reputation.

Little-League Competitors

Elements of little-league strategies include:

- Specialization. Adam Smith pointed out long ago that the degree of specialization was determined by the size of the market. Other things remaining the same, industry internationalization means a larger market for specialists. At the same time, it avoids direct competition with big-league firms. Specialization may take any one or all of the following forms:
  —Specialization of product (e.g., Ferranti's specialization in custom-built integrated circuits). Specialization of technology. Certain technologies and subtechnologies do not lend themselves to the high-volume product targets of the major-league competitors; these may be licensed or otherwise acquired by little-league firms.
  —Specialization by geography. One, in effect, concentrates company efforts in those countries that, because of tariffs, government regulations, or other reasons, are not subject to the full force of major-league competition.
- Extensive resort to partnerships, technology exchange agreements, joint ventures, and links with other organizations to make the most effective use of the limited resources available to the smaller firm.
- Maximum use of national strengths. This usually occurs in the firm's home as points of leverage to secure agreements such as those noted above. This often refers to strengths in national distribution and sales to government.
- Resort to complementarities with major-league firms (e.g., ICL's switch to products that are plug-compatible with IBM's).
- Internationalize. The larger international market for specialized products is only available to those firms geared to take advantage of it.

• Avoid big-league firms. Steer clear of head-on competition with international big-league firms.

Conclusion

The three industries in the above examples were all predominantly international, having changed rapidly in recent years. Hence, it was, perhaps, not surprising that no positive relationship between national ROI and national market share was found.

More significantly, it was evident in all three cases that the internationalization of the industry had brought about major changes in the positioning of competitors and the appropriate competitive strategies. These changes were apparently not perceived by the management of the three national companies. It was only after a financial crisis that two of these three firms changed their strategies to take into account the enlarged nature of their industry. All three cases indicate that the definition of which customers and competitors are to be included within management's operative definition of the firm's industry and market cannot be taken as either given or obvious. Identification of the scope of the industry is itself part of the strategic problem and a key aspect of strategy formulation.

This study also tends to confirm the Hatten-Schendel-Cooper findings on the difficulty of generalizing about industry strategies. Within any industry, strategies appropriate to one strategic group (or league) may not be appropriate for another. Identification of which competitive league the firm is in can provide considerable insight regarding the apppropriate strategy. Mistaken notions about which league the firm is in may adversely affect strategic planning.

Finally, in the context of industries changing from the national to international, the above points are interrelated. Identification of the firm's competitive league requires that management first defines the geographic boundaries of the industry.

References

1. Hatten, K; D. Schendel; and A. Cooper. "A Strategic Model of the U.S. Brewing Industry: 1952–1971." *Academy of Management Journal,* 1978.
2. OECD Report, *Gaps in Technology,* 1968.
3. Porter, M. *Competitive Strategy.* 1980, pp. 129–55.
4. Rapp, W. V. "Strategy Formulation and International Competition." *Columbia Journal of World Business,* Summer 1973.
5. Sciberras, E. *Multinational Electronic Companies and National Economic Policies.* 1977.
6. *The Scotsman,* June 21, 1982.
7. U.K. Government Report, *British Leyland: The Next Decade* (1975).

What this article is about: The value of strategic planning is a continuing topic for debate. As evidence mounts that many business strategies are poorly conceived and badly implemented, there is a growing disenchantment of key participants. The author explores several reasons why strategies fail and identifies seven questions that need to be asked if strategic failures are to be avoided.

2-8 Tough questions for developing strategies*

George S. Day

George S. Day is the Magna International Professor of Business Strategy at the University of Toronto.

Corporate management is concerned with the paucity of creative new ideas and evidence that crippling implementation problems are being overlooked. They wonder why many businesses are continually caught off-balance by unanticipated market and competitive actions. This leads naturally to doubts that the effort put into strategic planning is being returned by superior performance. Experience has also taught senior managers to be deeply suspicious of the rosy forecasts of revenue and profit performance that come from the business units. As one CEO complained, ''I'm tired of looking at hockey stick forecasts. . . . The focus of most business managers is on the first year of the plan, because this is the basis for their budget and performance appraisals. The rest of the planning period is simply wishful thinking designed to persuade us to give them the budgets they want. . . . It's frustrating because we don't have the detailed information to challenge them.''

Meanwhile, many operating managers seem uncertain about what corporate management is seeking. As one division general manager admitted, ''We hadn't done our homework on some key questions, and were badly cut up when the executive committee reviewed our strategy. . . . But frankly, I don't know what they are looking for, and since the questions we get seem to change every year I'm not sure they know either.''

The real cost of an arid and unfocused strategy dialogue between corporate and operating management is felt when the strategy fails to deliver the promised outcomes. Postmortems of these failures conducted by several multidivisional companies have found that most problems are eventually traced to unrealistic assumptions, distorted resource allocations or a lack of management commitment. Other studies of problems with planning systems have also been pointing to these as endemic problems. These insights have

* This article is reprinted with permission from *The Journal of Business Strategy* 6, no. 3 (Winter 1986), pp. 60–68.

Figure 1
Earnings history and forecast

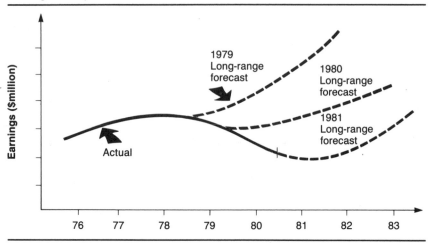

been very helpful in improving the strategic dialogue within planning teams and between operating and corporate management, and reducing the prevalence of these types of failure. At the heart of all efforts at improvement is the development of robust and mutually acceptable criteria for testing and refining business strategies.

Wishful Thinking

The bane of managers and planners is the "hockey stick" forecast, also known as the rolling-J-curve forecast. The following comparison of three sets of long-range earnings forecasts against actual business performance is a familiar illustration of this type of wishful thinking (Figure 1). Despite the growing discrepancy between actual and forecast earnings in 1979 and 1980, the management of this business was still holding to optimistic assumptions about share stability and strengthening margins. Their only concession to reality was an admission that the turnaround would be more difficult than first anticipated.

What accounts for this pattern of wishful thinking? Does it simply reflect a natural desire of those making the projections to do better in the future? While this impulse colors all forecasts, the real reasons are more deeply rooted in the way managers cope with ambiguity.[1] Three sources of bias have been identified:

1. *Anchoring.* Decisionmakers tend to "anchor" on a particular outcome they believe will occur. This outcome dominates their thinking about the option and suppresses consideration of uncertainties. As a result, downside risks are understated.

---

[1] See Amos Tversky and D. Kahneman, "Judgment Under Uncertainty: Heuristics and Biases," *Science*, 1974, pp. 1124–31; and Robin M. Hogarth and Spyros Makridakis, "Forecasting and Planning: An Evaluation," *Management Science*, Feb. 1981, pp. 115–38.

2. *Selective perception.* There are several biasing elements here: People tend to structure problems in light of their past experience (marketing people will interpret a general management problem as a marketing problem), the anticipation of what one expects to see will influence what one actually sees, and as a consequence conflicting evidence will be disregarded.

3. *Illusion of control.* Planning activities may give decisionmakers the illusion they can master and control their environment. At the same time, decisionmakers have a tendency to attribute success to their own efforts and failures to external events and "bad luck."

These three problems are compounded when top management has unrealistic expectations and requires operating management to make commitments that may not be possible. Texas Instruments (TI) is reputedly a company where senior management created a number of long-term problems by forcing operating managers to accept nearly impossible goals.[2] Meetings to review operations and plans were designed to generate a "we'll make it happen" attitude. The result was that after senior management got the commitment they wanted, operating management then had to figure out how to make it happen. In the view of one consultant who worked with TI, "The planning sessions generate false hope, not business plans."

As in all facets of planning, the key is hard-nosed reality, and willingness to support challenging objectives with adequate resources. This has worked well for TI in some areas, such as its terrain-following radar system for the F-18 jet fighter and its seismographic system for oil exploration that shows underground formations in three dimensions. These were ambitious programs based on capabilities that TI managers were able to assemble from within their organization. Adroit reassignment of people ensured that these programs would succeed. But the pressure of ambitious objectives also can force operating management to attempt programs beyond their capabilities, as when TI lost ground in the home computer market by trying to write most of its own software.

Myopic Analysis

Evaluations of strategies are likely to be dominated by facts and opinions that are easy to retrieve. Often this is evidence of the past success of a strategy. Because this hard data is given more weight than soft assessments of future threats, management may be unrealistically complacent. This is an especially dangerous posture within industries such as life insurance or telecommunications, which are in the midst of a major restructuring. Larger companies tend to underestimate the ability of new competitors to get needed resources, gain market acceptance, and penetrate previously stable markets. They may also rely for too long on actions—such as shoring up regulatory barriers—that have worked in the past without facing up to the inevitability of change.

---

[2] Bro Uttal, "Texas Instruments Regroups," *Fortune,* Aug. 9, 1982, pp. 40–45.

Myopia can cut both ways, however, and lead managers to give too much weight to their immediate problems. This is an understandable posture for managers in capital goods industries who have been preoccupied until recently with the problems of managing plant utilization rates of 60 percent or below. Yet the strategies of cost containment developed under these conditions often are not very robust because they cannot easily be adapted to new conditions. While strategies should be changed when the underlying assumptions are no longer valid, frequent changes are both expensive and disorienting. Here is where corporate management has a major role in forcing business units to consider the questions of the long-run adaptability of their strategy.

The myopia and biases that afflict managers' judgments have especially serious consequences for financial evaluations of investments in strategies and projects. For example, while much effort is devoted to projecting market growth, simplifying assumptions are often made that prices will move and shares will behave as they have in the past. But subsequent price levels may be depressed, either by too much added capacity or by low-cost capacity additions that displace high-cost facilities. The problem is even encountered in straightforward discounted cash flow analyses of the gains from cost-reducing investments. Such analyses often overlook the effects of competitors making parallel investments to reduce their labor, material, or processing costs. If prices reflect the changing cost structure of a competitive industry, the actual earnings may be lower than expected. This helps explain why the profitability of most business units falls far short of the corporate hurdle rates for investment.

Distorted Resource Allocations

Corporate allocations of resources for maximum impact are often thwarted by the "gamesmanship" of operating managers manipulating the planning process to serve their own ends. The resulting distortions are magnified when the measures of prospective performance used to compare strategies are themselves misleading. The result is a bias toward short-run payoffs from investment in mature businesses. In one company, this is called the Golden Rule of Planning: "Those that have the gold set the rules."

Gamesmanship

"Our planning process has a life of its own that often has little to do with competitive realities or market opportunites," complained one division general manager recently. "Business-unit managers pad their plans and resource requirements because they know corporate will cut everyone back. Corporate knows we do this so they try and outguess us and adjust their approvals of budgets and programs accordingly. So they're at least condoning the game." As each business unit maneuvers to get more than its fair share of the resources, important differences in strategic prospects get blurred.

This problem is a serious concern in many companies. A recent study[3] of

---

[3] Marjorie A. Lyles and R. T. Lenz, "Managing the Planning Process: A Field Study of the Human Side of Planning," *Strategic Management Journal*, 1982, pp. 105–18.

planning problems in six regional commercial banks found that two of the three most critical behavioral problems were that managers primarily bargained for resources rather than identifying new resources, and "padded" their plans to avoid close measurement. What was more revealing, however, was that these problems appeared to be a response by the managers to uncertainty about the expectations of corporate management. "When in doubt, leave lots of room for maneuvering," is a credo in many companies.

Misleading Signals

Sales growth and earnings remain the most popular benchmarks for evaluating strategies. As they are readily available from the financial accounting systems they are also influential measures of performance. Mounting criticism of these measures has properly emphasized the ease with which they can be manipulated and their inability to reflect differences in risk exposure or the timing of the earnings flows.[4] A more fundamental problem is that they may deflect the strategic dialogue within a company from the important questions. A promise of high rates of profit is not credible unless it is based on solid evidence of anticipated scarcity or competitive advantage.

Lack of Cohesion and Commitment

Strategy failures often boil down to the whole being less than the sum of the parts. Too often we have seen individually competent departments working at cross-purposes with one another, and behaving as though their success were coming at the expense of some other department. How else can one account for the manufacturing department that resisted investments in quality assurance programs, and seriously jeopardized a major product line, because they didn't bear the costs and consequences of warranty repairs?

A lack of cohesion is often evident in strategies that have evolved over time and are held together by shaky alliances among functional departments. These are vulnerable to changes in the environment that demand major adjustments, for the mechanisms to make those changes are not in place. However, the consequences of a lack of cohesion—the resulting absence of commitment to integrated action—are greatest when the business embarks on a new strategy. If the new direction is based on a network of reluctant compromises, the temptation to revert to the old strategy will be great. Many insurance companies are finding it difficult to disengage themselves from costly agency networks despite compelling reasons to find more economical ways to go to market. At the heart of the problem is often found a group of managers who are not convinced of the need for change, or whose authority might be compromised by the new approaches.

New strategies are like new ideas. Without a determined and credible champion—who has a vision that galvanizes the management team and the energy to overcome the resistance that change provokes—the odds of a strategy failure are great.

---

[4] Alfred Rappaport, "Selecting Strategies That Create Shareholder Value," *Harvard Business Review*, May–June 1984, pp. 139–49.

Asking the Tough Questions

What could be done to avoid the predictable reasons for strategy failure identified during the postmortems? The answer lies in the observation that a contributing factor in all failures was the absence of useful debate and dialogue at critical points in the formulation of the strategy. The right questions had clearly not been asked at the right time, and indeed it was not even clear there was agreement on what questions should be asked. This leads to the development of a series of evaluation criteria, with the participation of corporate and operating managers. These criteria are cast in the form of seven "tough" questions that are understood and accepted as appropriate ground rules by all participants in the strategic dialogue.

1. Suitability: Is There a Sustainable Advantage?

The essence of strategy formulation is the matching of competencies with threats and opportunities. An important first question is therefore whether a strategy makes sense in light of anticipated changes in the environment. Until the early 1980s, "systems houses" dominated the market for turnkey computer systems.[5] These firms prospered by offering a total solution to a customer's problems by providing both applications software and computer hardware. The market growth of packaged systems of 40 percent per year unfortunately attracted the attention of hardware manufacturers. Faced with rapidly declining hardware prices, these new competitors were beginning to emphasize software. Thus any strategy option for a systems house had to recognize the impact of much larger, better-funded, and highly visible hardware makers and computer service companies.

But strategy is also about the pursuit of competitive advantage. Unless a strategy offers some basis for future advantage, or adaptation to the forces eroding the current competitive position, then it does not stand the test. By mid-1980, it was apparent that systems houses that continued to emphasize general business applications such as accounting and payroll were most vulnerable because it was relatively easy for new entrants to acquire expertise in these applications. By contrast, systems houses specializing in technically complex markets—chromatography systems, for example—with the capability to provide a range of products, including remote data processing and systems consulting, had a protected advantage and attractive growth prospects.

Here are four key steps to follow when subjecting each alternative strategy to the suitability test:

> *Step 1. Review the potential threats and opportunities to the business.*
> The major sources of these threats or opportunities include: changes in the environment, and especially changes in customer and distribution requirements, the actions of present and prospective competitors, and changes in the availability of critical skills and resources.

---

[5] "New Rivals in Turnkey Systems," *Business Week*, June 23, 1980.

Step 2. Assess each option in light of the capabilities of the business. How well can the business ward off or avoid threats, exploit opportunities, or enhance current advantages or provide new sources of advantage? At this stage it is worth asking whether the strategy can work under a broad range of foreseeable environment conditions. Some strategies are only effective when inflation is high, or low, for example. Other strategies don't travel well to new geographic markets. A robust strategy that can be readily adapted to a variety of conditions is generally prefered.

Step 3. Anticipate the likely competitive responses to each option. Can competitors match, offset, or "leap frog" any advantages conferred by this option? Role playing by management teams, taking the perspective of different competitors, can be valuable in assessing competitive responses. To complete this step, ask how the business would cope with the anticipated competitive actions.

Step 4. Modify or eliminate unsuitable options. If the strategy option does not meet these suitability tests, it should either be modified or dropped from further consideration.

2. Validity: Are the Assumptions Realistic?

Choices among alternative strategies are among the least structured of all decisions that any manager must make. The manager has little hard data on which to rely. He must choose based on judgments, forecasts, and assumptions.

At the heart of these choices lie assumptions.[6] All those with a stake in choosing and implementing the strategy must share those assumptions. Otherwise the strategy will be formulated through compromise and implemented without understanding or conviction.

The difficulty lies in distinguishing sound assumptions from faulty ones. One must be on the lookout for assumptions that are accepted as conventional wisdom, but have either never been thoughtfully examined or cannot be justified in light of past events or probable trends. Whenever a major departure from past performance is anticipated, it is important to test whether there is adequate basis for the forecast. Figure 2 shows how this was done in the case of a proposed strategy for an industrial components business that forecast an increase of $51 million in sales and $7 million in net income between 1983 and 1987.

The first step in the validity test is to isolate each of the assumptions about the reasons for the forecast changes: for example, sales and profits are expected to benefit from a combination of price increases close to the rate of inflation, real market growth of 7 percent per year in the forecast period, and substantial share gains in both market segments. The next step is to evaluate the evidence used to support each assumption. Here the basis for the assumptions about share gains and real market growth appears epecially tenuous.

---

[6] Richard O. Mason and Ian I. Mitroff, *Challenging Strategic Planning Assumptions: Theory, Cases and Techniques* (1981).

Figure 2
Testing key strategic assumptions

Sources of Change	1983–1987 ($ in millions)		Key Assumptions/Actions	Validity
	Sales	Net Income		
Price increase	$23	$12	5.5% per year (inflation rate forecast = 6%)	7.6% increase in 1981 5.3% increase in 1982 80% industry capacity and Japanese threat Simultaneous growing share
Share improvement	$17	$ 4	31–34% in industrial segment 20–27% in commercial segment	.6% per year increase in 1979–1982 but with minimal price increase Industrial segment is a high-price sensitivity market New products in the commercial segment are catch-up
Real market growth	$10	$ 2	7% per year	2% per year, 1980–1982 20% from unproven new market x
Cost Productivity increase	$ 1	$ 1	3% per year	70% of annual productivity increase (3% per year, 1978–1982) was a single technical process breakthrough
Compensation increase	___	($12)	24% increase in head count	1983 head count same as 1980 with 10% less volume
Total change	$51	$ 7		

How can any share gains be realistically justified when the new products in the commercial segment do not appear to offer a competitive advantage, and the business is trying to hold prices in the industrial segment close to inflation while countering potential Japanese competition? On this evidence, one has little confidence the proposed strategy could deliver the promised results. New evidence has to be provided and the forecasts adjusted to fit market realities and reflect trade-offs between conflicting performance objectives.

Quality of Information All assumptions rely on information which itself may be inaccurate, misleading, or simply out of date. Thus it is important to constantly ask how the data was collected, by whom, and for what purpose. These questions apply equally to internal information (such as costs or salesmen's calling frequency) and environmental data (on growth, market size, and price levels). Information on changes in competitor's capabilities and customer requirements should be scrutinized with special care. The consequences of not doing so were graphically described by the president of the Becton-Dickinson Consumer Products Group in 1980 as he reflected on their experience with strategic planning:

Four years ago I went through a planning session with the Diabetic Care SBU, which makes, among other products, the syringes diabetics use to give themselves insulin. We had an excellent profiling session, and the strategy we developed seemed like a perfect one.

During the next year we suffered a serious loss of market share.

What happened was that a competitor introduced a syringe with a finer-gauged needle. We had known the competitor's plans and had tested the finer gauge on a machine that showed no appreciable reduction in drag from the thinner needle. But we didn't test it with the consumers, who have to stick these needles in themselves five or six times a day. They could feel the difference without even asking our machine, so they switched brands. Our problem was that even though we understood our competitors very well, we didn't have a good enough understanding of the market's unfulfilled needs. The planning session had given us a clear picture of the industry and the market, but only a static one. We weren't looking ahead.[7]

3. Feasibility: Do We Have the Skills, Resources, and Commitments?

The feasibility test poses two questions for each strategy option:

1. Does the business possess the necessary skills and resources. If not, is there enough time to acquire or develop them before the strategic window closes?
2. Do the key operating managers understand the underlying premises and elements of the option, and are they likely to be committed to implementing the option?

Assessing Skill and Resource Constraints Financial resources (capital funds or cash flow requirements) and physical resources are the first constraints against which the strategy option is tested. If these limitations are so constraining that undertaking a strategy would actually jeopardize the competitive position, then the strategy has to be modified to overcome or live within the constraint or perhaps be rejected. Imaginative solutions may be necessary, such as innovative financing methods using sale and leaseback arrangements or tying plant mortgages to long-term contracts.

The next constraints to be tested are access to markets, technology, and servicing capabilities. Do we have adequate sales force coverage? Is the sales force adaptable to the selling job demanded by the strategic option? Is the advertising effort and effectiveness likely to be sufficient? What about the cost, efficiency, and coverage of the present distribution system—including order handling, warehousing, and delivery? Are relationships with jobbers, distributors, and/or retailers sufficiently secure to adapt to the proposed new strategy? Similarly, do we have sufficient knowledge and experience with the next generation of appropriate product and process technology? Negative or uncertain answers should trigger a search for modifications to overcome problems, or perhaps will lead to eventual rejection of the option.

The most rigid constraints stem from the less quantifiable limitations of individuals and organizations. The basic question is whether the organization has even shown it could muster the degree of coordinative and integrative skills necessary to carry out the change in strategy. Any strategy option that depends on accomplishing tasks outside the realm of reasonably attainable skills is probably unacceptable.

---

[7] *Becton-Dickinson Corp.* (D) Case, University of Virginia, 1982.

Measuring the Capacity for Commitment   A broad-based commitment to successful implementation requires these two conditions:

1. The premises and elements of the strategy must be readily communicable. If they are not understood, then not only will the strategy option likely be flawed, but its capacity to motivate support will be seriously compromised. A good strategy is one that can be easily understood by all functions, so they are not working at cross-purposes. For this reason a good strategy is one that can be adequately explained in two or three pages.
2. The strategy should challenge and motivate key personnel. Not only must the option have a champion who gives it enthusiastic and credible support, but it must also gain acceptance by all key operating personnel.

If managers either have serious reservations about a strategy, are not excited by its objectives and methods, or strongly support another option, the strategy must be judged infeasible.

4. Consistency: Does the Strategy Hang Together?

A strategy is internally consistent if all its elements "hang together"; that is, there is minimal conflict among these elements. Planners need to be concerned about two levels of consistency. The first level is the fit of specific functional strategies with the basis for competitive advantage and the investment strategy that make up the strategic thrust. The second level of fit is concerned with the couplings among the functional strategies. Without an acceptable degree of fit at either level, effective coordination cannot be achieved. The obvious price is management energy needlessly devoted to organizational conflict and functional "finger pointing" to shift blame. A less obvious price is the diffused and uncertain impression of the business in the market.

The "consistency test" is seldom pivotal in that few strategies are rejected outright for inconsistency. But it can be useful in improving and refining the strategy to ensure that all elements are pointing in the same direction. This test may also indicate that the degree of change necessary to bring the elements into line is simply not feasible within the limitation of the available resources. Functional managers can only cope with a few changes simultaneously while trying to maintain continuing operations. Thus it may not be possible to upgrade old product lines, enter new markets, modernize the costing system, and build a new manufacturing plant all at once.

5. Vulnerability: What Are the Risks and Contingencies?

Each alternative strategy and the associated projects have a distinct risk profile. The overall level of risk reflects the vulnerability of key results if important assumptions are wrong or critical tasks are not accomplished. For example, an aggressive build strategy that increases investment intensity will increase the break-even point. This alternative is riskier because it makes the firm more vulnerable to shortfalls in sales forecasts than a "manage for current earnings" option.

Figure 3
Vulnerability/Opportunity grid for a mining company

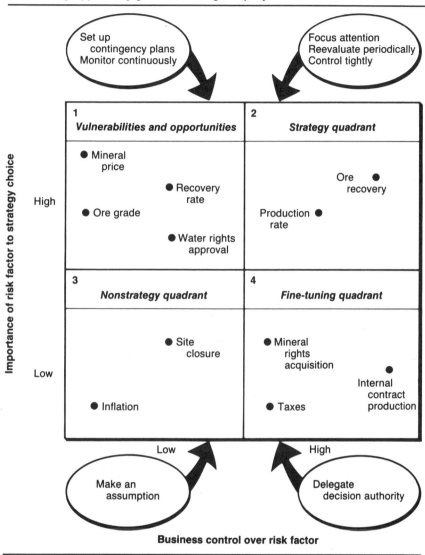

The Vulnerability/Opportunity Grid   As virtually any trend and internal capability is a potential risk factor, it is essential to isolate those few that would cause the most damage and deal with them explicitly. The vulnerability grid in Figure 3 is useful for this purpose. The *strategic importance* of the risk factors is a combination of (1) a sensitivity analysis of the potential consequences of extreme but plausible values—either positive or negative— of each factor on an overall performance, and (2) the likelihood that these extreme values could occur during the planning period. The appropriate response to important risk factors will depend on an assessment of the *degree*

of control the business has over the factor. For example, those that are strategically important, and also subject to company control, need to be understood very well, made the focus of major strategic action steps, and controlled tightly.

The specific risk factors illustrated in Figure 3 come from an assessment by a mining company of a major development proposal. The risky nature of the proposal is highlighted by the large number of strategically important risk factors, such as mineral prices, that are not controlled by the business. These become the focus of contingency plans, and must be continuously monitored. For less important risk factors it is sufficient to simply make an assumption or delegate authority to deal with the issue.

6. Adaptability: Can We Retain Our Flexibility?

In an uncertain environment it is important to ask whether, and at what cost, the strategy could be reversed in the future. The purpose of the questioning is to direct strategic thinking toward finding the best ways to make major investment commitments so that, if a major contingency occurs, it will not be necessary to write off the entire investment. Therefore, one must evaluate how each strategy offers possibilities for flexibility in design, multiple uses, or risk hedging—perhaps at a higher initial capital cost.

The question of adaptability applies as much to decisions about delaying changes in strategic direction as to decisions about undertaking major investment programs. The implications of a delay are difficult to assess, especially when they are buried in the implicit assumption of discounted cash flow analysis that investments are reversible.

In capital budgeting decisions, it is typically assumed that if an investment is postponed, it can always be made later with no penalty other than that implied by the company's discount rate. In fact, to regain this lost ground the business may have to spend a good deal more than if it had made the investment when first proposed. If the strategic window has closed, there may be no opportunity to adapt to the new situation, and all flexibility will have been lost.

7. Financial Desirability: How Much Economic Value Is Created?

The ultimate test of the final candidate options is the attractiveness of their forecast performance relative to the probable risk. At a minimum, an acceptable strategy must satisfy growth and profit objectives negotiated with corporate management. However, these are fallible measures and susceptible to manipulation. They may also myopically emphasize a short-run orientation.

Clearer signals may come from evaluating the merits of a strategy option in light of its capacity to enhance the economic value of the business or to improve competitive position. A forecast of substantial creation of economic value—or of high rates of profitability—cannot be taken as automatic indicators of the acceptability of a strategy option. Both these measures must be based on persuasive evidence of competitive advantage. Thus, further tests of the outcome require forecasts of the likelihood the option will gain or sustain an advantage.

Toward a Productive Strategy Dialogue

Effective business strategies are formed in a crucible of debate and dialogue between and within many levels of management. The challenge is to encourage realism in the dialogue—so critical decisions are not distorted by wishful thinking and myopic analysis—while not suppressing creativity and risk-taking. If the dialogue is limited to an annual confrontation in which new ideas are challenged by corporate management, then few business-unit managers will be inclined to venture beyond safe extensions of their present strategies.

What is needed is a continuing dialogue based on a shared understanding of strategic issues and mutually accepted and understood criteria for evaluating strategy options or strategies in progress. These criteria work best when they are embedded in the organization as "tough questions" that cannot be evaded. These tough questions also clearly communicate that an effective strategy does the following:

- Exploits environmental trends and creates an enduring advantage.
- Is based on realistic assumptions and accurate information.
- Can be achieved with available resources.
- Is internally consistent.
- Is acceptable to the operating managers who will be responsible for implementation.
- Is flexible enough to respond to unexpected developments.
- Will create economic value within acceptable risk limits.

Strategies that do not meet these criteria are unlikely to succeed. No champion will be willing to step forward and galvanize the operating managers into action, and no CEO will award it total support. Such strategies are especially vulnerable to the actions of competitors with a strong commitment to their own well-reasoned strategy.

3 Strategic analysis in diversified companies

Section 3 presents seven articles that address some of the issues facing strategic planners in diversified companies. Setting the stage for this section is a candid description of how Norton Company's strategic planning process works, written by Norton's president, Robert Cushman. This is followed by Richard A. Bettis and William K. Hall's article on the shortcomings of portfolio planning techniques. The next three articles deal with the timely subject of acquisitions. Robert J. Terry offers "Ten Suggestions for Acquisition Success"; David R. Willensky discusses "How to Execute an Acquisition"; and Lionel Fray, David Gaylin, and James Down address "Successful Acquisition Planning." The last two articles in this section are by prominent names in the field of strategic management—William K. Hall and Ian C. MacMillan. In the first article, the strategies for surviving in a hostile environment are discussed. MacMillan and his coauthor Robin George discuss the challenge of corporate venturing as a strategic option.

What this article is about: The portfolio approach to strategic planning that is used by the Norton Company is described, along with an account of how top management ensures the necessary involvement of a broad range of people in the planning process. This is an excellent article to see how actual companies use the tools of corporate strategy evaluation and business portfolio matrices to diagnose and appraise their situations.

3–1 Norton's top-down, bottom-up planning process*

Robert F. Cushman

Robert Cushman is the chairman of the board and chief executive officer of the Norton Company.

Eight years ago when I examined the corporate planning process at the Norton Company, I had one major complaint—the wrong people were doing the job. Possibly no one else sees the same problem, but ever since then, I have asked managers in other companies how their planning is organized and how it operates. At this point, I must conclude there are some very well-known companies that have ineffective systems, for the same reason that I felt ours was ineffective then.

So, what is my message? My message is simply this—in three parts:

• A corporate planning process of some kind is essential to any and all businesses.

• Top management cannot delegate the corporate planning process.

• Managers of the individual business units in the corporate portfolio should have incentives appropriate to their specific task.

With reasonable assurance that everyone agrees a planning process is essential, I will move to the second part of my triad and describe how we maintain at the Norton Company the kind of top management involvement I consider essential to an effective, ongoing process.

* Reprinted with permission from the November, 1979 issue of *Planning Review,* published by Robert J. Allio & Associates, Inc., for the North American Society for Corporate Planning. Copyright 1979.

Three Key Questions

Even though the organizational structure required to get the job done will vary with the size and complexity of the business, in every case, top line and staff managers must be personally involved in developing corporate strategies and plans. They cannot delegate to a group of individuals in a department called Corporate Planning because they cannot delegate answering three key questions:

- Where and what are we now?
- Where do we go and what do we want to become?
- How can we best get there?

In addition, they cannot or should not delegate the second and ongoing job of determining the character and content of the corporation's portfolio of business investments.

There's a fairly obvious reason for this. The degree of success in the execution of a corporate strategic plan will be in direct proportion to the degree of dedication to it. Dedication to it depends on the degree of involvement in its creation. This means planners cannot go around talking to division managers and staff departments like R&D, product planning, and sales, then put their own corporate plan ideas down in big, black, well-tabbed binders and make a major presentation to senior management. Corporate planners must insist that they work with top management—not for it—in this vital function.

Prior to World War II, there were relatively few large diversified companies. General Electric was an exception. Single or limited line companies were and still are headed by individuals who grew up with their products, understood the manufacturing, and knew the marketplace. In fact, I believe America's greatest companies succeeded because one man or a small group of individuals with strong convictions made things happen. They had vision and used intuition in varying degrees—and they did their own planning. It would not have occurred to them to delegate to anyone else the task of planning the future direction of their company.

Today, in the larger diversified organizations, it is obviously necessary to delegate to others many vital functions. But overall corporate strategic thinking always should involve top management. It is, in fact, up to the chief executive officer (CEO) to involve the board of directors to the extent that they agree and are committed to the company's plans and objectives.

The same is true of each division or strategic business unit (SBU). The division's manager and its top management must be involved in developing divisional strategic plans and objectives.

The total planning process involves many activities that I will not describe. I will not cover our annual financial planning cycle, our material or human resource planning, our acquisition and merger activities, or our research and internal development process.

I will describe what I consider to be the heart of our total process—the portfolio management concept. It is by working with various portfolio charts such as growth/market share matrices that we answer these key questions:

- What are we now?

• What are we trying to become?

• Can and how will we get there? (i.e., strategically not tactically)

The portfolio management concept is based on the fact that every business is really made up of many businesses when properly dissected into discrete product/market segments. To understand the competitive position of an individual unit, one needs to know its position in its industry's life cycle, its rate of growth, and its market share as related to that growth (Figure 1). Then, using the experience curve theory together with an evaluation of future trends and available resources, one can predict a particular unit's likely financial return (Figure 2).

Each SBU at Norton is responsible for developing its own overall strategy and the various segments within it.

Monitoring Committee

Six and a half years ago, we formed a top management committee whose function is to continuously assess the company's various businesses, to develop and monitor the company's portfolio, and to consider possible goals and objectives.

At the moment the committee is composed of the chairman and CEO, the president and chief operating officer, the executive vice president of finance, the corporate controller, the corporate development vice president, and 10 key operating officers.

Each SBU is asked to prepare a detailed strategy for each major segment of its operations and come before the committee, normally every 24 months. This is required for two reasons. Management wants to ascertain the viability of the unit's strategies unto themselves, but also to be certain they are still in harmony with overall corporate objectives and strategy.

The meetings open with a review of the corporate portfolio and the position of the SBU to be discussed within it.

Figure 1
Product life cycles curves

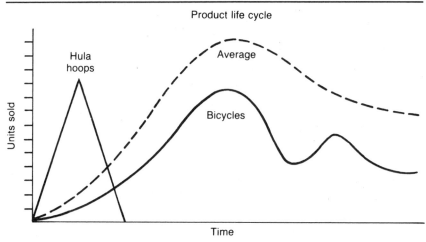

Figure 2
Experience curve

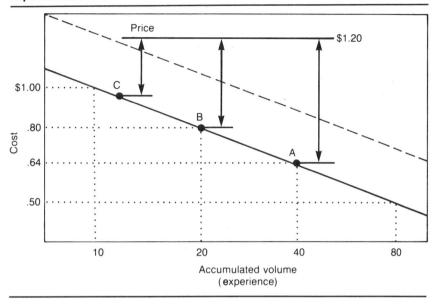

Figure 3 shows the strategic business units classified by market share strategy on the left, and by the organizational groups in the three columns labeled Abrasive Operations, Diversified Products, and Christensen. Note that an SBU may be a particular business in a country, region, or worldwide or it may be our operations in a particular country. In the strategy reviews, SBUs are always analyzed in further detail by whatever segmentation is appropriate.

The chart in Figure 4 illustrates how Norton ranks SBUs by return on net assets—or RONA—showing clearly the relative position of the business being reviewed. Similar rankings are used for return on sales and asset turnover.

Figure 5 shows how the company compares the recent actual RONA for each unit to its long-range RONA objective, while Figure 6 shows a ranking of the "par"[1] RONA results indicated by the PIMS Model for each unit.

In Figure 7, we show the company portfolio on a "balloon chart" or "growth—market share matrix." On this matrix, the vertical axis is the market growth rate in real terms, while the horizontal axis is relative market share. The balloon (or circle) sizes are proportional to sales, and the balloons are coded by market share strategy. (The information on this chart has been disguised somewhat, but the actual Norton portfolio has a similar appearance.)

[1] The PIMS (Profit Impact of Marketing Strategies) Model is developed and operated by the Strategic Planning Institute, Cambridge, Massachusetts, using information from member companies. "Par" RONA is the expected return on net assets indicated by the model for the particular business given the characteristics of its market, competition, technology, and cost structure.

Figure 3
Norton Company portfolio broken out by SBUs
(Figures = 1977 sales—$ million)

Market Share Strategy	Total Sales ($ million)	Abrasive Operations	Sales	Diversified Products	Sales	Christensen	Sales
Build	xxx	Country A	xxx	Country H—Bus. r	xxx	Business w	xxx
		Business a	xxx	Region J —Bus. r	xxx	Business x	xxx
		Business b	xxx	—Bus. s	xxx		
				—Bus. t	xxx		
				—Bus. u	xxx		
Build/ maintain	xxx	Business c	xxx				
		Country B —Bus. d	xxx				
		Country C	xxx				
		Region D —Bus. d	xxx				
Maintain	xxx	Region D —Bus. g	xxx	Country H—Bus. v	xxx	Region D —Bus. aa	xxx
		Country H—Bus. g	xxx	Business W	xxx	Country H—Bus. aa	xxx
		Region D —Bus. h	xxx				
		Country H—Bus. h	xxx				
Maintain/ harvest	xxx	Business p	xxx	Region D —Bus. v	xxx		
		Business g	xxx				
Harvest							
Total	$848		xxx		xxx		xxx

Figure 4
Norton RONA rankings

Norton Company Portfolio
Ranking by RONA (return on net assets)

		Average 1966-1977	1976	1977
1. Business	a	xx%	xx%	xx
2.	b	:	:	:
3.	c	:	:	:
4.	d	:	:	:
5.	e	:	:	:
6.	f	:	:	:
7.	g	:	:	:
8.	h	:	:	:
:	:	:	:	:
24.	x	xx	xx	xx
Norton average (operations)		xx	xx	xx
25.	y	:	:	:
26.	z	:	:	:
27.	aa	:	:	:
28.	bb	:	:	:
29.	cc	:	:	:
30.	dd	:	:	:
:	:	:	:	:
40.	nn	xx	xx	xx

Figure 5
RONA comparison to 1980–1981 objectives

Norton Company Portfolio
RONA comparison: 1981-83 objectives vs. 1977 actual

		Actual 1977	Objective 1981-83	Objective higher/ (lower)
1. Business	a	xx%	xx%	xx%
2.	b	:	:	:
3.	c	:	:	:
4.	d	:	:	:
5.	e	:	:	:
:	:	:	:	:
22.	v	xx	xx	xx
Norton average (operations)				
23.	w	xx	xx	xx
:	:	:	:	:
40	hh	xx	xx	xx

Figure 6
Norton "par" RONA rankings

Norton Company Portfolio
Ranking by PIMS "PAR" RONA — regular model

		PIMS "PAR" RONA 1974-76 average after tax
1. Business a		xx%
2.	b	:
3.	c	:
4.	d	:
5.	e	:
:	:	:
:	:	:
20.	t	xx
PIMS Average (all companies)		11%
21.	u	xx
:	:	:
:	:	:
40.	jj	xx

Figure 8 is an example of a particular business in a region showing the breakdown of this business by market.

The balloon chart (Figure 9) shows the same business segmented by country.

The chart in Figure 10 illustrates our test of cash generation versus market share strategy. The matrix includes cash generation in the vertical direction and market share strategy in the horizontal direction. The shaded-coding indicates which locations in the matrix are either acceptable, unacceptable, or questionable. Past and expected future locations of businesses and appropriate segments are plotted as shown by the examples (a) and (b). Note that example (b) has been in an unacceptable location but is expected to move to an acceptable location.

Figure 11 is a test of sales growth rate versus market growth rate versus market share strategy. Let's look at example (c)—the third column of figures.

The market share strategy is M or maintain (line B2). The expected market growth rate including inflation is 8 percent annually (line B5)—3 percent real growth plus 5 percent inflation.

Our expected sales growth is 12 percent annually (line B6)—significantly higher than the market growth rate. Therefore, the expected sales growth rate is not consistent with the market share strategy (line B8).

Top-down, Bottom-up Orientation

Each of these charts may produce a great deal of useful discussion and questions such as:

• What are the contributions of that unit in the overall scheme of things?

• Does it help balance or add stability to the total?

• Does it increase or decrease the cyclical nature of our abrasive business?

Figure 7
Comparison of relative market shares

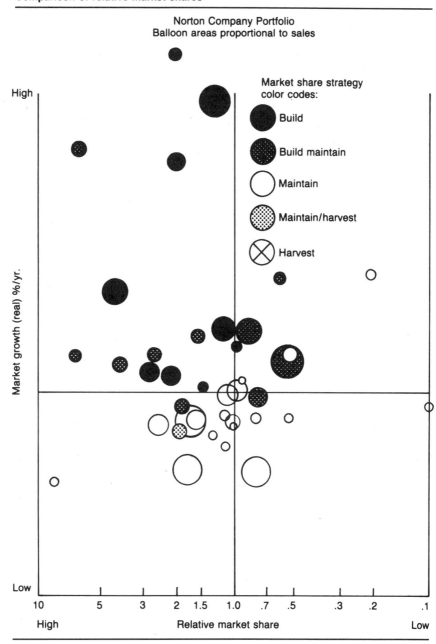

Norton Company Portfolio
Balloon areas proportional to sales

Figure 8
Business identified by market

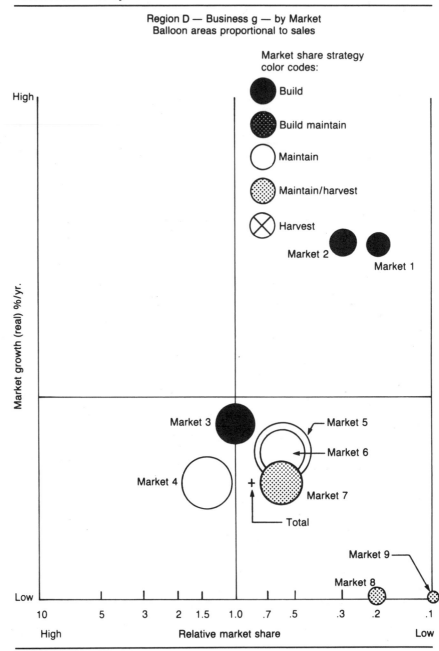

Region D — Business g — by Market
Balloon areas proportional to sales

Market share strategy
color codes:

Build
Build maintain
Maintain
Maintain/harvest
Harvest

Figure 9
Business identified by country

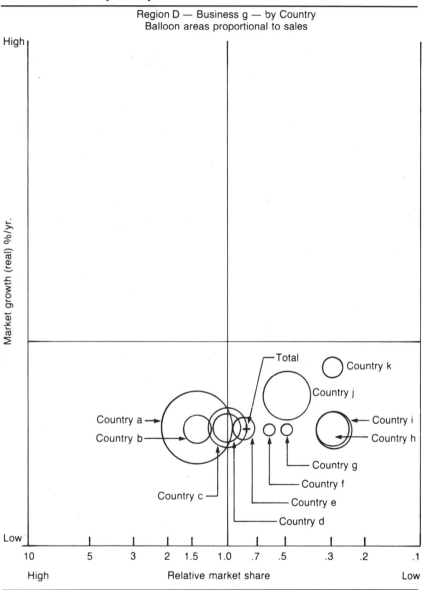

Region D — Business g — by Country
Balloon areas proportional to sales

• To what extent does it relate to other Norton technologies, processes, or distribution?

• Does it hurt or improve our image in the investment community?

Since committee members receive all material in advance of the meeting, there is no formal presentation. Discussion, and probing questions start immediately and normally follow a pattern which includes:

• Facts as presented, trends, and assumptions.

Figure 10
Cash generation versus market share test

Norton Company
Test: cash generation
vs.
Market share strategy

Market share strategy

		Build	Maintain	Harvest
Cash generation {	Use cash	(a)	(b)	
	Provide own cash			
	Disengage cash		(b)	

☐ Acceptable combination   ▨ Unacceptable combination   ▨ Questionable combination

Funds generated/(consumed)-average/yr.

Business	Market share Strategy	Actual last 5 yrs. $000 % to N.A.		Expected next 5 yrs. $000 % to N.A.	
(a) ----•----	Build	(200)	(8)%	(100)	(2)%
(b) ---------	Maintain	(150)	(5)%	200	5%

Figure 11
Sales growth versus market growth test

Norton Company
TEST: Sales growth rate vs. market growth rate
vs. market share strategy

	Percent per year		
	Businesses		
	(a)	(b)	(c)
A. Last 4 years			
1. Sales growth	15%	7%	10%
B. Next 5 years			
2. Market share strategy	B	M	M
3. Real market growth	10%	3%	3%
4. Price increase rate	6%	5%	5%
5. Market growth incl. inflation (3 & 4)	16%	8%	8%
6. Expected sales growth	20%	7%	12%
7. Growth: partic. incr./ (decr.) (6-5)	4%	(1)%	4%
8. Participation change (7) consistent with market share strategy (2)? (yes, no, or ?)	Yes	Yes	No

- The mission and mode of operation in terms of build, maintain, or harvest.
- Current appropriateness of strategy.
- Reasons for changes since last review.
- An analysis of the PIMS data obtained from the Strategic Planning In-
  stitute, which provides a feel for what each unit should expect in
  profitability compared to similar businesses, what results might be ex-
  pected from certain strategic changes, and a number of other "what if"
  questions.
- Relationship to other Norton businesses.
- Fit with corporate portfolio.

While there are a large number of separate strategic and substrategic business units, they are currently grouped to enable the committee to review about 40. We meet about 25 times per year for two to five hours per session. An SBU which has a problem may ask or be asked to meet more frequently. The committee may also meet to discuss an acquisition candidate. It meets annually to update our ongoing five-year financial model, a major progress check on our planning. When appropriate, it meets to review a collection of broad corporate strategy statements which are communicated to our employees in several different ways.

While this committee is obviously very powerful, it takes no votes as such, and approves neither capital expenditures nor budgets. In no way does it replace the company's executive committee.

In fact, it has no chairman. The job of moderator or facilitator is always assigned to a committee member whose own responsibilities do not include the business unit being discussed.

The committee is a sounding board, a diverse top management group that probes, critiques, and advises in matters relating to the company's portfolio of businesses and its future. But its most important function is to keep senior managers focused on corporate direction rather than just on areas of personal accountability. It provides the top-down direction necessary for effective management, while maintaining bottom-up involvement.

Management's commitment to the process indicates its importance to all. And because managing a portfolio is dynamic, it is a never-ending involvement.

Finally, Appropriate Incentives

We all realize that managing and maintaining a healthy cash business is quite different from managing a high-growth star—and that managing a high growth business in an emerging new industry is yet another job. So, we look for individuals suited to each task.

Whatever the business, though, it is important that each manager and his subordinates be challenged and made to realize that each assignment is vital to improving the total corporate portfolio.

To make that challenge credible we have developed over 50 different incentive plans, tailor-made to match each specific situation. It is not a difficult task. Once the basic formula is established, different goals and objectives are weighted differently. For example, gaining market share, and extensive investments in research may be more important than current profit margins in a high-growth industry. But good asset management, such as low inventory to sales ratios, low manufacturing costs, and high productivity are more important to maintaining the cash generator. So, our managers' incomes are related directly to specific results.

I said before I was sure we could agree on the importance of a strategic planning process. I believe that without top management's continuing involvement in the process, it is unlikely to be effective. In backing up my belief, I have described how one medium-to-large-sized company insures the necessary involvement among a broad range of people.

There are undoubtedly other methods of managing a multiproduct, multinational business; blind obedience to any one theory is dangerous. But the portfolio management technique has been found to be useful at the Norton Company as a way

- To manage.
- To control an increasingly diversified company.
- To assure that capital appropriations are not considered in isolation but in comparison with the needs of other units.
- To assure working toward a balance of cash generation and growth opportunities.
- To highlight divestment of units when appropriate.

We do not consider our planning to be nearly as sophisticated as those in operation at companies like General Electric and Texas Instruments. While it is constantly becoming more sophisticated, it is probably appropriate to a company of our size and complexity at this time.

We feel there are benefits to keeping such functions simple, because we can be sure a maximum number of employees understand the process and feel involved in what the company is now and what it is trying to become.

What this article is about: During the past decade the SBU (or portfolio) concept has enjoyed widespread popularity as a basis for corporate-wide strategic planning systems within large, diversified firms. This article discusses the implementation of the SBU approach at 13 companies, what has worked well and where some of the pitfalls are.

3-2 The business portfolio approach—where it falls down in practice*

Richard A. Bettis and William K. Hall

Richard A. Bettis is assistant professor at Edwin L. Cox
School of Business, Southern Methodist University. William
K. Hall is professor at the Graduate School of Business
Administration, University of Michigan.

The purpose of this paper is to integrate and summarize some of the authors' research into the implementation of SBU-based strategic planning systems in large, diversified firms. Specifically, the paper describes a useful contemporary approach to implementing such systems. This approach is based on interviews in a sample of 13 firms, using the SBU concept, which were conducted during 1977–79. The sales of these firms ranged from about $1 billion to over $15 billion in 1977. All were publicly held industrial companies and all were significantly diversified, although none would be considered conglomerates. Over 60 individual managers at corporate, group, and divisional levels were interviewed (some several times) in these firms. Planning manuals and actual plans from firms in the sample were examined. Also, public domain materials relevant to these firms were studied. Furthermore, six consultants with experience in implementing SBU-based planning systems were interviewed.

The research reported here summarizes some of the major features of SBU-based planning systems as they were seen to be evolving in the sample of firms by 1979.

The SBU Concept

Although there are numerous slight variations of the SBU (or portfolio) concept, they all rely on a matrix or grid similar to the one shown in Figure

---

* This article is reprinted from *Long Range Planning* 16, no. 2 (April 1983), pp. 95–104.

Figure 1
The portfolio concept: Conceptual matrix

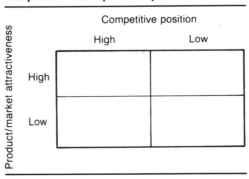

1. The matrix classifies businesses by product/market attractiveness along one axis and competitive position along the other axis. There are two basic approaches to measurement along these scales. One approach relies on a single measurable criterion along each axis, while the other approach uses multiple measures (including subjective ones) along each axis (see Figures 2 and 3). Typically the matrices or grids are divided into either four or nine "boxes," although the authors have observed some with significantly more. Figures 2 and 3 illustrate two of the most commonly encountered matrices. (The matrix in Figure 2 is usually attributed to the Boston Consulting Group, and that in Figure 3 to General Electric and/or McKinsey & Co.)

Regardless of the particular layout chosen for the matrix, the basic idea behind the SBU concept remains the same: the position (or box) that a business occupies on the matrix should determine the "grand thrust" or "mission" around which the strategy for the business is developed. Although these missions vary somewhat depending on the particular matrix, the top half of Figure 2 provides a typical illustration. (The discussion of implementation below is independent of the particular matrix used.) In one set of missions, the authors have seen that the mission of the "cash cows" is to generate cash flow that can be redeployed to promising "question marks." The mission of the "question marks" is to aggressively gain

Figure 2
Example matrix

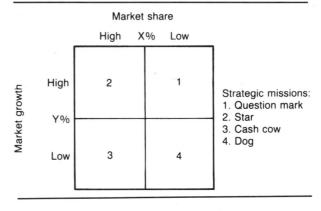

Figure 3
Example matrix

Business strengths

	High	Medium	Low
High	1	1	2
Medium	1	2	3
Low	2	3	3

Industry attractiveness (vertical axis label)

Strategic missions:
1. Invest/grow
2. Selectivity/earnings
3. Harvest/divest

competitive position with the needed investment funds coming from the cash cows. (Obviously the number of question marks in the corporate portfolio must be balanced with the cash generation capabilities of the cash cows.) The mission of the stars is to ensure their own long-term competitive position. Finally, the mission of the dogs is to generate positive cash flow until they can be opportunistically divested. Although this introduction to the SBU concept has been brief, it will be adequate for the authors' later developments. The key point is that different boxes on the matrix (or grid) denote different grand thrusts or missions for the business. The reader who is unfamiliar with the SBU concept or who desires a deeper understanding can refer to several references.[1]

This paper is concerned only with the situation in which the SBU concept is used as the basis of a corporate-wide strategic planning system. This situation is operationally defined when corporate-level management decides to make the SBU concept the primary basis for the corporate-wide strategic planning system. From now on in this paper reference to the SBU concept will refer only to this type of application.

What the Basic Model Says about Implementation

In order to show the evolution of the SBU concept in practice, it is necessary to first construct a "basic model" against which changes in implementation can be measured. Such a model is merely a simple baseline case against which changes can be delineated. However, it should be noted, the logic of this basic model can be found in popular articles, in the classrooms of several business schools and management development programs, and in the executive office of some companies with limited exposure to the SBU concept. The logic of the basic model is at once simple and

---

[1] William K. Hall, "SBU's: Hot New Topic in the Management of Diversification," *Business Horizons*, February 1978; Gerald B. Allen and John S. Hammond, *Note on the Boston Consulting Group Concept of Competitive Analysis and Corporate Strategy*, ICCH, 9-175-175; and Charles W. Hofer and Dan Schendel, *Strategy Formulation: Analytical Concepts* (St. Paul, Minn.: West Publishing, 1978).

compelling. When analyzed and distilled, it holds that there are three major steps in implementing the SBU concept as the basis of a planning system:

1. The firm is divided into strategic business units or SBUs. This involves determining the different businesses the firm is in by specifying the economically distinct product/market segments and the firm's resources that are dedicated to each segment. The objective is to divide the firm into the most relevant strategic entities.
2. Each of these SBUs is evaluated against the dimensions of the matrix. On the basis of this analysis the appropriate grand thrust or mission is assigned to each SBU.
3. A strategy is developed within each SBU and reviewed by corporate management to ensure congruence with the assigned mission and the appropriate balance of cash and/or resource flows.

This view of implementation is a straightforward extension of the basic logic of the SBU concept. Unfortunately, the authors have found that this approach does *not* work in most large, diversified firms. In a study of 10 firms with varying levels of experience with the portfolio concept, one of the authors[2] found that none had been successful using the basic model. Instead a significantly different approach evolved within these firms. Further research into three other firms by both authors confirmed this result. Several reasons underlie the failure of the basic model, and to them we now turn.

Why the Basic Model Is Often Inappropriate

The basic model is inappropriate for most large, diversified firms because it implicitly assumes that a firm can be unambiguously divided into a "reasonable number" of independent (in terms of markets and production processes) "single businesses." If a firm can be unambiguously divided into independent, single businesses, then these businesses can be defined as SBUs and each assigned a mission independent of the others. Furthermore, the term *reasonable number* means that the number of businesses (constituted as SBUs) is small enough (in a sense to be discussed later) that corporate-level management can develop the matrix positions, assign the missions, and review SBU strategies and performance to ensure congruence with the assigned missions. However, the authors' research has shown that for large, diversified firms: (1) SBUs cannot be unambiguously constituted as single businesses; (2) the extent of diversification precludes the "reasonable number" criterion mentioned above; and (3) the relatedness of diversification can preclude the independence of the SBUs.

The Ambiguous Notion of a Single Business

The concept of what constitutes a single business is difficult to operationalize. For example, is International Business Machines in the computer business, the information processing systems business, the hardware and software business, the big and small computer businesses, or the mainframe

---

[2] Richard A. Bettis, "Strategic Management in the Multibusiness Firm: Implementing the Portfolio Concept," doctoral dissertation available from University Microfilms, 1979.

and peripherals businesses (or other businesses)? The nature of the problem stems from the fact that a product/market segment can be defined in a variety of ways. In fact, there is generally a whole hierarchy of product/market segments. As an example, consider a firm that among other things manufactures and markets appliances. A logical breakdown might be into specific products (e.g., washers, ranges, microwave ovens, etc.). Alternative breakdowns (from among many possibilities) could be into commercial and home appliances, into different price/quality segments, or into different geographic segments. These breakdowns could be combined to yield increasingly finer segments (e.g., the commercial, microwave oven business, or the European, high-quality, home dishwasher business). So, in sum, SBUs could be defined in a myriad of different ways ranging from the entire appliance business to much smaller segments such as the European, high-quality, home dishwasher business. Regardless of which segments are eventually chosen to define these businesses, arguments could be advanced for other segments. Since segments finer than those finally selected will generally exist, arguments could be advanced that the definition aggregates several single businesses. Furthermore, it is easy to see that the position of the business on the matrix may depend on the definition chosen for the SBU. For example, if the entire appliance business is defined as an SBU, then a "cash cow" mission may be appropriate. However, in a finer breakdown by product the microwave oven business could quite conceivably be defined as an SBU with a "question mark" mission. The hierarchical nature of product/market segments frustrates the unambiguous definition of single businesses as SBUs. (Note that when the SBU concept is used for a specific application instead of as the basis of a corporate-wide strategic planning system, the level of aggregation may often be matched to the problem at hand.)

The Extent of Diversification

Closely related to the problems caused by the ambiguous nature of a single business are the problems inherent in the extent of diversification present in large, diversified firms. The basic nature of the problem is that the number of product/market segments in which these firms participate is so large that it completely swamps the "reasonable number" criterion described above.

As an example, consider the Eaton Corporation, a firm which had sales of $2.11 billion in 1977 and is certainly *not* considered to be a conglomerate. In the Eaton 1977 annual report reference is made to over 400 product/market segments that are said to consist of "a single product or family of related products which go into a well-defined and unified market." Examples given include economy truck transmission, narrow aisle lift trucks, agricultural scales, and gas control values. Is it reasonable to expect that for each of these over 400 product/market segments meaningful strategy and performance reviews can be conducted by corporate management? Furthermore, what size staff would be needed merely to develop the information necessary for positioning these segments on the matrix. The scope of such efforts at the corporate level would certainly need to be heroic if not foolish. The application of these results to most large, diversified corporations will obviously yield similar results.

The Relatedness of Diversification

Intimately interwoven with the ambiguous nature of a single business is the related manner in which most large firms are diversified. Wrigley and Rumelt showed that most firms tend to diversify into areas related to their "core" business.[3] Typical examples of such firms include General Electric, Union Carbide, Fiat, and Coca-Cola. The notable exceptions are, of course, the conglomerates such as Textron and International Telephone and Telegraph. This relatedness of diversification exacerbates the already ambiguous nature of a single business and simultaneously prevents the achievement of independent SBUs. The residual dependency among SBUs frustrates the assignment of missions independently to each SBU because the SBUs themselves are no longer strategically independent entities.

As an example of these ideas, consider the previous example of appliances, only this time assume a firm initially only manufactures and markets home washers and dryers. Diversification could logically take this firm into the manufacture and sale of home microwave ovens and trash compactors. This move itself will exacerbate the problems associated with business definition as previously discussed. Furthermore, assume that the washers and dryers are defined as a "home laundry" SBU and that the microwave ovens and trash compactors are defined as a "home kitchen" SBU. These two SBUs are obviously not strategically independent since, among other things they may share distribution channels, be often bought in combination (i.e., by housing contractors), share a common assembly facility, and mutually benefit from brand name advertising efforts. Inevitably there must be some coordination of strategy among the two, and this will be extremely difficult if different strategic missions are assigned (e.g., cash cow for the laundry SBU and question mark for the kitchen SBU). Grouping them all together into an appliance SBU will probably result in the assignment of an inappropriate mission to some parts (i.e., overall cash cow mission would probably be inappropriate for the trash compactors). The alternative of breaking them down further (e.g., washers, dryers, microwave ovens, and trash compactors) will only increase the interdependency between them. As this example illustrates, the related nature of much diversification prevents the achievement of independent SBUs and hence reduces the usefulness of the basic model for implementing the portfolio concept. In view of this and the arguments of the previous two sections, the basic model would seem to be of limited usefulness operationally. We now turn to a more useful approach which summarizes the major features of SBU-based strategic planning systems as they were seen to be evolving in the sample of firms. This approach departs significantly from the basic model.

An Alternative Approach to Implementation

The alternative approach is much less dogmatic than the basic model. It relies more on a flexible, situational matching of implementation to the

---

[3] Leonard Wrigley, "Divisional Autonomy and Diversification," doctoral dissertation, Harvard Business School, 1970; and Richard P. Rumelt, *Strategy, Structure, and Economic Performance* (Cambridge, Mass.: Harvard University Press, 1974).

circumstances of the particular firm. Specifically, the alternative approach involves the hierarchical application of the portfolio concept at multiple organizational levels, the coordination of inputs among these levels, and the purposeful but limited variation of managerial systems and processes across different strategic missions.

Hierarchical Application

Under the conventional wisdom, the management of a firm confronts a dilemma in the definition of SBUs. If each distinct product/market is used as the basis of an SBU, then the number of SBUs is likely to be unmanageably large from the corporate level. On the other hand, if only a manageable number of SBUs are defined, then the mission assigned to any particular SBU is likely to be inappropriate for substantial segments of the SBU (since the SBU is actually an aggregation of businesses). Furthermore, a strategic plan based on a single mission for such an aggregated SBU will likely ignore substantial differences among the component businesses.

To overcome this dilemma it is necessary to recognize that the application of the portfolio concept must be hierarchical in order to mirror the hierarchical nature of product/market segments. In this manner descending levels of the hierarchy can be used to refine the analysis and to achieve a better matching of strategic entity to product/market segment.

Although the authors believe that several levels of analysis may be ultimately necessary in some firms, they have observed that two overcome many of the problems associated with the basic model. (Interestingly, General Electric apparently has five levels of analysis: sector, SBU, segment, product line, and product. Such a five-level hierarchy could reasonably incorporate a breakdown at the product level of more than 10,000 products.) The subsequent discussion will concentrate on a two-level hierarchy. The extension of these ideas to hierarchies with more levels should be obvious.

To illustrate the nature of these ideas again consider the appliance example. Among other things, a firm produces and markets home appliances. From the corporate level an SBU called "home appliances" is created and assigned a cash cow strategic mission. At the same time, although a home appliance SBU is created, both corporate management and SBU management recognized that this represents a coarse or "aggregated" level of analysis that must be subsequently refined. In turn, the management of the SBU refines the analysis by "disaggregating" it into segments such as home laundry (washers and dryers), microwave ovens, dishwashers, and trash compactors. Figure 4 details the nature of the differences between the two levels of analysis. While the corporate level depicts a monolithic cash cow mission, the SBU level shows several strategic entities with both cash cow and question mark missions. Examination of this example shows that there are three essential steps.

1. *Group related business together to form aggregated SBUs.*

The essential logic of this step is that (as discussed earlier) each SBU must make sense as a single, though aggregated, product/market segment. How else can product/market attractiveness and competitive position be evaluated,

**Figure 4
Aggregation/disaggregation example**

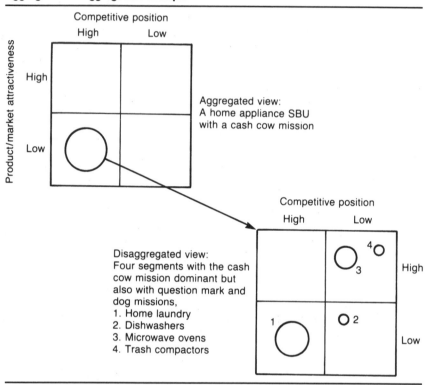

and how else can a meaningful (aggregated) strategic mission be assigned? The necessity of such a step arises because (as previously discussed) a division of a firm into all of its product/market segments results in a number that is unmanageable from the corporate level (i.e., the need to aggregate arises). The obvious question is how much to aggregate. No simple answer is possible, but there are some general guidelines. The number should be manageable from the corporate level. This will obviously depend on the management style of the CEO and on the amount and quality of staff support available. However, the authors have not personally observed any stable planning system with more than 45 SBUs, and hence this number may be taken as an approximate, practical upper limit. (The authors have observed firms starting implementation with over 100 SBUs, but this number rapidly decays as the management overload at the corporate level is felt.) Second, the more related the businesses of the firm, the fewer the SBUs that are required. In essence the more related a firm is, the fewer different businesses it is in. One of the authors[4] studied the relatedness of six large firms using the SBU concept as a basis for strategic planning. The results are illustrated in Figure 5 and show that the number of SBUs ranged from 6 for the smallest and most related to 43 for the largest and least related. So, in sum, the

---

[4] Bettis, "Strategic Management in the Multibusiness Firm.

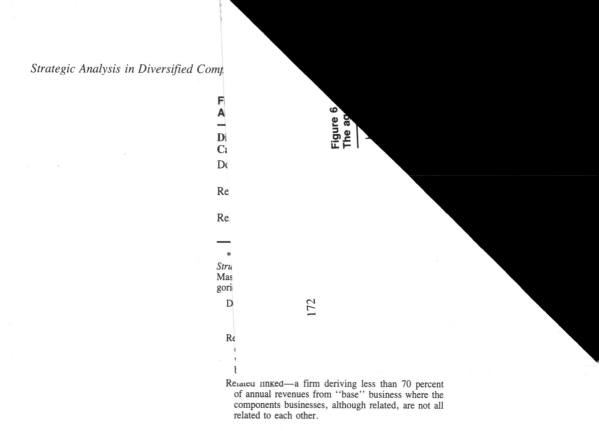

F|
A|
—
D|
C:
D(

Re

Re

—
*
Stru
Mas
gori

D|

172

R(

Reiaicu linked—a firm deriving less than 70 percent of annual revenues from "base" business where the components businesses, although related, are not all related to each other.

practical range would seem to be (very) approximately from 2 to 50 (aggregated) SBUs.

One interesting implication of this aggregation process would seem to be that use of the SBU concept as a basis for a corporate-wide planning system by large conglomerates is limited. By definition a conglomerate participates in unrelated businesses. Therefore, they cannot meaningfully be aggregated. Consider Textron as an example. Typical of the hundreds of products Textron produces are military helicopters, gold bracelets, chain saws, writing paper, polyurethane foam, and fine china. What is meant by product/market attractiveness and competitive position of an SBU composed of a military helicopter business and a fine china business or a chain saw business and a polyurethane foam business? Hence, if the conglomerate participates in more than about 50 different businesses, the portfolio concept is not a practical approach. (Interestingly, the authors are not aware of any large conglomerate which has adopted the SBU concept as the basis of a corporate-wide strategic planning system.) Figure 6 illustrates the nature of the aggregation problem in terms of the extent and relatedness of diversification as it applies to conglomerates and other types of firms. (Note that as previously developed the basic model only works for low levels of diversification and for low relatedness of diversification.)

Vertical Integration

One specific type of relatedness, vertical integration, requires further comment at this point. Since in vertically integrated businesses the output of one stage (business) represents the input of another stage (business), changes in any particular stage can have considerable impact on the other businesses.

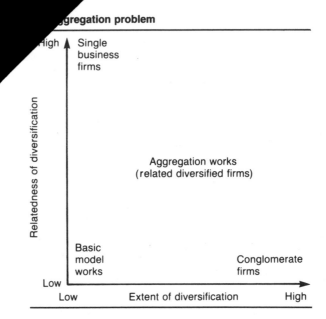

Aggregation problem

Such intense relatedness requires considerable management outside of an SBU framework since definition of various stages as SBUs leaves considerable dependencies among them. Furthermore, in the three vertically integrated firms the authors studied, the portfolio concept was being adopted as a result of attempts to diversify away from core businesses with little growth potential and generally low profit potential. The SBU concept was seen as a means for managing this diversification in addition to identifying appropriate strategic missions for various stages of the vertically integrated core business.

Once the definition of aggregated SBUs is complete, they may be evaluated against the dimensions of the matrix.

2. *Develop the aggregated strategic mission.*

The second step is straightforward and similar to the basic model except that the aggregated nature of the SBU is recognized. For the home appliance example, a cash cow mission as shown in Figure 6 could conceivably be appropriate. The next step is to proceed down the hierarchy to the next level of analysis.

3. *Define the component businesses of the SBU, and develop appropriate strategic missions for them.*

This step represents the disaggregation of the previous corporate-level analysis and takes place at the SBU level. The logic is that a refinement of the corporate-level analysis is made to incorporate the finer product/market structure of the firm at an organizational level where the appropriate expertise is available. Figure 3 illustrates this for the home appliance example. Although at the disaggregated level a cash cow mission still predominates, other missions for other segments of the SBU are apparent.

The experience of the authors (based on a sample of 13 firms) has been that generally from 2 to 15 segments of each SBU are identified and evaluated in this step. Given the earlier discussion about the practical limits on the number of SBUs, one can now envisage a total of several hundred product/market segments being identified and evaluated. Even for extremely large firms such numbers can provide a reasonably clear picture of the product/market structure. For example, in 1977 the Norton Corporation, a producer of abrasives and other products (1977 sales were $848 million, making Norton one of the smallest firms studied) had 30 SBUs whose strategy was regularly reviewed and monitored at the corporate level. These 30 SBUs were aggregated from 62 "sub-SBUs" whose characteristics were sufficiently different to warrant individual strategy development. Several of these sub-SBUs represented less than $5 million in sales. Furthermore, analysis was occasionally conducted within the sub-SBUs at even finer levels. At this point the argument has been developed to where the necessity to coordinate the two analyses should be obvious.

Coordinating the Inputs

If there is no coordination between the two levels of analysis, then inevitably substantial disagreements can develop among corporate and SBU managers. Each will hold a single partially exclusive view of any particular SBU. For example, a particular SBU may be seen at the corporate level as pursuing a "pure" cash cow mission. If the plans and capital budget of this SBU are devised using a disaggregated analysis (as they should be), then the corporate review will likely focus on the gap between the cash cow mission and the actual content of the plans. In our home appliance example (see Figure 4) the corporate expectation may be for a $50 million annual cash throw-off from the SBU. However, the SBU plans may reflect only a $25 million throw-off with the remaining $25 million being invested in the microwave oven and trash compactor businesses. Naturally a process of negotiation always occurs around plans, but this negotiation cannot resolve a fundamentally different view of an SBU.

To overcome such difficulties the authors believe that it is necessary to consciously build in mechanisms for coordinating the two levels of analysis. Although no single definitive set of mechanisms applicable specifically to the SBU concept is currently known to exist, some which are known to be useful can be discussed.

One of the more obvious mechanisms is explicit recognition at both levels of analysis of the perspective of the other. In essence this facilitates the planning process by legitimizing the different perspectives of both participants as complementary instead of mutually exclusive. This can be accomplished through planning conferences, management development programs (which stress the hierarchical nature of the portfolio concept), and the actual design of the planning systems. The planning manual, if one is used, should recognize both levels of analysis and their necessity. For example, consider the following quote from the planning manual of one large firm:

Due to differing business conditions, the current business situation, differing markets served, or other reasons, a breakdown below the Business Unit (SBU) level will be required to effectively convey the elements of your plan. Use your discretion in determining the most appropriate breakdown.

The strategic planning system should be designed around the two levels of analysis. The system should be structured so that the basic planning entities are the individual segments of each particular SBU. The SBU plans reviewed at corporate level should be aggregations of these plans stressing overall SBU strategy with short summaries of the individual segments and their missions included (perhaps in an appendix). Furthermore, the basic financial objectives of an SBU can be stated within the plans in a summary form (perhaps in an appendix) which shows how they are arrived at by aggregation.

Each year the detailed plans of a limited number of segments of SBUs can be carefully scrutinized at the corporate level. These segments can be chosen randomly or for their strategic relevance to the firm as a whole. Such an audit in addition to its direct benefits communicates the importance of the individual SBU segments as planning entities and reinforces the basic hierarchical nature of the planning system. A published case study of the Mead Corporation (available from the Intercollegiate Case Clearing House) provides an excellent example of such a mechanism. Here one of 13 segments within a particular SBU (the packaging division, one of 25 SBUs in 1977) is receiving intense corporate-level scrutiny because of its strategic relevance even though its sales are less than one thousandth of total company sales ($1.8 billion) and less than 4 percent of SBU sales.

Probably the most important coordinating mechanism of all is simply the SBU manager himself. He is positioned at the interface of the two views and is truly in the middle. He must be able to conceptualize the SBU in terms of the perspective of corporate management while simultaneously being sensitive to the varying strategic missions of his segment managers. He must be able to see the world in two different but complementary ways. This linking role appears to be somewhat different from the traditional division manager. Although the authors have not yet closely studied this new role (it is an agenda item on our current research), preliminary work has delineated some of the general considerations that are important.

In defining and approaching his job, the SBU manager must first determine how absolute and inviolate the corporate-level categorization of the SBU actually is. In other words, is the corporate-level categorization viewed as a final matching of strategic missions to businesses, or is it viewed more in the context of a first-cut approximation or preliminary matching. The authors believe that the degree of absoluteness in the corporate-level categorization should be critical in determining how the SBU manager approaches his job. In other words, effective coordination of the two levels of analysis depends on the SBU manager matching his approach to the absoluteness of the corporate-level categorization. Consider, for example, a firm in which the corporate-level categorization is totally absolute and inviolate. (The authors present this as a polar case only. They have not encountered such a totally dogmatic example. Furthermore, they conjecture that few, if any, such cases exist. Such a case is useful, however, in understanding the dimensions of the

SBU manager's job.) In such an unambiguous environment the SBU manager has no freedom regarding the assigned strategic mission. He essentially becomes an implementer who must work with his segment managers to produce an aggregate strategy that is totally congruent with a single given mission. In essence the interface becomes one-sided. He must work downward to fulfill corporate-level expectations without a feedback channel to influence those expectations. His job is one of convincing subordinates of the necessity to conform to corporate-level expectations.

The opposite case would be characterized by a corporate-level expectation that the SBU manager will work with his segment managers to develop the appropriate disaggregated missions (and strategies) and that these will then be communicated upward for corporate review. In this instance the SBU manager becomes more of a formulator. He has the general approach specified (SBU grid-type analysis) but has total freedom in using this heuristic to determine the strategic missions.

Given these two polar cases one can see a spectrum between them with varying levels of absoluteness in the corporate-level categorization. The authors conjecture that the SBU manager's job will vary depending on the location on this spectrum. Hence an SBU manager should consciously strive to determine how absolute the corporate-level categorization is. Once this is determined, the SBU manager can structure his role (within the strategic planning system) in terms of an appropriate balance of formulation and implementation. This will then lead to the structuring of relationships with superiors and subordinates.

Differentiating Management across Missions

An inherent assumption of the SBU concept is that different businesses may have different strategic missions. Furthermore, as Bower showed, management systems and processes should be tailored to the strategy. Combining these two leads to the conclusion that different strategic missions require different types of management[5] or alternatively that management should be differentiated across strategic missions (e.g., a "star" and a "question mark" should be managed differently).

What components of management should be varied, and how should these components be varied? The appropriate guideline is to make variations across missions only when these variations will not frustrate aggregation or disaggregation. The authors have generally found that it is useful to make some variation of managerial selection, the reward system, and the capital budgeting system across strategic missions. This variation should occur at both levels of analysis.

It is a widely observed fact that some executives make excellent managers for certain "types" of businesses but are ineffective for other types. Such an observation is, of course, neither new nor revolutionary. What is new is that

---

[5] John W. Slocum, Jr., and Don Hellriegel, "Organizational Design: Which Way to Go?" *Business Horizons,* December, 1979.

the different strategic missions embodied in the portfolio concept provide a new and more specific template for measuring managers against the job. This template can and should be used at both the aggregated and disaggregated levels of analysis. As an example, the authors are aware of one corporation which uses a matrix similar to Figure 2 where a star mission is associated with an "analytical" type of manager, a cash cow with an "engineer" type, a question mark with a "salesman" type, and a dog with a "cost accountant" type. Executives in this firm indicate that although these stereotypes are far from completely accurate, they are roughly correct for many of the firm's managers. The important point is that in selecting a manager for a particular business, the fit between the style and personality of the manager and the strategic mission of the business should be a major consideration.

Another component of management which should be varied across the strategic missions is the reward system. The logic involved here is once again simple. A manager should be rewarded for performance against his assigned strategic mission as embodied in his strategic plan. Hence, for example, managers of cash cows should be rewarded for generating cash and managers of question marks should be rewarded for gaining competitive position even at the expense of current profits. One implication is that a manager of a question mark may receive a significant bonus for gaining competitive position even though profits were minimal and substantial investment funds were used from other businesses. On the other hand, a cash cow manager may receive no bonus because, although his ROI was substantial, it fell considerably below the agreed-upon objective in his plans. For example, General Electric differentiates the incentive compensation of SBU managers. Managers of "Harvest/divest" SBUs (see Figure 3) have the preponderance (72 percent) of incentive compensation based on current financial results while managers of "invest/grow" SBUs (see Figure 3) have only 40 percent of incentive compensation based on current financial performance with most of the remainder based on longer term goals. (In the "selectivity/earnings" SBUs a balance is struck between these two extremes.) The important point is that managerial motivations need to be aligned with differing strategic missions (aggregated or disaggregated) instead of a uniform corporate directive to increase earnings/ROI each year.

A final component of management that needs to be differentiated across strategic missions is capital budgeting. Resource allocation is one of the main (if not *the* main) levers[6] available to corporate management to ensure that the missions are implemented. To do this requires that the essence of justifying a capital project should revolve around the strategic mission. For example, a capital project for a question mark could have a relatively long payback and low return if the competitive position could be significantly improved. By contrast a capital project for a dog might require an immediate and high return to justify using funds there. As a further example, a government-mandated pollution control system should be almost automatically approved for a star, but with a dog abandonment would have to be

_____

[6] Joseph L. Bower, *Managing the Resource Allocation Process* (Homewood, Ill.: Richard D. Irwin, 1972).

considered. In general, specific criteria should be developed for approval of projects for each of the strategic missions and these criteria should be applied at the disaggregated and aggregated levels of analysis. In this manner resources can be distributed in congruence with the differing strategic missions.

The Alternative Approach: A Review

To summarize the alternative approach to implementing the SBU concept as the basis for a planning system, a short review should be useful.

The alternative approach starts with the assumption that in order to obtain a manageable number of SBUs at the corporate level and yet to reflect the full diversity and complexity of the firm's product/market structure, a hierarchical application of the analysis is necessary. At the corporate level of the hierarchy the authors' research shows that the practical upper limit is about 50 SBUs. The actual number will depend on the diversity of the firm, the management style of the CEO, and the amount and quality of staff support available. At the SBU level a disaggregated analysis of from 2 to 15 segments composes the second level of the hierarchy. (A further breakdown at the segment level may also be useful in some firms.) Hence, with two levels of hierarchy in the planning system, a product/market diversity of up to several hundred segments can be reflected.

To help coordinate the inputs between the two levels, specific mechanisms such as those suggested earlier need to be designed into the system. Furthermore, each level needs to recognize the legitimacy and necessity of the other level of analysis. As previously discussed, the SBU manager is probably the most important coordinating mechanism of all. As discussed, he must structure his role and relationships to match the absoluteness of the corporate-level categorization.

After the two levels of the hierarchy have been defined, certain management parameters (as discussed earlier) need to be varied across the varying strategic missions at both levels, the underlying assumption here being that different strategic missions require different types of management.

The alternative approach to implementation as just reviewed represents a significant departure from the basic model. The authors believe this departure overcomes many of the problems firms encounter in developing a strategic planning system based on the SBU concept. Complementing this approach is a new perspective on the use and meaning of the SBU concept in large, diversified firms.

The SBU Concept: A New Perspective

The basic model is essentially a dogmatic approach. It stresses a single uniform approach to implementation that is localized at the corporate level. Corporate-level executives (including staff assistance) unambiguously define the independent SBUs, evaluate them against the dimensions of the matrix, and assign the appropriate strategic mission. The basic model is essentially a corporate-level framework. The authors have found that a substantial appeal of this approach is that it promises to recentralize a significant portion of the business strategies. What CEO has not wished for additional control over the direction of individual businesses? Such control is illusory, however.

Instead of centralized control of business strategies, the authors believe the SBU concept offers a general approach to strategy development throughout the firm that can be matched to the specific circumstances of a business or managerial level, but still retain a uniformity of approach. Specifically the SBU concept is a common set of strategic assumptions and a common language for dealing with strategy in a diversified firm. Furthermore, both the language and the assumptions are independent of the individual characteristics of any particular business.

Inherent within the SBU concept is a common set of assumptions about strategy. This includes how the strategic mission of the business is established (by evaluation against the dimensions of the matrix). Furthermore, the strategic mission contains certain assumptions about the broad strategic role of a business. These assumptions are, in fact, the strategic mission. For example, a cash cow should generate substantial cash for deployment elsewhere. Similar assumptions are contained in any other strategic mission, regardless of the particular matrix used. Notice that these assumptions are independent of the detailed characteristics of any particular business. A cosmetics business and a home appliance business may have the same generic strategy even though the detailed nature of these two businesses is substantially different. Furthermore, the *method* of establishing or questioning this common strategic mission is the same (i.e., by evaluation against the dimensions of the matrix) and does not depend on the individual characteristics of the different businesses.

The SBU concept also provides a common language independent of the idiosyncrasies of any particular business for talking about strategy. The cosmetics business and the home appliance business can be discussed in terms that are independent of each business. There are, of course, many features of the total strategy, as opposed to the strategic mission, that can only be discussed in industry-specific terminology. Still, a significant, independent terminology is contained within the portfolio concept.

The implications of this common set of assumptions about strategy and common language for communicating about strategy are straightforward and yet significant. This set of assumptions and language permits the hierarchical determination of strategy discussed earlier while still maintaining a consistent and interrelated approach. The determination of a business's strategy can be logically split between the aggregated and disaggregated analyses, and yet consistency of approach and coordination between the two processes can be maintained. Furthermore, strategic communication is facilitated both horizontally and vertically.

Contrast this to the situation without the SBU concept. Here the strategies are seen as entirely dependent on detailed knowledge about the specific businesses. A common view of strategy was set forth by Andrews[7] in *The Concept of Corporate Strategy.* Consider the following from this book:

---

[7] Kenneth R. Andrews, *The Concept of a Corporate Strategy* (Homewood, Ill.: Richard D. Irwin, 1971).

Deciding what the strategy should be is, at least ideally, a rational undertaking. Its principal subactivities include identifying opportunities and threats in the company's environment and attaching some estimate of risk to the discernible alternatives. Before a choice can be made, the company's strengths and weaknesses must be appraised. Its actual or potential capacity to take advantage of perceived market needs or to cope with attendant risk must be estimated as objectively as possible. The strategic alternative which results from a matching of opportunity with corporate capability at an acceptable level of risk is what we may call an economic strategy. (p. 37)

Notice how Andrews' concept of strategy is highly dependent on idiosyncratic knowledge of a particular business. Specifically, one must be knowledgeable of both the environment (threats and opportunities) and the internal strengths and weaknesses, and this requires in-depth knowledge of the business. Furthermore, for each business in a diversified firm this knowledge will be substantially different. The only generally imposed strategic direction from the corporate level will be the imperative to "maximize or improve earnings/ROI" in each business. There is no generally shared set of assumptions (i.e., question marks should rapidly gain competitive position) and no common language for talking about strategy under this approach. The business strategies become highly decentralized at the divisional or product/ market profit center level. It is difficult or impossible for managers not directly involved to understand and hence question the strategy of a particular business. Contrast this to the situation under the SBU concept, where the same language and assumptions are used by managers throughout the firm. Although many components of a business strategy must still be developed within the guidelines suggested by Andrews, the language and assumptions of the portfolio concept still provide the core of the strategy. It would seem that the SBU concept can be used in large, diversified firms to facilitate and rationalize strategy throughout the firm. However, this can only be achieved by adopting a flexible viewpoint instead of the dogmatic approach of an unambiguous corporate-level strategy framework. Such a flexible viewpoint incorporates the features discussed and illustrated previously: (1) recognition by corporate management that SBUs *cannot* be unambiguously defined as uniform, independent entities, each with a single, assigned, monolithic mission; (2) a hierarchical planning system with substantial involvement at all levels; (3) mechanisms for coordinating the different levels within the planning system; and (4) matching of selective components of management to strategic missions.

What this article is about: CIBA-GEIGY's experiences with acquisitions are summarized in the form of 10 suggestions to consider in an acquisition program. If these suggestions are followed, the author believes the result will be stronger, more profitable companies.

3-3 Ten suggestions for acquisition success*

Robert J. Terry

Robert J. Terry is vice president for planning and analysis of the CIBA-GEIGY Corporation.

Last summer, in the heat of the fierce bidding battle for Conoco, press criticism of acquisitions and mergers was also heating up. *Time* magazine expressed some "Big Doubts about Big Deals." *Newsweek* explored "The New Urge to Merge," and wondered "Is Business Getting Too Big?" *Fortune* was a lonely holdout on the newsstand as it pleaded, "Don't Stop the Mating Game."

Some people are very critical of acquisitions and mergers, saying that they take money away from capital investment. "America is sinking in a productivity swamp," they say, "struggling against foreign competition . . . staggering under high interest rates and runaway inflation. And what are its largest corporations up to? They're not spending their money constructing factories . . . or creating jobs . . . or increasing R&D. Instead, they're gobbling each other up."

Fortunately, some economic observers have a more encouraging view. They say that acquisitions lead to economies of scale that improve productivity in the long run and eventually show up in lower prices for consumers.

So, to acquire or not to acquire: that is the question. Whether 'tis nobler to grow through acquisition . . . or to expand internally through increased R&D and capital investment. But do we have to make a choice? Can't we do both?

---

* This article is reprinted from *Managerial Planning* 31, no. 5 (September–October 1982), pp. 13–16. Copyright © 1982, by the Planning Executives Institute, Oxford, Ohio.

CIBA-GEIGY has done both. We spend 8 percent of our sales on R&D—more than most other chemical companies. But, during the 1970s, we also embarked upon an acquisition program. It was ambitious, and I think it was also successful.

I'd like to tell you about our acquisition program and share some of the lessons we've learned. I don't believe we have all the answers about acquisitions. But I do believe that we understand some of the questions. The reader may be able to benefit from our mistakes, as well as our successes.

CIBA-GEIGY itself is the product of a merger. It was formed in 1970 by combining two large Swiss chemical companies, CIBA and Geigy—companies of almost the same size but very different management styles. One of the reasons for the merger was the rising cost of research in both companies. Leaders of the two firms agreed that a merger could make their research expenditures more productive.

CIBA's strengths in pharmaceuticals and epoxy resins and Geigy's strengths in agricultural chemicals and polymer additives complemented each other. The result was a much stronger competitor in the international chemical industry.

In the United States, CIBA-GEIGY has four divisions—Agricultural, Pharmaceuticals, Dyestuffs and Chemicals, and Plastics and Additives—plus Airwick Industries, a subsidiary. Our U.S. sales are about a quarter of the worldwide total. Our parent would like us to increase this amount. That was part of the reason for the acquisition program that I'm about to describe.

During the 70s, CIBA-GEIGY made 19 acquisitions in the United States. The purchase prices ranged from under a million dollars to almost $100 million. All together we spent about $300 million on the program—rather meager in comparison to what Du Pont paid to acquire Conoco, but a significant amount for CIBA-GEIGY.

Why This Acquisition Program?

First, we wanted to improve our competitive position by reducing our dependence on a few products. In 1975, a quarter of our sales came from one product—AAtrex, a corn herbicide. We expected a big loss of sales when our patent expired in 1976. Also, several of our other businesses, such as dyestuffs and epoxy resins, were becoming mature.

Second, we wanted to complement our internal R&D. As I noted earlier, we're strongly committed to basic chemical and pharmaceutical research. However, it seemed to us that, in many cases, it's cheaper to buy than it is to build, and it's faster too.

For instance, take our acquisition of the Hercules pigments business. We had been importing our pigments from Europe and were searching for an alternative. Our choices were to abandon the business—a business where we had research, technological know-how, and customers—or to build our own plants from scratch in the United States—or to go shopping. The first choice—abandonment—was unacceptable. The second—construction—made no sense financially. So we went shopping, and acquired the Hercules pigments operation.

The Hercules purchase, and most of our other acquisitions, were designed to complement internal strengths. We have R&D know-how in chemistry; we have experience in making specialty chemicals; and we have experience in marketing them. But we realized that this knowledge and experience would not necessarily enable us to make and sell hamburgers, for instance, because we clearly have no understanding of the fast-food industry.

Third, we wanted to cushion ourselves against the growing regulatory burden. Several of CIBA-GEIGY's core businesses—pharmaceuticals and agricultural chemicals, for instance—are highly regulated. In fact, the entire chemical industry is becoming one of the most regulated businesses in this country. Having other legs to stand on, where we don't have to satisfy an FDA or and EPA, helps to lighten the regulatory burden.

Those three reasons—a desire to reduce our dependence on a few products, a desire to complement our internal strengths, and a desire to expand into less regulated industries—sent us looking for suitable corporate partners.

How did our search work out? We're reasonably pleased with the results. We made some mistakes. But given the number of acquisitions we made, and the relatively short time in which we made them, winners still outnumber losers.

Ten Suggestions to Consider In an Acquisition Program

There are so many unknowns in the process of buying and selling companies that it can hardly be called a pure science. Anyone who's been involved in a successful acquisition has some pet theories about the process. Based on our experience, I've compiled 10 suggestions for those who may be considering an acquisition program.

First, *establish acquisition criteria*. And make sure everyone agrees on what those criteria are.

Buying a business is something like shopping in a supermarket. It helps to have a shopping list before you leave for the store. If you don't have a list, you may find yourself buying groceries, or businesses, that you don't need, just because they're available on the shelves. During the course of your acquisition program, you may stray, as we sometimes did, from the criteria on your shopping list, just as you sometimes buy an item or two on impulse at the market. But that's no excuse for not having a shopping list to start with.

At CIBA-GEIGY, we said our acquisition candidates should be in growing markets, should have patented products or well-known brand names in their field, should be able to benefit from our R&D know-how, should be product-oriented, rather than service-oriented, should have sales of at least $50 million, should be able to yield a return on investment of at least 15 percent, and should have a top purchase price of $400 million. Then, having made our shopping list, we headed for the acquisition supermarket.

Second, *if you think you see synergies, make sure they're real*.

Professor Rumelt of UCLA has published a study of acquisitions made by the 500 largest industrial companies over a 25-year period. He concluded that the best results were achieved by companies that diversified into areas of related skills or resources. The poorest results were achieved by companies that diversified into totally unrelated areas. An article in the current issue of *Fortune* magazine called "The Bottom Line on Ten Big Mergers of 1971" reached a similar conclusion.

An example of real synergism is Herbishield brand sorghum seed, which was developed jointly by our Agricultural Division and one of its acquisitions, Funk Seeds. Before Funk introduced Herbishield three years ago, sorghum growers couldn't use certain CIBA-GEIGY herbicides because they would damage the seed. Herbishield changed that. The sorghum seed is treated with a herbicide antidote, which protects the sorghum seedlings from the active ingredient in the herbicide. Funk has significantly increased its sorghum seed sales, and the Ag Division has increased its sales of herbicides to sorghum growers. Everybody's happy.

Another example of synergy is CIBA-GEIGY's investment in ALZA Corporation. ALZA's area of strength is in inventing unique drug delivery systems—a strength in research and technology. We teamed ALZA's strength with CIBA-GEIGY's strengths in pharmacology and in pharmaceutical marketing. The result: the first transdermal drug delivery system. It delivers the drug right through the skin and is used to combat motion sickness. We also have a second transdermal system on the market, containing nitroglycerin. Other new products combining unique ALZA delivery systems with CIBA-GEIGY drugs are in the development pipeline.

Third, *don't try to go into a completely new field* by telling yourself that good managers can manage anything. They can't. They can't because every industry has its own culture and it's own language. Perhaps any language can be learned, but by the time you learn it, the acquisition could be going down the drain.

We learned this lesson with Airwick's Pool Products business, which we'd acquired by accident rather than by plan. Airwick had acquired Pool Products shortly before we acquired Airwick itself. It came with the deal. But we were saddled with a business we didn't really want and didn't know anything about. We kept telling ourselves that swimming pool chemicals were somehow related to our other chemicals businesses, but they weren't. We never gave Pool Products the R&D support it needed, and the financial results were disappointing. In the end we sold Pool Products to a company in the mainstream of that industry.

Fourth, *don't pay more for the acquisition than it's worth*. W. T. Grimm & Co. says that price premiums were averaging 41 percent above market price in 1975. That figure rose to 50 percent by 1980. Some were far above the averages.

To avoid this pitfall, put a ceiling on your acquisition budget. Then stick to it. Decide what return on investment you need to get. At CIBA-GEIGY, we make the same internal rate of return calculations for acquisitions as we do for capital investments.

Fifth, *don't think small*. We found that Charles S. Tanner Company, the little $12 million company we wanted to tuck neatly into our Dyestuffs and Chemicals Division, took almost as much overall effort as the acquisition of the $50 million Airwick business. So you might as well go for the larger one—if it matches your acquisition criteria and if you can smoothly fold it into your operation.

There's a corollary to this. You don't have to be a big company to make an acquisition. CIBA-GEIGY has become 25 percent larger in the United States, and a lot stronger, through acquisitions. Keep in mind, too, that you don't have to buy an entire company. More business segments are being purchased, as opposed to whole companies. Five of our 19 acquisitions were parts of companies.

Sixth, *consider the quality of management in the acquired firm.* "Acquire and fire" is not a good policy. But don't just hold on to the managers you acquire—listen to them. They probably know their business a lot better than you do; at least in the beginning.

When Airwick first told us about its idea for Carpet Fresh—a powder that you sprinkle on the carpet, then vacuum up again, leaving a fresh, clean scent—there was a lot of disbelief among many members of CIBA-GEIGY's management. We didn't know much about consumer product market research and marketing. But we did have the good sense to listen to the management at Airwick. Carpet Fresh created a whole new product category—rug and room deodorizers. If imitation is the sincerest form of flattery, we're doing spectacularly. There's been a rash of "me-too" products, yet Carpet Fresh still holds a 43 percent share of the new $70 million category which it created.

Seventh, *don't overacquire.* Allow enough time to digest, integrate, and consolidate the acquisitions you make. Particularly, if you make a lot in a short period of time.

Our 19 acquisitions were made in three distinct phases. We bought two small companies during the early 70s. In 1974, after we decided to undertake a major acquisitions program, we bought Funk Seeds, Airwick, and Charles S. Tanner Company. Then we took a breather, partly dictated by the recession, but mostly to digest those sizable purchases. In the late 1970s we bought another 14 businesses. Now, once again, we're in a holding pattern. Looking back, our last push to diversify was too fast. We didn't allow enough time for some of our acquisitions to blend smoothly into our company. Our profits fell during the late 1970s, partly because of this too rapid acquisitions push. So we stopped short, consolidated, and put our house in order.

Eighth, *be prepared for surprises.* In other words, allow for some acquisition indigestion. Have some Tums or Rolaids handy. Sometimes the only way to spell relief is *d–i–v–e–s–t.*

One of our "tickets on the heartburn express" was Charles S. Tanner. Tanner had on the drawing board a new plant to produce EVA polymers. They, and we, thought the polymers would be very useful in the textile industry. When the plant was finished, it turned out that the textile industry didn't want the product. Most of the demand for the polymers was in the adhesives market. We recognized that our expertise is in textiles, not adhesives, so we sold Tanner to National Starch.

Another surprise was Hamblet and Hayes. It had leather tanning and finishing chemicals that we thought would complement our Dyestuffs and

Chemicals Division sales to the leather industry. Hamblet and Hayes has done very well, but not because of its sales to the leather industry. The leather industry is in a slump. But the acquisition included an excellent chemical distribution business. That business has grown steadily since we acquired Hamblet and Hayes in 1978. So that acquisition surprised us too, but pleasantly.

Ninth, *have patience*—lots of it. It may take a long time to reach an acceptable level of profitability.

When we bought Airwick, there were practically no competitors for solid air fresheners. But almost before the ink was dry on the closing papers, S. C. Johnson introduced a competitive product to Airwick Solid—at a lower price. Airwick declined rapidly from a profitable business to a break-even business. But then Airwick brought out some innovative products—Stick Ups, and then Carpet Fresh. By 1980, it had grown sixfold.

I've already related Funk Seeds' success with Herbishield. When we bought Funk, we found that the company was taking its research in an entirely different direction from the type of seed genetics which interested us. Now the company's on track with its research, and the synergy between Funk and our Ag Division has been proven. We're beginning to see financial success—eight years after the purchase.

Which brings me to my last piece of advice. *Don't hang on too long* hoping that losses will turn into profits. We didn't want the Pool business when we got it as part of the Airwick acquisition. But we kept it for seven years before we finally pulled the plug.

Summary

To summarize these 10 points again briefly: Establish acquisition criteria. Make sure the apparent synergies are real. Don't try to diversify into a completely new field. Don't overpay. Don't think small. Consider the quality of management. Allow time for integration. Be prepared for surprises. Be patient, but don't hang on too long.

I stated earlier that I didn't have nice pat answers about whether to start an acquisition program. That's because there are no nice pat answers. What seems important to me in appraising acquisitions is the end result. Will there be increased productivity? Will there be a stronger competitive position? Will there be more effective R&D? Will there be a better bottom line? If the answers are yes, then the acquisition route may be the one to take.

Many acquisitions result in stronger, more profitable companies; companies that can deliver high-quality products at reasonable prices. Other corporate marriages are ill-conceived, poorly executed, almost destined to fail before they're consummated. "To acquire or not to acquire" is a question that all present-day Hamlets and their companies will have to decide for themselves.

What this article is about: Successful acquisition requires judgment and sensitivity along with accurate information and careful analysis. The author describes the steps in conducting research and evaluation, developing an approach strategy, making the initial contact, and beginning negotiations. He explains how acquiring companies can avoid the numerous pitfalls at each stage and successfully differentiate themselves from other bidders.

3-4 Making it happen: How to execute an acquisition*

David R. Willensky

David R. Willensky is director of research for McKinsey & Co., Inc., in Los Angeles. Previously he was manager of corporate development for Telecor, Inc.

How to plan an acquisition and how to integrate an acquired company into the parent organization are two topics that have generated more than their share of books and articles over the years. In contrast, what comes between planning and integration—everything from contacting the prospective partner to signing the final papers—remains virtually unexplored in the literature. Yet these activities, comprising the actual execution of an acquisition, can tax management's time, energy, and negotiating skills most heavily. It is here that many business combinations are made or broken.

In view of the importance of this execution stage, the gap in the literature is remarkable. To help fill it, this article, drawing on the collective experience of some seasoned practitioners, outlines a practical approach to one category of mergers and acquisitions: those "friendly" transactions, typically initiated by the buyer, where operating management represents the selling shareholders in the negotiations and normally will be retained for some time after the acquisition has been consummated.[1]

In the words of one prominent investment banker specializing in acquisitions, "Execution is more important than ever today because of changing techniques, strategies, and competitive forces." Sellers are becoming more sophisticated, while the rivalry among deep-pocketed corporate buyers for attractive acquisition candidates has intensified. In a seller's market, the buyer who has something extra to offer usually increases his chances of

---

* This article is reprinted from *Business Horizons,* March–April 1985, pp. 38–45.

[1] There is, of course, another major subset of mergers and acquisitions in which a company becomes the target of a takeover attempt as a consequence of incumbent management's real or alleged failure to put the company's assets to best use. Such acquisitions, if they result in more efficient economic utilization of the assets in question, may, like the friendly transactions to be discussed here, benefit both the owners and society as a whole; but the strategic and tactical considerations involved in the two cases are worlds apart.

success. In the corporate marketplace, however, that "something extra" does not necessarily mean dollars—witness several recent competitive bid situations where the highest bidder failed to win for reasons ostensibly unrelated to price. Frequent accounts of misguided acquisitions have alerted desirable candidates to the pitfalls that may lurk in the nonfinancial aspects of business combinations. And as sellers become more wary, enlightened corporate buyers are beginning to recognize that they no longer can count on conventional techniques and price considerations alone to achieve their goals. To succeed, they must find ways during the execution phase to differentiate themselves from other bidders.

Execution, however, is more art than science. Experience, judgment, and human sensitivity are as important as information and analysis in arriving at the correct decisions and taking the right actions at the right time. The acquirer will much improve his chances of success if his approach reflects a recognition that each acquisition is unique. And since even willing sellers generally have mixed feelings about being acquired, the acquirer will be wise to position the proposed transaction as more merger than acquisition.

Because of the many uncertainties and imponderables in the execution process—not least the human element—there can be no infallible system or formula for success. This article merely describes how some successful acquirers improve their chances of reaching agreement, skirting the numerous pitfalls along the way that stretches from candidate research and evaluation, through the formulation and execution of an approach strategy, to the signing of the final agreement.

Conducting In-Depth Research and Evaluation

The part played by "outside-in" research and evaluation during the execution phase depends to some extent on the origin of the merger idea and the way the candidate first becomes known to the buyer. When the first contact between potential acquirer and potential acquiree comes about as a result of the latter's initiative, "outside-in" research and candidate evaluation become the first steps in the execution of an acquisition. In the other cases, when the candidate has been identified as the result of searching and screening by the would-be acquirer, considerable research on the potential acquisition will already have been done before the initial contact takes place.

In either situation, external, market-oriented research normally will be called for as a background to thoughtful examination of the factors underlying the candidate's competitive position and financial performance. Later, when the seller has granted access to his organization, the evaluation can be expanded to encompass operating, organizational, technological, and other issues requiring direct exposure to the candidate's people, plans, and facilities. After he has gotten "behind the numbers" and understands the economics of the candidate's business, the buyer will be better positioned to determine the company's value to him. To determine the price range that value implies, he will need to identify and analyze a range of financial and strategic issues, including:

• The investment/value creation trade-off applicable to alternative future performance scenarios, and the maximum price suggested by each.

- The sources and range of downside risk and upside potential.
- The financial impact of the transaction on the buyer, especially its cash flow, balance sheet, and stock market implications.
- Post-merger deployment of top management and first-level executives.
- Options for structuring the transaction.[2]

The level of effort this in-depth candidate evaluation requires will depend on the experience and caliber of the analysts and the availability of needed information. Before deciding to pay $1 billion for Beckman Instruments in 1982, SmithKline Corporation invested more than 500 man-hours in candidate research and evaluation. At the other extreme, at least one experienced acquirer—Insilco, a $600 million manufacturer of high-technology and specialty consumer products—claims that it is normally prepared to close a deal within two weeks after a candidate has been identified.

Other factors influencing the level of effort required for evaluation are the buyer's familiarity with the candidate's business, the amount of candidate-specific research already done in the course of preacquisition planning, the nature and extent of issues requiring further analysis, and the probability that initial contact will lead to serious discussions, thereby justifying the necessary expenditure of resources.

The importance of in-depth, timely candidate evaluation in today's "caveat emptor" acquisition environment can be seen in the case of a large, diversified drug company that acquired a young, fast-growing manufacturer of advanced medical equipment. In announcing the deal, the acquirer justified its high offering price by citing the candidate's leading market position in rapidly growing market segments. Since then, however, the parent company has discovered that the growth projections were highly exaggerated, that bad working relationships between R&D and manufacturing have repeatedly led to trouble in bringing promised new products to market, and that discord is rife among the top executives of its costly new subsidiary.

Developing the Approach Strategy

A carefully planned approach strategy can smooth the would-be acquirer's way and materially increase the chances of an outcome satisfactory to both parties. Once contact has been made, it enables the buyer to differentiate himself favorably from other would-be acquirers: even more important, it reduces the risk of things going wrong once discussions have begun. In the words of a classic Chinese treatise on military strategy dating from the sixth century B.C., "He who excels at resolving difficulties does so before they arise." In terms of the acquisition process, that implies an execution plan that anticipates events during the negotiation process, allows for contingencies, and provides an overall framework for the interactions between the parties. Willard F. Rockwell, past chairman of Rockwell International and

---

[2] For specific methodologies for in-depth candidate analysis and evaluation, see Alfred Rappaport, "Strategic Analysis for More Profitable Acquisitions," *Harvard Business Review,* July–August 1979, pp. 99–110; and Michael E. Porter, *Competitive Strategy—Techniques for Analyzing Industries and Competitors* (New York: Free Press, 1980).

architect of many merger transactions, puts the point crisply: "Conducting an acquistion is like playing chess. You do not plan just your next move; you plot out the whole game."

Create Theme

An effective approach strategy has two main elements: a thoughtful rationale or theme that brings out the mutual benefits of a proposed transaction to both parties, and a systematic plan of contact. Some successful buyers develop such a theme during the early planning stage when general corporate acquisition objectives and investment criteria are first spelled out, then refine it to fit individual candidates as they are identified. Others wait until initial contact has been made and encourage seller management to participate in developing and articulating the rationale for the business combination. The circumstances surrounding each transaction and the personal styles of those involved will dictate which approach offers the greatest prospect of success.

Ideally, a convincing rationale should show how the strengths of the buyer—for example, superior marketing skills, low-cost production facilities—dovetail with the candidate's objectives, and vice versa. At a minimum, the theme should set forth:

1. The potential business advantage for each party (for example, access to new technology for the buyer, stronger distribution channels for the seller).
2. The candidate's place in the new organization (for example, autonomous subsidiary, new business sector, broader responsibility for the candidate's management), and the deployment of the candidate's management group.
3. Potential benefits to the various stakeholders of the seller oganization, especially its shareholders. (In a cash transaction, buy-out price is usually the key variable; in a stock transaction, long-term value to shareholders is key.)

One company that used such a theme to good advantage is a European manufacturer of consumer products. It decided, after extensive study, that diversification into the U.S. market would be the most promising route to continued profitable growth. To secure an entry vehicle into the U.S. market and serve as a base for acquisitions, it first established a well-funded holding company, then set about searching for and screening potential partners. Eventually it settled on a leading U.S. consumer products manufacturer as its preferred flag-ship candidate. In making its approach, it stressed how the parent's capital resources and global consumer marketing know-how could help the combination achieve high long-term process and outlined the candidate's potential leadership role in the new holding company. Thanks to the care management had taken to develop a credible rationale and the sensitivity it displayed to the needs of the candidate's management, the transaction went off with exemplary smoothness.

The combination of a responsive theme and realistic pricing recently helped American Standard, a large international producer of building products, to win a three-way race to own Trane Company, a leading U.S. air

Figure 1
Illustrative acquisition themes

Acquiring Company	Theme	Representative Acquisitions
Penn Central	Acquire high-profit, high-growth industrial companies with leadership positions in markets subject to minimal government regulation: retain management, shelter earnings with substantial tax loss carryovers and integrate into parent holding company with strong divisional operating chiefs	G.K. Technologies Marathon Manufacturing Williams Energy
Hughes Tool	Reduce dependence on drilling side of energy business by acquiring small companies with proprietary technology in production segment; add Hughes name and distribution to achieve rapid growth	Byron-Jackson Oil Base Regan Offshore Brown Oil Tools Centrilift
Gould	Transform company into a broad-line, integrated producer of electronics products for factory automation markets	Modicon DeAnza Systems Systems Eng. Labs
Emerson Electric	Acquire high-cost-structure companies with superior products that could benefit from Emerson's cost-reduction skills	Appleton Electric Skil Xomox
General Mills	Acquire and build small companies that could benefit from GM's expertise in marketing services and products to upscale consumers	Good Earth Restaurants Lark Luggage Ship 'n Shore
General Foods	Acquire food processing companies likely to benefit from GF's research, raw material procurement, and distribution capabilities	Entenmann's Oscar Mayer
Beatrice Foods	Acquire regional companies and use parent's nationwide marketing distribution expertise to build volume	Tropicana Phoenix Candy Martha White Foods

conditioner manufacturer. According to press accounts, American Standard was able to show convincingly how both parties stood to benefit from a combination: Trane would provide American Standard with a broadened, nonoverlapping product line in existing markets, while American Standard would help Trane enter and compete in international markets. Trane's top management was assured of its importance to the company's continued success, and American Standard's CEO publicly declared that his counterpart at Trane would help run the parent company.

These are only two examples of themes that helped to differentiate the buyer in the seller's mind. Others are briefly outlined in Figure 1.

Even though price, more often than not, will become the central issue at some point in the merger negotiations, a carefully developed theme that focuses on the other distinctive advantages of a proposed combination can sometimes provide the decisive edge. In any case, by describing the combined entity envisioned by the buyer, such a rationale provides a common frame of reference that can keep neogiations from breaking down over potentially explosive minor issues.

Even where a "not for sale" sign is apparently up and price inducements seem to be unavailing, a candidate may be persuaded by a convincing written rationale supported by appropriate analyses. As one experienced acquirer puts it, "The seller's top management people always have a strong interest in the nonfinancial aspects of a merger. It may be latent, but it's there."

Devise Contact Plan

The other element of a successful approach strategy is a well-though-out plan of contact that identifies the key people associated with the target company and sets out preferred methods and timing for the initial and subsequent approaches, taking likely contingencies into account.

Large shareholders, directors, and officers are all potential audiences for a buyer's message. Often it is far from obvious which might prove to be the most effective initial communications channel. Advice on this point from investment bankers may be vital. In any case, how the first contact should be made will depend to a considerable extent on who the real decision makers are, and whether the candidate was identified through an active search, or, so to speak, just walked in the door. Michael Rolland, managing director of Warburg Paribas Becker, believes that "the way in which you bring two parties together is as important as the idea that perhaps these people ought to be partners."

Who should make the initial contact? In cases where the two chief executives know one another, the answer is usually obvious. Even where they don't, it is sometimes best to make the first approach "top-to-top." As one investment banker remarks, "A chief executive is apt to react better to a peer." But another tells his clients, "You can go ahead and make the call, but remember: If a banker gets thrown out, he can always go back in a second time. You can't."

When the companies concerned are strangers to each other, there is certainly a case for using recognized intermediaries such as bankers, lawyers, or consultants. But no general rules apply, except that the would-be acquirer, when planning the initial contact, needs to be sensitive to the potential seller's psychology. A tactical false step at this point can cripple the discussions from the start. A good many promising business combinations never get off the ground for reasons having little to do with business.

The manner in which the initial contact is made is at least as critical as the choice of messenger. Several years ago, when Seagram Company launched an unsolicited bid for St. Joe Minerals, St. Joe management first heard the news when Seagram's lawyers filed the required documents with government agencies. Predictably, they were not amused. While St. Joe apparently had several motives for rejecting Seagram's overtures, Jack Duncan, then chairman, was quoted as saying, "If Seagram had talked to us first, we might have reached an agreement." Instead, Fluor Corporation entered the picture and ultimately purchased St. Joe for $2.7 billion.

Too direct and blunt an approach can be equally counterproductive, however. Consider the example of a major consumer-oriented company that attempted, a few years ago, to buy a big soft-drink bottler. Reportedly, the would-be buyer's chairman simply picked up the phone, rang his counterpart at the bottling company, and blandly informed him of the takeover plan. Astonished and angered, the bottling company chairman immediately persuaded his board to seek bids from friendlier companies. After battling the would-be acquirer in the press and in federal court, the company was finally sold to a less high-handed partner.

Increasingly, acquisition experts deplore such unilateral, spur-of-the-moment approaches. They argue in favor of a systematic, carefully orchestrated, long-term approach. A vice president of a leading Wall Street firm notes that more and more buyers make a practice of identifying companies they believe are likely to be sold in the next three to five years and cultivate contacts with members of top management and/or major shareholders, letting their personal interest be known. Seller-initiated contact, they reason, enhances the buyer's prospects and negotiating leverage. By keeping in touch with a possible future acquisition and monitoring developments over time, a buyer will increase his chances of being approached when and if the candidate decides to sell.

EG&G, a $700 million manufacturer of electronic products with a voracious appetite for small technology-based companies, has systematized the process thoroughly. Each of its operating groups maintains a regularly updated list of acquisition targets, which are closely monitored for signs of any inclination to sell. United Technologies maintains an updated dossier on each of 50 or so attractive acquisition candidates that fit in well with its stated mission as an integrated supplier of high-technology systems. Four years ago, when Mostek, Inc., spurned the advances of another would-be acquirer, United Technologies was able to respond quickly with a successful offer.

Another compelling reason for the increasing use of this type of approach is candidate xenophobia. Understandably, most sellers are disposed to favor the familiar suitor over the total stranger, at least if the price is equal. When the CEO (and majority shareholder) of a profitable and well-known producer of specialty food products decided to sell his closely held company, he and his board sought offers only from those qualified potential buyers who had shown interest during the previous three years.

Making Initial Contact

Once the approach strategy has been developed and steps have been taken to set up an initial meeting between CEOs, the buyer approaches a critical go/no-go point. Says one investment banker, "The purpose of the first meeting is to make sure there's a second meeting"—in other words, to build goodwill and gain the seller's agreement to proceed with discussions. But there is more to it than that. Besides giving the would-be buyer his first chance to explore the theme of cooperative growth, this meeting will enable him to gauge the candidate's interest and to judge whether the personal chemistry between them seems to promise a successful working relationship.

Experience suggests three important tactical requirements for success at this juncture. First, the would-be buyer should *keep the first meeting small and relatively informal* in order to build personal rapport with his counterpart. Second, the *site should be chosen with care.* A neutral location is usually preferable to the buyer's or seller's turf, especially when it is important to foster a "merger" atmosphere. Finally, the *agenda should be flexible and discussions kept fairly general,* so that negotiations will not bog down prematurely in details and perhaps even be brought to a halt. In initial merger talks between Crane Corporation and Westinghouse Air Brake some years ago, Crane management reportedly pushed for an early discussion on organization and compensation issues. Westinghouse, unfortunately, interpreted this as an attempt to "buy" top management, an issue that became an important element of Westinghouse's successful defense against the takeover.

Once the buyer has had an opportunity to tell his story, it is important to reach explicit agreement on next steps. More than one merger discussion has broken down because the candidate mistook the buyer's intentions or the buyer misjudged the candidate's level of interest at the outset. A case in point was one conglomerate's abortive attempt to acquire a large manufacturer of recreational products. At an initial meeting, the conglomerate's CEO apparently misinterpreted the response to his proposal. After the meeting, he sent the candidate's chief executive a letter announcing an offer for the company's shares. Within hours, the candidate's top management group had gathered to plan its defense. Three days later, it publicly attacked the would-be acquirer, which ultimately backed off when the candidate, in an extreme defense maneuver, sold off its most profitable subsidiary to a third party.

To prevent such blunders and reduce the chance of unwelcome surprises, the buyer is well advised to make every effort at the first meeting to get a clear commitment from the candidate to proceed—ideally, to meet on a specified date to begin more formal discussions.

Beginning Negotiations

When and if exploratory discussions have convinced both buyer and seller that the proposed combination makes sense, negotiations should begin promptly to avoid loss of momentum.

Most successful merger practitioners strive for early agreement on the broad conceptual underpinnings of the proposed combination—how and why the two companies will fit together, broad organizational issues, transaction structure and terms. They avoid, at this stage, specifics such as proposed purchase price, who will report to whom, or which units will be liquidated. Here a visionary growth theme based on mutual accommodation can be immensely helpful. No less important is an appreciation of the motives and objectives of the seller's management team. Says a senior director of Lehman Brothers, "You spend more time trying to structure how the people will get together than you do on structuring whether the deal is part cash, part stock, or preferred."

When it comes time to address specific details, the negotiating positions of both parties should incorporate their ideas as to how the transaction might be structured and how valuation ought to be approached. All the negotiating team members on both sides—corporate officers, major shareholders, and/or outside professionals such as investment bankers, lawyers, or consultants—should, of course, be fully briefed on all these points by their respective parties.

Once buyer and seller have decided to pursue a transaction, investment bankers generally can provide advice on a fair price—"fair" not in the sense of "worth acquiring" but in the sense of how much, given the current market, the buyer should expect to have to pay. Whether the deal is a good one from a strategic standpoint for either party depends heavily on their respective situations and objectives, matters an investment banker is rarely in a position to judge. Says one experienced merger practitioner: "Relying on your investment banker for strategic judgments is like giving a plumber the job of designing your new bathroom instead of going to an architect."

How should the negotiation process be orchestrated, and who should be the conductor? Tony Hass, General Foods' chief merger negotiator, believes that there is a "natural rhythm" to the negotiation process.[3] "At best," Hass says, "it's like a beautiful tennis match where everyone has a smooth stroke. But if the rhythm gets interrupted, discussions may break down." To minimize such disruptions, Hass and other successful buyers try to keep control of the meeting dates, regulating the flow of discussions and key events so as to forestall the misgivings and second thoughts that tend to arise in the intervals between negotiating sessions. As another investment banker puts it: "Any time you can speed something up, you eliminate some risk. Risk is inherent in time."

The experience of active merger practitioners suggests a handful of other basic negotiating guidelines for the buyer.

1. *Maintain direct CEO-to-CEO contact.* This normally facilitates quick reactions to issues raised, offers concrete evidence of the candidate's importance to the buyer, and can provide a safety valve if talks should bog down.
2. *Assign responsibility for day-to-day negotiations to a single senior executive.* The risk of mixed or even contradictory messages is much reduced if a single lead negotiator is made responsible for managing the activities of his team and for monitoring and coordinating requests for information.
3. *Ascertain the exact authority of the seller's lead negotiator,* and ensure that the issues to be discussed already have been reviewed by the appropriate management and board committees, lawyers, auditors, and others.
4. *If a finder is involved, get him out of the picture.* Do this diplomatically; he may have a close relationship with the candidate. As a rule, the finder lacks clear-cut authority and is less than objective. At best, he introduces a further element of uncertainty; at worst, his presence can doom the negotiations.
5. *Define and communicate a consistent message on the key issues*— organizational fit, level of autonomy, valuation methodology, synergistic opportunities, and so on. Try to develop a sense of how far the other party is willing to go on these issues, so you will know whether and when to back off. Have an alternative.
6. *Concentrate on understanding the motives and objectives of the candidate's management* in order to identify any issues on which you may be able to differentiate your company and improve your chances of reaching an agreement.
7. *Maintain strict confidentiality.* Leaks to third parties could force your

---

[3] See "Dealmaker Profile," *Mergers and Acquisitions,* Fall 1982, pp. 19–21.

hand during negotiations, in effect inviting other bidders into the picture.

Merger negotiations, like any others, can be viewed as a process aimed at realizing common interests and achieving compromise on points of conflict. Both parties involved are naturally pursuing their own interests, but it often turns out that these overlap more than was apparent at the outset. Moreover, individual perceptions of self-interest may well shift during negotiations in such a way as to enlarge the area of overlap.

A would-be acquirer who goes into negotiations with the idea of "winning" usually hurts his chances of a long-range success. In a transaction based on sound planning, analysis, and realistic mutual accommodation, everyone wins—though everyone may not aways be prepared to admit it. Says one attorney specializing in merger negotiations: "If neither side is crowing over the outcome, it's probably a fair deal for both sets of shareholders."

Reaching Agreement

Reaching agreement on price and terms is the culmination of the negotiating process. Some merger advisors argue that the buyer can best protect his interests by preparing a letter of intent (or agreement in principle) and presenting it to the candidate at an appropriate moment, preferably early in the negotiations. They concede, however, that unilateral action should be pursued with caution when there is a risk of antagonizing or scaring off a skittish candidate.

Other experienced advisors suggest that it is almost always best to lay out the key aspects, both financial and nonfinancial, of the proposed union in a memorandum of joint understanding developed by both parties. This document should outline the overall objectives of the merger, its organization and legal structure, price considerations, and any specific conditions imposed by either party. Though not legally enforceable, it serves as a useful forcing device for identifying, discussing, and resolving outstanding issues. As such, it marks a major milestone during the execution phase. In the United States, this memorandum is frequently the means by which both parties make their intentions public.

Where a cooperative growth theme has been developed early and subsequently refined during negotiations to the satisfaction of both parties, it takes on, in effect, the character of a letter of intent. In such cases, negotiations should proceed directly to the "due diligence" phase. This period, ideally a matter of 60 days or less, involves a legal investigation of the candidate's business and contingent liabilities by the buyer's representatives (for example, accountants, lawyers, investment bankers) to satisfy the buyer's fiduciary responsibility to shareholders. It is a time when many deals tend to fall apart. Notes Alexandra Lajoux, editor of *Mergers and Acquisitions:* "Acquiring companies often cite changing business conditions in the industry in question, new information obtained about the target late in the game, fears about the size of an acquisition, or a change in (their own) long-range strategy as motives for backing out of a deal." Figure 2 illustrates an array of further stumbling blocks.

Figure 2
Announced causes of failed transactions

Cause	Examples (buyer/seller)	Value ($ millions)
Regulatory obstacles	Great Western Savings & Loan/Financial Federation	$ 231
	ENSERCH/Davy Corp.	300
	Heileman Brewing/Schlitz	—
	Smith International/Galveston-Houston	183
	Gulf Oil/Cities Service	5,000
Transaction structure and terms	Beatrice Foods/Bob Evans Farms	200
	Kohlberg, Kravis/Kirby Exploration	154
Lack of shareholder approval	Texas International/Phoenix Resources	114
	Supermarkets General/Pantry Pride	130
	Penn Central/Colt Industries	1,400
Internal seller dissension	Allegheny International/Blue Bell	504
Financing problems	Penn Central/Cooper Manufacturing	250
	Firestone/Hertz	750
	Eastern/Braniff	—
Contingent liabilities	Coca-Cola/Outlet Co.	185
	Penn Central/GK Technologies (later successful)	—
Competitive bid	IC Industries/Sunbeam	507
	Storage Technology/Memorex	85
	Private Investors/Lane Bryant	86
	Harold Geneen/Cannon Mills	376
	Mattel/MacMillan	329
	Connecticut General/ERC	548

SOURCE: *Merger & Acquisitions.*

The experience of those who have shepherded merger negotiations through the postagreement review period suggests five main guidelines for the buyer:

1. *Make sure you understand the multitude of disclosure requirements,* their timing, and their likely impact on the agreement.
2. *Assign central responsibility for managing the regulatory reporting process* and coordinating the activities of specialized advisors.
3. *Make sure arguments and contingency plans are developed to counter regulatory objections to the proposed combination,* based on guidelines such as the Justice Department's Herfindahl Index of market concentration.
4. *Anticipate and plan to deal with pressures* that may be brought to bear by various buyer or candidate constituencies who may now be learning about the proposed transaction for the first time.
5. *Have an orderly plan of withdrawal* that allows for either party to back out of the agreement in a manner that will minimize ill will and loss of face.

In summary, the likelihood of reaching agreement can be enhanced if the buyer differentiates himself by creating and executing a sound approach strategy based on a cooperative growth theme and a systematic plan for contact. Careful candidate research and evaluation can generate vital insights into the candidate's business, bring to the surface issues in need of resolution, and ensure informed decision making. The parties' respective negotiating positions should be reconciled in a memorandum of joint understanding describing the salient features of the proposed combination. Once agreement is reached, postagreement review activities should be carefully managed to ensure a smooth conclusion to the execution phase. By understanding and planning each step in the execution process, the would-be acquirer can greatly improve his prospects of success.

What this article is about: Although acqusitions are a popular means of creating shareholder value, almost 50 percent fall short of expectation. This article notes recent acquisition trends, reviews the basic strategic logic, and explores some ways acquiring companies can improve their chances of success.

3-5 Successful acquisition planning*

Lionel L. Fray, David H. Gaylin, and James W. Down

*Lionel L.Fray is a vice president and David H. Gaylin and
James W. Down are senior consultants with the management
consulting firm of Temple, Barker & Sloane, Inc.,
Lexington, Massachusetts.*

Why do many acquisitions fail to increase the wealth of the acquiror's shareholders as promised? While some deals have made good economic sense, the record for the past five years or more is, on balance, somewhat disappointing. One indication is the increasing frequency of divestiture of previous acquisitions.

Recent history provides no clear guidance on the causes of these disappointments. Observers of the merger scene have pointed to a variety of contributing elements, including major dislocations in the economic environment, the failure to integrate the different styles, goals, and cultures of the two organizations, and the personal agendas of key executives, which may be in conflict with shareholder interests.

Our own experience suggests at least one more reason: The difficulties of making sound decisions under the uncertainty, fast pace, and high pressure that often attend the acquisition process, particularly during the final deal-making stages. The twists and turns of recent takeover bids, involving proxy fights, bidding wars, and such exotic defensive maneuvers as "poisoned pills" and "shark-proofing" initiatives, only exacerbate that difficulty.

Can the Acquisition Record Be Improved?

Since the pressures are unavoidable—even attractive, to some—the odds of success can be increased only by greater investment in preparation up front. Such preparation should consist of a disciplined approach to acquisi-

---

tion strategy and decision making. The logic and structure of this approach, which is systematic yet flexible, are not difficult to grasp. The difficulty comes in implementation.

This is not to suggest that CEOs are not disciplined or rational. Quite the contrary. The general assumptions and rationales underlying an acquisition program are often initially well-grounded. But, caught in the rapid pace of deal making, CEOs rarely have the luxury of time to fully pursue and internalize a rationale and its ramifications. Consequently, it is imcumbent on those managers charged with responsibility to assist in the acquisition process to take a strong leadership role in its design and to build a disciplined, proactive approach that can be established well before the chase begins.

Recent Trends

Merger and acquisition activity over the past 20 years has fluctuated—peaking in 1969 with more than 6,000 mergers, decreasing during the early 1970s, and leveling in the late 1970s and early 1980s at around 2,000 mergers per year. (See Figure 1.) This reduction in the number of mergers, however, has been more than offset by an increase in their size, led by the "megamerger" phenomenon of recent years. The number of acquisitions in excess of $100 million has risen sharply. (See Figure 2.) In 1981, there were a record 12 mergers in excess of $1 billion, the largest being Du Pont's $8 billion acquisition of Conoco. (There were 11 such mergers in 1982 and 6 in 1983.) Culminating this trend, as of this writing, is the $13 billion Socal-Gulf deal. The surge in merger activity has engulfed some of the most famous names in U.S. industry: Getty Oil, Cities Service, Marathon Oil, Bendix, Salomon Brothers, Norton Simon, Heublein, Schlitz, and El Paso.

Analysts differ as to the long-term effects of the recent merger wave. Many see the early 1980s mergers as fundamentally different from those of

Figure 1
Net merger and acquisition announcements
(1969–1983)

Year	Number	Year-to-Year Percentage Change
1969	6,107	+37%
1970	5,152	−16
1971	4,608	−11
1972	4,801	+ 4
1973	4,040	−16
1974	2,861	−29
1975	2,297	−20
1976	2,276	− 1
1977	2,224	− 2
1978	2,106	− 5
1979	2,128	+ 1
1980	1,889	−11
1981	2,395	+27
1982	2,346	− 2
1983	2,533	+ 8

SOURCE: W.T. Grimm & Co.

Figure 2
Increase in the value of acquisitions
(1975–1983)

Year	Acquisitions in Excess of $100 Million	Total Dollar Value Paid (billions)
1975	14	$11.8
1976	39	20.0
1977	41	21.9
1978	80	34.2
1979	83	43.5
1980	94	44.3
1981	113	82.6
1982	116	53.8
1983	138	73.1

SOURCE: W.T. Grimm & Co.

the 1960s, when many companies tried to increase earnings per share and spread risk through investment in widely diverse enterprises. While this strategy worked for a time, the longer-term performance of such conglomerates led the stock market to accord them below-average price/earnings (P/E) ratios. By contrast, mergers in the late 1970s and early 1980s seem to have involved attempts to add value by producing synergy between companies. The recently proposed mergers in the steel industry, for example, seek synergy through cutting costs and downsizing in order to battle lower-priced steel imports.

Critics of the recent merger movement cite concerns over the high premiums paid and the significant debt incurred to finance the deals, and question whether the claimed synergies will materialize. Nonetheless, as businesses seek to maintain profits in the face of increasing global competition and technological change, a continuing realignment of assets and portfolios is likely.

The following sections examine the motives behind acquisitions, the elements of the acquisition process, and some of the reasons for success and failure.

Planning Acquisition Strategy

A common rationale for acquisitions is to maintain or increase profits and/or reduce risk. The pursuit of so general a purpose, however, is a major reason many acquisitions fail. An acquisition program should be based on much more specific and well-conceived objectives and strategies. Acquisitions can be made for a variety of specific reasons. Some of the more common ones are discussed below.

Strengthen or Protect the Base Business The desire to acquire key personnel, purchasing power, or assets that are directly related to the base business is often the driving force, subject to antitrust considerations. Examples include many of the recent energy deals—e.g., Shell's purchase of Belridge Oil and Sun Company's purchase of Texas Pacific from Seagram.

Similar horizontal acquisitions are made to adapt to competitive or environmental changes. As regulation of the railroads was beginning to ease in 1978, two connecting railroads, Chessie System and Seaboard Coast Line Industries (SCL), merged to create CSX. In response, Chessie's major competitor, the Norfolk and Western, merged with SCL's direct competitor, the Southern Railroad.

Diversify Acquisition can be a means to gain entry into new markets or businesses so as to reduce the risk inherent in the base business of a company or provide more opportunity for long-term development. Sears Roebuck & Co., facing slow growth in retailing, expanded its base in financial services (Allstate Insurance) by acquiring a major stockbroker (Dean Witter Reynolds) and real estate broker (Coldwell Banker). Diversification has its risks, however, particulary when the capital base is weak. The recent bankruptcy of Baldwin-United, a piano maker turned financial services conglomerate, highlights this point.

Avoid a Takeover Acquisition can be used to defend against an unfriendly takeover attempt. Frank B. Hall acquired Jartran in 1981 to fend off an acquisition attempt by Ryder Systems. Since Ryder and Jartran were direct competitors, Ryder consequently could not acquire Hall without violating antitrust statutes. A takeover target can even counterattack by going after the would-be acquiror (Martin Marietta and Bendix).

Improve Financial Returns A company sometimes makes an acquisition to improve its return on capital, take advantage of tax benefits, or improve the profitability of the acquisition itself (when management thinks it can do so). Owing to their different circumstances, the buyer may often value an acquisition candidate differently from the seller. Penn Central, following its bankruptcy and the divestiture of its railroad operations, used its substantial tax loss carryforwards to embark on a series of acquisitions to improve its return on capital. Gulf & Western, under its chairman, Charles Bluhdorn, employed a policy of acquiring companies whose assets were believed to be undervalued, with mixed results. (Since Bluhdorn's death, Gulf & Western's new management has reversed course, selling off some 25 businesses and a large stock portfolio.)

Corporate Evaluation

In considering possible goals of an acquisition program, a corporation must begin by evaluating itself. This should include an evaluation of its external environment and its ability to compete in this environment, and an assessment of corporate objectives and its ability to fulfill them. The external environment includes the economic, competitive, political, legal, social, and institutional pressures that bear upon any company. The internal environment includes functional strengths and weaknesses, shareholder goals, management style, and corporate culture. Some of the key strategic questions to ask during the evaluation are:

• What is the corporate mission?
• What are the long-term financial and nonfinancial corporate objectives?

- How mature are the company's present businesses, and what growth potential remains, especially through innovative additions or redefinitions of the business?
- What technological trends are taking place, and what threats or opportunities do they pose?
- What is the company's competitive position? How is it changing?
- Should the company deepen the penetration in existing businesses or expand into new business areas?
- Should the company change its mission?

The result of this evaluation is typically an assessment of the capability of the company's present business to satisfy its long-term objectives, including the identification of any expansion or diversification needs.

Acquisition Alternatives

Before embarking on an acquisition program, a company should also evaluate any alternative means of achieving its objectives.

Joint ventures are one alternative, although experience has shown they can be difficult to manage. Over time, the goals of many joint venture partners often diverge, resulting in disputes, attempts by one partner to abandon or buy out the other, and, in some cases, protracted legal battles. On the other hand, joint ventures spread the risk and may give a company access to capabilities it could not otherwise acquire.

The internal start-up of new ventures should also be evaluated as an alternative to acquisition. This strategy is probably most appropriate where a company has skills, resources, and time to develop new venture areas. Biggadike [2] determined that such new ventures typically suffer substantial losses and negative cash flows in their early years; on average, they require 8 years to achieve profitability and 10 to 12 years before their return on investment equals that of a mature business.

Acquisition Strategy

Once a decision has been made to embark on an acquisition program, a strategy must be developed to guide the program. Issues such as the strategic direction of the firm, the size and type of candidate to be acquired, and the acquisition approach desired must be addressed.

Strategic Direction   Should one seek horizontal expansion (Nabisco-Standard Brands), vertical integration (Conagra-Banquet Foods), diversification into related businesses (American Express-Shearson Loeb), or unrelated ones (ITT-Sheraton)?

While there are no hard-and-fast answers to such questions, a review of prior U.S. industrial experience is enlightening. Rumelt [6] demonstrated that, since World War II, there has been a strong and continuous trend for large U.S. corporations to diversify away from single businesses. One of Rumelt's most compelling points is that the financial performance of diversifying companies is closely correlated with the way in which they relate new business ventures to their old businesses, rather than to the magnitude or pace of diversification.

On average, companies that exhibit the best financial performance (i.e., highest returns to capital, least variability in earnings relative to earnings growth) are those that have consistently focused their diversification efforts by building on a single core of existing skills, knowledge, or experience. In contrast, companies that have either disregarded their existing core of skills and knowledge or tried to build in several directions, each new direction drawing on a different core skill, have not performed as well. Peters and Waterman's so-called excellent companies [5], for example, have all grown by building on their strengths. Not one is a conglomerate of unrelated businesses.

Related diversification, analyzed by Salter and Weinhold [7], can be usefully divided into two types:

1. *Related-supplementary diversification* is accomplished by diversifying into new markets requiring functional skills identical to those already possessed. The purest form of this strategy is horizontal integration, adding new markets with minimal departure from key functional activities.
2. *Related-complementary diversification* is accomplished by adding new activities in order to participate more broadly in the same market. The purest form of this strategy is vertical integration, adding new skills with minimal change in market orientation.

The main criteria for choosing between related-supplementary and related-complementary are the attractiveness of the market (e.g., rate of growth) and the parent company's competitive position within it (e.g., market share). In general, companies with strong positions in low-growth markets should pursue related-supplementary diversification; companies with limited positions in attractive markets should pursue related-complementary diversification.

Another form of strategic analysis used in determining acquisition strategy is the "product/market portfolio model." A commonly used version of this model, developed by the Boston Consulting Group, segments businesses into four categories by separating their cash use and cash generation characteristics. A key assumption of this model is that cash generation is a function of relative market share and that cash use is a function of market growth. The model suggests that acquisitions should be evaluated in light of balancing a company's portfolio of businesses, so that the surplus cash from mature businesses is feeding less mature, high-potential businesses.

Type of Company Should one seek a private company, a public company, or a division being divested? To a great extent this decision is influenced by what is available. Despite the fanfare surrounding the recent megamergers of public corporations, the predominant activity has involved divestitures and private companies. (See Figure 3.)

Size of Company Is one looking for a $10 million company or a billion-dollar company? This usually depends on objectives and resources. Alco-

Figure 3
Composition of acquisition announcements
(1980–1983)

Year	Divestitures	Acquisitions of Public Companies	Acquisitions of Private Companies	Total
1980	666	173	988	1,827
1981	830	168	1,330	2,328
1982	875	180	1,222	2,277
1983	932	190	1,316	2,438

SOURCE: W.T. Grimm & Co.

Standard acquired relatively small companies that can be operated on a decentralized basis but still benefit from association with a multibillion-dollar parent. Sears, on the other hand, had to acquire very large companies to diversify significantly away from its $20 billion retailing business.

Type of Approach   Is one looking for a "friendly" deal (Dart and Kraft), or is one willing to be "unfriendly" (Mesa going after Gulf; Brown-Foreman and Lenox)? Does one want to play the role of the "white knight" (Allied opportunistically coming to the rescue of Bendix)?

Pursuing a friendly acquisition usually increases the chances of retaining the acquiree's management but limits the range of available candidates, since many companies are not interested in being acquired. Pursuing unfriendly acquisitions, however, has some serious risks as evidenced by the notorious four-cornered battle among Bendix, Martin Marietta, United Technologies, and Allied. Unfriendly bids that fail can nonetheless be very profitable, but the risks are high.

Acquisition Process

Once a decision to make an acquisition has been made, an implementation plan should be developed. The plan should be either formal or informal, depending on management style and the time available. Formal plans can be inflexible and stifling; informal ones are usually inefficient and risky. The best plans typically strike a balance, allowing for speed and flexibility while taking an organized, comprehensive approach.

Development of Criteria

Acquisition criteria should not be formulated so tightly that nothing passes through, nor so loosely that too much passes. They should be flexible, possibly changing over time to reflect new experience and priorities. There are many types of acquisition criteria, but those outlined below are typical.

- *Industry focus.* Is one looking for a company involved in *any* manufacturing industry or is one seeking a company involved, for example, in the manufacture of heavy truck equipment?

- *Synergy with acquiror.* What relationship should the acquisition have to present operations? While holding companies and conglomerates do not necessarily seek a close relationship, most acquirors want to strengthen or broaden existing businesses. Potential synergies include the following:

- *Functional synergy,* e.g., a strong marketing company acquiring a company with a solid product line but limited marketing expertise (Philip Morris acquiring Miller Beer and 7UP) or a company with strong distribution acquiring a company in need of it (Sears and Dean Witter, Chesebrough-Pond and Bass Shoe). Other areas of functional synergy could involve technology, manufacturing, or R&D.
- *Financial synergy,* for example, a cash-rich company acquiring a company with growth potential but limited capital (United Technologies and Mostek).

Financial and Economic   Financial and economic criteria typically include the following:

- *Growth.* Is one looking for rapid growth potential or is growth less important? (It is important to consider how the candidate's future performance, under new ownership, might vary from its historical record.)
- *Return on equity/return on total capital.* How should the expected returns from an acquisition compare against those of existing operations or to industry averages?
- *Financial leverage.* Is one seeking a company with high or low leverage, a company compared against existing operation or against the candidate's competitors?
- *Operating leverage.* What should be the acquisition candidate's relative level of fixed and variable costs? What level of capital and labor intensity does one want?

Competitive Posture   Is one looking for a company that is a leader in its industry and that could, therefore, command a premium price? Does one seek a troubled company that has the potential for turnaround and a substantial increase in value? Would one be comfortable with a high level of competitive or technological risk?

Management   Does one want a company with an experienced incumbent management team that will stay or does one plan to provide one's own managers? How important is similarity in management style and culture?

Geography   Does one want a company with primarily domestic or international revenues? Does one expect to physically consolidate both companies?

Acquisition Search

There are several approaches to the acquisition search process, the choice of which depends on a company's objectives, timetable, prior planning, resources, and corporate culture. Freier [3] identified three types of approaches:

1. *Opportunistic approach.* This method first identifies companies available for sale and then determines which are attractive. It permits immediate movement into the flow of deals while not wasting time on companies that may not be for sale. Some disadvantages are that it

entails reliance on third-party brokers, can yield inappropriate candidates, and may not support an overall strategic direction.

2. *Research approach.* This entails detailed screening and research to determine which industries and companies fit the acquiror's strategy and criteria and then determining which may be for sale. This approach is highly focused and likely to yield candidates that fit well with the acquiror. The major disadvantage is that it involves significant research time and effort, requiring patience and discipline.

3. *Combination approach.* This blends both opportunistic and research elements. It involves researching and identifying industries and companies that should be pursued while still being open to attractive deals that may become available.

The research and combination approaches typically begin by screening industries to identify those that meet broad acquisition criteria (e.g., a consumer products company). The next step is to identify all standard industrial codes (SICs) that fall into this category. Financial and secondary research is then conducted (using trade journals, directories, and on-line data bases, such as Disclosure and Compustat) to provide a preliminary evaluation of each industry. The industries may then be ranked by relative attractiveness, and several of the highest ranked should be chosen for in-depth analysis. This analysis should be performed using (1) interviews with industry participants, trade associations, and so on; (2) secondary research (e.g., published industry reports, consultants, investment reports); and (3) a complete literature review aided by the on-line data bases. The output of this process should be a comprehensive report on each industry containing the following information:

- Industry size, growth, and projections.
- Industry structure and dynamics:
    - —Number and market shares of participants.
    - —Revenues and profitability.
    - —Historical and projected changes.
    - —Cyclicality.
    - —Cost-price experience.
- Competitive profile of significant participants:
    - —Financial.
    - —Products.
    - —Organization.
    - —Management.
    - —Performance.
- Critical factors for long-term success.
- Determination of interest in entering each of the industries analyzed and list of target companies for further analysis.

In addition to industry analyses, acquisition prospects can be generated from many other sources, including directors, consultants, investment and commercial bankers, attorneys, accountants, and brokers.

Initial Contact With Candidates   If the candidate is likely to resist the takeover, an unfriendly attempt may be necessary, and initial contact is often bypassed to avoid giving the candidate time to plan countermeasures. But if a friendly takeover will be attempted, contact may be initiated directly by letter or telephone and indirectly through mutual friends or professional intermediaries. This initial contact serves many purposes, including evaluating potential cultural and business fit, assessing value added, and determining interest in merging.

Detailed Company Investigation and Appraisal   The next phase is an intensive appraisal of the candidate. The following activities are the minimum that should be included:

- Conducting preliminary operations, legal, and financial audits (e.g., are major lawsuits pending? What accounting policies govern reported earnings? Are pension liabilities adequately funded?)
- Performing an appraisal of the assets.
- Consulting with experts on accounting, financing, legal, and regulatory issues (e.g., pooling versus purchase, tax-free options, antitrust).
- Developing detailed information on operations, markets, technology, and competition.
- Determining the impact of merger on both parties under various scenarios:
  —Possible purchase prices.
  —Financial and operating plans (e.g., pricing, volume, cost).
  —Industry and other microeconomic outlooks.

Negotiations   It is important to develop a negotiating strategy prior to serious discussions. This strategy should cover the following: price, type and terms of financing, employee benefits, how the candidate will report to the acquiring company, and whether key managers will get special contracts and incentives.

Documentation, Confirmation, and Closing   Acquisition negotiations can often be lengthy, during which time changes may take place within the candidate company. Often, "agreements in principle" are reached, subject to confirmation of the validity of certain claims about the candidate. Prior to closing, all studies and analyses should be carefully reviewed and updated. This includes final legal and accounting audits, final forecasts, and analysis of any major changes that have occurred in specific functional areas. In addition, the closing itself usually involves significant legal review for both parties.

Implementation of Transition Plan   The closing of the deal does not end the acquisition process but instead begins the transition phase. It is helpful to develop a detailed transition plan *before* the closing. The turnover of top managers in an acquired company is usually high in the first few years. They often cite the new parent's burdensome information reporting requirements, a real or perceived loss of status, or a change in the acquiror's motives. A good transition plan can reduce turnover, if desired, and its negative effects by addressing the following:

- Integration with parent's systems (e.g., accounting, personnel, budgeting, planning).
- Level of autonomy.
- Reporting relationships and requirements.
- Compensation and benefits.
- Perquisites (e.g., company cars, bonuses, travel).
- Other policies and procedures.

Acquisition Valuation and Payment Issues

Valuation

Almost every company is for sale if the price is high enough. A key to the success of any acquisition, therefore, is the purchase price, which must be carefully considered before an offer is made. A good deal at $75 million may be less attractive at $100 million and a grave mistake at $150 million.

There are no precise determinants of value. If the candidate is a public company, the market has already valued it; however, the candidate usually requires significant premiums over market value in order to obtain a controlling interest. (See Figure 4.) Premiums over market are usually a function of (1) the value the acquiror feels it can add to the operation and (2) the market supply and demand characteristics for this type of company.

One way to value a candidate is by analyzing recent acquisitions of similar companies. The P/E ratio of the tender offer, its premium over market, and the market-to-book ratio may all be analyzed for as wide a sample of comparable companies as possible. This is rarely straightforward since the definition of "comparable" is often subjective, particularly for companies that participate in several businesses. Comparative analysis by itself, therefore, is not a good valuator but it can provide useful guidelines.

Another approach is to examine the candidate's historical performance. Simple extrapolation of past trends, however, while useful, is also inadequate by itself. How the candidate can be expected to perform in the future, under new ownership, is vital. Before an offer is made, therefore, the acquiror should engage in planning for the prospective acquisition in much the same fashion as it plans for its existing businesses.

Probably the most widely used method of valuing acquisitions is to discount their expected cash flows over a specified period of time. Although this process is mechanically straightforward, projecting future earnings and cash requirements usually requires considerable familiarity with the company and its environment, and even then will involve much judgment.

Figure 4
Average premium paid over market
(Percent)

1978	1979	1980	1981	1982	1983
46.2	49.9	49.9	48.0	47.4	37.7

SOURCE: W.T. Grimm & Co.

Figure 5
Acquisition valuation model

Proposed Acquisition Assumptions:
  Revenue: $200 million
  Net income: $10 million
  Reinvestment = Depreciation + 10 percent of Earnings
  Residual value multiple: 8
  Discount rate: 14 percent

	10 Percent Growth			20 Percent Growth		
Year	Earnings	Cash Throw-Off	Discounted Value	Earnings	Cash Throw-Off	Discounted Value
1	$ 11.0	$ 9.9	$ 8.7	$ 12.0	$10.8	$ 9.5
2	12.1	10.9	8.4	14.4	13.0	10.0
3	13.3	12.0	8.1	17.3	15.6	10.5
4	14.6	13.2	7.8	20.7	18.7	11.1
5	16.1	14.5	7.5	24,9	22.4	11.6
6	17.7	15.9	7.2	29.9	26.9	12.3
7	19.5	17.5	7.0	35.8	32.2	12.9
8	21.4	19.3	6.8	43.0	38.7	13.6
9	23.6	21.2	6.5	51.6	46.4	14.3
10	25.9	23.3	6.3	61.9	55.7	15.0
Residual value	$185.0		$ 49.9	$442.1		$119.3
Total discounted value			$124.2			$240.1
Maximum multiple payable		•	12.4			24.0

Figure 5 illustrates a simple model valuing an acquisition under two different earnings growth rates. This example shows how critical the assumptions are—increasing the expected growth rate from 10 percent to 20 percent doubles the acquisition's value and the P/E multiple that could be justified. To account for risk and uncertainty, it is usually advisable to value the company under a variety of scenarios (e.g., optimistic, most likely, pessimistic), considering the probability of each, and to examine the impact of specific strategic jeopardies. Discounted cash flow models are driven by assumptions about the following:

- *Time period.* The cash flows should be projected for a time period that the forecaster feels comfortable with, typically 5 to 10 years.
- *Cash flow.* Cash flow is defined as net income plus noncash items, minus planned capital expenditures, minus increases in working capital. The example in Figure 5 asssumes that capital expenditures will equal depreciation plus 10 percent of earnings, although actual projections should be based on rigorous, case-by-case analysis.
- *Residual value.* The residual or terminal value of the acquisition—its market value at the end of the forecast period—often plays a major role in valuation. The example in Figure 5 uses an anticipated P/E ratio. Another common method is to discount the value of the perpetual cash flows beyond the forecast period [1].
- *Discount rate.* This allows the acquisition to be compared with other investment opportunities of similar risk. The most widely used method is

to use a discount rate equal to the acquiror's weighted average cost of capital. If the acquisition is riskier than the acquiror, however, or will increase the acquiror's overall risk, a higher discount rate should be used.

Payment

In addition to price, the form of payment is also a critical factor in negotiations. Options include cash, common stock, preferred stock, debt, or a combination of stock and cash. According to W.T. Grimm [4], in 1983 stock was used in 35 percent of all acquisitions, cash in 32 percent, and a combination of cash, stock, and debt in 33 percent. The advantages and disadvantages of cash versus stock relate to their tax implications, the risk involved with stock, and the effect on earnings per share.

While cash probably offers a buyer more flexibility, if stock is used for at least 51 percent of the payment, the transaction usually can be structured so that federal taxes can be deferred until the stock is sold. (See Figure 6 for various types of mergers and their tax implications.) Feld [8] states that "most mergers are not done primarily for tax reasons. But in the analysis of any deal you look at the numbers, and some of the numbers depend to a considerable degree on tax consequences." Even if cash is used for payment, the deal can often be structured to reduce the tax liabilities.

Figure 6
Types of mergers

Characteristics, Requirements, Implications	Statutory Merger	Exchange of Stock for Stock	Purchase of Assets for Stock	Purchase of Stock for Cash or Nonvoting Securities	Purchase of Assets for Cash or Nonvoting Securities
Nontaxable to shareholders of acquiree if specific requirements met	Yes, except for "boot"	Yes, except for "boot"	Yes	No	No
Transaction medium and steps	Generally 50 percent or more of purchase price must be in stock to meet continuity of interest rule	Voting stock only; voting preferred stock may be possible but not for pooling treatment	1. Voting stock with possibility of up to 20 percent nonstock 2. Corporate shell of acquiree remains and may be liquidated	No restriction as to purchase medium	1. No restrictions as to purchase medium 2. Corporate shell of acquiree remains and may be subsequently liquidated to avoid double taxation
Type of accounting treatment	Purchase or pooling of interests	Purchase or pooling of interests	Purchase or pooling of interests	Purchase only	Purchase only

SOURCE: J.W. Bradley and D.H. Korn, *Acquisition and Corporate Development*, (1981), p. 170.

A potential disadvantage of a stock deal from the acquiree's standpoint is that it becomes tied to the future performance of the acquiror's stock. This disadvantage is exacerbated if the acquiree's shares are encumbered by agreement in some fashion. For the acquiror, a stock deal may dilute earnings per share. Potential dilution can be anticipated by calculating the expected earnings per share issued, i.e., the acquiree's earnings divided by the shares issued to buy it.

In addition to tax effects, the form of payment also has an effect on the acquiror's accounting for public reporting purposes. There are two main methods of merger accounting: the purchase and the pooling of interests. Purchase accounting is required when the acquisition is made for cash or nonvoting stock. This method can have a negative effect on reported earnings for the merged entity when the purchase price exceeds the fair market value of the assets acquired, since goodwill is created which must be amortized against earnings. Under the pooling method, which may be used in certain noncash exchanges, the balance sheets of the merged parties are essentially integrated without creating goodwill.

Guidelines for Success

Despite the continuing popularity of acquisitions as a means of creating shareholder value, research indicates that on average almost 50 percent of all acquisitions fall short of expectations. According to Young's data, 45 percent of all acquisitions fail and 6 percent more are likely to fail [9]. His sources further indicate little change in this failure rate for the past 40 years.

While there has been scant quantitative research on the reasons for failure, much of the qualitative evidence points to a general lack of acquisition planning and too little emphasis on the human aspect of absorbing a new organization.

What can be done to ensure a successful acquisition? There is no single answer. Each acquisition is unique, and success is never guaranteed. Our experience, however, suggests some guidelines that, if applied to each acquisition, should significantly increase its chances of success:

1. Develop a comprehensive diversification plan as part of an overall corporate development strategy. It is essential that a buyer have a clear definition of what business it is in and what business it wishes to be in. It should also understand its own strengths and weaknesses.

2. Buy a firm that meets sound strategic and economic criteria—not what is available. Too many firms become impatient or "lovestruck," unwisely abandoning their screening criteria in the heat of the chase. Exercise patience.

3. Understand the business being purchased *strategically*—industry position, the bases for competition, possible competitive reactions to the acquisition, and any changes in strategy. Presumably it will be in the business a long time. Even if it is not, the acquisition's strategic position at the time of exit will determine the exit price.

4. Understand opportunity; have the resources to develop it and the management commitment to exploit it. Companies should seek a good fit with their own operations, but expecting perfection is not realistic.

5. Evaluate the management of the acquisition candidate for competence, style, energy, and motivation. Would you want them as members of the "corporate family"? Experienced management is important, but fit with your corporate culture and values is equally important.

6. Make the right advances—acquisition requires courtship. Gains for owners of both firms should be specified, and people should be absorbed into an organization with sensitivity to their needs for status and autonomy. People problems need to be anticipated.

7. Determine the price beyond which the deal ceases to be attractive. Keep in mind that at some price almost any company can be bought—the key is to purchase at a price that allows for an attractive return.

8. Be prepared for contingencies—industry changes, competitive reactions, and, most important, management failures or departures. In an acquisition, contingencies are more likely to occur than not. Some thought to contingency planning and backup management can take one a long way.

9. Avoid a big mistake. Small mistakes can be absorbed. But if you bet your company on an acquisition, the options for recovering from a mistake are likely to be limited indeed.

References

1. Ackerman, R. W., and L. Fray. "Financial Evaluation of a Potential Acquisition." *Financial Executive,* October 1967.
2. Biggadike, R. "The Risky Business of Diversification." *Harvard Business Review,* May–June 1979, pp. 105–6.
3. Freier, Jerold L. "Acquisition Search Programs." *Mergers & Acquisitions: The Journal of Corporate Venture,* Summer 1981, pp. 35–39.
4. W.T. Grimm & Co., *Mergerstat Review,* 1983.
5. Peters, T. J., and R. H. Waterman, Jr. *In Search of Excellence.* 1982.
6. Rumelt, R. P. *Strategy, Structure, and Economic Performance.* 1974, p. 53.
7. Salter, M. S., and W. A. Weinhold. *Diversification through Acquisition.* 1979, pp. 61–63.
8. "Tax Law's Effects on Mergers." *The New York Times,* Sept. 7, 1982, p. D-8.
9. Young, J. B. "A Conclusive Investigation into the Causative Elements of Failure in Acquisitions and Mergers." *Handbook of Mergers, Acquisitions and Buyouts,* 1981, p. 605.

What this article is about: An in-depth study of 64 companies in such domestic manufacturing industries as steel, tire and rubber, automotive, heavy-duty truck and construction equipment, home appliance, beer, and cigarettes reveals that success comes to those that achieve either the lowest cost or most differentiated position.

3-6 Survival strategies in a hostile environment*

William K. Hall

William K. Hall is professor of business administration at the Graduate School of Business Administration, University of Michigan.

As economists, managers, and industry analysts pause to look back on the past decade, there remains little doubt that the business environment in the United States grew increasingly hostile during the 1970s. More important, there is now little doubt that this hostile environment will continue (and perhaps even worsen) during the decade ahead, reflecting the combined effects of:

- Slower, erratic growth in domestic and world markets.
- Intensified inflationary pressures on manufacturing and distribution costs.
- Intensified regulatory pressures on business conduct and investment decisions.
- Intensified competition, both from traditional domestic competitors and also from the new wave of foreign competitors entering U.S. markets with different objectives and frequently lower ROI expectations.

As a result of these growing pressures, large U.S. manufacturing corporations are witnessing a major evolution in industry structures and competitive behaviors. Many structures that were stable and highly profitable during the "go-go" decade of the 1960s are now moving toward instability and marginal profitability.

* Reprinted by permission of the Harvard Business Review. "Survival Strategies in a Hostile Environment" by William K. Hall (September/October 1980). Copyright © 1980 by the President and Fellows of Harvard College; all rights reserved.

Moreover, the broad range of corporate strategies and business "success formulas" which brought prosperity in those earlier years are no longer working. Instead, these are being replaced with a much narrower range of strategic choices that are becoming essential to survive in the hostile environment ahead.

The purpose of this article is to present some preliminary findings from an ongoing research project that my colleagues and I are conducting to explore these strategic and structural changes in more depth. This project is focusing on two broad questions:

1. How are industry structures in the mature markets evolving in the face of the adverse external pressures of the late 1970s?
2. Given this evolution, what business strategies are appropriate? Which strategic choices give the best chances for survival, growth, and return in the hostile environment ahead?

In-Depth Investigation

To examine these issues, I selected eight major domestic manufacturing industries for comprehensive study because of their importance to national and/or regional economic development and also because the adverse external trends of the 1970s have been especially severe in their impact on them. As a result, during the 1970s, all eight industries underwent a significant structural change which is expected to continue into the 1980s. Within these industries, I examined the strategies and evolving competitive positions of the 64 largest companies by using a combination of public data sources and field interviews.

In examining the impact of external pressures on these companies, I found that the eight industries either matured during the 1970s or will mature in the 1980s, resulting in lower growth records and growth expectations as shown in Figure 1. While the industries (on average) exceeded national economic growth rates in the 1950s and 1960s, they grew only slightly faster than the GNP in the 1970s, and they are projected to grow significantly more slowly than the U.S. economy in the 1980s.

During this maturation period, these eight industries, which are capital, raw material, and labor intensive, have been subjected to heavy inflationary pressures that cannot easily be price recovered. All are being forced by regulatory agencies to make major investments to comply with new occupational safety and health regulations and with new product safety, performance, and environmental protection standards.

In addition to the domestic pressures, foreign competition has been harsh in the eight basic industries selected for study. Foreign competitors have achieved significant market shares in three of the industries—steel, tire and rubber, and automotive; moderate shares in two—heavy-duty trucks and construction and materials handling equipment; and entry positions in the other three—major home appliances, beer, and cigarettes.

Because many of these foreign competitors are either nationalized, quasinationalized, or highly salient in their own countries, they are frequently willing to accept lower returns in U.S. markets, offsetting these lower returns against unemployment, balance of payments, and capital gains

Figure 1
Compound annual real growth rates in demand—United States
(Eight basic industries)

	1950–1970	1971–1980	1980 Forecast*
Industrial goods			
Primary products			
Steel	4.0%	2.2%	1.5%–2.5%
Tire and rubber	4.2	1.4	1.0–1.5
Intermediate products			
Heavy-duty trucks	7.0	2.8	2.5
Construction and materials handling equipment	7.8	3.6	2.3
Consumer goods			
Durable products			
Automotive	4.8	3.5	2.0–3.0
Major home appliances	6.2	2.9	2.3–2.8
Nondurable products			
Beer	3.1	2.5	2.3
Cigarettes	1.6	1.0	0
Average growth rates— eight industries	**4.8%**	**2.4%**	**1.9%**
Average growth rates— U.S. GNP	**3.7%**	**2.3%**	**2.5%**

* Based on economic forecasts and industry projections.

at home. While these foreign approaches have been criticized as unfair, the results have altered U.S. domestic industry structures in all eight cases.

Needless to say, the net effect of these adverse trends has made life anything but pleasant for managers and companies in these basic industries. Profitability and sales growth levels have generally fallen to or below the average manufacturing returns in the U.S. economy (Figure 2). And industry spokesmen frequently speak out, urging either public assistance or some type of return to the simpler, less painful world of the 1960s.

Figure 2
Financial returns and revenue growth rates, 1975–1979
(Eight basic industries)

	Return on Equity	Return on Capital	EPS Growth	Revenue Growth
Steel	7.1%	5.7%	5.5%	10.4%
Tire and rubber	7.4	5.9	3.9	9.6
Heavy-duty trucks*	15.4	11.6	13.8	13.8
Construction and materials handling equipment	15.4	10.7	16.8	13.0
Automotive*	15.4	11.6	13.8	13.8
Major home appliances	10.1	9.0	3.2	6.8
Beer	14.1	10.2	6.2	12.4
Cigarettes	18.2	10.5	8.9	12.2
Average eight industries	**12.9%**	**9.4%**	**9.0%**	**11.5%**
Average *Fortune* "1,000" company	**15.1%**	**11.0%**	**13.1%**	**13.1%**

* All vehicle manufacturers.

As one senior executive I interviewed commented: "Maybe I should have accepted that job as an IBM systems engineer after graduation from college. It sure would be fun to look forward to going to work in the morning." Despite the outcries, the adverse external trends haven't gone away, and structural evolution continues at a slow, but inevitable, pace.

The heavy-duty truck manufacturing industry provides an excellent example of this evolution. In the early 1960s, spurred by rapid growth in the economy and by the completion of the U.S. interstate highway system, the industry grew at more than 8 percent per year. Eight major manufacturers—International Harvester, General Motors, Ford, Mack, White Motor, Diamond Reo, Chrysler, and Paccar—participated fairly equally in this growth, producing 60 truck models to serve the rapidly growing light-heavy and heavy-duty segments (19,000 pounds and greater gross vehicle weight).

However, by the late 1970s, annual growth had slowed to less than 3 percent. Emission regulations and inflation had raised unit costs. Investments for new truck model development had slowed to the extent that the number of models had dropped from 60 to 35 by 1979.

As a result of this movement toward a hostile environment, Chrysler closed its heavy-duty truck manufacturing operation, Diamond Reo was in bankruptcy, and White lingered near receivership. Both Mack and International Harvester had lost significant market share and were searching for foreign assistance or major cost-cutting programs to maintain their viability. Of the eight healthy domestic competitors in the early 1960s, only three—General Motors, Ford, and Paccar—maintained free-standing, vibrant, competitive positions as they entered the decade of the 1980s.

Similar moves toward lower profitability and consolidation occurred in all eight industries as the hostile environment took its evolutionary toll. In steel, Bethlehem announced in 1977 the largest corporate quarterly loss in U.S. history up to that time (exceeded by Chrysler two years later and U.S. Steel in late 1979), Jones & Laughlin and Youngstown merged under the failing firm provision of U.S. antitrust laws in 1978, and Kaiser tried to sell its steel-making operation to the Japanese in 1979. In rubber, industry analysts waited impatiently for Uniroyal to exit the industry; and in automotive, Chrysler made front-page headlines in its race against time to achieve federal loan assistance. Words like "dinosaur" and "dog" were coined by industry observers to describe the evolving competitive profiles in all eight industries.

However, the profiles of basic industry problems and corporate failures tell only part of the story. These "disaster" tales need to be juxtaposed against some success stories to see how some companies have survived and even prospered in the same hostile environment. The resulting comparisons provide important insights into survival strategies and industry dynamics not only for general managers in the eight industries under study but also for managers in other industries as they lead their companies into the new decade. For example, a careful comparison of success and problem strategies in the eight industries in this study demonstrates that:

- Great success is possible, even in a hostile environment.
- Strategies leading to success share common characteristics.

- Successful strategies come from purposeful moves toward a leadership position.
- Problems come from failure to gain or defend a leadership position.
- For a deteriorating position, diversity may not be the proper recovery approach.
- Structural evolution moves toward a dynamic equilibrium as basic industries face a hostile environment.

I will amplify and discuss each of these insights in subsequent sections of this article.

Great Success Is Possible Even in a Hostile Environment

When one looks at the eight industries in this study, as well as at other basic manufacturing industries facing the hostile environment of the 1980s, it is easy to slip into generalizations by extrapolating from aggregate industry problems to the individual companies within the industry.

Recent articles in the business press, asking ''What Killed the U.S. Steel Industry?'' ''Is Chrysler the Prototype?'' or proclaiming ''Tire Industry Goes Flat'' or ''Last Chances for Cigarette Producers,'' are typical of those that tend to project adverse trends uniformly onto all competitors in the industry. In fact, however, nothing could be further from the truth. Some of the most vibrant, successful companies in the world reside and prosper in these seemingly hostile industry environments.

If one eliminates from my eight-industry sample of 64 companies all competitors who gain a majority of revenues and profits from diversification efforts outside their basic industry (e.g., Armco Steel and General Tire), then the most profitable remaining competitors (the industry leaders) in terms of corporate return on equity are those shown in Figure 3.

While some variation in returns exists among these leading competitors

Figure 3
Financial returns and growth rates, 1975–1979
(Leading companies in eight basic industries)*

	Average Return on Equity	Average Return on Capital	Annual Revenue Growth Rate
Goodyear	9.2%	7.0%	10.0%
Inland Steel	10.9	7.9	11.4
Paccar	22.8	20.9	14.9
Caterpillar	23.5	17.3	17.2
General Motors	19.8	18.0	13.2
Maytag	27.2	26.5	9.1
G. Heileman Brewing	25.8	18.9	21.4
Philip Morris	22.7	13.5	20.1
Average	**20.2%**	**16.3%**	**14.7%**
Median *Fortune* "1,000" company (same time period)	**15.1%**	**11.0%**	**13.1%**

* Excluding those companies which gained a majority of their returns from diversification efforts.

Figure 4
Financial returns and growth rates, 1975–1979
(Leading companies in other and more rapidly growing industries)

	Average Return on Equity	Average Return on Capital	Annual Revenue Growth Rate
International oil			
Phillips Petroleum	19.5%	14.7%	16.6%
Technology leaders			
Xerox	17.8	14.4	15.5
Eastman Kodak	18.8	17.7	11.8
Texas Instruments	17.2	16.3	14.6
Digital Equipment	17.0	15.5	37.4
Diversification leaders			
General Electric	19.4	16.9	10.5
United Technologies	18.3	12.6	19.0
Average of these "high performance" leaders	**18.3%**	**15.4%**	**17.9%**
Average (leading companies in basic industries from Exhibit III)	**20.2%**	**16.3%**	**14.7%**
"Blue chip" competitors			
IBM	21.9	21.2	13.5
3M	20.7	17.7	13.1

(Goodyear Tire and Rubber Co. and Inland Steel had significantly lower returns and growth rates than the other six), the corporate average return on equity earned over the last half of the 1970s easily places these companies in the top 20 percent of the *Fortune* "1,000" industrials and well ahead of the median *Fortune* company on return on capital and annual growth rate.

Moreover, the average returns on both equity and capital in my sample of industry leaders are well ahead of those earned by the leading international oil company (Phillips Petroleum). These average returns are also well ahead of those earned by companies heralded by the business community as technology leaders (Xerox Corporation, Eastman Kodak Company, Texas Instruments Incorporated, and Digital Equipment), and these returns are likewise well ahead of those earned by corporations singled out as models of progressive diversification and acquisition planning (GE and United Technologies).

In fact, as Figure 4 shows, the industry leaders shown in Figure 3 outperformed all of the highly touted companies during the most recent five years. In addition, the industry leaders grew faster than premier corporations like 3M and IBM, and they returned only slightly less to their shareholders and capital investors than these same "blue chip" competitors in high-growth industries.

In retrospect, perhaps the much publicized article, "TI Shows U.S. Industry How to Compete in the 1980s,"[1] should have been written about

---

[1] *Business Week,* September 18, 1978, p. 66.

one of the leading companies in my sample instead of about Texas Instruments, because 75 percent of the leaders in the basic industries I studied outperformed TI during the latter half of the 1970s. Moreover, they outperformed TI in industries that averaged only 2.4 percent real growth during the past decade, significantly less than the 15 to 20 percent compound growth rates of the semiconductor industry during this same period.

Thus even a cursory analysis of leading companies in the eight basic industries leads to an important observation: survival and prosperity are possible even when the business environment turns hostile and industry trends change from favorable to unfavorable. In this regard, the casual advice frequently offered to competitors in basic industries—that is, diversify, dissolve, or be prepared for below-average returns—seems oversimplified and even erroneous.[2] A hostile environment offers an excellent basic investment opportunity and reinvestment climate, at least for the industry leaders insightful enough to capitalize on their positions.

Strategies Leading to Success Share Common Characteristics

A more detailed, in-depth examination of the business strategies employed by the top two performing (nondiversified) companies in each of the eight industries sampled reveals that these success strategies share strong common characteristics, irrespective of the particular industry. Indeed, throughout their modern history, all 16 of these leading companies have demonstrated a continuous, single-minded determination to achieve one or both of the following competitive positions within their respective industries:

1. Achieve the lowest delivered cost position relative to competition, coupled with both an acceptable delivered quality and a pricing policy to gain profitable volume and market share growth.
2. Achieve the highest product/service/quality differentiated position relative to competition, coupled with both an acceptable delivered cost structure and a pricing policy to gain margins sufficient to fund reinvestment in product/service differentiation.

A rough categorization of the strategies employed by these 16 companies, based on selective field studies and observed behavior over time, is shown in Figure 5. In most cases, the industry growth and profit leaders chose only one of the two strategic approaches, on the basis that the skills and resources necessary to invest in a low-cost position are insufficient or incompatible with those needed to simultaneously invest in a strongly differentiated position.

The rudiments of this strategic trade-off can be found as early as the 1920s in Alfred P. Sloan's statements regarding GM's selection of a cost-reduced strategy:

---

[2] See, for example, Theodore Levitt, "Dinosaurs among the Bears and Bulls," *Harvard Business Review,* January–February 1975, p. 41; also the section on basic industries in Richard P. Rumelt, *Strategy, Structure, and Economic Performance* (Boston: Division of Research, Harvard Business School, 1974), pp. 128–39.

Figure 5
Competitive strategies employed by leading companies
(Eight basic industries)

Industry	Achieved Low Delivered Cost Position	Achieved "Meaningful" Differentiation	Simultaneous Employment of Both Strategies
Steel	Inland Steel	National	
Tire and rubber	Goodyear	Michelin (French)	
Heavy-duty trucks	Ford	Paccar	
Construction and materials handling equipment		John Deere	Caterpillar
Automotive	General Motors	Daimler Benz (German)	
Major home appliances	Whirlpool	Maytag	
Beer	Miller	G. Heileman Brewing	
Cigarettes	R. J. Reynolds		Philip Morris

Management should now direct its energies toward increasing earning power through increased effectiveness and reduced expense. . . . Efforts that have been so lavishly expended on expansion and development should now be directed at economy in operation. . . . This policy is valid if our cars are at least equal to the best of our competitors in a grade, so that it is not necessary to lead in design.[3]

However, in at least three cases, the leading companies in my sample chose to combine the two approaches, and each has had spectacular success.

Caterpillar has combined lowest cost manufacturing with higher cost but truly outstanding distribution and after-market support to differentiate its line of construction equipment. As a result, Caterpillar, ranking as the 24th largest and 39th most profitable company in the United States, is well ahead of its competitors and most of the *Fortune "500"* glamour companies.

Similarly, the U.S. cigarette division of Philip Morris Incorporated combines the lowest cost, fully automated cigarette manufacturing operation in the world with highest cost, focused branding and promotion to gain industry profit leadership, even without the benefit of either the largest unit volume or segment market share in both domestic and international markets.

And finally, Daimler Benz operates with elements of both strategies but in different segments, coupling the lowest cost position in heavy-duty truck manufacturing in Western Europe with an exceptionally high quality, feature differentiated car line for European and North American export markets.

A more complete picture of the strategic and performance profiles of all major competitors in these eight hostile environments can be obtained by positioning on a matrix those businesses whose axes reflect the relative delivered cost position and the relative product/service differentiation with respect to other competition. The result is a conceptual diagram like that shown in Figure 6.

While the quantification of competitive profiles in this format is typically inexact—because of the proprietary nature of relevant cost, sector, and

---

[3] Alfred P. Sloan, Jr., *My Years with General Motors* (Garden City, N.Y.: Doubleday, 1964), pp. 65–66, 172.

Figure 6
Strategic profile analysis
(Basic mature industries)

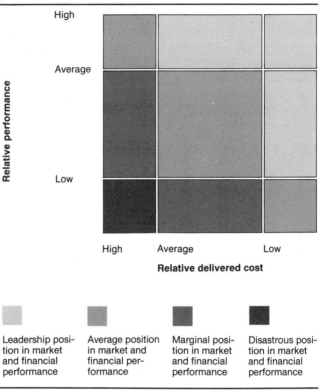

Leadership posi-
tion in market
and financial
performance

Average position
in market and
financial per-
formance

Marginal posi-
tion in market
and financial
performance

Disastrous posi-
tion in market
and financial
performance

performance data—a qualitative attempt to perform this anlaysis for the heavy-duty truck manufacturing industry is presented in Figure 7. This representation, based on an analysis of industry interviews and public records, is imprecise, yet it correlates perfectly with the industry performance profiles over time.

For example, from Figure 7, it is clear why Ford and Paccar continually lead the heavy-duty truck industry in growth and financial performance. It is equally clear why White lingers near bankruptcy and also why Freightliner and International Harvester are rethinking their strategies for heavy-duty trucks. (Freightliner recently entered into a distribution agreement with Volvo in an attempt to differentiate its distribution system in the light-heavy segment, and International Harvester initiated a major cost-reduction effort in truck design and manufacturing in an attempt to improve its weak relative cost position.)

A similar analysis of business-level returns for all 16 leading competitors in the eight industries (Figure 8) indicates some interesting aspects of the respective strategies, as the following comparison reveals:

• The *lowest delivered cost* leader typically grows more slowly, holding price increases and operating margins down to gain volume, fixed-cost

Figure 7
Strategic profiles in U.S. heavy-duty truck manufacturing

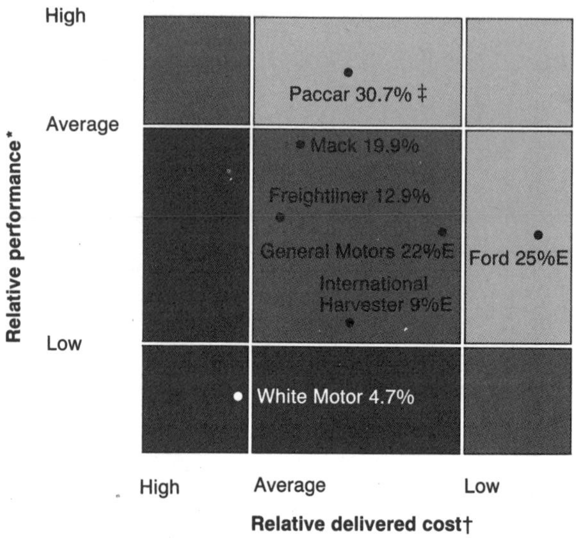

* Based on customer and industry interview data.
† Based on manufacturing and distribution cost analysis, evaluating economies of scale, and vertical integration profiles.
‡ Operating return on assets; E = Estimated from industry sources.

reductions, and improved asset turnover. In addition, this competitor will typically have a lower sales turnover than the differentiated producer, reflecting the higher asset intensity necessary to gain cost reductions in production and distribution.

• The *differentiated position* leader typically grows faster, with higher prices and operating margins to cover promotional, research, and other product/service costs. At the same time, this competitor typically operates with lower asset intensity (higher sales turnover), reflecting both higher prices and a lower cost, "flexible" asset base.

Successful Strategies Come from Purposeful Moves toward a Leadership Position

In examining the business strategies and subsequent performance of the leading competitors, it becomes clear that purposeful movement toward and defense of a "winning" strategic position—either lowest cost and/or superior, price-justified differentiation—has been the fundamental long-term objective of all 16 high-performance companies. There is little doubt that consistency and clarity of purpose have helped to mobilize and coordinate internal resources in gaining and defending a leadership position.

It is important to note that the time-phased pattern of investment decisions used to attain and hold these winning positions was based on "doing the right things" to gain leadership in lowest costs and/or differentiation. As a result, all the high performers in my sample used careful strategic analysis to guide their investments, avoiding simplistic adherence to doctrinaire approaches

Figure 8
Business level returns and revenue growth sales

Leading industrial goods producers 1978*	Operating Margins	Sales Turnover	Operating ROA	Revenue Growth Rates, 1975–1979
Steel				
Inland Steel	8.3%	1.3	10.8%	11.4%
National	12.0	1.5	18.0	12.0
Tire and rubber				
Goodyear	8.6	1.5	12.9	10.5
Michelin	10.0 (est.)	N.A.	N.A.	N.A.
Heavy-duty trucks				
Ford	11.0 (est.)	2.3	25.0 (est.)	12.7
Paccar	12.7	2.4	30.5	15.5
Construction and materials handling equipment				
Caterpillar	15.5	1.8	27.9	14.9
John Deere	10.0	1.3	13.0	17.5
Leading consumer goods producers* 1978				
Automotive				
General Motors	9.6%	2.0	19.2%	13.2%
Daimler Benz (automotive)	11.0	2.4	26.4	15.1
Major home appliances				
Whirlpool	8.4	1.0	8.4	5.3
Maytag	21.8	1.8	39.2	9.1
Brewing				
Miller	8.2	1.5	12.3	29.2
G. Heileman Brewing	9.5	3.5	33.3	32.2
Cigarettes				
R. J. Reynolds	17.1	2.3	39.3	15.0
Philip Morris	17.7	1.4	24.8	20.1

* Lowest delivered cost producer listed first, followed by most differentiated producer.

toward strategy formulation which come from the naive application of tools like:

- Share/growth matrices—planning models which suggest that mature market segments should be ''milked'' or ''harvested'' for cash flows.
- Experience curves and PIMS—planning models which suggest that high market share and/or lowest cost, vetically integrated production are keys to success in mature markets.[4]

Instead, based on a case-by-case analysis, the performance leaders made investment decisions which frequently conflicted with these doctrinaire theories:

[4] PIMS (Profit Impact of Market Strategies) is a multiple regression model which relates profitability to a number of associative variables. See Sidney Schoeffler, Robert D. Buzzell, and Donald F. Heany, ''Impact of Strategic Planning on Profit Performance,'' *Harvard Business Review*, March–April 1974, p. 137.

1. The leadership positions in mature markets were not being milked by any of the 16 competitors, contrary to the advice of consultants who emphasize the portfolio approach to asset management. In fact, the top managers in two of the leading companies I interviewed laughed when they discussed this concept. They pointed out that their future success and growth opportunities were far greater if they aggressively reinvested in their base business than if they redeployed assets into other (diversified) industries.

2. Low-cost production is not essential to prosper in mature markets, contrary to the belief of strong proponents of the experience curve. Instead, high sustainable returns also come from reinvesting in an average cost, highly differentiated position, as the data of the previous section and Figure 8 demonstrate, and as the ongoing track records of companies like Paccar and Maytag clearly illustrate.

3. High market share and accumulated experience are not essential for cost leadership in a mature market, as indicated by proponents of the experience curve and some large-sample empirical studies like PIMS. In fact, four of the eight low-cost producers in this study—Inland Steel, Whirlpool Corporation, Miller, and Philip Morris—have achieved their lowest cost positions without the benefit of high relative market shares.

Rather, these producers have focused their plants by emphasizing modern, automated process technology, and they have heavily invested in their distribution systems to gain scale economies and other cost reductions in their delivery systems.

4. Vertical integration is not necessary to exploit cost leadership in mature markets, as suggested by a number of empirical and economic studies. In fact, all of the low-cost producers in the industries under study were less vertically integrated into upstream and downstream activities than at least one other major competitor in their industry.

Instead of emphasizing vertical integration as a policy, all looked for selective integration into high value-added, proprietary componentry, following the type of integration policy first delineated by General Motors in the 1920s of "not investing in general industries of which a comparatively small part of the product is consumed in the manufacture of cars."

Instead of fully integrating, the low-cost leaders invested to have the most efficient process technology in at least one selective stage of the vertical chain. Consider, for example, Ford in truck assembly and Inland in order entry-distribution. The result in all cases is focus—the ability to orient management attention to gain low costs in a partially integrated operation. As one of Ford's major competitors observed:

Ford is the least integrated of any of the high-volume, heavy-duty truck manufacturers in the world, yet it is still the low-cost producer and gains one of the highest ROIs in the industry. In retrospect, Ford's strategy was brilliant; they let the rest of us learn to manufacture componentry while they learned to manufacture profits.

Problems Come from Failure to Gain or Defend a Leadership Position

A more detailed examination of the marginal or failing competitors in each of the eight basic industries (Figure 9) also reveals some interesting observations:

Figure 9
Marginal or failing companies in U.S. markets

Steel	J&L-Youngstown
	Kaiser
Tire and rubber	Uniroyal
	Mohawk
	Cooper
Heavy-duty trucks	White Motor
Construction and materials handling equipment	Massey Ferguson Allis Chalmers
Automotive	Chrysler
Major home appliances	Tappan
Beer	Most regional breweries
	Schlitz
Cigarettes	Liggett & Myers

1. The historical strategies and policies pursued by these companies have placed them in an unstable position. All are the high-cost producers in their segments, and all have a product that not only is largely undifferentiated in any meaningful sense but also in many cases is below average in quality and performance.

2. The external pressures that these companies complain about—unwarranted regulation and unfair foreign competition—are simply the final blows, sealing a fate that was predestined by improper strategic positioning or repositioning in the 1950s and 1960s, a period when there was still growth and time to maneuver.

3. Many of these marginal producers held low-cost or differentiated positions in these earlier years, and made strategic errors in their reinvestment decisions which contributed to their marginal or failing positions today, as the following examples show:

- *International Harvester* led the U.S. heavy-duty truck manufacturing industry in 1965 with a market share of 30 percent. However, over the next decade, IH failed to reduce costs as rapidly as Ford and GM. As a result, the IH truck division is now a high-cost, low-margin producer.
- *White Motor,* a strong number-two truck producer in the mid-1960s, invested in backward integration into cabs, frames, axles, and engine manufacturing, assuming that this would reduce costs. Unfortunately, these investments, all made at suboptimal capacities for efficient scale economies, resulted in a relative high-cost position, adding momentum to White's deteriorating situation.
- *Tappan,* the technology leader in ranges in the early 1960s, chose to broaden that product line, to diversify, to reduce R&D expenditures, and to out-source certain key engineering activities. As a result, it failed to gain the low-cost position in ranges (today held by GE). And by failing to reinvest in technology, it lost its differentiated position in ranges to Caloric (gas), Jenn-Air (electric), and Raytheon (microwave).
- *Chrysler,* the technology leader in the U.S. automotive market in the early 1950s with a 25 percent market share, chose to make questionable

international expansion decisions while adopting a "me too" participatory strategy in the domestic market. The subsequent decline in Chrysler's position and returns was predictable, and this disaster trajectory was certainly accelerated in the early 1970s when its management team announced a revised (but highly inappropriate) strategy to "try to be a General Motors in whatever segments of the market we choose to compete in."

For a Deteriorating Position, Diversity May Not Be the Proper Recovery Approach

Over the past several years, it has become fashionable to recommend product/market diversification as a way out of an unstable or failing position for mature companies in hostile environments. Unfortunately, in the 64 companies I examined in this research, diversification has "helped" overcome major competitive/performance problems in only three—The B.F. Goodrich Co., General Tire, and Armco Steel (now Armco Group). These three competitors recognized the tenuous nature of their positions early in the maturity cycle and took steps to resegment their base businesses into more advantageous positions by redeploying assets in carefully chosen diversification moves.

* *Goodrich* moved into high-margin, specialty segments of the tire industry while diversifying to attain a low-cost position in PVC and other basic chemicals.
* *General* shifted into low-cost production of tires for commercial vehicles while diversifying to attain a participatory position in very high-growth, fragmented industries such as communications and aerospace.
* *Armco* proceeded into low-cost steel production in selected regional segments like oil country pipe, while diversifying into high-growth markets like oil field equipment, oil and gas exploration, and financial services. (A recent public relations release from Armco announced that most of its new capital investment would go toward growing these diversification ventures, while maintaining only current capacity levels in steel making.)

These early efforts to resegment and to gain meaningful diversification have paid off. General and Armco lead all competitors in the rubber and steel industries in return on capital and growth, while Goodrich has moved into a stable third place among the surviving tire and rubber producers.

On the other hand, efforts to gain meaningful economic diversification have eluded most of the other problem competitors in the eight industries. By waiting too long to begin diversification efforts, most lack the capital and managerial skills to enter new markets and/or to grow businesses successfully in these markets. Thus their diversification efforts to date have been too small or have been managed in too conservative a fashion to obtain sustainable performance improvements, as witnessed by the very minor performance contribution of U.S. Steel's diversification program into chemicals and the continuing problems of Liggett & Myers Tobacco Company, Inc., despite a 43 percent diversification program out of the tobacco industry.

As a result of these modest, participatory efforts, some of the marginal performers in the eight industries have even divested diversified assets to gain capital and "hang on" for a few more years in the base business. Two notable examples are White Motor's recent sale of its construction equipment operation and Uniroyal's sale of its consumer goods division.

On the whole, it would appear that diversification comes too little and too late for most companies caught in a hostile environment. However, for a courageous few, continued managerial commitment and refocus on the base business to provide a steady flow of capital for promoting meaningful positions in diversified businesses may work to ensure ongoing growth and vitality.

Structural Evolution Moves toward a Dynamic Equilibrium as Basic Industries Face a Hostile Environment

A summary of the underlying data in my study suggests that basic industries in mature, hostile environments are moving through a structural evolution, leading ultimately to four industry and performance subgroups (Figure 10):

Figure 10
Strategic and performance subgroups
(Basic industries)

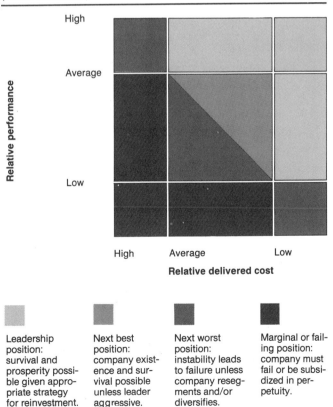

Leadership position: survival and prosperity possible given appropriate strategy for reinvestment.

Next best position: company existence and survival possible unless leader aggressive.

Next worst position: instability leads to failure unless company resegments and/or diversifies.

Marginal or failing position: company must fail or be subsidized in perpetuity.

1. *Leadership position*—Competitors who achieve the lowest delivered cost and/or the highest differentiated position. These positions are gained either on a full product line (Caterpillar) or on an economically viable segment (Whirlpool in washers and dryers). At maturity these competitors will have the highest growth rates and returns in the industry, the best reinvestment prospects, and they should be able to prosper and coexist in dynamic equilibrium even though external pressures continue.

2. *Next best position*—Competitors who attain the second best position in either cost or differentiation (again on either a full or partial line basis). These companies will have moderate but generally acceptable growth rates and returns, and reinvestments can (and will typically) be made at return levels slightly above the cost of capital. For these companies, vulnerability to strategic and performance deterioration occurs mainly when the industry leaders or a set of externally subsidized competitors choose to aggressively attack. (For example, the recent problems of Ford in the U.S. automotive market can be directly traced to GM's more aggressive market share strategy, coupled with the European and Japanese attacks on U.S. small car markets.)

3. *Next worst position*—Competitors who finish in third place as the industry matures. Given a hostile environment, growth rates and return prospects for these companies are bleak unless they resegment into uncovered niches and gain a sustainable leadership position in these segments (AMC in utility vehicles, Goodrich in performance tires), or unless they can make major asset redeployment into meaningful diversified markets (like Armco and General). Without the ability to resegment or diversify, competitors in this class ultimately will move toward a marginal or failing position. (Chrysler in automotive, Uniroyal in tires, and Schlitz in brewing are examples of companies currently going through such a transition.)

4. *Marginal or failing position*—Competitors who end up last in mature, hostile environments ultimately must fail or be subsidized, either through government ownership or aid (Chrysler) or through cash infusions from a diversified parent (Kaiser in steel, Allis Chalmers in construction equipment). Despite efforts to use such subsidies to resegment and refocus their operations, the survey data shows no successful efforts in such turnaround attempts among the 64 competitors in the eight basic industries, raising a fundamental question as to whether there is any real possibility of strategic turnaround. Consequently, a society or a company subsidizing this type of marginal competitor should expect the worst—perpetual subsidies, perhaps slightly offset by infrequent operating returns during high peaks in basic economic cycles.

In Summary

The strategic and performance data from this eight-industry study suggest that both great successes and failures are occurring as basic, mature industries move into a hostile business environment created by slower growth, higher inflation, more regulation, and intensified competition. Uniformly, the successes come to those companies that achieve either the lowest cost or most differentiated position. Simultaneously, survival is possible for those companies that have the foresight to downsize their asset commitments into niches in their basic industry and to use their incremental capital for meaningful diversification moves. For the weaker companies, the inability to achieve a lowest cost or most differentiated position results in high vulnerability and ultimate failure or perpetual subsidy.

For general managers guiding their companies into the economic environment of the 1980s, the implications of these findings are clear. The laws of the jungle change as maturity comes and hostility intensifies. In such a jungle, the range of strategic options narrows, requiring both an early warning of the coming hostility and an early strategic repositioning for a company to survive and prosper.

Hence intensified efforts must be made to create internal administrative structures and mechanisms to recognize and efficiently manage this repositioning. (GM's effective organizational restructuring in the early 1970s to respond to the down-sizing imperative stands as a brilliant case study in the use of such an administrative effort to create strategic change.)

For public policymakers monitoring and attempting to influence the business environment, these results suggest that failures will be inevitable, as industry structures evolve in the face of maturity and hostility. The currently popular attempts at forced consolidation and subsidies are one way of dealing with these failures. However, these actions should be taken with full knowledge that they will not stop the driving market forces.

The question that remains in the decade ahead is whether the short-run employment, balance of payments, and fiscal stability provided by such public policy actions is worth the long-run cost of maintaining an inefficient industry structure that conflicts with the driving market forces created by a hostile environment.

What this article is about: Creating new business within a company is often the only way to grow. But many attempts result in abysmal failure. The authors describe what CEOs and senior managers must do to increase the chances of success for new ventures.

3-7 Corporate venturing: Challenges for senior managers*

Ian C. MacMillan and Robin George

Ian C. MacMillan is director of the Center for Entrepreneurial Studies at New York University. Robin George is vice president at Rain Hill Group, Inc.

Companies are increasingly looking to corporate venturing (the creation of new businesses within the company) as a means of achieving long-term growth. Yet many of the real obstacles to developing businesses within corporations occur at the corporate level. Venturing efforts that founder often do so because senior management in the corporation fails to recognize that it has significant responsibilities to discharge.

This prompted the authors to conduct a multistage study of the problems of implementing new business development in corporations. In the first stage, 35 managers who had at one time or another been heavily involved in the new venture activities of their firms were approached. The managers were asked to generate a list of factors that they felt had contributed significantly to problems of venture execution. These results were then collected and displayed to the assembled group of managers, who in the next stage were asked to provide comments and suggestions for overcoming the problems. In the final stage, a discussion was held with the management of 20 of the Fortune 500 companies. The discussion involved implementation problems and solutions.

This article describes the key challenges that were identified in the study. These challenges must be met by senior management if a corporate venturing effort is to be successful. So that there is no confusion about terminology, the accompanying box lists definitions of terms.

Level of Ventures

Six types or levels of ventures are listed below in order of increasing difficulty:

---

* Reprinted by permission from *The Journal of Business Strategy* 5, no. 3 (Winter 1985), pp. 34–43. Copyright © 1985, Warren, Gorham, & Lamont Inc. All rights reserved.

Level 1. New enhancements to current products and services.

Level 2. New products and services to be sold to current markets within one to two years.

Level 3. Existing products and services that can be sold to new markets within one to two years.

Level 4. New products or services that can be sold to current markets, or existing products or services that can be sold to new markets. These new ventures will take more than two years to reach the commercialization stage.

Level 5. New products or services that are unfamiliar to the company but are already being produced and sold by other companies.

Level 6. New products or services that do not exist today but could be developed to replace current products or services in known markets, or entirely new markets that could be created for the new products or services.

Level 1 "ventures" aren't really ventures at all. These ventures, or perhaps more appropriately, projects, will never result in new business or sources of revenue, per se; they are only described to complete the spectrum. It is levels 2 through 6 that describe the major avenues of growth available for corporate venturing.

Unfortunately, the organizational and managerial challenges of the ventures increase almost exponentially as one moves down the list of levels.

While there may be exceptions, the ability of a company to handle each level of venture follows a distinct pattern:

• Level 2 ventures, which are destined to deliver new products or services to existing markets within two years, are easier for divisional management to support out of their operating funds and resources than ventures with longer-term focuses. There is a simple organizational reason for this: Most bonus programs are designed to reward short-term performance, so new products that are projected to generate revenue within this time frame can be presented in annual plans and tolerated within the divisional reward system (although they often still disrupt ongoing operations).

• Level 3 presents a very different type of problem that must be surmounted. For level 3 ventures, existing products or services must be sold to new markets within two years. The structure of most corporations is so focused on their current markets that operating divisions just cannot enter new markets at will. They must either collaborate with other divisions already serving those markets (a very difficult thing to do in most organizations) or acquire or develop a whole new marketing and sales force.

• Level 4s are essentially level 2s or level 3s that will take longer than two years to commercialize. Although they will ultimately be incorporated into an existing operation and benefit from the resources and expertise of the existing organization, the managers in the study argued that these longer-term ventures tend to be ignored, overmanaged or, in hard times, totally stripped of support if they are attempted inside operating divisions. By and large, these ventures must be grown outside the operating entity into which they will ultimately be incorporated.

- Level 5 ventures are never close enough to an operating entity for them to be logically initiated from within one. On rare occasions, an entrepreneurial general manager in a division has been known to initiate and support level 5 ventures. More generally, these diversification ventures must usually be initiated at the corporate level with appropriate support from the senior levels of the organization.
- Level 6 poses the greatest number of problems. The development of new products or services with which the world is unfamiliar demands a very long time horizon and enormous tolerance for uncertainty on the part of senior management. The authors do not know of a single level 6 venture that was successfully undertaken within an operating group.

This study suggests that it is only the rare company that can successfully manage level 4, 5, or 6 ventures inside divisions that must also keep up with current operating responsibilities. Most companies that really want to use venturing as a vehicle for substantial growth have had to establish separate entities through which they create and develop level 4, 5, and 6 ventures.

Important imperatives that senior management must meet if the corporate venturing process is to succeed at all can conveniently be divided into two groups: (1) imperatives that have to do with initiation of the venturing process, and (2) imperatives that have to do with execution of the ventures.

Initiation of the Venturing Activity

Senior managers, particularly CEOs, do not have the time to manage each individual venture. However, senior management cannot totally abdicate either. There are cases where only senior management can prevent or solve major problems. The experiences of two major companies, whose first venturing attempts were disastrous, are reviewed below to illustrate a few of the aspects that must be managed in initiating a venture effort.

In a mature heavy machinery and equipment company, a second new management in three years was recruited by the board to develop a strategy for rejuvenating the somnolent company. The new management determined that the company was currently participating in approximately 165 of the 500 steps involved in producing the world's foodstuffs; that is, their equipment was used to plant seeds, harvest crops, process raw food into prepared products, deliver food to distributors, and so on. The new management decided to participate in all 500 steps, whether equipment was involved or not. They enthusiastically identified seed companies, biotechnology programs for producing improved seeds, food packaging technology, and so on, and created a task force comprised of several senior long-term employees who were responsible for endorsing the candidates and integrating the resulting ventures into the organization. The task force met monthly and gave token endorsement to the proposals, but always found additional review steps that should be conducted prior to action. The problem here was that each task

---

KEY CONCEPTS

- *Senior Management:* In general, by senior management, the authors mean the corporate leadership. However, some organizations delegate significant strategic responsibility to major operating sectors. In these cases, the top managers of the sectors could be regarded as the senior management referred to in this article. However, in order to qualify as senior management, the relevant individuals must have the resources and the full authority to support ventures that will take longer than two years to commercialize.
- *Venture Managers:* These are the individuals who are directly responsible for moving the business idea from concept to full commercialization.
- *Venture Ombudsman:* This is a representative of senior management who interfaces directly with the venture managers. He can have a formal title and direct responsibility for the venture process, or he can perform the function on an ad hoc basis.

---

force member also had line responsibilities, and was convinced that growth was easy to achieve—but not through venturing. They felt growth was best achieved through a larger sales force. The task force members took their roles so lightly that, on their way back to their divisions after each meeting, they would stop off at the local pub and make bets on how long the new management team would last.

In the second case, the CEO of a large chemical company started announcing 10 years before the fact that the company was going to build new businesses to achieve significant profit contributions from specialty chemicals, thus taking advantage of the technology created by the company's massive R&D effort. Statements appeared in every annual report, and were repeated at each stock analyst briefing. However, no significant internal changes were made to execute this plan. The capital allocation process continued as before, and the few new business proposals that made it to the review stage of the new venture process were rejected for lack of adequate documentation. For seven years there was no formal review of progress for new business development. When the recession of the late 1970s finally precipitated a full analysis of the business (to try to explain the heavy losses), the CEO finally realized that in all those years, no significant progress had been made in shifting to a specialty chemical business. The company now has in place a reorganization plan that created eight units where there used to be three. Each unit is required to report annually the sales and profits associated with products and markets that the company had not had five years earlier. Each unit must also submit an annual report of progress on individual current projects that are expected to contribute to significant sales and profits in the next 1 to 5 and 5 to 10 years. Two of the three original general managers have been replaced, and the eight general managers now finally believe that the CEO is serious about venturing, and the managers are beginning to address the problem of balancing current operations with new business developments.

These examples, plus the input obtained from managers in the study, indicate that there are four major initiation challenges that senior management needs to meet. These are:

1. Selection of context.
2. Design of structure.
3. Provision of adequate support.
4. Appointment of a venture ombudsman.

Select the Context

It is vital for senior management of the company to scope out and delimit what the appropriate range of venture activities should be, particularly if a clear organizational need can be specified [7]. Appropriate venturing activities can be indicated via a clearly articulated development strategy [4]. Both the equipment manufacturer and the chemical company cited above started off expecting too much of their organizations. Too often, a CEO arbitrarily decides that it is "time we innovated" and announces some grandiose plan to start venturing, without concern for the required quantum jumps in organizational capabilities, or massive redirection of effort and commitment in the firm. This is irresponsible, and generally sows only confusion, frustration, and eventual disillusionment in the corporation. The net result is a huge waste of time, energy, enthusiasm, and resources because of having tried ventures at too ambitious a level.

It is a major responsibility of senior management to ensure that the company pursue an appropriate portfolio of ventures. Because of the inherently high failure rate in new ventures, it is usually necessary to pursue more than one venture. Yet it is equally important not to pursue too many ventures. This overstrains the organization's capabilities. Senior management needs to shape the portfolio of ventures rather carefully so that there is a match between the amount of venturing activity and the evolving organizational capability at venturing. This means that the organization may have to "learn to venture" by focusing initially on a high proportion of level 2, 3, and 4 ventures, and a very limited number of level 5 or 6 ventures. By keeping the early ventures rather modest, the chances of success increase [5]. This also builds morale and confidence within the organization [7].

Design the Appropriate Structure

The two case studies also demonstrate the importance of creating the right structure. In both cases, the CEOs failed to recognize the capacity of the ongoing operation to ignore, smother, or actively resist new business development. This is quite natural. It is unrealistic to expect line managers of current operations not to devote most of their attention to today's crises and to assign lowest priority to fledgling ventures whose impact may only be in the next decade's operating results.

Responsibility for progress has to be "owned" and so it should formally be assigned to clearly identified venture managers who acknowledge ownership of this responsibility.

The appropriate structure called for is very much related to the level of venture:

- In most cases, level 2 and level 3 ventures are best handled by the divisions themselves. Here, division heads act as senior management. Responsibility for results should be assigned to a divisional product development manager or divisional market development manager who is supported by a product or market development team. This team is appointed by the division head. It should be comprised of functional representatives from all the division functions and have direct accountability for results and progress [8].
- On the other hand, level 4, 5, and 6 ventures call for specialized structures that match their increasingly significant challenges. Many managers in the sample argued that such ventures could never succeed if they remained in the divisions, and that an entirely separate organizational unit is required, much like Teleflex Corp. or the Brunswick Corp. have established. These companies set up separate venture departments with independent funding and freedom to get any outside resources that are not available in-house.

Managers in the study made the following points regarding the design of appropriate structures for levels 6, 5, and 4.

Level 6 ventures must have direct endorsement, support, and attention from the senior management of the company. So few of these ventures have ever proven successful that the personal attention of the CEO is required when one is undertaken. When those in charge of level 6 projects report directly to the CEO, this assures that these projects will receive the support they need. And venturers will not commit themselves to too many ventures because CEOs will not be able to devote time to more than two or three well-managed, focused level 6 projects.

Level 5 opportunities fall into this category as well. Since level 5 ventures have no natural home within the organization, they need to be "grown" in a completely separate unit.

Level 4 projects can be developed in their future home division, but then they must be developed and nurtured separately from the division's operating activities. The pragmatic fact is that most operating divisions are not able to provide the requisite nurturing and attention to fledgling level 4 ventures, so these ventures merely wither and die.

Whatever the detailed design for each venture, senior management must recruit an individual venture manager or champion [6] who accepts direct ownership of the venture and the responsibility for delivering results. If these venture managers are to be successfully recruited, they must believe that the organization is committed to the venturing effort. This is the next challenge.

Commit to Providing Adequate Support

The venturing effort will surely fail if senior management does not demonstrate that it is truly committed to delivering the financial and organizational resources that are necessary for the venturing effort. Depending on the company's history of initiating venturing efforts, this commitment may need to be amply demonstrated in dollars and in organizational structure before career employees will volunteer to become venture managers.

In company after company, attempts at new venture development efforts have failed abysmally because management cut back on critical resources when the rest of the organization fell on hard times. If senior management is likely to do this, the new venture development should not even be started.

This does not mean that the firm should doggedly hold on to useless individual ventures or ineffective managers; it does mean that there must be the feeling in the organization that management will continue to supply the resources needed to sustain a new venture development effort. If needed resources may be withdrawn as soon as ongoing activities run into adversity, no competent and intelligent subordinate will place career bets on an activity that has such an obviously low level of senior management commitment. When senior management cannot demonstrate its convictions with courage, why should the employees?

It is equally fatal to deny talent to the venture effort. Developing a new venture requires top talent, not mediocre performers. If some of the very best people are not assigned to new venture development, management is again wasting effort. It is strategically wiser to go back to running the existing business better.

In one company, a senior scientist was appointed to run the newly created venture development effort four years before he was eligible for early retirement. His selection stemmed from the fact that he had played a major role as an inventor of a multimillion-dollar product early in his career. However, he had devoted most of the intervening years to coming up with various enhancements to the product. In the four years he worked on new venture development, he reviewed dozens of opportunities, but always decided that they were too risky, would take too long to develop, or would not make a big enough impact on the organization. In reality, he had no incentive to risk his track record in the few years before he retired.

Another error is to make new venture activity a training ground for junior executives who can hardly wait to do something else. For example, in a large beverage company, new venture development was viewed as a staff job and the director spent all of his time paving his way to becoming general manager of a $500 million existing product group. He was never around to focus on new venture development. The question becomes how to find, recruit, and motivate the right type of venture management talent.

Appoint a Venture Ombudsman

A few organizations have had significant successes in handling the "talent" issue by appointing a venture ombudsman [3, 6, 9]. The venture ombudsman is now becoming a key factor in the success of corporate venturing.

The ombudsman plays a vital part in making sure that certain key issues are addressed. Only he has the clout to insist that senior management clearly identify which strategic areas to investigate or pursue. He plays a major role in identifying or recruiting venture managers. He keeps the focus on action rather than endless analysis of opportunities. Without an ombudsman, the business of approving the areas to pursue, of identifying, recruiting, and relocating the venture managers, and of actually getting the venture started can prove insurmountable to many corporations. They will often remain stalled in the selection and approval stage because the other components do not fall into place.

The person chosen should be thoroughly familiar with the corporation's strategy and culture. He should have high tolerance for uncertainty, which calls for a secure individual. He must be capable of inspiring and guiding the venture managers and arguing their case with senior management. On the other hand, he needs to make sure that senior management's interests are represented.

The critical role that this venture ombudsman plays cannot be underrated. It calls for objectivity, judgment, and dedication to fulfilling the corporation's growth goals as well as strong, persuasive powers and solid influence within the company.

The venture ombudsman will generally have direct responsibility for level 5s and level 6s. He may sponsor or only support level 4s, and his role in level 2s and level 3s should be minimal—he should only serve as a godfather to those product or market development managers responsible to their divisional managers for venture results.

Once the venturing activity is initiated, senior management still has the responsibility for managing the execution of the venturing process.

Senior Manager as Sponsor

It is almost essential to have a senior-level manager as the sponsor for new developments within the corporation. In some cases, where a formal structure is created, this senior manager has a formal title, a lean but competent staff, and even several level 4, 5, or 6 venture managers under his direct control. In other situations, he may primarily help solve problems as they arise in ventures of type 2, 3, or 4 evolving at the divisional level while continuing to perform other management functions. The role will depend on the corporate environment and the attitudes of senior management.

Execution of the Venturing Activity

In managing the execution of the venture effort, senior management faces the following three challenges:

1. Impose discipline.
2. Fully assess and understand the risk.
3. Manage the process, but not the projects.

Impose Discipline

As shown in the two cases illustrated, one of the most important contributions that senior management must make is to insist on disciplined venturing. Just as venture capitalists demand discipline in the independent ventures they support, so senior managers should demand that corporate venturing be disciplined. Senior management exerts discipline in the following ways.

Insist on Output   The problem of many of the corporations that do decide to grow through internal venturing is a tendency to focus on endlessly developing, refining, and modifying the criteria they use in screening opportunities. Instead of launching new business ventures, they circumnavigate the globe in search of opportunities to screen. One screening system, for example, requires that for each venture a series of analyses be performed. In fact, the list of analyses is 10 pages long—that is just the list, not the analyses themselves.

Venture managers need to be focused on output, not on analysis. It is an important responsibility of the senior management to insist on, and expect, output in the form of actual revenues from new business. Within a reasonable time frame, the venturing effort should deliver a realistic target percentage of sales from new business. Both the equipment manufacturer and the chemical producer in the illustrative cases failed to do this, so their venturing effort never really got started. If the senior managers do not persistently and continuously insist on output, no one else will.

In level 2 and 3 ventures, the role of senior management is relatively simple: assign responsibilities to the relevant divisions so that they deliver results in the form of revenues from new activities, persistently monitor the divisions to see whether this is being delivered, and take appropriate appreciative or punitive action on the basis of results. Little further intervention is needed. However, in the case of levels 4, 5, and 6, it becomes necessary to demand more detail for monitoring purposes.

Demand that Each Venture Plan Have Clearly Identified Milestones and Kill Points As Block [2] suggests, in level 4, 5, and 6 ventures, venture budgets should be formulated on the basis of key milestones to be achieved, rather than on an annual basis. As each milestone is achieved, the progress of the venture can be evaluated to see whether it is worth pursuing further, and what resources and efforts should be committed in light of the most recent information. Senior management plays a vital role by demanding that the venture managers think through and present these milestones and their associated kill points, so that the progress of the ventures can in fact be monitored.

Shoot the Wounded It is senior management's sometimes painful responsibility to exercise the "kill" option. Once a venture is under way, either within a division (levels 2 and 3) or as a separate venture (levels 4–6), it is unreasonable to expect the manager of the venture to maintain a high level of enthusiasm and commitment while also keeping his thumb hovering over the "kill button."

This is why it is important for senior management to insist on the formulation of a clear definition of kill points for each major milestone in the evolution of any proposed venture. After the "launch," the venture ombudsman can monitor the progress and maintain the magisterial objectivity required to declare failure if the venture reaches a milestone without having accomplished what was deemed critical in the plan. Then, however painful this may be, the kill option may have to be exercised. Obviously, senior management also retains the option to revise the criteria based on the information acquired during that implementation phase.

Many corporations in the study did not have clearly established kill points and so, via creeping commitment, were drawn into spending millions of dollars beyond the original budgets. For example, the energy companies that pumped billions of dollars into tar sands and oil shale projects should have set up kill points. It would have saved them huge sums. The net result was that resources and talent were vaingloriously wasted, when they could have been diverted to other, viable ventures, which in turn failed for lack of critically needed resources.

Fully Assess and Understand the Risks

It is important that ventures be launched with a full understanding and anticipation of the dangers involved. Often, only senior management is in a position to make the required risk assessments. While the process is initiated with the selection of areas in which to venture, it must be reexamined when specific ventures are proposed. Several senior managers cited the importance of determining the "full cost" of failure. They found that failure of the venture meant much more than the financial write-offs, such as substantial damage to the company's public image, prestige, or credibility with unions, suppliers, and distributors. If there is a potential for such expanded risk, the attendant problems must be anticipated.

A second risk is the danger of finding exit barriers that prohibit abortion of the venture if it fails. For instance, in the case of a failing construction venture underwritten by one U.S. conglomerate company in South America, the host government took the position that if the company abandoned the venture, it would have to withdraw its other business activities as well. The venture became a "bleeding ulcer" that the firm regretted for years. A third risk issue has to do with upside risk. There have been corporate ventures (such as stainless steel razor blades) that significantly exceeded the most optimistic forecasts of the company. These ventures precipitated enormous demand, which could not be supplied because this upside risk had not been considered. As a result, competitors moved in and walked away with the lion's share of the new business. Contingency plans for catering to such upside risks are needed, and must be developed in such a way that they do not add additional investment exposure to the venture.

The important issue with fully exploring the risk dimension is that as long as the full risks of the venture are thought through, management can develop plans to handle them. The worst time to discover these full implications is when they are "on-line." At that time, the margin for error is at its smallest, and the probability of error is greatest.

Manage the Process, Not the Projects

The final responsibility of senior management lies in being able to "manage the forest, not the trees." That means striking the correct balance between the undesirable extremes of continuous interference and positive neglect.

As both Block [2] and Burgelman [3] have strongly suggested, the frequent interference of senior management in the individual ventures is something to be assiduously avoided. The basic challenge is to manage the venturing process, not the ventures themselves.

The venture managers in the sample were adamant that this role is important and constructive if it is focused on the following activities:

Probe for, and Compensate for, Organizational Weaknesses Every company has weaknesses, and several managers in the study identified a fatal tendency for their companies to attempt all the tasks of development, manufacturing, and marketing when they were severely handicapped in one or more areas.

Roberts [8] has suggested several alternatives to doing it all oneself. Along these lines the authors developed Figure 1, which lists some joint venturing options that should be seriously considered as alternatives to doing the whole task oneself. Failing to recognize that one does not have the requisite skills in the particular endeavor virtually assures that the venture will be crippled by this weakness. Since it is difficult for subordinates to argue vehemently that their company has weaknesses, the senior management needs to create an atmosphere that positively encourages, or insists on, the use of external resources where appropriate.

For instance, Teleflex began an internal new venture funding program in 1972 and had 20 active projects in mid-1974. The program continues today and has been successful: 30 percent of their 1983 sales can be traced to their new venture fund's support. The company feels that one of the key elements to the program has been that the venture managers go outside of the organization to buy prototype development, manufacturing, and testing rather than trying to do it all in-house. While very little was "given up" by purchasing outside help, the fact that it was made available was essential to the success of many of Teleflex's ventures.

Probe to Ensure that Management of Venture Is Proceeding Well Venture managers felt that senior management has an important and constructive monitoring role to play. It needs to constantly probe the venture management's handling of common venture problems; "keep the ventures honest" in terms of their milestones; and only intervene in individual ventures when it is clear that the venture managers are having difficulties in resolving these problems. Briefly, these recurring venture management problems are:

Figure 1
Alternatives to compensate for skill deficiencies

Organization Skill Deficiency			
Product and Process Development	**Manufacturing and Sourcing**	**Marketing and Distributing**	**Feasible Strategies**
X			License in new products and processes
	X	X	License out new products/processes developed, or sell the patents
	X		Subcontract out the required manufacturing
X		X	Seek manufacturing subcontracts and/or private label business
		X	Franchise out marketing and distribution of products
X	X		Seek out marketing/distribution franchises for others' products
X	X	X	Acquire a successful going concern

- Difficulty in getting support from key stakeholders.
- Difficulty in securing internal support.
- Impatience in the firm with the venture's progress.
- Difficulty in coping with the rapid growth when success is finally achieved.

Often the intervention by senior managers on behalf of the venture management is all that is needed to rapidly resolve such problems. This is another area where the venture ombudsman can prove invaluable.

Devote Disproportionate Time and Attention to Venturing Effort
Unless senior management is prepared to give sustained personal attention to the new business ventures, there is little hope that other managers, occupied with day-to-day crises and ongoing distractions, will be prepared to do so. This calls for devoting a disproportionate amount of time and a disproportionate amount of resources to the nurturing of ventures. Note that this does not mean that the CEO spends all his time on the ventures. It means that venturing is:

- Kept on important agendas.
- Discussed frequently.
- Given priority when problems arise for specific ventures.
- Given the benefit of the doubt in marginal cases when venturing activities conflict with other operations.

These activities are necessary so that people in the organization realize that senior management takes venturing seriously.

Recognize the Difference between Poor Decisions and Poor Outcomes
This is a major lesson that firms new to venturing have to learn—venturing is inherently risky. Therefore a distinction has to be made between a situation where the venturer made a poor decision and a situation where the venturer made a good decision with all the limited information available at that time, but the outcome was poor because "the ball bounced the wrong way." If venture managers are to be taken to task for events beyond their control, venturing will collapse. This is once again why it is so important to do milestone planning rather than purely temporal planning.

In sum, as long as the progress of venturing is continuously probed, attention is paid to assisting venturing efforts, and people feel secure that they will be judged on what they control, there is little need for senior management to attempt to manage the individual ventures. A good ombudsman and committed venture managers will do much to ensure a venturing effort that produces results.

Conclusion

The results of the discussions with many corporations and managers suggest that there is little point in aspiring to expand the firm's sales via new venture development unless senior management recognizes and meets certain key responsibilities. These responsibilities call for: an appreciation of the very different organizational challenges posed by the levels of ventures the authors have identified; selection of a portfolio of ventures that matches the organizational capabilities; creation of appropriate organizational structures for undertaking ventures; selection and appointment of a venture ombudsman (from senior management ranks) who will mediate between the CEO and the venture managers; and finally a determination to pay sustained attention to managing the venturing process while avoiding getting embroiled in the details of the individual ventures. If these responsibilities are not met, the chances are rather high that the whole process is doomed to expensive and demoralizing failure.

References

1. Biggadike, R. "The Risky Business of Diversification." *Harvard Business Review,* May–June 1979, pp. 103–111.
2. Block, Z. "Can Corporate Venturing Succeed?" *Journal of Business Strategy,* Fall 1982, pp. 21–33.
3. Burgelman, R. A. "A Process Model of Internal Corporate Venturing in the Diversified Major Firm." *Administrative Science Quarterly,* June 1983, pp. 223–44.
4. Crawford, C. M. "Defining the Charter for Product Innovation." *Sloan Management Review,* Fall 1980, pp. 3–12.
5. Hanan, M. "Venturing Corporations—Think Small to Stay Strong." *Harvard Business Review,* May–June 1976, pp. 139–48.
6. Madique, M. A. "Entrepreneurs, Champions, and Technological Innovation." *Sloan Management Review,* Winter 1980, pp. 59–76.
7. Quinn, J. B. "Technological Innovation, Entrepreneurship, and Strategy." *Sloan Management Review,* Spring 1979, pp. 19–30.
8. Roberts, E. B. "New Ventures for Corporate Growth." *Harvard Business Review,* July–August 1980, pp. 132–42.
9. von Hippel, E. "Successful and Failing Internal Corporate Ventures: An Empirical Analysis." *Industrial Marketing Management,* 1977, pp. 163–74.

4 Managing strategy implementation

The final section takes an in-depth look at the problems and tasks of strategy implementation. There are two articles on designing organizations to aid strategy implementation, one by Ian C. MacMillan and Patricia E. Jones and one by Thomas Peters. Also, there are articles on linking the reward structure to strategic performance, the McKinsey 7–S framework, and the attention that must be paid to corporate culture; these are followed by applications articles on the corporate culture at IBM, the introduction of a competition-driven culture at AT&T, and the efforts to preserve the entrepreneurial culture at 3M. Next is a presentation by Barry Z. Posner and Warren H. Schmidt on their latest research findings concerning the values of American managers. The final article, by Ram Charan, gives an overview of the whole strategic management process and points to ways of avoiding some of the pitfalls of strategy review and strategic planning.

What this article is about: The ability of corporations to defend or take market share from competitors varies with the corporations' strengths and weaknesses, many of which spring from their own structures. The challenge is not to design organizational structures that are perfect, but to design structures that are better than those of competitors.

4-1 Designing organizations to compete

Ian C. MacMillan and Patricia E. Jones*

Ian C. MacMillan is a professor at New York University.
Patricia E. Jones is a staff manager at AT&T.

In 1979, Kiechel [1] claimed that 90 percent of American corporations have been unable to develop and execute successful strategies. He cited implementation as a critical issue, which has become the new rallying cry for growing numbers of managers and consultants [2]. In this article we go a step further and claim, as Davis [3] has done, that lack of success in implementing strategies has, in many cases, been due to a complete lack of a competitive organization design. The challenge of developing such a design can be likened to the challenge facing the general who has prepared a superb campaign strategy and must now design the army that will execute that strategy. Without the correct assembly of different battle units and their support services, the campaign cannot proceed, let alone achieve victory. By design we mean not only the selection of the organization structure but also the design of the support systems, planning systems, and control systems that deliver the strategy via the structure.

"Traditional" Design

Among others, Galbraith [4] and Nadler and colleagues [5] have done much to develop guidelines for "traditional" organizational design. Their three basic steps are:

1. Determine organization design "imperatives," that is, the demands and constraints placed on the organization by its environment and its strategy.
2. Design an organizational structure to meet these imperatives.

* Reprinted by permission from *The Journal of Business Strategy* 4, No. 4 (Spring 1984), pp. 11–26. Copyright © 1984 Warren, Gorham & Lamont, Inc. All rights reserved.

3. Manage the implementation of the design carefully and systematically.

We contend that these steps have to satisfy an essential prerequisite—that they be carried out in a competitive context. Nearly all organizations are engaged in some form of competition, if not for customers, then for scarce resources such as funds or staff. Previous authors have largely ignored competition, mentioning it only briefly as but one facet of the environment. The result can easily be a design that strives to homogenize the system and develop similar structural units with common policies, procedures, and measurement and reward systems, all of which are of little avail if the different parts of the organization are being attacked by very different competitors in very different environments.

The Foundation of Competitive Design

The reality is that every design has imperfections. Once this is acknowledged, one can further acknowledge that the organization is better served by designing to be competitive rather than striving for the holy grail of perfection in efficiency. Competitive design is an extension of the above three basic steps, expanded to take into account the competitive nature of the environment. Figure 1 lists a set of questions that has proven helpful in the

Figure 1
Questions for the competitive design process

1. What is the organization's strategy?
   - What is its contribution to society?
   - What is its strategic role?
   - By what strategy will the above be accomplished?
   - What critical functions will drive the strategy?
   - What are the key success factors?

2. How will we know that the strategy has been accomplished?
   - What strategic accomplishments spell success?
   - In pursuing this strategy, what ideology should shape our decisions?
   - What changes are necessary to achieve the strategic accomplishments?

3. How will competitors be impacted?
   - Who are target competitors?
   - What are their strategic strengths and weaknesses?
   - What are their design weaknesses?

4. What major task groupings are feasible design alternatives?
   - What groupings address the needs of the marketplace?
   - What groupings address the competitive advantages?
   - What are the vulnerabilities of each of these feasible groupings?
   - Can we accomplish the strategy without major reorganization?

5. What linkages are necessary between groupings?
   - What mechanisms link key groupings to critical functions?
   - What linkages address key vulnerabilities?

6. What support systems are needed?
   - Have necessary support systems been identified?
   - What new management and functional skills are needed?

7. What execution problems can be anticipated?
   - Have key events been simulated?
   - Has stakeholder impact been identified and managed?
   - Have problem owners been assigned?

competitive design process. Appropriately addressing these questions provides the foundation upon which an effective competitive design can be built.
Thereafter, it is possible to use the more traditional organizational design
guidelines, which are put forth in the current literature on the topic, to
complete the design. In this article, we shall not pursue the more traditional
detail, but rather will focus on discussing the questions outlined in Figure 1.

1. What Is the Organization's Strategy?

Rothschild [6] has developed a detailed and helpful list of questions to aid
in the strategic analysis process. Any analysis, however, should answer at
least the following:

What Will the Organization's Contribution to Society Be?   In other
words, what gives it the right to exist in society? It is important here to
identify what need is being satisfied by the organization *from the point of
view of society.* For instance, in its early days, IBM recognized that its
societal contribution was not to "manufacture and sell computers," but to
solve data storage, retrieval, and processing problems of large organizations.
This question not only puts the business into a societal perspective, it also
helps the business to recognize that there are many ways of satisfying its
societal need. It is also a useful question for support departments to ask with
respect to their corporation.

What Is the Strategic Role?   In other words, what strategic purpose must
the organization accomplish for itself? MacMillan [7] has identified eight
role choices, depending on the organization's position in a larger corporate
portfolio: build aggressively, build gradually, build selectively, maintain
aggressively, maintain selectively, prove viability, divest/liquidate, and
competitively harass. (The missions associated with each role are summarized in Figure 2).

By What Strategy Will the Above Be Accomplished?   A business strategy must be selected to accomplish the above challenges. This involves
selecting an array of products or services, targeting them at selected markets,
and making use of selected competitive advantages. Thus, in the 1950s, IBM
elected to build aggressively in the medium-to-large business market, the
government market, and the medium-to-large educational market by supplying an array of mainframe computers with modest modularity and with a full
range of peripheral devices. They elected advanced (but not cutting-edge)
products, cutting-edge technology, and high operational reliability of product
as key competitive advantages.

What Critical Functions Will Drive the Strategy?   If the strategy is to be
achieved, a limited number of functions must be performed and performed
well, as Rothschild [6] indicates. In fact, these functions must be performed
well for the company to attain the competitive advantage it seeks. And it's
these functions that dictate where major resource allocations and trade-offs
are to be made. For instance, IBM's commitment to advanced technology
and to the operational reliability of the product on site caused development
and service functions to take a critical role in the early days. Marketing and
finance, although aggressive and powerful, generally had to take a back seat
in trade-offs involving performance reliability of their computers versus

Figure 2
Possible strategic accomplishments for strategic roles

Role	Action Required	Relative Accomplishments	Absolute Accomplishments
Build aggressively	Build share on all fronts as rapidly as possible.	Rapid growth in share—all markets. Leadership in technology, service.	Limits on losses and negative cash flows.
Build gradually	Steady sustained increase in share of entire market.	Sustained growth in share—all markets. Leadership in quality, service.	Limited losses. Sustained cost reductions.
Build selectively	Increased share in carefully selected markets.	Share growth in selected markets. Leadership in customer satisfaction. Superiority in market research.	Growth in profits and profitability. Growth in cash flow.
Maintain aggressively	Hold position in all markets and generate profits.	Hold market share in all markets. Relative cost leadership—fixed and variable. Technology leadership—in product and process.	Improve asset utilization. Growth in profitability and cash flow. Improve expense-to-revenue ratio. Reduce force levels.
Maintain selectively	Select high-profit markets and secure position.	Overall share reduction. Hold market share in selected markets. Improve relative profitability. Distribution, service leadership.	Minimum investment. Improve asset utilization and cash flow. Reduce fixed cost/sales.
Prove viability	If there are any viable segments, maintain selectively, divest rest.	In this exhibit, see the sections to the left called "Maintain Selectively" and "Divest/Liquidate."	Minimize drag/risk to organization. Growth in profits and cash flow.
Divest/ liquidate	Seek exit and sell off at best price.	Reduce share except for highly selective segments. Enhance value added via technical leadership.	Minimize investment. Reduce fixed costs. Improve profitability. Maximize selling price. Reduce work force levels.
Competitively harass	Use as vehicle to deny revenues to competitors.	Attack competitor's high-share business but do not gain share. Relative price never above that of target competitors.	Minimize fixed costs. Sustained reduction of variable costs. Limits on losses and negative cash flows.

introduction of new technology, or new product releases, or inventory allocations to customers. As a result, IBM today continues to extract a premium price based on its image of reliability and superb service.

What Are the Key Success Factors? These will vary from company to company, but generally they include exceptional management of several of the following: product design, market segmentation, distribution and promotion, pricing, financing, securing of key personnel, research and development, production, servicing, maintenance of quality/value, or securing key suppliers. For example, companies in the grain trading business simply will not survive if they do not have exceptional sourcing and delivery logistics as well as superior options and contract management. Once the key strategic decisions are made, answers to the next important set of questions define the major design parameters of the strategic control system.

2. How Will We Know When the Strategy Is Accomplished?

The critical challenge in designing a strategic control system is to create a system that is self-controlling; that can respond autonomously to environmental challenges, but in which the various subunits still pursue their assigned strategic roles, according to their designated strategy. It has been our experience that this is accomplished by detailed attention to strategic accomplishments and ideology.

What Strategic Accomplishments Spell Success?   In competitive design, those charged with executing strategy should at least be able to gauge when they have been successful. Success is best monitored by specifying the set of accomplishments that will demonstrate that the organization has achieved what it set out to do—namely, pursue the strategic role, *via* the selected strategy. Therefore, we need to specify clearly what will indicate that the role itself has been accomplished, as well as indicate the means by which it was accomplished. For instance, IBM's accomplishment of an aggressive build role via its selected strategy could be demonstrated in the late 1960s by the following accomplishments:

- It had a major share of *all* markets it had elected to serve.
- Growth had exceeded that of all major competitors (in other words, IBM was also gaining share).
- Profits were increasing and cash flows were positive.
- It was acknowledged worldwide as having the most up-to-date equipment—both mainframe and peripherals.
- It was acknowledged worldwide as having superior product reliability and service.

Thus, there was no question that IBM had been successful in its aggressive build mission (a role that calls for substantial gains in share in all markets) and that this had been done via IBM's selected strategy of providing advanced products with unequaled operational reliability and service.

An imperative in the specification of strategic accomplishments is the selection of the *minimum* number of key criteria which management will pursue in the actual execution of strategy. Having too many criteria is a drawback since each additional criterion inhibits the flexibility and adaptability of those charged with strategy execution. Yet there should also be a sufficient number of criteria to ensure that the single-minded pursuit of one or two criteria is not carried out to the detriment of the long-term health of the organization.

Particularly important is the selection of at least one relative criterion and at least one leadership criterion. Absolute criteria are inclined to encourage an inward orientation, with attention to performance compared to past history rather than the current competition. By relative criteria we mean measuring performance relative to competitors', while leadership criteria are criteria in which our performance exceeds that of all competitors. Those criteria selected should be selected in such a way as to steer the organization toward fulfilling its selected role. In our experience, the relative criteria set the strategic direction by forcing the organization to focus on its competitive performance, while the absolute criteria set limits on the extent to which relative performance can be single-mindedly pursued to the long-run detriment of the organization. Finally, the leadership criteria force the organization to focus on the desired competitive advantage. Figure 2 lists some typical criteria that have been selected by firms in past competitive designs.

Having selected the criteria, the final challenge is the selection of appropriate measures of accomplishment. Absolute criteria and relative criteria generally pose less of a problem than leadership criteria, but for all criteria the important thing is to find measures that are objective or external, rather than subjective and internal. It is all too easy for the organization to convince itself that it is a technology or quality or service leader if·it listens only to itself or its loyal distributors and customers. However, leadership is in the eyes of the market, and it may be necessary to survey the market to establish whether the "leadership" is a fabrication of the organization's imagination. For example, AT&T, through its Telephone Survey Attitude Measurement (TELSAM) system, focused on customer evaluations of its service quality— in order to objectively assess its service performance.

Another problem arises with the need for *appropriate* measures. Often, a direct measure cannot be obtained. For example, cost leadership and, particularly, technology leadership are difficult to assess because hard data about the competitors are rarely available. It may be necessary to come up with imaginative surrogate measures which are indicators of the actual performance. One high-technology equipment manufacturer used the following as indicators of technology leadership:

- Ratings of its research and development department compared to those of its two leading competitors. Ratings were done by customers, suppliers, investment bank analysts, and three leading universities.
- Relative number of patents (compared to leading competitors) applied for in the past five years, and past two years.
- Relative number of new models introduced by the company compared to its leading competitors, and ratings of these models by key firms in the served market (*not* only its own customers).
- Number of research and development job offers to recent scientific postgraduates that were "lost" to competitors, compared to number of research and development job applicants "captured" from competitors.

Note that it may be possible for each of these measures individually to be "subverted" by a devious development department, or for each of these measures to give false signals as to the true status of the firm's technology leadership. However, the reality was that senior management stressed that the spirit of the measures was more important than each individual measure itself. The firm's development staff was aware that in spirit it was expected to achieve technology leadership and would be judged more on the "gestalt" of the above measures than on any individual measure.

For strategic control it is direction and commitment that are important, not precision of the measurement. With a limited number of criteria to steer the organization in the desired strategic direction, management is free to pursue this direction, responding autonomously to competitive conditions as they occur.

In order to create a self-controlling environment in which relatively autonomous decisions can be made, it is necessary to design and disseminate suitable ideology to guide such decision making.

What Should the Ideology Be?   Development of a suitable ideology has been discussed by many authors. By ideology we do not mean the corporate culture, which is a passive manifestation of corporate beliefs. Ideology is an explicitly generated, consciously managed, and clearly disseminated set of values by which senior management will judge the quality of internal behavior, attitudes, and external interactions of the organization and its members.

Peters and Waterman [8] in their study of excellent companies identified a number of factors that need to be included in ideology. These components of ideology were made more explicit in the analysis of several companies by MacMillan [9]. The fundamental principles held by the organization should broadly specify the following:

• Scope—what constitutes desirable types of products and markets?
• Drivers—which shall be the critical functions?
• Style—what style of management shall prevail?
• Ethics—what are the determinants of ethics?
• Attitude to risk-taking—how much risk is encouraged?
• Attitude to competition—how aggressively should competition be pursued?
• Attitude to customers and channels—are they regarded as intelligent decision makers or people who are easily manipulated?
• Attitude to employees—are they considered robots or intelligent contributors?
• Attitude to external groups—what is the attitude toward various special interest groups, government, and so on?
• Self-image—how does the company feel about its control over its destiny?

The underlying philosophy is that once managers in the organization have internalized these key principles, the autonomous decisions they make in response to competitive or environmental challenges, while addressing the specific challenge, will also stay within the boundaries of behavior desired by the organization as a whole.

This set of explicit principles, plus the strategic accomplishments, creates a framework for autonomous but self-controlling responses by the managers to the competitive environment. Discussion of the problems and the management of this strategic control system can be found in the material cited above and will not be discussed here.

With the foundation of the strategic control system in place, it is necessary to consider what changes are required to effect these accomplishments.

What Changes Are Necessary to Achieve the Strategic Accomplishments?   If major strategic shifts must be made, this will certainly necessitate major changes: in staffing, in support systems, and particularly in skills required. It is imperative to identify what changes will be necessary for two reasons: First, change must be managed internally, or the organization will revert to past practices; second, such changes have to be supported by the external (and internal) stakeholders, and the process of generating their support will also have to be managed. The organization designer therefore must identify what the most critical changes will be if the strategy is to be accomplished; these changes then become the focus of the change management process, which is extensively discussed in the literature [5], and will not be discussed here.

The answers to the set of questions covered so far are equivalent to the military specification of mission. The "senior officers" responsible for conducting this specific secondary task have been apprised of how their action is to fit into the overall campaign, what key results must be achieved, what resources will be available, and what guidelines they should use to shape their tactical decisions. The next set of questions involves assessing the design of the "enemy"—namely, the competition.

3. How Will Competitors Be Impacted?

In reality, no strategy impacts all competitors evenly. In fact, a good indicator that a strategy has not been thoroughly thought through is when the strategists cannot pinpoint which of the competitors will bear the main brunt of the impact of their strategy.

Who Are the Target Competitors? If the strategy formulation process did not start with target competitors in mind, the analysis of the impact of strategy on the competitors will highlight those companies that *will* be target competitors—namely, those that bear the brunt of the strategic attack. Responses of these competitors and their capacity to respond need to be evaluated. This assessment results from determining the competitors' strategic and design weaknesses.

What Are the Target Competitors' Strategic Weaknesses? This question ensures that we have in fact identified the *real* target competitors. These are competitors whose strategic weaknesses render them most vulnerable to our strategy. If we have a strategy that is based on a competitive advantage in distribution and service, then clearly the brunt of our attack will be borne initially by those firms that are weak in these areas, not those that are strong. (On the other hand, if *none* are weak, then we are not undertaking an attack, but a defense; essentially, we are playing catch-up.)

What Are the Design Vulnerabilities of the Target Competitors? It is important to also analyze the organization design of the competition, particularly the structure of the competition. This analysis could provide some interesting opportunities for an aggressive competitive design. At each level in the organization, work can be grouped in one of three basic ways: by activity (typically, a functional design), by output (typically, a product division), or by client (typically, a market segment division). The first few levels of design are critical; each combination of groupings at these levels brings with it substantial strengths and weaknesses. For example, a computer firm had for years been successfully organized by activity/output. Within the marketing department (activity), sales of its two product (output) groups—

large and small computers—were organized separately. However, in the 1970s, the distinction between large and small computers started to blur. The result was that salespeople from each product group were calling on the same customers, creating customer confusion and irritation. "Turf" wars started between competing sales forces, service difficulties increased, and eventually the company became vulnerable to a small-computer competitor which designed its structure around key accounts under the marketing function (thus using an activity/client structure).

Competitors are in business to defend or take market share from the organization, and their ability to do so varies with their individual strengths and weaknesses, *many of which spring from their own structure*. One tool for assessing potential design advantages has been presented in the Appendix to this article. First, consider how target competitors have grouped work at the top two layers, and then identify the potential strengths and weaknesses inherent in these particular groupings. Then, when we are considering alternative groupings for our own design, we can select combinations of groupings that recognize the competition's strengths. And, if we are fortunate, we can also take advantage of their weaknesses.

For example, if the target competitor is organized by activity/activity, then by grouping by output/user-client we will create a much higher sensitivity to market needs. Because of its organization, the competitor inherently will have a much slower response to these needs. This is the situation in which AT&T found itself in the late 1970s when MCI attacked specific high-density routes, and focused on specific client segments on these routes (business and consumer).

Note that the more usual case where the target competitor does happen to be grouped effectively does not preclude us from grouping our own organization in the same way. In fact, we are even more obliged to design effectively. There may be weaknesses in other parts of the design, such as the linking mechanisms (specific arrangements designed to facilitate and control the flow of critical information between groups, such as standing committees, product managers, liaison officers, or task forces) that the competitor uses (or does not use). For instance, direct responsibility to respond to our strategy may not fall within the jurisdiction of one particular department, as happened when Merrill Lynch "raided" the commercial banks' big retail customers by offering to these consumers one-stop cash management accounts. The banks had several departments which were affected, no single one of which had the authority to respond.

Alternatively, other support systems of competitors, such as their planning, control, and reward systems, standard operating procedures, or even ideology, shape the rate at which they become aware of, and respond to, strategic moves we make [7]. The organization that can build superior linking mechanisms or major support systems into its own structure may yet capitalize on the design vulnerabilities of a competitor whose major groupings mirror its own.

With the competitors' design strengths and vulnerabilities identified, it is possible to turn to the design of our own organizational structure. There are many considerations that go into designing the formal organizational structure: work grouping, linking, job design, methods and practices, standards and measurements, physical work environment, human resource management systems, reward systems, and support systems. All of these must reflect the organization's strategy and its competitive environment. It is here that it becomes all too easy to lose the *competitive* imperatives in the detail. In competitive design, it is the top few layers of the organization that are vital, and the key decisions are in the areas of grouping and linking. These are discussed next.

4. What Major Task Groupings Are Feasible Design Alternatives?

The first key decision addresses major task groupings [11]. It is here that the organization designer may be tempted to design with the focus on the internal activities rather than on the external challenges of the organization. The questions that follow force an external focus.

What Groupings Address the Needs of the Marketplace? The organization is in business to deliver products or services to the target markets. The first step in grouping should thus address how the organization plans to serve, and compete in, the selected markets. The strategic and competitive analyses recommended above suggest what factors should be considered.

For example, an industrial foods firm decided that in order to compete with its larger competitors, it had to keep prices competitive. At the top level, this called for a function design (activity). However, the firm's business and institutional markets were drastically different, and each required very different and specialized marketing skills. So, management elected to segment the marketing efforts by client (see Figure 3) at the next

Figure 3
Key groupings for industrial foods manufacturer

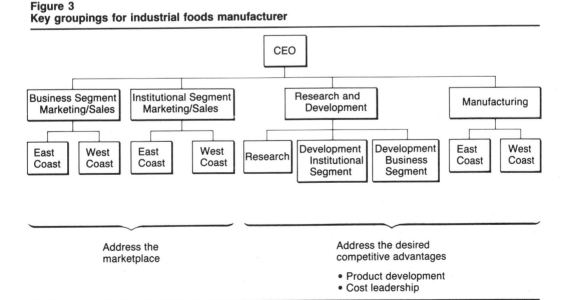

level. At the third level, the marketing for each segment was grouped geographically to reflect discerned regional differences on the East and West Coasts. Thus, the marketing activity was grouped according to a client/client grouping (see Appendix). Had the regional sensitivity been identified in the strategy as the key difference, their second- and third-level groupings (in marketing) might have been reversed.

What Groupings Address the Competitive Advantages? The next grouping decision must address the organization's desired competitive advantages. Continuing our example in Figure 3, the industrial foods firm selected two areas in which it felt it had to develop a competitive advantage: product development and cost leadership. In order to retain competitive prices, the firm maintained its activity groupings for basic research and development and for manufacturing. It decided on an activity/client design for research and development and another form of activity/client design for manufacturing. Some interesting points emerge as we look at these subgroupings. Under research and development, two development functions were established: one in support of the business segment, the other in support of the institutional segment. While it may be argued that such a grouping reduces efficiencies available from economies of scale, it produced an organization capable of responding quickly to needs and changes in each market segment, thereby *designing in* effectiveness. If serving particular market segments well with rapid and market-responsive product introductions is key to the success of the organization, then effectiveness must take priority over efficiency. Also, note that the research function was separated from the development function. The "blue sky" nature of basic research would be ill-served by grouping it with the shorter-term development function.

However, there remained the problem of keeping the research function in line with the rest of the organization and with the demands of this environment. This called for effective linkages [12] and the company created a formal linking position: product managers for each market, who interacted constantly with the development function on the subject of new products.

The next area of interest was in manufacturing. The geographical groupings at the second level were in response to the need for a price leadership position: economies of scale were essential, so each regional plant manufactured products for both markets. However, the market focus within these plants was maintained once more by the product managers, whose linking role here was to manage conflicts between the needs of marketing and those of manufacturing.

Note that if the firm had been a much smaller one, such a structure may have highlighted the impossibility of price leadership *and* product leadership as competitive advantages in a small firm. Such a discovery in the design phase is not at all inconceivable, and may lead the organization to reexamine its selected strategy.

What Are the Vulnerabilities of Each of These Feasible Groupings? The best grouping mix is one that enables the organization to most effectively maximize its strengths and minimize its vulnerabilities vis-à-vis the competition. At this point in the design process, several structures might seem feasible. However, some alternatives can be eliminated by weighing the advantages and disadvantages of the various groupings, as reflected in the Appendix. Some of these vulnerabilities could be defused with appropriate linking mechanisms (which will be addressed in the next section), but none should be tolerated that interfere with the organization's ability to effectively address the needs of marketplace; this automatically disqualifies a potential grouping.

Can We Accomplish Our Strategy without Major Reorganization?   If one of the feasible groupings closely resembles the current method of grouping, this should become a prime candidate for final selection, particularly if this grouping structure seems to have relatively minor vulnerabilities vis-à-vis those of the key competitors. The reason for this is that a major reorganization is also a tremendous source of trauma for the company. Enormous amounts of time, energy, talent, and competitive vigor are consumed as the new structure is developed under the new set of relationships. It is estimated that it takes a minimum of three years to "recover" from a major reorganization. So, if it is at all possible, it is preferable to try to use the existing groupings, supported if necessary by well-conceived new linking mechanisms (which we discuss next) in order to avoid the disruption created by reorganizing. Once again, the pragmatic challenge is not to design systems that are perfect but systems that are merely better than those of the competitors and that are appropriate to the strategy.

5. What Linkages Are Necessary between Groupings?

The very act of grouping certain functions together will also mean that certain natural work flows are separated. For instance, it may be appropriate to divide production into two geographically separate plants, even if some of the production of one plant is needed at the other. But if there are no coordinating or linking mechanisms, disruptions or exceptions at the first plant can create problems for the second. Linking mechanisms must be designed to coordinate and control critical interfaces. The focus at this stage should be on those interfaces that are critical to the organization's strategic and competitive success. Figure 4 lists the key mechanisms that have been used to link interfaces. The details of how to use such linking mechanisms are not discussed here since they are freely available in the literature [5, 12]. We have, however, tried to indicate the circumstances under which each should be employed by focusing on the nature of the disruptions/exception conditions which create the need for intergroup coordination. For instance, if the expected disruptions are not likely to be serious and will occur frequently, and their nature is fairly predictable, the most appropriate linking mechanisms is the appointment of formal liaison people in each department who will coordinate actions when these disruptions occur. A typical example would be to assign a plant foreman the responsibility of coordinating the acquisition of supplies from another of the company's plants. To do this, he would coordinate his activities with those of the foremen in the other plant. Sequential dependence means that one group depends on the input of another, such as in a production line. With reciprocal dependence, the output of one group becomes the input of another, which in time provides input back to the first. Typical reciprocal situations are relations between units that use equipment and units that maintain equipment (airlines, railroads). Another

Figure 4
Key linking mechanisms*

Exception Conditions			Grouping Interdependency	Linking Mechanism
Impact	**Predictability**	**Frequency**	**Grouping Interdependency**	**Linking Mechanism**
Low	High			Rules
Low	Low	Low		Contact
Low	Low	High		Liaison
High	High	Low		Contingency plan
High	Low	Low		Task force
High	High	High		Teams
High	Low	High	Sequential	Integrating role
High	Low	High	Reciprocal	Matrix

NOTE: Critical to success of linking mechanisms is to ensure that they take place at the correct level with correct delegation.

* Adapted from [12].

reciprocal situation is the relationship between the design, production, and marketing departments as new products and their supporting production systems are developed.

For the purposes of Figure 4, the following definitions apply:

• Task force: A group is selected from various activities to tackle a specific intergroup problem. It is automatically disbanded after the problem is solved.

• Team: A group is selected from various activities in the organization to respond to *recurring* problems that cross over group boundaries. It is a permanent coordinative arrangement that is only disbanded by a higher level in the hierarchy.

• Integrating role: An individual is charged with formal responsibilities for coordinating between two groupings. A common example is the product manager whose task it is to see that specific products get adequate attention from the marketing, production, and service functions.

• Integrating department: A department with independent resources and staff whose task is to ensure coordination between different functions. A typical example is an expediting department in a manufacturing firm whose task is to coordinate between marketing and production. In a defense contracting firm, an expediting department might coordinate between specific projects and the various technical departments supplying skills to execute the projects.

• Matrix structure: A person simultaneously reports to and has responsibility for a number of managers, each in charge of different activities or resources which must be coordinated. In addition, below this matrix manager is a structure in which competing tasks must be executed. The classic example is the project manager in a construction company who is required to report both to operations (for project programs) and to the technical manager (for staffing requirements) while managing a specific project under her control. In effect, the matrix manager absorbs conflicts between groupings and thus shields the subordinates from the intergroup conflicts, so allowing the subordinates to pursue their tasks without such disruptions. The matrix structure is extremely difficult to operate and should be avoided in favor of a simpler linking mechanism.

What Mechanisms Will Link Key Groupings to Critical Functions? As mentioned above, the critical functions are those that must deliver the competitive advantage and the strategic role. Here, the designer must build linking mechanisms to ensure that these critical functions perform their tasks and at the same time remain responsive to the markets being served. In our example of the industrial foods company, it is futile for the development department to create new products that the market does not want. It is also fatal for the manufacturing department to seek cost reductions if this means the company would have to deny an appropriate variety of products to the market or reduce the availability or reliability of supply to the customers in order to reduce inventory and scheduling costs.

The research and development function *must* deliver new products appropriate to the market, and the manufacturing function *must* accomplish cost reductions appropriate to the marketing effort. To accomplish this, the company in our example created teams in which a senior marketing manager from each segment worked with a senior development manager and a senior manufacturing manager. It was the charter of these teams, together with any ad hoc members co-opted as deemed appropriate, to *drive* the coordinated development of new products and processes, and the coordinated development of cost-reduction programs, in directions that were appropriate to the markets being served.

What Linkages Address Key Vulnerabilities? Every structure has its vulnerabilities. Vulnerabilities arising from the organization's structure can be reduced, if not eliminated, with the design and installation of additional linkages. Some of the grouping alternatives identified in the previous step will lend themselves easily to the design of linkages that overcome vulnerabilities. This will weed out the less desirable grouping options. For instance, the industrial foods company was aware that its fundamental design was an activity/client one. The key vulnerability was from low-cost competitors who might undercut prices to secure price-sensitive clients. This is why the firm *had* to select continuous cost reduction as a key strategic imperative, and why teams of marketing, development, and production managers were created to pursue cost reductions on a continuous basis.

6. What Support Systems Are Needed?

The grouping and linking decisions which shape the organization's formal structure still do not adequately address the requirements for a complete design. Nadler [5] and Peters and Waterman [8], among others, point out the need for additional, highly interrelated support systems and the need for congruence between these components if the organization is to perform effectively.

Have Necessary Support Systems Been Identified? If the questions above have been answered adequately, it is now possible to use the more traditional approaches to organization design to plan the necessary support systems. The idea is to design detailed planning, control, and reward systems focused on the pursuit of the strategic accomplishments and the ideology established in earlier stages.

What New Skills Will Be Needed to Produce the Accomplishments?   It is critically important to identify what changes in the skill mix may be required if the strategy is to be accomplished, since there is usually a substantial lag between recognition of a required change in skill mix and its accomplishment. Furthermore, the required skill mix may extend well beyond the traditional boundaries of the business: IBM during its aggressive build phase in the 1950s and 1960s was astute enough to recognize that it was vital to develop the programming skills of potential clients, and so spent millions of dollars on educating and training its clients' employees worldwide. To accomplish this, IBM's own capabilities to devise and deliver such training required development. The result was a huge program to train programming instructors and software applications instructors within IBM.

The management attitudes and skills needed to carry out a particular strategic role may also call for a change in the human resource management systems. Selection, promotion, and compensation guidelines must be designed and installed to encourage the development of the needed attitudes and skills. Without systems that support the strategic role, traditional American business values [13] such as the tendency to maximize short-term profits and minimize risk, will quite naturally take precedence, whether or not they suit the role.

If the strategy is to be effective, it may also be important to recognize the skill requirements of suppliers and distributors. For decades, the large U.S. auto manufacturers had a formidable advantage against foreign competition due to their networks of dealers who offered service and repair capabilities. It was only by designing highly reliable vehicles that Japanese auto producers considerably reduced the need for such service skills, thus defusing the advantage of domestic producers.

To get a better idea of the importance for implementation of required change in the skill mix, it is useful to ask what the impact on strategic accomplishment will be if there is a shortfall in the skill categories needed to support a particular strategy. One electrical equipment manufacturer estimated that a 10 percent shortfall in trained repair technicians would be enough to both severely damage its service reputation and also virtually destroy a proposed aggressive maintenance strategy which had been based on distribution and service leadership. This discovery precipitated a major reallocation of senior management attention to internal technical training and a substantial redirection of corporate resources and support for technical training in regional public school systems.

7. What Execution Problems Can Be Anticipated?

Answers to this last set of questions reduces the organization's exposure to major implementation pitfalls to which so many of the most well-conceived strategies and designs fall prey.

Have Key Events Been Simulated?   By this we mean "walking through" the major events that the organization must be able to handle if its strategy is to be executed. This is in essence a reality check, an attempt to answer the question "Will it work?" This analysis must be done, and done in detail, if the emerging design is to effectively implement the strategy.

The first step is to identify and then list the key challenges the organization is likely to encounter. A good place to look for the identification of these key challenges is in the organization's strategy. If, for example, the organization seeks to achieve market leadership via new product introductions, then a new product is a major event and should be walked through the proposed design to make sure that the design is set up to handle the identification, development, and introduction of new product ideas as well as the responses of distributors, customers, and competitors to its introduction.

Another important check is to identify competitive triggers. For example, if a target competitor counterattacks, how will the proposed design identify and respond to this move? Once the key inputs are identified, the progress of each can be traced through each design alternative.

From the simulations will emerge conflicts, redundancies, or misunderstandings about groupings, questions about how coordination and control mechanisms will function, and any missing or incomplete functions. Based on the results, further grouping alternatives will be ruled out entirely, or other new or different linking mechanisms will be designed. At this point, if more than one design alternative remains, the final choice can be made by checking each against the answers to Questions 1–3, choosing the one that best meets the resulting strategic and competitive imperatives. Specifically ask: Have all the strategic and competitive imperatives been met?

Has Stakeholder Impact Been Identified and Managed?   The impact of the design on stakeholders cannot be ignored. Strategic accomplishment may be considerably delayed by resistance from key stakeholders, or considerably facilitated by their active support. The extent to which stakeholders will be impacted as the strategy is executed needs to be analyzed, and major threats or opportunities emanating from stakeholder reaction must be identified and managed. Specific plans for managing both positive and negative stakeholder reactions must be made and appropriate action taken before the first move, as well as throughout the implementation phase.

Have Problem Owners Been Assigned?   A very effective mechanism, invented by IBM, has been the identification and appointment of problem owners for implementation. All major problem areas for implementation identified in the prior simulation—for example, technical difficulties, motivation problems, human resource management challenges, and stakeholder resistance—are assigned to a "problem owner" who acknowledges and accepts the responsibility for managing this problem area. Problem owners are not necessarily given resources and authority, but they are held accountable for managing all problems that may arise in their problem area during implementation. They do have the right to veto (if they *have to*) any move that negatively impacts their problem area. Two benefits are obtained with this mechanism: The problem owners themselves receive important developmental experience, and the organization receives the smoothest possible change implementation. It is interesting to note that in IBM the "problem ownership" role is eagerly sought by those executives who seek to demonstrate that they can manage their problems despite lack of formal authority and official resources, since senior management regards such skills as important indicators of promotion potential.

This completes the key questions that shape competitive organization design. More detailed design considerations are handled quite adequately by the conventional design approaches.

Adequate answers to the above list of questions lead to a design that addresses the need to compete as well as to seek efficiency. There is no question that such designs are somewhat more complex, and less efficient, than designs that focus primarily on efficiency. But in actuality, competitive design is concerned with effectiveness—after all, it is not essential to deliver a perfect design, but rather a design that is better than that of the best competitor.

Another way of looking at competitive design is to return to the military analogy with which we started. In designing the army to conduct the campaign, the general can ill afford to seek perfection on the parade ground. Rather, he must assemble his forces and materials to create an army superior to that of the enemy in the actual terrain. Our questions have consistently assisted managers in achieving this more modest, but pragmatic, purpose of designing competitive, if imperfect, designs. They go a long way toward delivering designs that are competitively superior—a key challenge of the 1980s.

References

1. Kiechel, W., III. "Playing by the Rules of the Corporate Strategy Game." *Fortune,* September 24, 1979.
2. "The Future Catches Up with a Strategic Planner." *Business Week,* June 27, 1983.
3. Davis, S. Personal communication to author.
4. Galbraith, J. R., and D. A. Nathanson. *Strategy Implementation: The Role of Structure and Process.* St. Paul, Minn.: West Publishing, 1978.
5. Nadler, D. A., J. R. Hackman; and E. E. Lawler III. *Managing Organizational Behavior.* Boston: Little, Brown, 1979.
6. Rothschild, W. E. *Putting It All Together.* New York: AMACOM, 1976; *Strategic Alternatives.* New York: AMACOM, 1979.
7. MacMillan, I. C. "Seizing the Competitive Initiative." *Journal of Business Strategy,* Spring 1982.
8. Peters, T. J., and R. H. Waterman. *In Search of Excellence: Lessons From America's Best-Run Companies,* New York: Harper & Row, 1982.
9. MacMillan, I. C. "Corporate Ideology and Strategic Delegation." *Journal of Business Strategy,* Winter 1983.
10. *Implementation Strategies.* AT&T, 1980.
11. Hax, A. C., and N. S. Majluf. "Strategic Organization." *Journal of Business Strategy,* Fall 1983.
12. Galbraith, J. R. *Designing Complex Organizations.* Reading, Mass.: Addison-Wesley Publishing, 1973.
13. Hayes, R. H., and W. J. Abernathy. "Managing Our Way to Economic Decline." *Harvard Business Review,* July/August 1980.

APPENDIX: Design Strengths and Weaknesses

First/Second layer groupings (examples)	Potential strengths	Potential vulnerabilities
Activity/Client 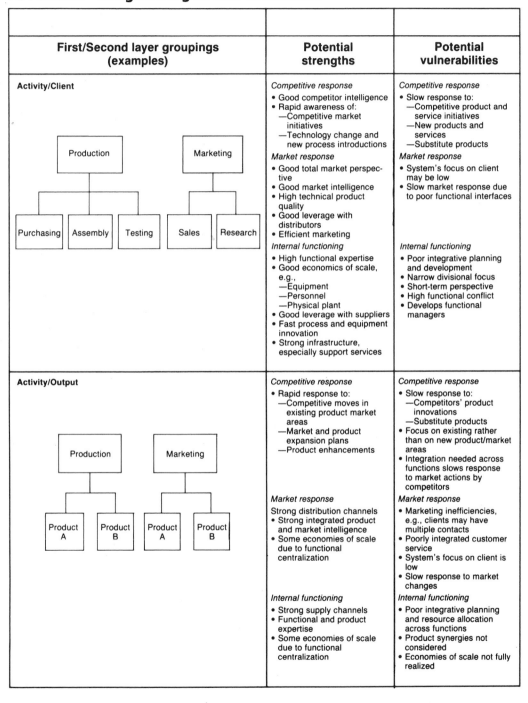	*Competitive response* • Good competitor intelligence • Rapid awareness of: —Competitive market initiatives —Technology change and new process introductions *Market response* • Good total market perspective • Good market intelligence • High technical product quality • Good leverage with distributors • Efficient marketing *Internal functioning* • High functional expertise • Good economics of scale, e.g., —Equipment —Personnel —Physical plant • Good leverage with suppliers • Fast process and equipment innovation • Strong infrastructure, especially support services	*Competitive response* • Slow response to: —Competitive product and service initiatives —New products and services —Substitute products *Market response* • System's focus on client may be low • Slow market response due to poor functional interfaces *Internal functioning* • Poor integrative planning and development • Narrow divisional focus • Short-term perspective • High functional conflict • Develops functional managers
Activity/Output	*Competitive response* • Rapid response to: —Competitive moves in existing product market areas —Market and product expansion plans —Product enhancements *Market response* Strong distribution channels • Strong integrated product and market intelligence • Some economies of scale due to functional centralization *Internal functioning* • Strong supply channels • Functional and product expertise • Some economies of scale due to functional centralization	*Competitive response* • Slow response to: —Competitors' product innovations —Substitute products • Focus on existing rather than on new product/market areas • Integration needed across functions slows response to market actions by competitors *Market response* • Marketing inefficiencies, e.g., clients may have multiple contacts • Poorly integrated customer service • System's focus on client is low • Slow response to market changes *Internal functioning* • Poor integrative planning and resource allocation across functions • Product synergies not considered • Economies of scale not fully realized

APPENDIX *(continued)*

First/Second layer groupings (examples)	Potential strengths	Potential vulnerabilities
Activity/Client 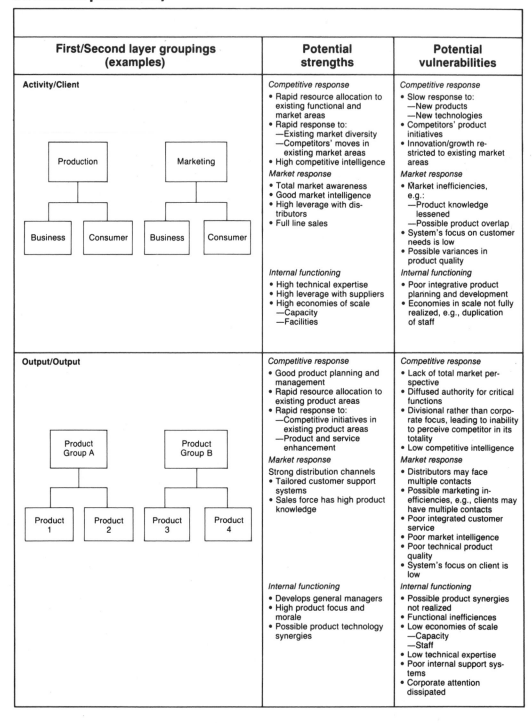	*Competitive response* • Rapid resource allocation to existing functional and market areas • Rapid response to: —Existing market diversity —Competitors' moves in existing market areas • High competitive intelligence *Market response* • Total market awareness • Good market intelligence • High leverage with distributors • Full line sales *Internal functioning* • High technical expertise • High leverage with suppliers • High economies of scale —Capacity —Facilities	*Competitive response* • Slow response to: —New products —New technologies • Competitors' product initiatives • Innovation/growth restricted to existing market areas *Market response* • Market inefficiencies, e.g.: —Product knowledge lessened —Possible product overlap • System's focus on customer needs is low • Possible variances in product quality *Internal functioning* • Poor integrative product planning and development • Economies in scale not fully realized, e.g., duplication of staff
Output/Output	*Competitive response* • Good product planning and management • Rapid resource allocation to existing product areas • Rapid response to: —Competitive initiatives in existing product areas —Product and service enhancement *Market response* Strong distribution channels • Tailored customer support systems • Sales force has high product knowledge *Internal functioning* • Develops general managers • High product focus and morale • Possible product technology synergies	*Competitive response* • Lack of total market perspective • Diffused authority for critical functions • Divisional rather than corporate focus, leading to inability to perceive competitor in its totality • Low competitive intelligence *Market response* • Distributors may face multiple contacts • Possible marketing inefficiencies, e.g., clients may have multiple contacts • Poor integrated customer service • Poor market intelligence • Poor technical product quality • System's focus on client is low *Internal functioning* • Possible product synergies not realized • Functional inefficiencies • Low economies of scale —Capacity —Staff • Low technical expertise • Poor internal support systems • Corporate attention dissipated

APPENDIX *(continued)*

First/Second layer groupings (examples)	Potential strengths	Potential vulnerabilities
Output/Activity 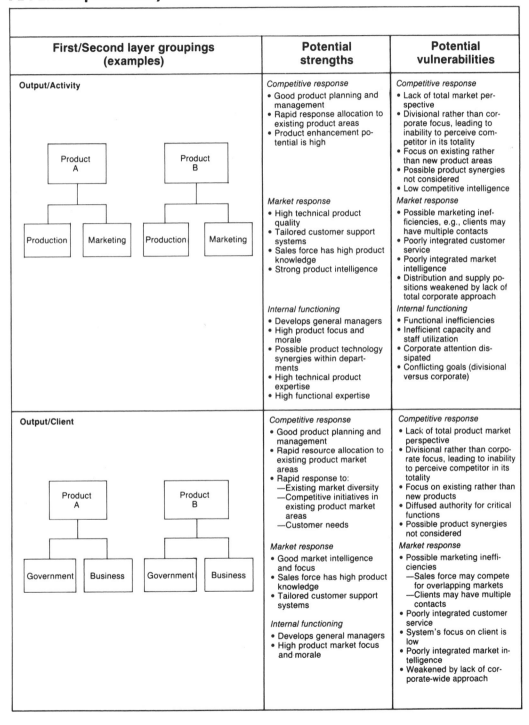	*Competitive response* • Good product planning and management • Rapid response allocation to existing product areas • Product enhancement potential is high *Market response* • High technical product quality • Tailored customer support systems • Sales force has high product knowledge • Strong product intelligence *Internal functioning* • Develops general managers • High product focus and morale • Possible product technology synergies within departments • High technical product expertise • High functional expertise	*Competitive response* • Lack of total market perspective • Divisional rather than corporate focus, leading to inability to perceive competitor in its totality • Focus on existing rather than new product areas • Possible product synergies not considered • Low competitive intelligence *Market response* • Possible marketing inefficiencies, e.g., clients may have multiple contacts • Poorly integrated customer service • Poorly integrated market intelligence • Distribution and supply positions weakened by lack of total corporate approach *Internal functioning* • Functional inefficiencies • Inefficient capacity and staff utilization • Corporate attention dissipated • Conflicting goals (divisional versus corporate)
Output/Client	*Competitive response* • Good product planning and management • Rapid resource allocation to existing product market areas • Rapid response to: —Existing market diversity —Competitive initiatives in existing product market areas —Customer needs *Market response* • Good market intelligence and focus • Sales force has high product knowledge • Tailored customer support systems *Internal functioning* • Develops general managers • High product market focus and morale	*Competitive response* • Lack of total product market perspective • Divisional rather than corporate focus, leading to inability to perceive competitor in its totality • Focus on existing rather than new products • Diffused authority for critical functions • Possible product synergies not considered *Market response* • Possible marketing inefficiencies —Sales force may compete for overlapping markets —Clients may have multiple contacts • Poorly integrated customer service • System's focus on client is low • Poorly integrated market intelligence • Weakened by lack of corporate-wide approach

APPENDIX *(continued)*

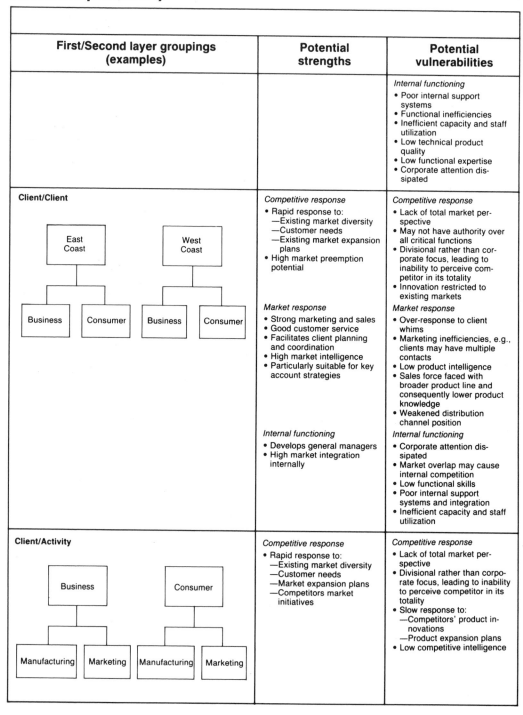

First/Second layer groupings (examples)	Potential strengths	Potential vulnerabilities
		Internal functioning • Poor internal support systems • Functional inefficiencies • Inefficient capacity and staff utilization • Low technical product quality • Low functional expertise • Corporate attention dissipated
Client/Client	*Competitive response* • Rapid response to: —Existing market diversity —Customer needs —Existing market expansion plans • High market preemption potential *Market response* • Strong marketing and sales • Good customer service • Facilitates client planning and coordination • High market intelligence • Particularly suitable for key account strategies *Internal functioning* • Develops general managers • High market integration internally	*Competitive response* • Lack of total market perspective • May not have authority over all critical functions • Divisional rather than corporate focus, leading to inability to perceive competitor in its totality • Innovation restricted to existing markets *Market response* • Over-response to client whims • Marketing inefficiencies, e.g., clients may have multiple contacts • Low product intelligence • Sales force faced with broader product line and consequently lower product knowledge • Weakened distribution channel position *Internal functioning* • Corporate attention dissipated • Market overlap may cause internal competition • Low functional skills • Poor internal support systems and integration • Inefficient capacity and staff utilization
Client/Activity	*Competitive response* • Rapid response to: —Existing market diversity —Customer needs —Market expansion plans —Competitors market initiatives	*Competitive response* • Lack of total market perspective • Divisional rather than corporate focus, leading to inability to perceive competitor in its totality • Slow response to: —Competitors' product innovations —Product expansion plans • Low competitive intelligence

APPENDIX *(concluded)*

First/Second layer groupings (examples)	Potential strengths	Potential vulnerabilities
	Market response • Strong marketing and full-line sales • High leverage with distribution channels • High product quality • High market intelligence *Internal functioning* • High function expertise • Good internal support systems • High leverage with suppliers	*Market response* • Marketing inefficiencies —Product knowledge lessened —Product priority conflict —Possible market product overlap • Low product intelligence *Internal functioning* • Product priority conflict (if multiproduct) • Low economies of scale (across divisions) • Poor integration between functions
Client/Output Business Consumer Product A Product B Product A Product B	*Competitive response* • Rapid response to: —Customer needs —Market and product expansion plans —Competitive moves in existing product/market areas —Product enhancements • Rapid resource allocation to product market areas *Market response* • Strong marketing and sales, e.g., sales force has high product knowledge • Good market intelligence and expertise • Good customer service *Internal functioning* • Develops general managers • High product and market focus and morale	*Competitive response* • Lack of total market perspective • Divisional rather than corporate perspective leading to inability to perceive competitor in its totality • Low competitive intelligence • Slow response to competitors' product innovations *Market response* • Marketing inefficiencies, e.g., client may have multiple contacts • System's focus on client is low • Possibly over-responsive to client whims *Internal functioning* • Low functional expertise • Poor internal support systems • Low capacity and staff utilization • Product innovation/enhancement overlaps • Possible product synergies may be overlooked

What this article is about: Twenty years ago management analysis focused on organization—structure and systems—with the external environment being given short shrift. The pendulum has now swung to the opposite extreme, with the analysis of external strategy dominating contemporary thinking about management. This article proposes a third view, that the best performing companies are packagers of superb skills that lead to constant adaptation to changing circumstances.

4-2 Strategy follows structure: Developing distinctive skills*

Thomas J. Peters

Thomas J. Peters is coauthor of In Search of Excellence *and* A Passion for Excellence, *founder of the Tom Peters Companies, and a lecturer at the Stanford Graduate School of Business.*

David Ogilvy, in his delightful new book, *Ogilvy on Advertising*, quotes Marvin Bower, McKinsey & Co.'s legendary leader:

> If a company rests its policy of not letting its agencies serve competitors on the need for security of information, it does not have a very solid base. As a matter of realism, the interests of competing clients would not be harmed by an almost complete exchange of information among the people serving the two competing companies. Of course, no responsible service firm would do that—and indeed they go to great lengths to avoid even inadvertent exchanges. Nevertheless, as one who has been a repository of confidential information over many years, I am convinced that the history, makeup, ways of doing business, attitudes of people, operating philosophy, and procedures of even directly competing companies are ordinarily so different that information could be exchanged between them with no harm to either.[1]

Or, strategy follows structure. Distinctive organizational performance, for good or ill, is almost entirely a function of deeply engrained repertoires. The organization, within its marketplace, *is* the way it *acts* from moment to moment—not the way it thinks it *might* act or *ought* to act. Larry Greiner recently noted:

> Strategy evolves from inside the organization—not from its future environment. . . . Strategy is a deeply engrained and continuing pattern of management behavior that gives direction to the organization—not a manipulable and controllable

---

* Reprinted from *California Management Review* 26, no. 3 (Spring 1984), pp. 111–25 Copyright © 1984, The Regents of the University of California.
[1] David Ogilvy, *Ogilvy On Advertising* (New York: Crown Publishers, 1983), p. 69.

mechanism that can easily be changed from one year to the next. Strategy is a nonrational concept stemming from the informal values, traditions, and norms of behavior held by the firm's managers and employees—not a rational, formal, logical, conscious, and predetermined thought process engaged in by top executives. Strategy emerges out of the cumulative effect of many informal actions and decisions taken daily over the years by many employees—not a "one shot" statement developed exclusively by top management for distribution to the organization.[2]

Of course we understand, at one level, exactly what Greiner is saying; few would disagree with it. At the same time, however, we more often than not manage as if the principal variable at our command—in order to bring about an adjustment to a changing environment—is the "strategy lever."

Execution Is Strategy

SAS (Scandinavian Air System) just completed a monumental "strategic turnaround." In a period of 18 months, amidst the worst recession in 40 years, it went from a position of losing $10 million a year to making $70 million a year (on $2 billion in sales), and virtually the entire turnaround came at the direct expense of such superb performers as SwissAir and Lufthansa. The "strategy" (he calls it "vision") of SAS's Jan Carlzon was "to become the premiere businessperson's airline." Carlzon is the first to admit that it is a "garden variety vision: "It's everyone's aspiration. The difference was, we executed." Carlzon describes SAS as having shifted focus from "an aircraft orientation" to a "customer orientation," adding that, "SAS *is* the personal contact of one person in the market and one person at SAS." He sees SAS as "50 million 'moments of truth' per year, during each of which we have an opportunity to be distinctive." That number is arrived at by calculating that SAS has 10 million customers per year, each one comes in contact with five SAS employees on average, which leads to a product of 50 million "opportunities."

Perdue Farms sells chickens. In the face of economists' predictions for over 50 consecutive years (according to Frank Perdue), Perdue Farms has built a three-quarter billion-dollar business. Margins exceed that of its competitors by seven or eight hundred percent, yet Perdue Farms maintains market shares in the 50s and 60s in every major area in which it competes— even in tough markets such as Richmond, Baltimore, Philadelphia, Boston, and the New York metropolitan area. Frank Perdue argues, and a careful analysis of his organization would lead one to argue, that his magic is simple: "If you believe there's absolutely no limit to quality [remember we're talking about roasters, not Ferraris] and you engage in every business dealing with total integrity, the rest [profit, growth, share] will follow automatically." Interestingly, Perdue's number one customer is Stew Leonard's, "the Disneyland of dairy stores," as it is called by The *New York Times*. Leonard, too, engaged in a most mundane business—selling dairy products in a giant Norwalk, Connecticut, store—yet his results are nothing less than astonishing.

---

[2] Larry E. Greiner, "Senior Executives as Strategic Actors," *New Management* 1, no. 2 (Summer 1983), p. 13.

A colleague of mine once said, "Execution *is* strategy." The secret to success of the so-called excellent companies that Bob Waterman and I looked at, and the ones that I have looked at since, is almost invariably mundane execution. The examples—small and large, basic industry or growth industry—are too numerous to mention: Tupperware, Mary Kay, Stew Leonard's, Mrs. Field's Cookies, W. L. Gore, McDonald's Corporation, Mars, Perdue Farms, Frito-Lay, Hewlett-Packard Company, IBM, and on it goes.

My reason for belaboring this point is to suggest that, above all, the top performers—school, hospital, sports team, business—are a *package of distinctive skills*. In most cases, one particularly distinctive strength—innovation at 3M, Johnson & Johnson, or Hewlett-Packard; service at IBM, McDonald's, Frito-Lay, or Disney; quality at Perdue Farms, The Procter & Gamble Co., Mars, or Maytag—and the distinctive skill—which in all cases is a product of some variation of "fifty million moments of truth a year"— are a virtual unassailable barrier to competitor entry or serious encroachment. David Ogilvy quotes Mies Van Der Rohe as saying of architecture, "God is in the details,"[3] Jan Carlzon of SAS puts it this way, "We do not wish to do one thing a thousand percent better, we wish to do a thousand things one percent better." Francis G. (Buck) Rodgers, IBM's corporate marketing vice president, made a parallel remark, "Above all we want a reputation for doing the little things well." And a long-term observer of Procter & Gamble noted, "They are so thorough, it's boring." The very fact that excellence has a "thousand thousand little things" as its source makes the word "unassailable" (as in "an unassailable barrier to entry") plausible. No trick, no device, no sleight of hand, no capital expenditure will close the gap for the also rans.

Distinctive Competence—The Forgotten Trail

The focus on execution, on distinctive competence is indeed not new. Philip Selznick, as far as I can determine, talked about it first:

> The term *organization* suggests a certain bareness, a lean, no-nonsense system of consciously coordinated activities. It refers to an *expendable tool*, a rational instrument engineered to do a job. An "institution," on the other hand, is more nearly a natural product of social needs and pressures—a responsive adaptive organism. The terms *institution, organizational character,* and *distinctive competence* all refer to the same basic process—the transformation of an engineered, technical arrangement of building blocks into a purposive social organization.[4]

Early thinking about strategy, which was the focus of my M.B.A. schooling a dozen years ago at Stanford, was driven by the industry standard: Edmund P. Learned et al.'s textbook, *Business Policy*.[5] The focus of strategy making at that point was clearly on analyzing and building distinctive competences.

---

[3] Ogilvy, *Ogilvy*, p. 101.
[4] Philip Selznick, *Leadership in Administration* (New York: Harper & Row, 1957), p. 5.
[5] Edmund P. Learned, C. Roland Christiansen, Kenneth R. Andrews, and William D. Guth, *Business Policy: Text and Cases* (Homewood, Ill: Richard D. Irwin, 1969).

In the years since Selznick and Learned et al., the focus on distinctive competence has been downgraded. Analysis of strategic position within a competitive system has all but butted out concern with the boring details of execution (which sum up to that elusive competence). Presumably the "people types" (the OB faculty) take care of such mundane stuff. The experience curve, portfolio manipulation, competitive cost position analysis, and the like have reigned supreme for the last decade or so.

I have no problem with the usefulness of any of these tools. Each is vital and few of them, indeed, were used very thoughtfully or regularly just a dozen years ago. However, we seem to have moved (rushed?) from a position of "implementation without thought" (analyzing structures on the basis of span of control, rather than on the basis of external forces) to "thought without implementation." We have reached a wretched position in which Stanford, annually voted by the business school deans as America's leading business school (and thus the world's), has only *three* of 91 elective MBA courses focusing on the making (manufacturing policy) or selling (sales management) functions of business.[6] This distortion of priorities was poignantly brought home to me late last school year. A local reporter attended my last class (an elective based on *In Search of Excellence*) and asked my students if the course had been useful. One student, quoted in the subsequent article, tried to say the very most complimentary thing he could: "It's great. Tom teaches all that soft, intangible stuff—innovation, quality, customer service—that's not found in the hard P&L or balance statements." Soft? Hard? Has that youngster got it straight or backwards—is there a problem here?

Roots

Let me back track for a moment, and describe my own odyssey. I became involved in the issue of "doing strategy" in 1976. Returning to McKinsey & Co. from a sabbatical during which I completed my business Ph.D. at Stanford, I was given a project that dealt with "looking for the next generation of organizational structure." (Prior to 1976, I had been a garden variety strategy consultant, dealing mainly with oil exploration simulation models.) McKinsey's new managing director asked me to undertake the study for three reasons:

1. The matrix structure—which was the kneejerk structure being installed by every company, especially if the company called in McKinsey—was clearly showing that it was less than ideal in practice (it was great on paper) and we needed to know why—quickly.
2. McKinsey's new managing director had earned his own stripes primarily by being a champion of radical decentralization and was thus a proponent of the critical importance of organizational structures to business success (i.e., strategy execution).
3. McKinsey was, without much conscious thought, going willy-nilly

---

[6] "Course Descriptions for Electives Taught in the 1983–84 Academic Year," Stanford University Graduate School of Business.

down the path of becoming a "strategy boutique," in response to competitive threats (the first serious ones in the company's history) from the Boston Consulting Group and Bain & Company. Indeed, McKinsey in the mid-70s was populated by young men almost totally enamored with the nuances of the ideological debate going on amongst strategists—the Porter view, the PIMs view, and the McKinsey (or GE) portfolio/nine box, versus the BCG/four box versus the ADL/24 box.

I began my search rather randomly and traveled from Stockholm, to London, to Dusseldorf, to Detroit, to Palo Alto. As time went by, it became obvious that neither strategy nor structure—nor even the two together—was sufficient to explain organizational differences. I began to focus on "management style" (which, as I defined it at the time, would fall under the heading of "culture" today), on the subtle role of management systems in directing habitual forms of organizational behavior, and on "guiding values" which seemed to somehow be the most significant in directing institutional energy (these have now come to be called by many, myself included, such things as "vision," "superordinate goals," "shared values," or, again, "culture").

Eventually, in mid-1978, my colleague Bob Waterman and I, with the help of Anthony Athos and Richard Pascale, developed the so-called McKinsey 7-S framework.[7] In a nutshell, it was a response to a single phenomenon that we had all observed: what I now call the strategy-execution gap. The 7-S structure, as many doubtless know, consists of the following variables: strategy, structure, systems, style, shared values (called superordinate goal originally), staff (people), and skills.

The 7-S structure was once a 5-S structure, then a 6-S structure, and then the last variable to be added was skills. When writing the first lengthy description of the model,[8] I went through each of the variables in what was then a "6-S" model. I was trying to figure out, since our sole objective was to do better organizational diagnosis, "what the six S's added up to." It was not a very rigorous or perfectly logical question, but it was a very pragmatic one. Did some five of the S's add up to the sixth—strategy? That didn't feel right. Or did five of the S's add up to an alternate sixth—style, or another, staff (people)? All told, nothing felt quite right. As a product of frustration, more than inspiration, I decided to add the term *skills*. My observations seemed to suggest, above all, that organizations were packages of "somethings"—skills? —perhaps just another term for habitual ways they acted or reacted to crisis and opportunity alike. On the one hand, these things called "skills" seemed the most important of all—the most distinctive encapsulation of the organization's way of doing business. On the other hand, they seemed to be the things that, above all, dropped through the cracks in any analysis—typically reductionist analysis which usually focuses on structure,

---

[7] Robert H. Waterman, Jr., Thomas J. Peters, and Julien R. Phillips, "Structure is Not Organization," *Business Horizons*, June 1980.

[8] Thomas J. Peters, "Enhancing Organizational Capability and Effectiveness: The Never-Ending Juggling Act," McKinsey & Co., October 1978.

control systems, or strategy formulation processes. Fiddle with the structure, change the strategy, think about the style, work on the development of staff (people), articulate a new system. But just *what* was it that you were really up to? It is of course an unanswerable question, but skills seemed to fit the bill acceptably well.

At the time our objective was simply to (in Bob Waterman's words, I believe) "enhance the pile of variables beyond the simple structure-strategy or structure-strategy-systems formulation." We wanted to do better—richer—diagnosis. We wanted to reduce the strategy-execution gap.

We Blow It Again

The chain of circumstances is unimportant, but a year or so later, in 1979, we began the so-called excellent company research, that of course resulted, among other things, in the publication of *In Search of Excellence*. And what did we observe in those companies? Well, history—that is, our shortcomings—repeated itself. We began with a very extensive, systematic 27-page interview guide. Our focus was on differences in sales force organization and differences in compensation or informal reward systems. The questionnaire, though we religiously followed it in all of our settings, turned out to be of little value in unearthing differences. The respondents, from top to bottom in the organizations we polled, were talking about other things. I *now* believe that what they were talking about was *skills*—or distinctive competences. Moreover, á la the opening quote by Marvin Bower, they talked freely about them, explicitly aware that to copy "the 3M way" is a virtual impossibility for others. David Ogilvy, in his new book, has a brief chapter solely devoted to the ins and outs of competing with Procter & Gamble. He has just two points. The first is a suggestion: Don't. The second is the reason why: They make better products. The same "oversimplifications" are true of virtually all the companies we looked at. IBM has a three-value set of beliefs. The driving force (in addition to the focus on people from whom it all emanates), is "to provide the *best* service of *any* company in *any* industry in the *world*." Mars, Inc., Perdue Farms, Maytag, and others—along with P&G—all focus slavishly on superior quality. Frito-Lay, Disney, Sysco, and the like focus on superior service. Raychem, Hewlett-Packard, Johnson & Johnson, and 3M focus on continuous innovation. The late Ray Kroc, McDonald's founder, once said, "If I had a brick for every time I've said Quality, Service, Cleanliness, and Value, I could pave a two-lane road to the moon." Debbie Fields of the remarkably successful Mrs. Field's Cookies says, "I am not a businesswoman. I'm a cookie person." To our utter—and growing—astonishment, these simple (albeit excruciatingly hard to execute), yet very distinctive skills turn out to describe a shockingly high percentage of the variance between these companies and their less effective competitors. Procter & Gamble understands brand management to be sure, and it manages and invests in advertising beautifully, but its 150-year dedication to absolutely unparalleled, top quality at the head of every category in which it chooses to compete is the true reason for its unparalleled effective performance (e.g., 7 of the top 10 package good products in the United States).

The Simple Substance

As best I can determine, there are only *three* truly distinctive "skill packages." They are evident in virtually all of the institutions which are top performers. They are:

1. A focus on total customer satisfaction.
2. A focus on continuous innovation.
3. A common denominator—the notion that the first two require "all hands," and virtually every one of these companies shares a bone-deep belief in the dignity and worth and creative potential of the individual person.

Total Customer Satisfaction

The most frequent accusation I face is that Waterman and I discovered "mere common sense." It is an accusation that I relish. What kinder thing than to be accused of having discovered common sense! The miracle, as I'm fond of pointing out, is that so few apply it, or are *able* to apply it in large, complex businesses. Nothing is more common sensical than TCS—total customer satisfaction. And yet seldom do more than one or two companies in any segment provide truly distinguished service and quality of product. IBM's corporate marketing vice president, Buck Rodgers, sadly comments, "If you get satisfactory service today, it's a darned miracle."

The superior service and/or quality provider is the winner wherever one turns. In 65 of the 70 companies that we looked at, the competitive distinction comes from what I've come to call "revenue line enhancement," which is apparently more important than a slavish devotion to "low cost at all costs."

An IBM officer makes a vital distinction, not found in the microeconomic texts: "There's a big difference between 'competitive cost' and 'low cost.' The former is vital. But I've never known a winner over the long haul with a 'low cost attitude'." His point *is* the key point, as it relates to distinctive competence, or skills. On *paper,* there's no earthly reason a business can't be the "high value added, industry-leading innovater, low-cost producer." However, it is nigh on impossible for big companies to be best at all things, to walk and chew gum simultaneously. The obsession necessary to do any one thing well is enormous. The whole debate focuses on paper possibilities (first at everything) versus real world skills (where first at any one thing is miracle enough).

A recent extensive study for the American Business Conference, the new lobby representing America's "mid-size growth companies" (those between $25 million and $1 billion in sales, which have doubled or more in size over the last five years), concludes exactly the same way. Forty-three out of 45 of its top companies focus on revenue enhancement.

Winners almost always compete by delivering a product that supplies superior value to customers, rather than one which costs less. Most strategists believe that the business winners are those who capture commanding [market] share through lower costs and prices. The winner mid- size companies compete on the value of their products and services and usually enjoy premium prices.[9]

The act of differentially focusing on quality, service, and nicemanship (revenue enhancement) would not be newsworthy, except for the fact that in the "real world" it is rarely practiced. Moreover, business schools and consultants have been a major part of the problem. Carlzon's transformation of SAS was an unabashed attempt to focus on revenue enhancement. He tells a wonderful story:

> I didn't learn much at business school. To be frank, I simply learned that if you had a problem, there were only two strategies that could be used to extract yourself from it—increase revenue or decrease cost. I made that apparently simplistic comment in front of a large [Swedish] group recently. One of my former economics professors, to my surprise, happened to be in the audience. He stood up and said, "Mr. Carlzon, as I suspected, you weren't listening. We didn't provide you with two tools, but only with one—reduce costs."

Using the venerated tool of content analysis (actions speak louder than words) and remembering my prior comments about the 91 electives at Stanford, the same thing could almost be said of at least one U.S. school, quantitatively: while only three courses at Stanford focus on selling and making, fully 34 focus on accounting, financing, and decision analysis.

Looking back at the 70s, it's amazing that we got so badly stung by the experience curve. From the mundane world of Dreyer's Ice Cream (50 percent equity returns and 50 percent p.a. growth in a $75 million business), to Mr. Perdue's chickens (with margins, remember, that are 800 percent above industry average), to Maytag's washers (which command top share and a $75 price premium per machine against tough competitors in a mature market), to Procter & Gamble's toilet paper (whose one-ply variety, even, sells at a full 50 percent price premium over generic "TP"), the higher value-added producers are the winners. Even U.S. Shoe, a tremendously successful company, calls itself the "sports car and convertible end of the shoe business." As Ted Levitt begins in his latest, very readable book, *The Marketing Imagination*, "There is no such thing as a commodity."[10] The often slavish devotion to the experience curve effect is not responsible for our forgetting all of this counterevidence, to be sure. Making more (selling at a lower price to gain share) in order to achieve a barrier to entry via lowest subsequent industry cost is certainly not a bad idea. It's a great one. But the difficulty seems to be the unintended resultant *mind-set*. As one chief executive officer noted to me, "We act as if cost—and thus price—is the only variable available these days. In our hell-bent rush to get cost down, we have given all too short shrift to quality and service. So we wake up, at best, with a great share and a lousy product. It's almost always a precarious position that can't be sustained." Also, I suspect, the relative ease of gaining dominant market position—first in the U.S., and then overseas—by most

---

9 Thomas J. Peters, "On Political Books," *The Washington Monthly*, October 1983, p. 56.
10 Theodore Levitt, *The Marketing Imagination* (New York: Free Press, 1983), p. 72.

American corporations in the 1950s through the 1970s (pre-OPEC, pre-Japan) led institutions to take their eye off the service and quality ball. The focus was simply on making a lot of it for ever-hungry markets. Moreover, this led to the executive suite dominance by financially trained executive-administrators, and the absence of people who were closer to the product (and thus the importance of quality and service)—namely, salespersons, designers, and manufacturers.

The net result is that our strategy-making focus in the United States has become cost containment rather than revenue emhancement. To put it bluntly, service and quality stink to high heaven in most U.S. markets. I revel in GE's ability to have increased its share (from 7 to 75 percent in 26 months) in the domestic U.S. locomotive market through "better listening to its customers." Then I find out that fully 60 percent of GE's machines *didn't* work just three years ago. Holy Smoke: 60 percent! Room for improvement is enormous—from shoes to locomotives.

Continuous Innovation

The second basic skill trait is the ability to constantly innovate. Virtually all innovations—from miracle drugs, to computers, to airplanes, to bag size changes at Frito-Lay, to menu item additions at McDonald's—come from the wrong person, in the wrong division, of the wrong company, in the wrong industry, for the wrong reason, at the wrong time, with the wrong set of end users. The assumption behind most planning systems, particularly the highly articulated strategic planning systems of the 70s, was that we could plan our way to new market successes. The reality differs greatly. Even at the mecca of planning systems, General Electric, the batting average of strategic planning was woefully low. In the 70s (when planners were regularly observed walking on water at Fairfield), GE's major innovative, internally generated business successes—e.g., aircraft engines, the credit business, plastics, and the information services company—came solely as a product of committed, somewhat irrational (assumed, inside, to be crazy) champions. When Jack Welch became GE's chairman in 1980—ending a 30-year reign by accountants—he moved to enhance entrepreneurship. One of his first steps was to reduce the corporate planning staff by more than 80 percent. The most truly innovative companies—Hewlett-Packard, the Raychem Corporation, 3M, Johnson & Johnson, PepsiCo Inc., and the like—clearly depend upon a thoroughly innovative climate. Radical decentralization marks Johnson & Johnson. Both J&J and IBM (via its new Independent Business Unit structure) give the innovating unit a board of directors with an explicit charter to "ignore the strictures of formal planning systems and to keep the bureaucrats out of the hair of the inventors." 3M is simply a collection of skunkworks. The highly profitable Raychem Corporation has grown to almost a billion dollars by adding over 200,000 products to its product line in a 25-year history. In the soft goods business, the extraordinary success of Mervyn's (a Dayton-Hudson subsidiary) is based on the fact that it can remerchandise a multibillion-dollar business in 10 days—an act which takes almost 10–12 weeks at its arch-competitors J. C. Penney Company, Inc. and

Sears Roebuck & Co. In the same tough business, Bloomingdale's is marked, according to its most intimate analyst, by having "more experiments going on per square foot than any other retailer in the country." It's a formula that Macy's Ed Finkelstein has copied for the last five years—resulting in Macy's extraordinary success.

The trend toward radical decentralization (as opposed to coordinated market attack via central strategic planning) as the only viable path to instilling entrepreneurship is beginning to intrude into an ever-larger number of corporations, especially mature businesses. Campbell Soup is tired of simply trading tiny fractions of share points. Its new chief executive officer, Gordon McGovern, has just reorganized the company into 50 independent business units. The objective for each of them is clear: innovate *around* their product lines rather than stick with the tried and true. Numerous other package good companies—PepsiCo chief among them—are vigorously pursuing new business development rather than relying upon grabbing another millionth of a share point (which may easily be lost next month). A most unlikely vital company is U.S. Shoe, yet the entrepreneurial vigor of this billion-and-a-half dollar company is extraordinary. A recent *Fortune* article attributed its success to "superior market segmentation." The next issue of *Fortune* carried a letter to the editor from the son of the founder which rebutted that argument: "My father's real contribution was not superior market segmentation. Rather, he created a beautiful corporate culture which encouraged risk taking." So from Hewlett-Packard and 3M, where we'd expect it, to PepsiCo, Campbell Soup, and U.S. Shoe, we find the gospel of salvation through internal entrepreneurship increasingly being practiced.

All Hands

The third and final regularly found skill variable is the *sine qua non* that goes hand in glove with the first two. Superior customer service, quality, and courtesy (total customer satisfaction) is not a product of the executive suite—it's an all hands effort. Constant innovation from multiple centers is similarly not the domain of a handful of brilliant thinkers at the top. Thus, virtually all of these institutions put at the head of their corporate philosophies a bone-deep belief in the dignity and worth and creative potential of *all* their people. Said one successful Silicon Valley chief executive officer recently, "I'll tell you who my number one marketing person is. It's that man or woman on the loading dock who decides *not* to *drop* the box into the back of the truck." Said another, "Doesn't it follow that if you wish your people to treat your customers with courtesy that you must treat your people with courtesy?" Many sign up for these three virtues, but only the truly distinguished companies seem to practice them regularly.

Common Thread: The Adaptive Organism

These three skills—and these three alone—are virtually the *only* effective sources of sustainable, long-term competitive advantage. Notice that each suggests the essence of an adaptive organism. The organization that provides high perceived value—service, quality, courtesy—invariably does so by constantly listening and adapting to its customers' needs. The innovative company is similarly radically focused on the outside world. And the expectation that all people will contribute creatively to their jobs—receptionist and product designer alike—means similarly that each person is a source of external probing and a basis for constant renewal, fulfillment, and adaptation. These organizations, then, are alive and are excited—in both the "attuned" and the "enthusiastic" sense of that word. Moreover, such organizations are in the process of constant redefinition. The shared values surrounding these skills—customer listening and serving, constant innovation, and expecting all people to contribute—are rigid. But, paradoxically, the rigid values/skills are in service of constant externally focused adaptation and growth.

The excellent companies—chicken makers to computer makers—use their skills as the basis for continually reinventing adaptive strategies—usually on a decentralized basis—to permit them to compete effectively in both mature and volatile youthful markets. Skills, in a word, *drive* strategy in the best companies.

Skills versus Strategy

I tend to see the word strategy, in the sense that it's currently taught in the business schools (or practiced by the leading consultants), as *not* having much meaning at the corporate or sector level at all, but as being the appropriate domain of the strategic business unit or other form of decentralized unit (the IBU at IBM, the division at Hewlett-Packard or J&J, the merchant organization at Macy's). To return to our 7-S model, this is the classic case for what we have constantly called "soft is hard." The driving variable in the model, which creates the preconditions for *effective* strategizing, is, above all, skills. Strategy is the dependent variable, operable at a lower level in the business.

We view the constantly innovating, constantly customer-serving organization as one that continually *discovers* new markets and new opportunities. The notion of the learning organization, the adapting organization, the discovering organization, reigns supreme. Sound skills are the basis for "finding" or "discovering" business-unit strategies in the cause-effect model that we see at play from IBM to Perdue Farms. IBM has had a giant success with the PC. The basis: IBM translated its unique view of customer friendliness into a market previously driven by engineering(technology)-run companies. 3M scored a remarkable success with Post-It Notepads. 3M is a blue-chip finder of odd-ball new markets, uniquely independent of prior category designations. By contrast, we watch the traditional "strategists" fall into the abyss time and again. Because a market looks good on paper, they believe the company should take it on. Yet they invariably underestimate the executional effort (skill base) required to do extremely well at *anything*.

Proactive Leadership

If there is some sense to all the above, what then is the leader's role? If not master strategist, then what? He or she becomes, above all, a creator or shaper or keeper of skills. Warren Bennis has called the leader of this sort a "social architect." Harry Levinson calls him an "educator." Larry Greiner coined "strategic actor." Xerox subsidiary (Versatec) CEO Renn Zaphiropoulos calls himself a "gardener." I have used terms such as *role model, dramatist,* and *value shaper.*

Above all the leader's role becomes proactive rather than reactive. Strategy formulation has usually seemed to me, as it actually gets practiced (certainly not as planned by the academics), to be a reactive process. Analyze what was and try to get ahead of the world by projecting from there. This is not the stuff of creation—of new markets in shoes or miracle drugs. I'm always reminded that Ray Kroc created McDonald's by following up on the order pattern of a single customer (when he was selling milkshake machines) who happened to be using about seven times as many machines as that store "should have been using." He learned from the store, bought it from the McDonald family, and the rest is history. A 3M executive says that the senior manager (many more than just those in the executive suite) "should above all be a *nurturer* of champions." He says that would-be champions ("monomaniacs with missions," in Peter Drucker's words) are "close to a dime a dozen." The important people are those that view their prime role as protecting the champions from the silliness of inertial bureaucracies. Former Chairman Ren McPherson, speaking of the Dana Corporation, sketches a similar role: "The manager's job is to keep the bureaucrats out of the way of the productive people." Sam Walton, founder of the remarkably successful WalMart Corporation, says, "The best ideas have always come and will always come from the clerks. The point is to seek them out, to listen, and to act." At the Rolm Corporation, an executive adds, "The leader is not a devil's advocate. He is a cheerleader." Gordon McGovern at Campbell says senior management's role is to develop "a business concept, challenging financial goals, guideline characteristics and an understanding of how to move its culture."

Larry Greiner also speaks eloquently to the proactive role, discriminating between the "trapped executive" (e.g., solves daily problems, meets formally with immediate subordinates, acts aloof and critical, pays attention to weaknesses) and his notion of a "strategic actor" (e.g., articulates philosophy, makes contract with employees at all levels, acts warm and expressive, pays attention to strengths of the business).[11] The skillbuilder, in my experience, is thus a nurturer, cheerleader, unabashed culture shaper, keeper of bureaucrats off the backs of productive people, listener, wanderer. All are direct statements about value shaping and skill building. All are proactive.

Leadership: Spirit in the Details and Daytimer

The leader is not a decision maker! Gordon McGovern describes his reorganization of Campbell Soup:

We first broke the business into manageable parts, multiplied the number of people running to an opportunity and with the wherewithal to get things done. We then

---

[11] Greiner, *Senior Executives,* p. 14.

established with these people a concept which is flexible and rich and open-ended, so they can go out and grab parts of it that we at the top wouldn't even imagine.[12]

If not a decision maker/strategist, then what? If a skill builder/value shaper, what does that mean? A while ago I had dinner with Andy Pearson, PepsiCo's president. Andy has a sparkling reputation in many circles as a "genius at package goods strategy." I want to argue that he's not! He's better than that. He is a skill builder in a once dormant, now vital $8 billion enterprise.

The dinner with Pearson, before a Strategic Marketing Society conference, illustrated the point. It was a lovely Montreal restaurant. The food and wine were first class. The discussion? It could have been about anything. Baseball would have been my first choice (it was October and my favorite team was in the playoffs). But no, for four nonstop hours we talked about waiting time bells in Pizza Huts, cookie shelf space acquisition tactics by Frito-Lay, a tiny new bakery PepsiCo recently acquired, and so on. Andy is not "a strategist." Andy *lives* the skill he is shaping: entrepreneurial, constant, opportunistic quick attacks on a variety of markets. Test. Do. Try. Fail. Learn. Try again. Get on with it. That is the skill that Andy and Chairman Don Kendall have built into PepsiCo. When Andy visits a subsidiary, stop one is *not* the executive suite. Instead, he camps out in the offices of the associate brand managers. "What are you up to?" Over and over he probes, day in and day out, decade in and decade out. Is Pearson a master strategist? Or a master skill builder/value shaper?

At a recent seminar, former P&G senior manufacturing manager (a 15-year veteran) takes agitated exception to an insurance executive's assertion that *In Search of Excellence* makes a case for "balancing rigid controls with some informal, looser stuff." The ex-P&Ger almost shouts:

We didn't have the MRP systems or lengthy reports. And I'll tell you how I learned about quality at P&G. As a young manager, I remember vividly the phone ringing one night at 1:30 A.M. It was a sales manager, and he screamed at me, "George, we got a problem with a [he emphasizes *a*] bar of soap down here!" [*Here* was 200 or so miles away] "Could you be down here by 7:00 A.M. to look at it?!" The tone told me it wasn't an invitation. After you've driven 200 miles, through the mountains, at 75 miles per hour, to look at one 35¢ bar of soap, you figure out pretty quick that these guys [P&G] are more than a little bit serious about product quality. It ain't soft or informal, I'll tell you.

P&G's stories—heroes, myths, anecdotes—are at the soul of its remarkable 145-year history of unparalleled quality. P&G's "strategy" is to maintain that skill and apply it creatively in a raft of markets, and even to fend off maturity when required (they explicitly deny that product life cycles exist and point to 100 or so reformulations of Ivory Soap as an example).

A large company president and friend states, "The maintenance of the lasting skill lives in the millions of executive actions, many or most nearly subconscious, that illustrate and dramatize a continuing, living commitment

---

[12] Gordon McGovern (Address to "1983 Midyear Executive Conference," National-American Wholesale Grocers Association, September 30, 1983).

to it. It's the visits, marginal notes, and content of articles in the company bulletin that really count—not the so-called bet the company decisions.''

The lasting strategic skill, the distinctive competence that acts as a decades-long barrier to competitive encroachment, *is* Andy Pearson's stories and visits, *is* the simple recollection, in public, of the harrowing ride through the Tennessee hills to rescue a single 35¢ bar of soap at P&G.

Enthusiasts, Passion, and Faith

Let's really stray afield from the world of traditional definitions of strategy formulation. Ray Kroc says, ''You gotta be able to see the beauty in a hamburger bun.'' Recall that Debbie Fields of Mrs. Field's Cookies says, ''I am not a businesswoman, I am a cookie person.'' Sam Walton loves retailing. From Steve Jobs to Famous Amos, the creators of effective organizations are unabashed *enthusiasts*. Bill Hewlett and Dave Packard had a passion for their machines. Herman Lay had a passion for his potatoes. Forrest Mars loved factories. Marvin Bower of McKinsey loved his clients. John Madden loved linebackers. The love was transmitted and transmuted into excitement, passion, enthusiasm, energy. These virtues infected an entire organization. They created the adaptive organization—the organization aimed externally, yet depending upon the full utilization of each of its people. This seemingly simple-minded definition of effective strategy for the ages even holds in mature organizations. The fervor with which Procter & Gamble revered quality has now been passed down through many generations. The ''salesman's bias'' of an IBM and 3M has similarly been maintained several generations beyond the founder. The passionate belief that the dominant skill reigns supreme is at the heart of business success. Johnson & Johnson, many generations beyond the founder, credits the power and continued vitality of its brief credo for its successful (remarkably so) response to the tragic Tylenol affair. The response was not analytic. The response was to re-interpret the basic values.

So where does all this leave us? The world of experience curves, portfolios, and 4-24 box matrices has led us badly astray. George Gilder notes in *Wealth and Poverty:*

> Economists who attempt to banish chance through methods of rational management also banish the only source of human triumph. The inventor who never acts until statistics affirm his choice, the businessman who waits until the market is proven—all are doomed to mediocrity by their trust in a spurious rationality.[13]

The devilish problem is that there is nothing wrong with any of these strategy tools. In fact, each one is helpful! I think of the same thing in the area of quality: quality circles, automation, and statistical quality control are extraordinarily powerful tools—but *if and only if* a bone-deep belief in quality comes first. Given the 145-year tradition at Procter & Gamble, the tools are then helpful. Absent the faith, passion, belief, value, and skill, the tools become just one more manifestation of bureaucracy—another attempt

---

[13] George Gilder, *Wealth and Poverty* (New York: Basic Books, 1981), p. 264.

to patch a fundamental flaw with a bureaucratic BAND-AID. In the same vein, if you have the well-developed skills of a J&J, 3M, HP, U.S. Shoe, WalMart, or Mrs. Field's Cookies, then the strategy tools can be helpful adjuncts indeed.

But we should never forget for a moment that the analytic models are not neutral. Any analyst worth his salt, with anything from a decision tree to a portfolio analysis, can shoot down any idea. Analysts are well-trained naysayers, professional naysayers. Yet it turns out that only passion, faith, and enthusiasm win. Passion can also lead to losses—many of them, of that there is no doubt. Yet there is no alternative. We simply can't plan our way to certain success. John Naisbitt, *Megatrends* author, asserts: "Strategic planning turned out to be an orderly, rational way to efficiently ride over the edge of the cliff." I think he's not far off. Above all, the winning companies that we've observed—small and large, regulated or unregulated, mature or new—are ruled by somewhat channelled passion in pursuit of distinctive skill building and maintenance.

What this article is about: Providing incentives for success requires that performance appraisal systems emphasize the strategic plan of the organization.

4-3 Linking strategy, performance, and pay*

R. Henry Migliore

R. Henryt Migliore is dean of the School of Business at Oral Roberts University.

The appraisal portion of the strategic plan has long been a problem. How do you reward the achievement and performance of individuals as they operate the organization's strategic plan? How do you use the performance appraisal area to motivate the management team to achieve the objective in the strategic plan? How do you provide incentive for your people to stay with your organization? How do you develop a commonsense approach to salary and bonus rewards?

The keys to performance appraisal and salary administration within the strategic plan are profit and performance. This discussion focuses on two factors: (1) appraisal and reward for individual performance and (2) group bonus reward systems.

Figure 1 represents the various possible reward alternatives each individual faces. In the lower left-hand Section A, the low performer in an organization whose objectives were not achieved would receive low pay and a low bonus. At the other extreme, in Section C, where the individual had achieved his objectives and the organization had achieved its objectives, then the individual would receive high pay and a high bonus. Sections B and D represent other situations. In Section B, the individual achieves his objectives yet the organization has modest success. Then he could receive high pay and a medium bonus. Section D is in a situation where a person didn't do

---

Figure 1
Reward alternatives

Individual objectives attained	10	High pay							High pay		
				(B)	(C)						
		Medium bonus							High bonus		
		Low pay							Medium pay		
				(A)	(D)						
		Low bonus							High bonus		
	1	2	3	4	5	6	7	8	9	10
									Organization objectives attained		

as well on achieving his individual objectives but the organization did well, and he would receive medium pay and a high bonus. The rest of this column will discuss specific programs that contribute to individual rewards along with the group bonus reward.

Individual Reward

Ideally, the organization meets its broad overall purpose and reason for being. Specific measurable objectives in key result areas are largely met on a constant, sustaining basis. This success is based on a management team that has the motivation, ability, and insight to manage the organization's resources. The individual manager meets or excels his specific, measurable, key result objectives.

The successful organization rewards its contributors: stockholders, owners, managers, and employees. As a spin-off, it now contributes to society in its roles as taxpayer, employer, etc. It encourages its suppliers to make long-term plans to meet its needs. The ripple effect of success works its way down.

The successful organization now must devote attention to rewarding its own managers and employees for their contributions. The organization's needs are met. Now how does the organization meet the extrinsic and intrinsic needs of its people?

Intrinsic needs are met through a properly functioning long-range planning/MBO philosophy. Organization members meet their higher-level needs of self-esteem, autonomy, recognition, and self-worth with this particular style of MBO.

The extrinsic needs have always been more difficult to deal with. Few salary and bonus systems do well over the long run. The big question mark among MBO scholars, students, consultants, and executives is: "How do you combine MBO with salary administration?"

In its simplest form, the person must be evaluated on how he performed against key objectives that were negotiated, thoughtfully considered, and obtainable. They usually number from 5 to 10.

The managers should also be evaluated. Then each year's pay increase should be based on performance of the 5-to-10 key performance objectives and the 10 criteria listed.

1. Use of long-range planning/MBO.
2. Developing people.
3. Contribution to morale.
4. Communication.
5. Creativity.
6. Emotional stability.
7. Job knowledge.
8. What kind of leader.
9. Problem solver.
10. Public image/social responsibility.

One method the author has devised would take already existing sets of objectives and turn them into appraisal forms as suggested in Figure 2. The individual's regular performance objectives are listed at the top of the sheet, and their final outcome is given a rating of 5 for excellent through 1 for poor performance. The 10 items listed above are then rated according to the same system.

These 10 items are nonmeasurable but should be considered. The main criteria should be the results of how the managers performed as compared to what they negotiated as their performance objectives. Each objective at year-end would have performance rated excellent through poor. Figure 3 might be followed in determining the specific pay increases. You would average the objectives and give them a 75 percent weight. The 10 nonmeasurable areas would get a 25 percent weight.

If the person fared well against these expectations and the organization has done well, he should receive a salary boost commensurate with the performance. In today's climate, this would be a 12 to 20 percent + pay increase.

Next, let's consider another circumstance: the organization hasn't done as well, but the individual performer posted a good record in all areas over which he had control. He should be paid by the same criteria. The organization has too much at stake to risk losing its high performers. Usually 20 percent of the people contribute 80 percent of the *key* results. Don't be niggardly with the 20 percent. The same rule of thumb, 12 to 20 percent pay increase, holds if the organization does poorly. The other 80 percent receive pay in the third 10 percent range.

In the third possible circumstance, the organization does poorly but the individual does very well. In this case, the high-performance individual is not in a position to expect the kind of organizational rewards listed in the first two circumstances. A mature management system should realize this. My best suggestion is that the same five performance levels be recognized but that the pay scales be exactly half of what they normally would have been.

In the circumstance where the individual does poorly, it doesn't make any difference what the organization did. The individual did not make the right kind of contribution and should not be rewarded. Rewarding for a poor performance is a guarantee to continue the same.

Figure 2
MBO performance appraisal form

	Excellent 5	Above Average 4	Average 3	Below Average 2	Poor 1	Discussion Notes
			Rating			
1. Operate within budget of $146,032 and cost per credit hour of $130	5					
2. Graduate 25 MBAs in May 1980	5					
3. Maintain enrollment of 100 FTE MBA students		4				
4. Publish in top third of the nation	5					
5. Average 35 aerobic points per week and reduce weight to 205	—	–	3			
	15	4	3			22 = Total
1. Use of LRP/MBO	5					
2. Developing people	5					
3. Contribution to morale	5					
4. Communication			3			
5. Creativity	5					
6. Emotional stability	5					
7. Job knowledge		4				
8. What kind of leader	5					
9. Problem solver			3			
10. Public image	5					
	35	4	6			45 = Total

Average of objectives = 22 ÷ 5 = 4.4.
Average of other items = 45 ÷ 10 = 4.5.
Weighted average = (4.4 × 75%) + (4.5 × 25%) = 4.425.

One complicating factor in this era of high inflation is what do you call a pay increase, and what do you call an adjustment for inflation? I know of no organization that has completely solved that problem. In reality, even with Figure 3, this past year with inflation at 15 percent, if a top performer received 20 percent, in effect he was receiving only a net 5 percent reward for his performance. This author believes the recommended pay percentages should be tied into the inflation rate. Theoretically, every organization should automatically modify its pay ranges based on the inflation level and then add the pay increase on top of inflation.

Bonus System

Working hand in hand with salary rewards based on individual achievement is the bonus system. This is nothing new of itself. But how does it work

Figure 3
Pay increase determinants

Performance Level	Recommended Pay
1. Performance less than satisfactory (has not met all minimum acceptable performance standards and objectives for the position). Point average below 1.5.	Zero percent increase
2. Performance meets minimum standards and objectives but not up to average. Point average 1.5 to 2.5.	Not more than 5 percent increase (0–5)
3. Performance meets at least average standards and objectives and may excel in some areas. Point average 2.5 to 3.5.	Not more than 10 percent increase (5–10)
4. Performance is better than average overall and excels in a majority of standards and objectives for the position. Point average 3.5 to 4.5.	Not more than 15 percent increase (11–14)
5. Performance is outstanding because it excels in all of the objectives and conditions previously listed. Point average 4.5 to 5.0.	Not more than 20 percent increase (15–20)

with MBO? If the organization meets certain understood, agreed-upon objectives and criteria, every organization member shares in the harvest. Objectives such as sales, profit, manufacturing efficiency, quality, and safety could be the bases. Criteria could be set for those deemed to be of importance based on the individual organization. The bonus system must be simple, straightforward, and understood.

The most important objective is profit. Good, solid, long-term-oriented profit is the golden word of capitalism. It's simple: no profit, no bonus. Other objectives can be a factor but only after the profit objective is met.

The criterion for profit might be 15 percent before-tax profit on sales. A pool is set up with 20 percent of all profit above the minimum criterion of 15 percent going into the pool. For example, a $40 million sales company with $6 million profit would have no bonuses. One company provides a nice working vacation at a popular resort area if the minimum criteria are met. Another idea would be to give some percentage (e.g., 1 percent of all profits) if the minimum criteria are met. However, a $7 million profit would put $200,000 into a pool. If there were 500 employees, this would be a bonus of $400 per person. All employees share equally in this pool. The bonus is a nonbudgeted item.

Another way the pool can be distributed is to give divisional managers shares of the pool to distribute as they see fit within their units. This method is of doubtful value because of the bias problem. This is one instance in which the author advocates treating everyone on the team the same. The bonus is the team reward. If the team wins the league championship, it goes to the Superbowl and everyone shares equally in the reward. If you don't win the league championship (in this case 15 percent profit before taxes), you stay home and everyone gets the same thing . . . nothing.

Under this system, a person has an opportunity to get ahead on his own and is also rewarded for being a team player.

This author still believes the most effective way to handle a bonus is to include everyone, including the management team, by setting up a bonus fund. The fund is not budgeted but comes out of aftertax corporate profits based on an audited financial statement. Another alternative is that funds should be available for bonus distribution unless the corporate performance exceeds all of the following: (1) 10 percent return on sales before taxes; (2) 5 percent return on sales after taxes; (3) manufacturing efficiency 80 percent; and (4) sales growth of 40 percent. The total fund available for distribution each year is not to exceed 10 percent of corporate aftertax net profit or 1 percent of sales. This sets some standards, is reasonably simple, and lets everyone in on the bonus if things go well. Another criterion is 20 percent of aftertax profit in excess of 8 percent gross revenue.

Again, pay particular attention to the 20/80 rules. Those 20 percent who contribute the 80 percent need to be rewarded. A rigid reward system that holds them back just encourages them to go elsewhere. The other 80 percent are not going anywhere anyway, so don't spend as much time worrying about them.

Some guidelines to keep in mind are:

The key is accountability, not activity.

Use job objectives instead of job descriptions as the focal point.

People who are committed to your organization are worth more than people who are not committed to it.

People who feel they are underpaid will act like it.

Don't give any kind of merit increase to someone not meeting his job responsibilities and objectives.

Bonuses should be paid only for beating an indicator.

Paying people below equitable market rates will assure you of marginal performance and high turnover.

Fair pay does not motivate, but unfair pay demotivates.

The higher the person is in the organization, the more you pay for strategies and creative thinking.

Performance appraisal and salary administration are part of the strategic planning process.

Conclusion

The performance appraisal approach outlined in this article is now being used in four organizations. Each adapted parts of it to fit particular needs in the organization. It has been in use for six months to two years. At this stage, this approach seems to be very positive. The management teams in all four organizations agree that this approach is superior to the one previously used. They now have a way of rewarding performance fairly, emphasizing the strategic plan, and providing a real incentive for people to see that they have a long-range future in the organization.

What this article is about: The successful implementation of a strategy requires that the internal organization be supportive of the strategy. The McKinsey 7-S Framework is a useful way for managers to judge the alignments and administrative "fits" within the internal organization as they attempt to implement strategy.

4-4 The seven elements of strategic fit*

Robert H. Waterman, Jr.

Robert H. Waterman, Jr., is editor of The Journal of Business Strategy.

In a recent article on strategy in *Fortune,* Walter Kiechel estimated that the vast majority of American companies have so far proved incapable of developing and executing meaningful corporate strategies. In fact, he estimated 90 percent.

While that figure is probably an exaggeration—I like to think our clients do a lot better than that—I have to agree with the gist of Walter's comments. One reason for the problem, I expect, is that the managers who would be strategists forget one of the most important lessons to be learned from the military generals, from whose Greek predecessors, Webster tells me, the word *strategy* is derived. The lesson is simple: The value of a strategy depends not only on the elegance of its conception but fully as much on whether the company proposing the strategy can really execute it. Given a particular company—and what I submit are a set of capabilities and weaknesses uniquely its own—what are the odds of a strategy getting done right?

The Proof Is in the Execution

This problem of execution, which in my judgment is quite common, is the civilian equivalent of an otherwise brilliant invasion plan that happens to overlook the fact that the logistics chain cannot supply the troops.

But many strategies proposed in the business world seem to me to be much like the Iranian sneak invasion. In the abstract they sound great, but they are simply too hard to execute. What works for IBM in computers has proved nigh impossible for its would-be competitors. A good strategy is not synonymous with a doable one. Nor is a doable strategy synonymous with a good one. The challenge is to find a good doable strategy.

Is there an easy way to tell which strategies are likely to run amok because a company does not have the wherewithal to make them work? My claim is that there is, and my aim is to propose an answer to that question. The answer lies in the use of the McKinsey 7-S Framework.[1] Originally developed as a way of thinking more broadly about the problems of organizing effectively, the framework also proves to be an excellent tool for judging the doability of strategies.

What the framework (Figure 1) says is this: It is not enough to think about strategy implementation as a matter only of strategy and structure. The conventional wisdom used to be that if you first get the strategy right, the right organization follows. And when most people in Western cultures think about organization, they think structure. We find in practice, however, that these notions are too limiting. To think comprehensively about a new strategy and the problems with carrying it out, a manager must think of his company as a unique culture and must think about the ability of the company to get anything really fundamental (i.e., not tactical) accomplished as a matter of moving the whole culture. It has not been just strategy that led to the big Japanese wins in the American auto market. It is a culture that

Figure 1
McKinsey 7-S Framework

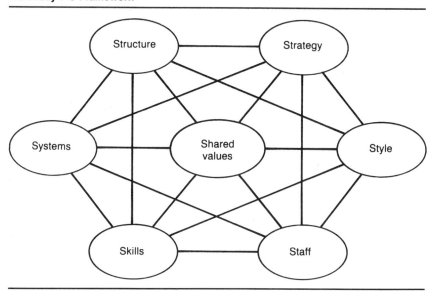

---

[1] Robert H. Waterman, Jr., Thomas J. Peters, Julien R. Phillips, "Structure Is Not Organization," *Business Horizons,* June 1980, pp. 14–26.

inspirits workers to excel at fits and finishes, to produce moldings that match and doors that don't sag. It is a culture in which Toyota can use the most sophisticated of management tools, the suggestion box, and in two years increase the number of worker suggestions from under 10,000 to over 1 million with resultant savings of $250 million.

In this context, the 7-S Framework is saying that culture is at least a function of seven variables (alliteration intended to aid memory): strategy, structure, systems, style, staff, skills, and shared values (see Figure 2 for summary definitions). Now think of the 7-S diagram as a set of seven compasses (Figure 3). When the needles are aligned, the company is organized; when they are not, the company has yet to be really organized even if its structure looks right.

A classic example is AT&T. No telephone company in the world was as well organized around its past chairman Theodore Vail's notion of "universal service." However, as management knew when it undertook it, it may prove very difficult for this company to implement its new concept of marketing in a deregulated environment. Not that there is anything wrong with the strategy; indeed, due to deregulation, AT&T probably has no choice. But it is extremely difficult to move all those compass needles in so large a company where the old culture runs so deep.

Another example: One of my most successful clients had decided that—as a strategic matter—all its major new products must come from acquisition rather than de novo start-up, a strategy that management had tried with scant success on several previous occasions. The strategy is right. Carrying it out means moving from a functional to a divisional structure, which is easy to draw on paper but difficult to execute. The top management is so used to running a functional organization that—as a stylistic matter—it has taken more than three years to come to grips with even starting to make the change.

Figure 2
A summary of the S's

1. *Strategy*. A coherent set of actions aimed at gaining a sustainable advantage over competition, improving position vis-à-vis customers, or allocating resources.
2. *Structure*. The organization chart and accompanying baggage that show who reports to whom and how tasks are both divided up and integrated.
3. *Systems*. The processes and flows that show how an organization gets things done from day to day (information systems, capital budgeting systems, manufacturing processes, quality control systems, and performance measurement systems all would be good examples).
4. *Style*. Tangible evidence of what management considers important by the way it collectively spends time and attention and uses symbolic behavior. It is not what management says is important; it is the way management behaves.
5. *Staff*. The people in an organization. Here it is very useful to think not about individual personalities but about corporate demographics.
6. *Shared values* (or superordinate goals). The values that go beyond, but might well include, simple goal statements in determining corporate destiny. To fit the concept, these values must be shared by most people in an organization.
7. *Skills*. A derivative of the rest. Skills are those capabilities that are possessed by an organization as a whole as opposed to the people in it. (The concept of corporate skill as something different from the summation of the people in it seems difficult for many to grasp; however, some organizations that hire only the best and the brightest cannot get seemingly simple things done, while others perform extraordinary feats with ordinary people.)

Figure 3
The 7-S compass

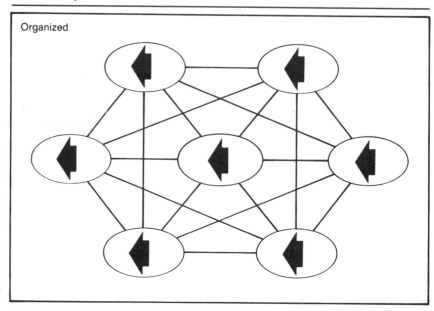

Organized

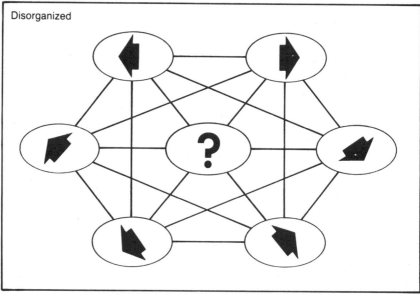

Disorganized

Another client's strategy is to be as customer-service-driven as IBM. However, a majority of its sales force does not make quota, whereas most of IBM's sales force does, or so I am told. But the message that is constantly being sent out by the client's compensation system is that every year over half of the salesmen will be losers. The system, it seems to me, is defeating the strategy.

Checking Strategic Fit

What we are starting to see in the examples is a wonderful way to check strategic fit.[2] Given a proposed strategy, do the other S's in the 7-S Framework support that strategy, or (more likely) will each have to be changed to fit? How difficult is it to change each of the other S's? Does management have the will and the patience to make these changes? These questions must be asked because it is the "fittedness" among the S's that turns a good strategic idea into a lean, mean program for corporate success.

How It Works: A Banking Example

To elaborate on how one might use the 7-S Framework to test strategic fit, let's take a bank. A strategic problem in banking has always been how to organize to serve the very different needs of all the different markets a bank serves. Few industries I know of serve such a broad spectrum of markets, all the way from the teenager with a savings account to the largest of corporations. Now, the problem has new urgency. As the industry is being deregulated, new nonbank competitors are attacking bank markets differentially. Money-market funds cream the affluent segments of the consumer market. Foreign banks and commercial paper offerings erode the loan market for large corporations. A bank must have a market-based strategy to survive. Citibank anticipated this, and in 1970 mounted a major reorganization around market segments, but almost no other bank followed suit. In an industry that typically follows suit with dispatch, the question is: Why have others been so slow to move? I think the answer lies in the lack of fit that the 7-S Framework would have predicted.

Suppose a bank does decide on a close-to-the-market strategy. If it has a big, diverse branch system, its immediate problem will be how to structure. The natural way has been to organize around branches as profit centers. The problem with structuring around markets is that most branches do not fall neatly into one market or another. Matrix organizations, in my view, don't work very well, so the dilemma is how to maintain the simplicity of the branch-as-building-block structure and at the same time differentiate by markets.

The style problem is no less difficult to solve. To pick just one dimension of the problem, the historic culture of banking has been that of the lending officer. People who have advanced in the mainstream of banking in the last 20 years have typically advanced through lending. As a result, top-management time and attention in most banks are biased toward lending activity. But a close look at some markets shows this function is less important to the customer and competitive situation than it used to be. In the large-business market, for example, lending has become a commodity, and the banks with unique services are those with unique cash and transaction services. The skills required to support these services are typically operations and EDP

---

[2] I am indebted to Tony Athos of Harvard University for his concept of "fittedness." Tony was not only helpful as we struggled with the concepts underlying the 7-S Framework, but he was also the first to insist that fittedness among the S's is what counts most.

skills, which as a stylistic matter most bank managements have paid little attention to in the past.

Let's look at bank staff (not in the line/staff sense, but staff as a way of making human dimension of organizations start with "S" so 7-S alliteration will work). Here it proves extremely useful to think of staff in terms of the demographics of the population of an organization.[3] One problem for the would-be market-oriented bank is that to be competitive direct selling of many services is required. But as a demographic matter, there are too few people in banking with real sales experience.

Bank managers will also stumble over systems. Unlike, say, a large mining company, where a new strategy can be implemented by investing in a major new mining venture, a bank does not implement strategies until bank officers start to negotiate individual deals differently. For example, bank managements can and have talked at length about the importance of profits versus asset volume alone. But unless the account officers are negotiating to make every customer profitable, the situation that typically exists today will not only allow but invite competition (i.e., inordinate variance in any given market segment between the most and the least profitable customers). One reason underlying this phenomenon is that performance measurement and compensation systems reward volume, not profitability. Until systems are put in place that accurately measure profitability (no mean trick in banking) and reward people on this basis, the strategy of market orientation remains a dream.

And so it goes through the remaining elements of the framework. No matter how sensible a concept sounds, unless there are good answers to the issues raised in the realm of each of the other S's, the concept is far from a real strategy.

In practice, we have used the framework to assess strategy in several different ways. One way is to fill out a matrix that, in the top rows, lists the areas in which a company now has congruence among the S's and, in the bottom row, summarizes what will have to change in each S category to make a proposed strategy work. It is the degree of difference between what a company now does well and the proposed strategy that determines the degree of difficulty of that strategy. While that by itself is no great discovery, the rigor and explicitness added by the framework give realism to strategic choice in a way I have not seen before.

Being more realistic, management can then be more intelligent about its choices. If the 7-S analysis says the strategy will be difficult, management can either search for other options or go ahead, realizing that if its company can pull it off, it will truly have a competitive edge and concentrate its attention where it counts—on all the manifold problems of execution suggested by the framework.

Conclusion

In conclusion, I want to return to what I think is at the heart of Kiechel's "dirty little secret," using a concept I first saw articulated in a marvelous

---

[3] I am indebted to Richard Pascale of Stanford University for the staff demographics idea.

book by Graham Allison called *Essence of Decision.*[4] In it, Allison postulates several models of the world of decisions and shows that not one but all are useful in explaining how the world really works. But most of what I see done and written about on corporate strategy is based on the assumption that only one of his paradigms, the strategic model, is really in force. The strategic model is one of rational choice: Organizations have reasonably clear goals, and the problems of strategic choice are resolved by analytically determining which options are the most effective in relation to the set of goals. The concept of the business portfolio as a strategic framework and a tool for guiding action swims in the mainstream of Allison's strategic paradigm.

But Allison poses another, and equally useful, paradigm: the organization model. In this view of the world, organizations are creatures of habit just like people. They are cultures, heavily influenced by the past. If one knows enough about how an organization has made past decisions, one can fairly well predict how an organization will respond to future problems of strategic choice. Many of the electronics companies may have had enormous difficulty in digital watches because their habit was to drive costs and prices down the learning curve, whereas making money in consumer markets requires different habits.

This then is the essence of strategic fit: It is to determine strategy with both models of the world at work. The 7-S Framework is a very useful way to ensure that this happens.

---

[4] Graham T. Allison, *Essence of Decision* (Boston: Little, Brown, 1971).

What this article is about: The focus of this article is on how top managers can overcome the invisible barrier of culture to speed up the process of strategic change. It explores how culture can not only inhibit strategic change but can be an invaluable aid to speedy and coherent strategic choices.

4-5 Managing culture: The invisible barrier to strategic change*

Jay W. Lorsch

Jay W. Lorsch is professor of business administration at the Graduate School of Business, Harvard University

Culture affects not only the way managers believe within the organization, but also the decisions they make about the organization's relationships with its environment and its strategy. In fact, my central argument is that culture has a major impact on corporate strategy. To clarify what I mean, let me define two key concepts: *culture* and *strategy*.

1. By culture I mean the shared beliefs top managers in a company have about how they should manage themselves and other employees, and how they should conduct their business(es). These beliefs are often invisible to the top managers but have a major impact on their thoughts and actions.
2. By strategy I mean the stream of decisions taken over time by top managers, which, when understood as a whole, reveal the goals they are seeking and the means used to reach these goals. Such a definition of strategy is different from common business use of the term in that it does not refer to an explicit plan. In fact, by my definition strategy may be implicit as well as explicit.

I define these two terms at the outset because culture and strategy are concepts widely used by scholars and managers, often without being clear about their precise meaning. My purpose is not to take issue with others' definitions. I only want to be sure the reader understands mine.

* Jay W. Lorsch, "Managing Culture: The Invisible Barrier to Strategic Change," in *Gaining Control of the Corporate Culture,* ed. Ralph H. Kilmann, Mary J. Saxton, and Roy Serpa (San Francisco: Jossey-Bass. This article also appeared in *California Management Review* 23, no. 2 (Winter 1986), pp. 95–109. Reprinted with permission.

Focusing on the con?
at no time in recent h
with such a wide arr
companies:

- Regulatory chang?
  as diverse as a?
  tions.
- Advancing elec?
  industry and
  financial ser
- The cost of t?
  giants of t?
  partners, f
- Automotive comp??
  eign competition are restru??
  productivity, and adopting foreign sour??
- Similarly, managers in a wide range of mature indus???
  consumer durables are reexamining and changing traditional manu???
  turing and distribution policies to remain competitive in the world
  market.

There is considerable evidence that such pressures will accelerate in the
years ahead, given the rapid rate of technological change, the increasing
interdependence of global markets, and continuing regulatory change in the
United States. This means that many top managers will increasingly find that
they are confronted with major questions of how to position their companies
in a new business and how to change fundamentally their firm's strategy in
their existing business.

In the face of such pressures for strategic change, a major concern for
managers must be to avoid missteps and to shorten the time required to
develop effective new strategic approaches. Unfortunately, strategic repositioning has historically been a complex and long-term process (even in highly
successful companies) and one that is heavily influenced by the company's
culture. The following examples illustrate the point:

- A consumer food company recognized in the late 1950s that changing
  consumer tastes were obsoleting its major products. It took over 15 years
  and two generations of top management to successfully reposition the
  company into growing businesses which built on its strengths in consumer marketing.
- A manufacturer of industrial supplies became aware in the late 1960s that
  the market for its major product was shrinking due to the development of
  alternate processing technologies. Top management needed almost a
  decade to develop and implement a strategy which today makes the
  company again a successful source of supplies to its customers.
- In the early 1970s, the top management of a growing electronics firm
  turned down a proposal from engineering and middle-managers who

manufacture and market a mainframe computer with inno-
w features. The reason—the project seemed too risky. It was
10 years before this top management found a suitable way to
ely position itself in the computer industry.

hese are successful top managers, those who are able to pull off major
tegic changes that allowed their companies to remain financially healthy
d growing in changing times.

ties of Strategic Change

Some might argue that the long time required to achieve strategic change is
a direct result of management's inadequacies in logical analysis or their
failure to use the latest tools for strategic planning. But the facts of the matter
are quite different.

Obviously, strategic changes necessarily involve many actions, which
require months and years to accomplish. Old businesses may have to be
divested or shut down. New products may have to be developed by scientists
and engineers. Market tests may be required. Manufacturing facilities may
have to be built or modified. An alternative approach to internally developing
new businesses may involve acquisitions, which require time to locate, to
negotiate, and to integrate successfully with the parent.

In a more subtle but equally important way, strategic change requires a
basic rethinking of the beliefs by which the company defines and carries on
its businesses. In a study of 12 successful companies, we found that there
exists among top managers a system of beliefs (a culture) which underlies
these strategic choices. These beliefs have been developed over many years
of successful operation. As a top manager in one firm stated:

It is a closed loop. You make the argument that in the beginning of the company, the
founders wanted to make certain products, which in turn led to our way of managing,
which reinforced our products. It all hangs together. It isn't the result of any
intellectual process, but it evolves. The pattern of principles which emerge out of a
lot of individual decisions is totally consistent, and it is a fabric which hangs together
and leads to success.

As this executive also points out, the beliefs in each successful company
truly have a systemic quality. Each individual premise fits into a pattern or
cultural whole which had guided managers' decisions to many years of
corporate success.

Managers learn to be guided by these beliefs because they have worked
successfully in the past. As one CEO said:

If you have a way that's working, you want to stay with it. . . . This is not the only
way to run a company, but it has sure worked for us.

Executives in successful companies become emotionally committed to
these beliefs because, having usually spent their entire careers in their
companies, they have learned them from valued mentors and have had them
reinforced by success at various stages of their career. This longevity was not
only true of the CEOs in the 12 companies studied, but of most Fortune 500
companies. The president of another company provided a specific example:

My predecessor became president about 1947. In our staff meetings he'd say, "We're caught between two giants—the retailers and our suppliers." We're the little unit in between. We need to grow so we can exercise power on both sides. I can't remember a staff meeting in the early 1950s when an officer didn't make some mention of this point. It led directly to our concern with growth.

These beliefs cover a range of topics: what the firm's financial goals should be; in what businesses it can succeed; how marketing should be done in these businesses; what types of risks are acceptable, which are not. But at the core of each system of beliefs is top management's particular vision of its company's distinctive competence. This vision is management's own assessment of the capabilities and limits of the company's employees, its market position, and its financial resources and technological base. In sum, it is management's core beliefs about what the company is capable of accomplishing. (Figure 1 illustrates the system of beliefs in a typical company.)

These beliefs can inhibit strategic change in two ways. First, they can produce a strategic myopia. Because managers hold a set of beliefs, they see events through this prism. Frequently, they miss the significance of changing external conditions because they are blinded by strongly held beliefs. For example, the management of the industrial supply manufacturer mentioned earlier was rudely awakened to the decline of its major product by a dramatic market study. The current CEO of the company recalled:

Back in the 1950s, a member of the finance department made a study of the industry which showed that it was in a mature phase. This was the first time that the company had done such a study and management was shocked by its implications that the industry and the company would stop growing. From that point on, everyone became concerned about the problem and what they were going to do about it.

In retrospect they recognized that they could have seen the decline several years earlier.

Second, even when managers can overcome such myopia, they respond to changing events in terms of their culture. Because the beliefs have been effective guides in the past, the natural response is to stick with them. For example, the food processing company mentioned earlier studiously avoided opportunities to grow internationally. Why? An early international failure convinced its top managers that such expansion was outside of the company's distinctive competence. Their vision was that: "We can succeed with products which are marketed to consumers in the United States. We understand them." While top managers are usually able to recognize the practical difficulties involved in accomplishing a major strategic change, they are much less likely to recognize that their deeply held beliefs represent an invisible barrier to strategic change which must be penetrated.

The Process of Strategic Change

An examination of strategic change (as we learned about it in our study of the 12 successful companies) illustrates how the invisible barrier of culture can be overcome. In those companies where major strategic change was a necessity because of changing product market conditions, managers for a time did suffer from strategic myopia. The severity of this ailment depended

Figure 1
Commodity products company—Top management culture

Beliefs about Capital Market Expectations

Have a return on equity of "x" %, which places us among the upper ⅓ of all manufacturing companies.

Have a steady improvement in market share.

Dividends should *never* be cut and should be "x" % of earnings.

Maintain "x" credit rating and keep debt less than "x" % of capital.

Strategic Vision

We can be the strongest and top-ranked company in our industry, but will not diversify outside it.

Beliefs about Internal Organization

We must have the strongest management structure in the industry.

Foster harmony and preserve the family feeling within the company through all levels of employees including those in the union.

We must keep employees who believe in the industry happy because the industry is what we are good at.

Preserve the drama and emotion of the industry.

We want to keep management open door and participating.

Top management must always include at least one person who understands manufacturing process and operations.

Good coordination between sales and manufacturing gives us the ability to serve customers better than competition.

Beliefs about Product Market Competition

Our geographic location provides us with a cost advantage.

We must offer better service than competitors to our customers.

Major customers like big suppliers committed to the industry.

We must improve profit position through lower costs, not higher prices.

Market share is important, but not through low prices.

We must compete on innovation in processes and basic products, not in price.

We must expand and modernize plants for the long haul.

In sum: Beliefs about capital market expectations reflect management's convictions about what is necessary to keep investors and lenders satisfied given their strategic vision of staying in a mature industry. Beliefs about product market competition reflect their conviction about why and how they can succeed in a highly competitive mature industry. Their beliefs about internal management reflect what management approaches will lead to competitive success and therefore will meet capital market expectations.

upon for how long and how well the old culture continued to achieve top management's cherished financial goals. Persistent problems in achieving the desired financial goals was, in each case, the trigger that made managers aware that something was wrong with their beliefs. The pattern of principles which had worked well no longer did so.

Incremental Change

The initial response to this discovery was a period of questioning various individual premises. Could the problem be fixed with minor modifications? In some instances, these attempts at incremental change succeeded. For example, in one of these companies, adverse financial results in 1974 and 1975 alarmed top management because they were simultaneously investing heavily in a major new product. They either had to undertake more long-term debt or abandon the new product. Either option meant departing from an important belief. Two executives recalled the dilemma:

> We were using our debt capacity too fast. The momentum of our capital expenditures program was carrying us out too fast, especially in one business where the outlook had been changing negatively. We had to decide what was useful to the future of the company.
>
> Well, in 1974–1975, survival was the name of the game. The first thing we had to do was perpetuate the company and not let it get away from us, but [the new product] represented the future and we couldn't let that go. It was a technological breakthrough. It was a big chip to bet on.

In the end, this company's top management altered their beliefs about what was an acceptable level of long-term debt so that they could continue the development of the major new product. In the past, such new products had fueled the company's profitable growth. To depart from the principle that major new products assured the future health of the company would have shattered their central cultural vision of the company's distinctive competence. It was far easier to bend one less-central principle than those at the core of top management's culture.

Such incremental changes in top management's beliefs occur periodically in most successful companies. One belief or another is altered, but the basic fabric of their culture remains the same. However, in the rapidly changing world of the 1980s, changing events are likely to require even more fundamental changes. This had also been the case in the history of several of the companies we examined. While their top managers had tried initially to adjust to external market change through incremental actions, they found such small steps did not achieve the desired results. This led to much more serious departures from past strategic beliefs and practices, which changed the fundamental nature of their belief system.

Fundamental Change

Top managers went through several distinct but interrelated stages in their thoughts and actions as they led their companies in fundamentally new directions.

Awareness The first stage grew directly out of earlier attempts at incremental changes. Top managers gradually developed a *shared* awareness that fundamental changes in their culture would be necessary to assure corporate survival. Because top managers were so emotionally committed to their beliefs, an awareness of the need for fundamental change did not come easily. During this early phase, top managers would engage in months of what psychiatrists label *denial*. They chose to ignore the possibility that key beliefs could and should be modified. But gradually, in each firm, an awareness did develop among the top group that external events had changed permanently. Incremental steps were not solving their problems. Drastic changes in the whole pattern of beliefs were needed.

Confusion . This recognition was followed by a period of confusion. While all the top managers could agree that the old beliefs were not working, there were often as many ideas as top managers about what to do next. No one idea attracted wide support. Strategic planners and their concepts offered little help, because the confusion went to the heart of top managers' own judgments about such matters as what the firm's distinctive competence had been and could be in the future.

As long as the firm's financial viability is not seriously in question, the period of confusion can continue for many months or even years. One executive described such a period in his company's past:

> We acquired business after business. There was no real support, so it failed. We flubbed around. People said we should be in a [particular business] because it had growth, but we never picked out what segment, and the president and chairman weren't comfortable with the program.

While aware of the need for major change in strategic direction, but confused about what to do, top management was ready for new leadership, and the boards of directors apparently shared that view. In these companies, the board turned to new leadership to find a path out of the period of confusion. In all but one instance, the new CEO was promoted from within. However, he always represented a new generation of management with fresh ideas. Because these CEOs were generally insiders, they also had an understanding and an appreciation of the old pattern of strategic beliefs. This, too, was important because their major task was to bring a clear new direction out of the existing confusion, while building as much as possible on existing strengths.

Developing a Strategic Vision   The first steps out of the confusion took place inside the heads of the new CEOs and may have even predated their ascension to corporate leadership. They developed a personal set of ideas about what their company could become. Their next task was to elaborate and clarify this strategic vision and to rally other top managers and the larger management organization to it. For a while, their activities in this regard were largely mental and verbal—thinking and talking and listening to their subordinates.

A company executive described this phase:

> What we did in the mid-60s was to assess the management group. We stepped back. There were several sessions with top management out of the office. It was a self-assessment. It was top management assessing itself and saying we didn't see the good prospects for technology in [a basic consumer products business] we had hoped for. If we had anything to bring to new industries, it was our ability to think about customers, how to do market research, market planning, etc.

Out of such discussions evolved a vision shared among the top managers about what the company's distinctive capabilities could be in the future. In the instance of this executive's company, it was to be a manufacturer and marketer of a wide range of nondurable branded products to U.S. consumers; and to do this in such a way that the company would be an "all weather company"—one that would do well in all phases of the business cycle.

In each company, the CEO and his associates developed a unique vision. What these strategic visions had in common, however, was that they took fundamentally new ideas and meshed them with some old beliefs about how to compete effectively, how to manage their employees, and about corporate finances. Such a fusion of old and new is realistic because it reflects the best assessment these executives could make about their own and their company's capabilities. Psychologically it made sense because it enabled them to retain as many beliefs from their cherished culture as possible, even as they fashioned new directions. Because the new CEO and his colleagues were almost all career-long managers in their companies, adherence to old beliefs was comfortable and minimized resistance to strategic change.

In fact, one of the two major accomplishments of this phase was to overcome the persistent doubts among the executives about departing too far from established beliefs. The other accomplishment was a refinement and clarification of the direction that was to carry the firm forward. While this clarification was achieved, initially by thought and discussion, at some point the ideas had to be converted into concrete decisions. Such decisions signalled the final stage of the process—experimentation.

Experimentation   Like scientists in a laboratory, executives in these successful companies experimented with their new ideas. Gradually and incrementally they committed money and people to the new direction.

An executive in a consumer products company described this phase:

> During the 1960s, we had four out of every five capital investment dollars going into acquisitions. There were many new venture teams going and we got into quite a number of businesses. We were searching for new business.

In this particular company, experimentation took the form of both acquisitions and internal development. For example, part of their vision was to open retail shops, so they could sell directly to the consumer. A number of different types of stores were opened. Results were evaluated, new ideas tried. But none of the ideas really caught fire. Frustrated but not discouraged by several years of trying, these executives discovered a small chain of outlets which they could acquire and which already embodied many of the ideas they had concluded were important as a result of their own internal development. These four stores were acquired and today have been expanded into a nationwide network of 300 outlets. Success with this acquisition led to additional acquisitions repeating the pattern with other products.

The top managers in the industrial supply company went through a similar process. They began a search for products which could build upon the strengths of their sales force and distribution network. A number of small acquisitions were made. Some were kept and other divested. Gradually, again over several years, they learned what products fit their vision and which did not. For example, it became clear to them that consumable supplies were desirable and that there was an upper limit on the technological content of the businesses they could enter.

In some of these companies, top managers also learned through experimentation that their new vision wouldn't work. A forest products company provides an example. Even though their company was a good performer in its industry, these top managers, frustrated by slow growth and low profitability in the base business, concluded that diversification into unrelated businesses would solve these problems. Several acquisitions were made and the company operated them for several years. The results were only mediocre and the top management concluded that their vision of the company as a diversified "conglomerate" was not viable. Instead they began experimenting with new products more closely related to their core business.

These examples illustrated one reason why fundamental strategic change can consume years. It simply takes that long for top managers to convert abstract ideas into concrete realities. As they do so, they are learning new beliefs which combine with the old ones they retain to shape the pattern of their culture and their corporate strategy for the future. As their predecessors before them, they become committed to a system of beliefs which work. Experimentation gradually subsides and top management finds itself with a stable pattern of beliefs which have created new corporate success, but which are fundamentally different from those with which they started the process of strategic change.

Breaking Through the Invisible Barrier

If this is the reality of fundamental strategic change—what can managers do to speed up the process in an era which demands more rapid adaptation to constantly changing realities. Is it possible to reduce the time required, which—as we have seen even in successful firms—could be as long as a decade? Of course, part of the answer rests in the speed with which top managers and their organizations can deal with the pragmatics of strategic change—acquisitions, diversification, new product development, test markets, building new facilities, and so on. And there are obviously real limits here, particularly if one agrees that experimentation (which is so characteristic of strategic change in successful companies) is important to minimize major missteps in defining new direction. But, as we have seen, there is another major reason for the long time required. This is the invisible barrier of the top manager's culture. Is it possible for managers to retain the benefits of strong beliefs, while still being capable of changing them more rapidly? I believe the answer is yes.

One key is for top managers to accept as a major premise in any company's culture the importance of flexibility and innovation. Whatever else they hold sacred, they must recognize that in the world of the 80s and beyond, the need for strategic change will be a constant. However else top managers define their unique strategic vision, they must recognize this fact. But such a commitment will only be meaningless words unless it can be converted into activities and actions which cause managers to use this conviction to examine and challenge their other strategic premises. Several ways of assuring that this happens are suggested by the experience of these successful companies.

Making Beliefs Visible

In a few of these companies, top managers had put their major beliefs into writing. In one, for example, the central beliefs were available for employees, customers, and visitors to read in a printed brochure distributed widely throughout the company's offices, visitors' waiting rooms, etc. Similarly, at Johnson & Johnson (which, while certainly a highly successful company, was not included in our study) the company's "credo" hangs on the wall of most executives' offices. Such formalized statements, while they may not capture all aspects of a company's culture, do remind managers that their decisions are guided by such principles.

The important lesson to be drawn from these attempts to develop formal statements of beliefs is that the invisible beliefs can be made more visible in this way. Of course, displaying these beliefs publicly may or may not be a sound idea depending upon whether managers feel they contain proprietary ideas. But that is not the critical point. What is more important is that top managers can and should make their implicit beliefs explicit, at least to each other. If managers are aware of the beliefs they share, they are less likely to be blinded by them and are apt to understand more rapidly when changing events obsolete aspects of their culture.

In companies which, like the vast majority of those we studied, do not have such explicit statements, top managers should undertake a *cultural audit* so that they are aware of their beliefs prior to having to deal with changing events. A culture audit involves the top management group developing a consensus about their shared beliefs. The process starts with each member of the top group answering questions such as those listed in Figure 2. Then, individual answers to these questions are compared and provide a basis for discussion among top managers. Through this process, the beliefs which are shared can be identified and codified. In answering these questions, it is critical that the emphasis be on what top managers believe as evidenced by their practices, not on some idealized view of their company.

This is important to emphasize in the wake of the current management obsession with excellence and corporate culture, a by-product of which has been a spate of statements of corporate philosophy. While these may be admirable statements of top management's intentions, they may have little to do with the strategic beliefs top managers actually operate upon, which is what the culture audit is intended to identify.

An effective culture audit cannot be delegated. It must involve the company's major decision makers, including the CEO. They must be willing to commit the thought and time, probably several days, to answer such questions individually and then to collectively compare and discuss their individual responses until they reach a consensus.

As they go through this process, top managers should be able gradually to identify the consistent pattern to their culture and how beliefs are related one to the other. If the audit is successful, top managers will have made the once invisible barrier of the culture visible. Then they can deal with it more rapidly in the face of change, retaining beliefs which still are valid and discarding those which are not.

Figure 2
Culture audit

	Questions	Examples
Beliefs about Goals	About what financial objectives do we have strong beliefs based on traditions and history?	Return on assets Rate of growth Debt/equity ratio Bond rating Dividend policies
	How, if at all, are those beliefs about financial goals related to each other?	Growth should be financed internally, which means no long-term debt and limited dividends.
	What other goals do we believe to be important?	To be in the top quartile of Fortune 500 companies. To be the best in our country. To be a responsible corporate citizen. To be an ''all-weather'' company.
Beliefs about Distinctive Competences	What do we believe to be the appropriate scope of our competitive activity?	We can manage any business. We can succeed in domestic consumer products. We can succeed with products based upon our technological expertise. We can only succeed in the paper industry. We can manage our business worldwide.
	To what earlier experience can we trace these beliefs?	
	Do they reflect a realistic assessment of the competence of management and the company?	
Beliefs about Product Market Guidelines	What broad guidelines do we believe should guide our managers in competing in product markets?	Have one or two share in each market. Provide the best quality product. Compete on service, not on price.
	Can these principles be traced to earlier historical events?	
	Are these guidelines valid today in our various businesses?	
Key Beliefs about Management Employees*	What do we believe employees want and/or deserve in exchange for their effort?	Safe working conditions Stable employment High wages Share of profits Equity ownership
	What beliefs do we hold about the importance of employees to company success?	Our scientists are key to innovation. We want managers and employees to work as one big team. Committed employees lead to satisfied customers.

* While these are not strategic beliefs, strictly speaking, they are important to understand because they are so closely related to strategic premises.

Assuring Flexibility

Making culture explicit is one way to facilitate more rapid strategic change. Also required, however, are other ways to stimulate top managers to maintain a commitment to flexibility, whatever else they believe. Successful companies use a variety of means to accomplish this.

Top Managers without Portfolio One device is the presence of a very senior and experienced top manager whose role is to raise questions, challenge beliefs, and suggest new ideas. Such managers, we found, generally had few other responsibilities. They often have the title of "vice chairman." At first glance, it might seem that they have been shunted out of the line management. But a more careful examination indicates that these managers-without-portfolio are valued members of the top management group. Always highly intelligent with long experience, often skeptical and inquiring, they interact constantly with other top managers, challenging their beliefs and suggesting new ideas. While they understand and are committed to the existing culture, they keep it fluid and dynamic through their presence in the management group.

The qualifications for such positions may seem unique, and there may be no way to assure that such a person is available to every top management group. Yet the presence of such managers in several of these successful companies suggests that the CEOs understood the value of intelligent dissent and creativity in their top management.

The Role of Outside Directors Outside directors can also play an important part in assuring strategic flexibility. While they usually are affiliated with companies for long periods of time and may therefore fall prey to sharing many of top management's beliefs, they are also far enough removed to provide objectivity and raise important questions about the appropriateness of these beliefs in changing times. While many top managers hold to the view that strategic decisions are the sole purview of management, outside directors can, even with limited time and information, play an important role in keeping top managers alert to their culture and to changing external events. Such activities may be conducted in informal contacts or may, as in some companies, be formally assigned to a strategy committee of the board.

Bringing in New Blood Another way to assure cultural flexibility, is to bring in an outside manager at a very senior level. Such an individual brings a new perspective and objectivity. But to be successful, he or she must deal effectively with two problems. First, any newcomer comes with a set of beliefs from his or her prior experience. What worked with the previous employer can become a dearly held set of principles for each individual. To be effective in a new setting, the newcomer needs to develop an awareness of these personal beliefs. Second, the new executive needs to develop an awareness of the culture of the new company. If these beliefs have been explicitly stated, the transition is easier; but if not, the newcomer will have to be an effective detective. Not understanding the existing beliefs can cause the newcomer to unwittingly step on too many sensitive toes and to be rejected before the objectivity and new ideas for which the newcomer was hired can be tried out.

Flexibility down the Line   Another way to assure flexibility at the top is to encourage flexibility of thinking at subordinate levels of management. This can assure that succeeding generations of top management will be less blindly rigid in their adherence to cultural traditions. It can also provide a source of new perspective to the present top managers as new ideas bubble up from subordinate levels.

Two different routes can be used to encourage flexibility among middle managers. One is to stimulate new ideas within the organization. An incompany education program for middle managers, with outside experts as instructors, is one frequently employed means. Another is to encourage systematic rotation of managers among functions and businesses. In this way, their perspectives can be broadened. Such inside activities always have the inherent limitation that new ideas are learned with company colleagues in the context of the company's culture.

There is a way to avoid this pitfall. High potential subordinate managers are provided an opportunity to broaden their perspectives outside the company. University executive education programs are one vehicle for achieving this. Whatever else they achieve, they do broaden the perspective of participants through contact with peers from other companies. Business and government exchange programs, like the White House Exchange Fellowships, can accomplish the same objective. Another possibility used successfully is to encourage travel to other companies in other countries to learn new methods and gain broadened perspective. Such programs have been used recently by several companies to challenge the beliefs and broaden the perspective of manufacturing executives. The result has been improved manufacturing practices which depart from strong traditions.

In whatever way top managers decide to broaden their subordinates' perspective, they must be ready to encourage new initiatives and innovations, after the broadening experience. Flexibility will flourish only if top managers, through their own words and actions, reward innovative initiators and allow experimentation.

Change and Stability

Our focus has been on how top managers can overcome the invisible barrier of culture to speed up the process of strategic change. As necessary as this will be in the future, we must not lose sight of the positive value of a strong culture. In the successful companies studied, these belief systems were critical components in corporate success, providing guidance to managers as they made complex decisions. As long as external conditions do not change dramatically, culture is an invaluable aid to speedy and coherent strategic choices. Even when conditions change dramatically, many old beliefs describe the essence of the company's character and competence. They cannot be abandoned without a high cost.

Thus, the real challenge for top managers is to encourage flexibility while still respecting and valuing their culture. Awareness of these beliefs is a prerequisite to achieving this balance, which will be critical to corporate survival in the dynamic decades ahead.

What this article is about: The IBM culture, as expressed through its rules, discipline, and goals, reinforces its successful strategy. This article explains how the interaction between culture and strategy works at IBM.

4–6 The corporate culture at IBM: How it reinforces strategy*

Susan Chace

Susan Chace is a staff reporter for The Wall Street Journal.

When Thomas J. Watson, Sr., died in 1956, some might have thought the IBM spirit of the stiff white collar was destined to die with him. But indications are that the founder's legacy of decorum to International Business Machines Corporation still burns bright. Consider the way an IBM man on a witness stand in San Francisco the other day replied when questioned about an after-hours encounter with a competitor:

Q. "All of you were in the hot tub with the Qyx district manager?"
A. "The party adjourned to a hot tub, yes. Fully clothed, I might add."

That an IBMer invited to a California hot tub should fear that propriety demanded a swimsuit wouldn't surprise many people who have ever worked for the giant company. For, besides its great success with computers, IBM has a reputation in the corporate world for another standout trait: an almost proprietary concern with its employees' behavior, appearances, and attitudes.

What this means to employees is a lot of rules. And these rules, from broad, unwritten ones calling for "tasteful" dress to specific ones setting salesmen's quotas, draw their force at IBM from another legacy of the founder: the value placed on loyalty. Mr. Watson believed that joining IBM was an act calling for absolute fidelity to the company in matters big and small.

Esprit de Corps

And just in case an IBM employee isn't a self-starter in the loyalty department, the company has a training regimen geared to instilling it. In brief, this consists of supervising new trainees closely, grading them, repeatedly setting new goals for them, and rewarding them amply for achievement. Suffused in work and pressure to perform, employees often develop a camaraderie, an esprit de corps.

What it all amounts to is a kind of IBM culture, a set of attitudes and approaches shared to a greater or lesser degree by IBMers everywhere. This culture, as gleaned from talks with former as well as current employees, is so pervasive that, as one nine-year (former) employee puts it, leaving the company "was like emigrating."

To George McQuilken, who left IBM to found his own company, Spartacus Computers, Inc., "the hardest part about being gone was the first few times I tried to make a decision on my own about anything, like what hotel to stay in, or who I wanted to hire."

For those who don't leave, IBM returns the loyalty. It prides itself on being able to reward those who follow its code and meet its expectations with success and security for life. The most valued of these employees are sometimes known within the world of IBM as "sorries"—people the computer company would be especially sorry to lose.

Divorce Court

Virginia Rulon-Miller was once an IBM sorry. A self-described "lifer" at IBM, she got into trouble when her interpretation of IBM's largely unwritten rules clashed with that of her superiors. Unlike most separations from IBM—quiet resignations to pursue other interests—hers was a messy divorce that ended up in court.

Gina Rulon-Miller joined IBM as a receptionist in Philadelphia in 1967 at age 19. After 12 years, five moves, and numerous stints at IBM training schools, she became a marketing manager, in San Francisco, supervising salesmen who sold fancy typewriters and other IBM equipment to such companies as Pacific Telephone & Telegraph and Standard Oil of California.

On a June day in 1979, Miss Rulon-Miller abruptly turned in her keys and her plastic identification card and fled IBM, after her boss confronted her with her relationship with Matt Blum, once an IBM supersalesman and at that time a manager at a competing office-products company. In an emotionally charged interview, her boss said she was being given a nonmanagement post at the same salary. To her, steeped in IBM's get-ahead culture, this was tantamount to being released, and she said so. She sued, charging wrongful dismissal.

Inherent Conflict?

At the trial, IBM conceded that Miss Rulon-Miller was a loyal employee with an outstanding record and that there was no indication she had ever passed company secrets to her boyfriend. But, it argued, the mere existence of a relationship between business rivals was a conflict. "She clearly cared very much for Matt Blum," IBM said. "And she clearly cared for his success. And if that is the case, she had a conflict of interest."

Miss Rulon-Miller's lawyers argued that what really worried IBM was the possibility she would defect to Matt's company, Exxon Corporation's Qyx, encouraging other IBM salesmen to defect as well. The jury sided with her, saying in effect that the company couldn't dictate an employee's off-the-job behavior. It awarded her $300,000 in compensatory and punitive damages. IBM has said it would appeal, but it won't discuss the case with a reporter.

Even though Miss Rulon-Miller has since spent two years wandering around the country, taking four different jobs and losing her boyfriend in the process, she has a typical IBMer's nostalgia for the company she left. She says the company "created me professionally," and her harshest comment about it is, "I'm not as positive about IBM as I was before."

How does IBM inspire positive feelings even in former employees who take it to court? Largely by following Mr. Watson's basic formula: systematic goading toward excellence, combined with constant supervision and frequent rewards. Its more flamboyant aspects are gone; probably no IBMer will ever again be feted as Otto E. Braimayer, an early 40-year employee, once was, with a formal dinner featuring 40 waiters carrying in 40 cakes. But management-by-merit-badge techniques continue to keep employees arriving at 7:30 A.M. to attend meetings before their regular duties begin.

Every year an employee gets a Performance Plan, a written set of very specific goals. The manager neatly lays out the employee's responsibilities. Meeting or exceeding Performance Plan goals leads to promotions and raises.

Tight discipline is also enforced by near-constant observation and grading. At sales training schools, trainees know what can happen if they fail to leave their rooms "broom clean": They may be called back to try again, or their manager may be charged for the cleanup. Vigilance even extends to the evening hours. Instructors take notice of who is burning the midnight oil preparing for the next day's product-demonstration tests and who seems to have a crush on whom. "Report cards" grade trainees on matters ranging from product knowledge and presentations to attitude—enthusiasm, confidence, sincerity, cooperation, work with others, desire to learn.

Rising Quotas

One way to stand out at training school is to finish work in time to help slower classmates. Those who help the most may be elected class officers. Then they may get choice sales territories when they return to the field.

Once out in the field, salesmen get a quota of IBM machines to be placed in their territories. Each year the quota is raised or the territory cut or both, partly to test employees' ingenuity in selling more products to the same people. Customers need to be sold hard; IBM takes back the commission if a customer decides to return rented equipment after a year or so.

The Performance Plan is law. Extensions to deadlines for handing in reports are given for good reasons only. (A broken leg will do.) Employees get an overall rating based on the various points in their plans. A "1" means exceeding expectations; a "5" is unsatisfactory.

Achievement is followed by immediate rewards. Insiders say the most cherished of these isn't money. It's having your name and quota on the bulletin board with a notation saying "100%." It's having a party thrown for you at your branch because you have satisfied a prickly customer. It's a steady flow of letters of commendation. Says one ex-IBMer: "If you burp the right way, they send you a certificate."

Thank-You Notes

Gina Rulon-Miller was a "1" who burped the right way. Her file over-flowed with notes. "Dear Gina, thank you . . . for the excellent job you did in setting up our casé studies at your branch last month" or "for helping to make this business show a success." Or, "Your performance in purchase and new equipment placements has been tremendous." Congratulations "for qualifying for your third 100% club. . . . May the force be with you."

The notes and the quotes, the training and the praise are very effective. "People work their brains out," says Miss Rulon-Miller's brother Todd, an IBM veteran who now works for an American Express Company unit. The results please IBM, too. Asked whether company officials ever wonder if IBM has too many rules, a spokesman replies: "IBM has an adequate number of rules. We think they are proper and necessary. But we always try to challenge bureaucracy, so that any time we felt a rule was extraneous or unnecessary, we would seek to eliminate it."

The hard work that the IBM atmosphere inspires has another effect, Todd Rulon-Miller believes. "A close clique forms from the pressure everyone feels," he says. "The first thing they want to do at night is go out and have drinks with each other. Then they start blending business and social life. They rent cabins in Tahoe together, buy a sailboat, join a softball team, play golf."

When a member of the clique leaves the office, he may want to keep up his IBM-based social life. So it was that Matt Blum, the IBM salesman, even after his defection to Exxon was playing third base for a softball team of IBMers the night an IBM man showed up dressed as a big typing ball from an IBM Selectric typewriter to cheer the team on. Mr. Blum shared beer and golf with his IBM buddies. He braved San Francisco Bay in a communal sailboat. And he invited the (clothed) IBMers into his hot tub.

Rapid Rise

Meanwhile, IBM offered Miss Rulon-Miller a management job. She accepted it enthusiastically, even though it meant temporarily lower pay. In quick succession she got a $4,000 raise, joined a group of top IBM salespeo-ple for a week's celebration in Bermuda, and pressured an IBMer who knew the intricacies of Qyx machines to talk to her people at 7:30 A.M. so they would know what they were up against.

Then one day Wayne Fyvie, another IBMer, spotted Miss Rulon-Miller with Mr. Blum. Mary Hrize, also of IBM's San Francisco office, began to worry that Mr. Blum might snoop in Miss Rulon-Miller's briefcase and discover information that would help Qyx and hurt IBM. And Philip Call-ahan, Miss Rulon-Miller's boss, who was under pressure to stem a tide of salesman defections, hastily told her she was losing her management position.

In California State Supreme Court in San Francisco last December, it became clear that IBM didn't have written rules about the propriety either of golf games with competitors' employees or of close personal relationships with them—to say nothing of hot-tub parties. The company officials who testified couldn't agree about whether moving Miss Rulon-Miller out of management was a disciplinary act, or about how it squared with IBM's code of "respect for the individual." One IBM loyalist said the switch was merely a way to accommodate her personal relationship by removing her from a potential source of conflicts.

The jurors didn't buy that, concluding that IBM had acted with "oppression or actual malice" in its dealing with Miss Rulon-Miller. But their verdict didn't do much to clarify the company's encompassing but unwritten code of behavior, a code that pervades the life of every IBM professional. One former IBMer, reflecting on his years at corporate headquarters in Armonk, New York, describes the way that atmosphere affected him: "In my 15 years there," he says, "I never lost the feeling that I was breaking a rule. But I never knew what the rule was."

What this article is about: The author provides a framework for managing cultural change within the context of his involvement in AT&T's divestiture process. His view of the cultural impact of disassembling the world's largest corporation illustrates the challenges of adapting culture to changes in a large organization.

4-7 Cultural transition at AT&T*

W. Brooke Tunstall

W. Brooke Tunstall is assistant vice president and director of corporate planning, AT&T.

At AT&T Operational Headquarters in Basking Ridge, New Jersey, a remote 20 × 32-foot room serves as the status control center for the staggering job of disaggregating the Bell System. The magnitude and complexity of this job are only suggested by the component divestiture of $125 billion in operating telephone company assets from the parent AT&T Company. The walls of this "Corporate Divestiture Management Center" are adorned with timeline charts, schedules, and graphic representations of critical issues. A computer terminal in one corner instantly displays any one of the 300 corporate assumptions, 2,000 work activities, and/or 150 major events underlying divestiture planning. Yet nowhere in this room or in the computer's memory can be found the one single element that may ultimately be most critical to AT&T's success, through divestiture and beyond. That element is AT&T's corporate culture.

Clearly, the culture must be reshaped, adapted, and reoriented to bring the value systems and expectations of AT&T people into congruence with the corporation's new mission and to prepare them for the competitive telecommunications battles looming ahead. Yet no AT&T manager is charged specifically with the management of the corporate culture. No task force is studying its dimensions. No committee is planning approaches to altering its underlying aspects.

The reason is that the culture is as broad as the enterprise itself, as pervasive as a value system that evolved over a century of service, and as

---

* Reprinted from *Sloan Management Review*, Fall 1983, pp. 15–26.

amorphous as the attitudes and expectations of one million employees. Managing the required changes in culture is not an event underlying divestiture; rather, divestiture is one of the causal factors underlying change in the culture. No one manager is assigned responsibility for managing the change because all managers must be responsible for it.

The road to such responsibility is neither broad nor well marked. The idea of managing corporate culture has only recently surfaced and is still considered an unknown art. No disciplined analytic method exists for objectively assessing cultural attributes and their proportionate influence on corporate performance. No accepted conceptual model of corporate culture exists for diagnosis and orderly change of corporate culture requirements.[1] In fact, there is not, as yet, even a clear consensus on how to define culture, although a number of different approaches have been suggested in the research and business literature. For example, Pettigrew emphasized such elements as rituals, symbols, ideologies, and myths in reporting his longitudinal study of organizational culture.[2] Baker referred to an "interrelated set of beliefs, shared by most of their [corporations'] members, about how people should behave at work and what tasks and goals are important."[3] Kilmann described corporations' cultures as "the collective will of their members," manifested through the development of work-group norms, rites, rituals, and myths.[4]

More broadly, corporate culture may be described as *a general constellation of beliefs, mores, customs, value systems, behavioral norms, and ways of doing business that are unique to each corporation,* that set a pattern for corporate activities and actions, and that describe the implicit and emergent patterns of behavior and emotions characterizing life in the organization. Taken together, the elements in the culture encompass the very meaning of the organization, and increasingly, they are recognized as a virtual sine qua non for its ultimate success. In fact, it has been observed that the culture can play as significant a role as either strategy or structure in the long-term performance of the company, especially for the large corporate organization experiencing significant changes in its markets and/or business environment. This may be AT&T's greatest challenge. The concept of corporate culture holds the fascinated attention of many at AT&T who are charged with helping to steer the corporate ship through the stormy seas of divestiture. In fact, as we near the end of this figurative voyage, some see it as a virtual observatory of cultural change in "real time," not only because of the

---

[1] The development of such a model might most profitably proceed along four dimensions: (1) corporate identity, including purpose and mission, corporate symbols, community and government relations, and attitudes toward investors; (2) psychological contract, including employee perceptions of trust and fair treatment, reward systems, management expectations of employees, and employee communications; (3) concepts of responsibility and authority, including both management style and organizational structure; and (4) orientation to the customer, especially including attitudes of employees toward product quality and service. Generally, these four dimensions form the backdrop against which AT&T's experience is examined throughout this article.

[2] A. M. Pettigrew, "On Studying Organizational Cultures," *Administrative Science Quarterly,* December 1979.

[3] E. L. Baker, "Managing Organizational Culture," *Management Review,* July 1980.

[4] R. H. Kilmann, "Getting Control of the Corporate Culture," *Managing,* 1982.

challenge of adjusting a clear-cut, well-established cultural heritage to a new business environment, but also because of the critically compressed time frame in which the change must occur.

The Context of Change

The root causes for AT&T's impending transition lie in a decade of extended debate on whether the nation's telecommunications industry should be opened to competition and, if so, how. Throughout the 1970s, scores of FCC dockets, dozens of private anti-trust suits, several proposed legislative bills, and a Justice Department antitrust suit combined in an avalanche of change on the corporate consciousness of Bell management. Decision after decision by governmental bodies moved the industry incrementally toward greater competition. Finally, in late 1981 and early 1982, two cataclysmic federal government mandates opened the floodgates of change. The first was the FCC Computer Inquiry II Order; the second was the divestiture agreement with the Department of Justice.

The magnitude of the structural changes flowing from these mandates can hardly be overstated.

- The FCC ordered AT&T to form a separate subsidiary to provide, on a detariffed basis, all new customer premises equipment (telephones, push button systems, PBXs) and "enhanced services" (e.g., digital network) by January 1, 1983. The dimension of the change is enough to require a complete overhaul of the way AT&T markets, sells, and distributes its products and systems. This subsidiary, already a reality, is AT&T Information Systems.

- The divestiture agreement required that a major part of each of the 22 Bell Operating Companies be spun off from AT&T early in 1984 (now set for January 1), without specifying the precise form of their restructuring. Subsequently it was decided to regroup the 22 companies into seven regions and a centralized service staff. The charter of each region will be to provide local exchange service and access to local customer lines for long distance companies (e.g., AT&T, MCI, and Southern Pacific). An eighth entity, a mutually owned and operated service corporation, will provide central staff services for the seven regions. The surviving AT&T, the ninth entity, will also be reorganized to provide interstate and intrastate long-distance services, and to supply and maintain telephone equipment on the customer's premises through its subsidiary (AT&T Information Systems).

The seven Regional Bell Operating Companies (RBOCs) will, of course, be completely severed from the parent AT&T, joining the vast clan of 1,700 independent U.S. companies whose only relationship to AT&T is to interconnect lines in order to complete customer calls. The RBOCs, which are large corporations with assets ranging from $12 to $20 billion, are now in the throes of major reorganization. Each newly appointed RBOC chief executive officer must build a new corporation, a new identity, a new management team, and a new array of product and service offerings.

The surviving AT&T must also accomplish a vast restructuring because it lost its local lines. As the end of 1983 approaches, this task is almost complete. The restructuring involves the following essential elements:

- The large AT&T headquarters staff is currently being drastically reduced. When the divestiture agreement was signed, the headquarters staff numbered 15,000 people. The ultimate level of the new headquarters staff will be approximately 2,000 people. Former staff members will be redeployed to the RBOCs and its central staff and to the newly formed subordinate units of AT&T.
- Two large sectors are being formed. AT&T Communications will provide *inter*exchange service nationwide, and it will still be under the watchful eye of the FCC. AT&T Technologies will consist of Western Electric Manufacturing, Bell Laboratories Research and Development, AT&T Information Systems (to provide customer equipment), and AT&T International (to serve overseas markets).

Essentially, AT&T is moving from its former geographical profit centers (Bell Operating Companies) to nationwide lines of business serving discrete markets. As with the regional companies, this involves a radical change in many aspects of the way the company operates, including its culture. Its "interconnectedness" with its former operating subsidiaries will be through tie lines and contracts, as opposed to structure and culture.

While the critical research, manufacturing, and long-distance operating capabilities of AT&T remain intact, it must be recognized that the two government mandates will mean the *disintegration of* the Bell System as the nation has known it. This, of course, strikes at the heart of Bell's historical legacy—*its sense of unification* over the course of a century.

The "culture shock" created by these changes is difficult to exaggerate. In fact, when Bell System people began to verbalize their feelings on January 8, 1982 (the day divestiture was announced), they spoke in metaphors of personal grief, almost as if they had been deserted or there had been a death in the family. Gradually, the initial shock began to abate, helped along by occasional flashes of grim humor. "My initial reaction," one company president said, "was that my best horse had just been shot out from under me."[5]

Every one of its million employees knew that the company would be changed forever, that the postdivested entities would constitute a new ball game, and that they would be working for new companies requiring new skills and new ways of doing things.

Interest in Culture

All of this is happening at the precise moment when the American business community is experiencing a virtual explosion of interest in corporate

---

[5] "Bell System Workers Ponder Their Future. . . ." *The Wall Street Journal*, January 11, 1982.

culture. "Corporate culture," the *New York Times* recently reported, "is the magic phrase that management consultants are breathing into the ears of American executives."[6]

Corporate culture appears to be an idea whose time has come. Yet, it is vaguely reminiscent of Twain's observation on the weather—no one seems to be doing much about it. In fact, the authors of *Corporate Cultures*, a book devoted entirely to the subject, figuratively throw up their hands at the prospect of trying to manage cultural change. "Let's be candid about this," write Allan A. Kennedy, a former principal at McKinsey, and Terrence E. Deal, a professor at Harvard's Graduate School of Education. "We don't know this area any better than anyone else. Cultural change is still a black art as far as we are concerned."[7]

Unquestionably, culture within the corporation is difficult to pin down, nearly impossible to quantify or measure, and remarkably resistant to change. However, the culture can be positively influenced by consistent, thoughtful managerial action. Clearly, no "cookbook recipes" for change are possible since each corporation's culture, like each individual's personality, is made up of elements unique to itself. But certain concepts will not change from corporation to corporation. The most basic concept is that managing cultural change is a three-step process:

- First, management must understand the meaning and impact of corporate culture and must ascertain, largely through empirical methods, the elements of its own culture.
- Second, the "cultural wheat must be separated from the chaff." Decisions must be made about which elements support future goals and strategies and must be retained, and which elements are no longer appropriate and must be changed.
- Third, appropriate actions must be taken to effect the required changes in a way that leaves the desirable elements unaffected.

This article will explore each of these elements as they are currently going forward at AT&T.

I. Ascertaining AT&T's Corporate Culture

It has been said that the Bell System contained all the necessary attributes of a nation: territory, idiomatic language, history, culture, and government. The assertion may have been slightly exaggerated, but its cultural component was unarguably accurate. That culture, in fact, generated the energy to drive the enterprise to become the world's largest—in terms of both assets and employees.

To understand Bell's culture, one must understand that it evolved in a precise way to directly support the corporate mission: *achieving universal service in a regulated environment.* Everything related to culture was af-

---

[6] S. Salmans, "New Vogue: Corporate Culture," *New York Times,* January 7, 1983.

[7] T. E. Deal and A. A. Kennedy, *Corporate Cultures: The Rites and Rituals of Corporate Life* (Reading, Mass.: Addison-Wesley Publishing, 1982).

fected: the kind of people Bell companies hired, their shared value system, and the infrastructure of processes to run the business. For most of this century, Bell System people believed that the surest way to achieve universal service was to manage the entire telecommunications system "end-to-end" as a single entity, with both vertical and horizontal integration. (Within this context, universal service meant the design and implementation of a pricing structure that would enable everyone to afford a telephone.)

These two driving forces—the goal of universal service and the concept of end-to-end responsibility—shaped the network, guided Bell Laboratories' technology, permeated Western Electric manufacturing, forged operational methods and practices, and even influenced the depreciation schedules. Equally important, these forces fashioned a corporate culture that was entirely congruent with the corporate mission.[8]

It is significant that neither the mission nor the culture evolved accidentally. They were molded successively by two historic Bell System leaders: Theodore Vail and Walter Gifford. It has been said that if Alexander Graham Bell invented the telephone, then Vail invented the Bell System. Interestingly, Vail patterned the structure of the Bell System after the U.S. government's local/federal division of responsibilities. He then coined a six-word mission statement which would provide direction for the enterprise for more than 70 years: "One System, One Policy, Universal Service." This doctrine became the driving force behind the integrated telephone network, the pricing of products and services, and the unified administrative systems, from Vail's day to the present.

Just as Vail provided the structural blueprint and mission, AT&T President Walter Gifford in 1927 provided the "value system" to realize them. Gifford stated that the Bell System's goal was to strike a fair balance in the treatment of employees, customers, and shareholders. His philosophy was to "furnish the best possible service at the lowest possible cost, consistent with fair treatment of employees and shareowners."[9] This guideline permeated the Bell System's decision-making process and soon became symbolized as "the three-legged stool" (Gifford's vision of balanced responsibilities to customers, shareowners, and employees). Thus, Vail provided Bell System employees with a *clarity of mission* and *a sense of unification* and Gifford provided a *sense of fairness,* establishing patterns of managerial actions and employee relations that would continue to the present day.

Bell System Cultural Attributes

Vail's "oneness" and Gifford's "fairness" doctrines had an enormous impact on the attitudes of Bell's employees over the years. Vail's ideal of

---

[8] Every corporation has subcultures within its total culture, each with its own priority-oriented subset of values. In extolling technical competence as its first priority, Bell Laboratories originated values that were different from Western Electric (which espoused manufacturing efficiency and distribution know-how as primary) and from the operating companies (which cherished the service ethic first and foremost). However, this article addresses that set of overarching values that are common to all: values that transcend the subordinate organizational units.

[9] A. Page, *The Bell Telephone System* (New York: Harper & Row, 1941).

universal service provided the common purpose that would unite and motivate generations of management and craft people. Gifford's concept of balancing the interests of employees, customers, and shareholders further defined that purpose. A mutually reinforcing set of elements evolved into the intrinsic descriptors of Bell's culture. The first element involves treatment of employees, a prominent part of the psychological contract between company and employee.

Employees   *Lifetime careers* is an essential aspect of Bell's culture. A high proportion of Bell employees spend their entire working lives within the corporate boundaries of the Bell System; many managers may have as many as 15 different assignments in a variety of departments and territories. (Layoffs have been almost unknown except at Western Electric, which has closed factories in some episodes of economic decline.)

Career longevity is accompanied by *intense loyalty* to the company (a second attribute). Almost nationalistic in its fervor, corporate loyalty extends even beyond retirement when former Bell System employees are united in an immense and extremely active fraternity called Telephone Pioneers of America.

A quid pro quo for Bell employees' dedication and loyalty is their *perception of fair treatment by the company*. Employment security, good salary and benefits, and enormous emphasis on employee safety are facts of life under the protection of "Ma Bell." Over time, employee perception of fair treatment gradually crystallized into a general sense that senior management cared about each employee's welfare.

Bell's policy of *up-from-the-ranks management succession* is a deeply ingrained aspect of the culture. One veteran manager wryly observed that if faced with the need for a troop of ballerinas, the company would reassign and retrain a group of telephone operators.

Despite its strengths, such a self-contained human resources development system gives rise to mores which may, over time, become less than entirely productive. For example, throughout the Bell System there is a powerful *level consciousness*—an extreme deference to the status inherent in each level of the managerial hierarchy. There is also a powerful bias toward *consensus management*, which was exacerbated in past years by a functional organization structure that required a high degree of coordination between the functional departments. (It is interesting to note that the attributes already cited are prominent cultural characteristics of Japanese management. It is too early to know whether these attributes are appropriate to the U.S. business environment in general and to AT&T's environment after divestiture.)

Customers   Another cluster of cultural attributes relates to the second leg of the three-legged stool—customers. *Dedication to the service ethos* is an especially powerful value shared by Bell System people. The importance of quality service is instilled early in every employee's career and is constantly reinforced by senior management. A highly sophisticated and quantified "quality of service" measurement system has long provided the basis for evaluating managerial performance and is a critical part of the organizational infrastructure. Employees anxiously wait to receive the "Green Book," the monthly accounting of finite service indices in every Bell company in the nation. Prints of Angus McDonald, the 19th-century Bell System lineman fighting a blizzard to keep the lines open, have long been part of Bell office decor and are another reminder of the spirit of service.

Shareholders Finally, shareholder accountability, the third leg of the stool, is safeguarded by those elements of corporate culture that foster productivity and sound financial management.

Through the years, the emphasis on productivity measurements and customer service has been perhaps the most powerful shaper of the Bell value system. There has been intense competition among Bell Telephone Companies to achieve ever greater *operational efficiencies*. One of AT&T's major managerial challenges in the 1980s will be to redirect this internal competition toward the external environment. However, the shift of this internally directed competitive spirit toward the external marketplace can already be seen in the attitudes of many of the managers in AT&T's regional companies. In a *Fortune* article, one of AT&T's consultants observed, "I've never seen managers so willing to change."[10]

Another dominant aspect of Bell's culture has been its predisposition toward operational and technical skills. Since management of the network has been the central core of the Bell System's historic mission, managers with technical and operational skills have tended to predominate; this can be seen in Bell's senior management profile.

From a strategic standpoint, senior officers in the telephone companies and at AT&T have by necessity maintained a *strong focus on regulatory matters*. Former Chairman John deButts said that a colleague once asked, "Wouldn't it be nice if on coming to work some morning we found ourselves thinking not about the FCC or the Justice Department or the state commissions or even the Congress, but thinking first about the customer?"[11] In the absence of external competition, Bell management necessarily focused high-level attention on the industry's regulators, working assiduously to create a favorable "regulatory climate" in Bell territories.

When taken together, these important Bell System cultural attributes explain a great deal about the patterns of behavior and the expectations of generations of Bell System people. Their effect was extended and extraordinary success in protecting the well-being of employees, the investments of shareholders, and the quality of service to customers. Corporate mission and corporate culture have rarely been so well matched. Detractors ("outsiders") might have viewed the environment as a stifling cocoon. However, for most Bell people, the culture provided a "good place to work" and security against the economic vicissitudes of the competitive marketplace.

The match between mission and culture was sustained for decades, primarily because the environment remained largely unchanged. Then suddenly, as 1981 faded into 1982, it became clear that the principle of universal service had essentially been achieved, and that the principle of end-to-end

---

[10] B. Utall, "Breaking Up the Phone Company," *Fortune,* June 27, 1983.

[11] "Some Thoughts on Regulation" (Speech presented by former AT&T Chairman John deButts before the Communications Law Section, Federal Bar Association, Washington, DC on January 31, 1977).

responsibility would have to be abandoned. As the regulated environment gave way to a competitive one, many of the bedrock philosophical doctrines of the Bell System would have to be overhauled to fit the new realities of the marketplace.

II. Separating Cultural Wheat from Chaff

Sensing impending change, a conferee at an AT&T management seminar asked a senior manager if "in its ardor to become a successful competitive enterprise, the Bell System would become a 'shlock' outfit?" [12] The question strikes at the very heart of what many employees fear in the loss of cherished and still valuable aspects of an idealistic cultural heritage.

Clearly, both the FCC Computer Inquiry II Order and the divestiture agreement will bring about monumental changes. Any tampering with the corporate value system during the transition must be executed with great care. As noted previously, it is extremely important to make the distinction between those cultural attributes that are to be preserved and nurtured through periods of change and those that are to be discarded or, at least, reshaped and redirected.

For example, AT&T management recognizes that if employees begin to question whether the corporation has their best interests at heart, this would represent a severe setback that could not be easily repaired. Thus, as this "family" of one million is broken apart and hundreds of thousands of people are reassigned, management must consistently demonstrate that it continues to care about each employee as an individual. Although AT&T can no longer follow Vail's historic vision of "oneness," it is imperative that it not lose sight of Gifford's vision of "fairness."

AT&T also recognizes that in a competitive arena where service quality may provide the competitive edge, it must continue to foster the service doctrine as a strong corporate value. The importance of efficiency of operations must be preserved. Productivity rates of Bell companies have exceeded those of other industries because efficiency has been a "way of life" permeating every job and a primary element used in evaluating managerial performance. It must remain so.

Other cultural characteristics need to be changed. These begin with the way Bell people think about conducting daily business and extend to broadening the paths of managerial succession.

Adapting Managerial "Mind-Set"

As AT&T moves toward a fully competitive environment, the mind-set of its management will shift toward a market orientation, a welcome change for senior managers long embroiled in a quagmire of regulatory, legal, and legislative matters. Such a shift will impact not only the ways Bell people think about doing daily business, but also the ways in which business is done. For instance, strategic planning will employ competitive analysis techniques for the first time; a functional organizational structure will move

---

[12] W. B. Tunstall, "A Heritage of Idealism," *Bell Telephone Magazine*, ed. 6, 1980.

further toward market-segmented lines-of-business structures; costing and pricing methodologies will move from a basis of cross subsidies and national price averaging to product-by-product and service-by-service computation schemes; capital recovery formulae will be overhauled to recognize the shorter product life inherent in competitive products. Such changes reverberate intensely throughout the corporation.

Conforming to a More Risk-Oriented Management

As AT&T moves toward a more competitive environment, its management style must adapt accordingly. In the process its managers must recognize that marketplace uncertainty will replace regulatory uncertainty, and that the cultural mores will change to value more entrepreneurial types of managers that in the past. Attitudes toward risk taking vary considerably among corporations and are an essential ingredient in the total makeup of the corporate culture. Regulated firms like AT&T, with their more predictable forecasts of sales volumes, are not prone to promote risk taking as a valued managerial attribute. This is not a pejorative statement; indeed, it would be foolish to take risks where the rewards are not compensatory. However, in competitive industries which experience sharp shifts in market share and in which greater sensitivity to economic conditions prevails, conservatism is tantamount to default in the marketplace. Unquestionably, AT&T's managers of the future will be more inclined to risk taking than care taking.

Accepting Organizational Change as a Continuing Phenomenon

The "steady state" organizational structure, once part and parcel of the corporate culture in the Bell System, must continue to adapt and readapt to meet changing needs in the future. Certainly nothing in the realm of corporate culture is so ingrained as the corporate organization chart, perhaps because the hierarchical structure is the predominant way decision-making power is distributed among managers of the enterprise. By the same token, it is an entirely human trait to seek stability of structure in an uncertain world. For half a century the Bell System enjoyed a stable structure that was ideally suited to its regulated world. But in the past 10 years, two major reorganizations have been implemented, and now Bell is poised for the third and most far-reaching restructuring of all. As strategies change to meet changing market conditions, so must organizations adapt to implement these strategies. Such adaptation will be a continuing phenomenon which must become a part of every employee's system of expectations.

Broadening the Routes to Power

Under regulation, operational and technical skills were paramount. Line operating jobs were the developmental assignments for managers with high potential to progress first to the coveted operating vice president spot in the operating companies and then to levels of even greater responsibility at AT&T. In the future new patterns of executive succession may be more appropriate, because a substantial portion of the operating units will be divested, and because the success of competitive strategies will be highly dependent on technological development, marketing prowess, manufacturing know-how, and financial acumen. This is not to say that operating line experience in the surviving regulated sector will no longer be a path to the top; however, it may not be the only path. Conference Board studies show that the routes to top management in Fortune 500 companies are consistently through three channels: production and engineering, marketing and sales, and finance.[13] Future generations of top AT&T executives will undoubtedly include people from these areas, in contrast to the traditional, almost exclusive selection from telephone company operations.

Change at the Grass Roots

Not surprisingly, it is considerably easier to project generalized objectives for cultural change than to predict accurately how change will manifest itself at the grass-roots level of the organization. Intensive effort is required to discern, as fully as possible, the changes that employees are experiencing individually, in terms of their attitudes toward the company and toward their work.

In the various Bell System Companies, studies and surveys have monitored changes in employees' moods and attitudes virtually from the day divestiture was announced—often with dramatic results. As one recent study report noted, "The mere mention of the word 'divestiture' to employees can summon up visions of a legacy eliminated . . . of job opportunities foregone . . . of promises broken."

It is incumbent upon management to demonstrate, in both word and deed, that Bell's promises were made to be kept; that the future of its dedicated employees is secure; and that management's concern for their well-being, like its concern for the quality of service, will continue undiminished.

III. Management Actions to Effect Change in Corporate Culture

A recent article in *Fortune* addressed "just how tractable elements like shared values really are." It posed the following question: "Can a company deliberately change its culture, as it can its strategy or structure?"[14] Although there are no "cookbook recipes," once a corporation's culture is defined and its cultural attributes are analyzed to determine which should be preserved and which need modification, actions can be taken to effect the changes. Such actions are now under way at AT&T. (It should be noted that in some instances, influencing the corporate culture is not the exclusive objective—i.e., the actions themselves constitute well-established management practice.)

1. Set the Example

Cultural changes cannot be delegated to the employee information staff. They must begin at the top of the organization with the chief executive officer and have the support of his or her inner circle of top officers. There are numerous examples of how enlightened leadership can transform organi-

[13] R. G. Schaeffer, "Top Management Staffing Challenges: CEOs Describe Their Needs," *The Conference Board,* 1982.
[14] W. Kiechel III, "Corporate Strategies under Fire," *Fortune,* December 27, 1982.

zations in military as well as corporate histories. The chief executive officer whose behavior is consistent with the norms and values he or she has articulated for the company has an enormous head start.

Several years before the process of divestiture began at AT&T, Chairman Charles L. Brown began to set the stage for cultural change in a speech before the Commercial Club in Chicago. In that speech, Mr. Brown asserted that "there is a new telephone company in town . . . a high-technology business applying advanced marketing strategies to the satisfaction of highly sophisticated customer requirements." He questioned whether the label "Ma Bell" was appropriate to describe such a business. He then asked his audience to pass the word that "Mother doesn't live here anymore."[15] For Bell employees, the statement carried powerful messages about their culture, including the need to set aside symbols of the past (even so venerable a symbol as "Ma Bell").

It seems evident that AT&T has a clear vision of its new mission. The process of strategic change, which has already begun, includes the formation of an overseas subsidiary (AT&T International) and a subsequent joint venture with Phillips of Holland, the reorganization of Western Electric and Bell Laboratories into new lines of business, the introduction of a host of newly developed telephones and telephone systems, and the restructuring of long-distance pricing schemes to reflect the realities of competition.

These are just a few of the changes already achieved. However, the process of change is having a striking effect on Bell's employees. AT&T managers and craft people are beginning to think of themselves as competitors. As the corporate managerial focus shifts from regulators to the marketplace, the culture will also reflect the shift in outlook.

2. Revamp the System of Management

Even the influence of leadership, of course, has its limits, particularly in large corporations where the principal management is far removed from day-to-day middle and lower management functions. Cultural norms, then, must be reoriented by changing the system of management—the many management processes, the organizational structure, and the management style that drive the corporation. AT&T is clearly communicating the patterns of values and behaviors it wants to achieve by changing reward systems, reorienting resource allocation processes, and restructuring the organization and establishing its new identity.

For example, the basic job of restructuring postdivestiture AT&T involves a move from its former geographical profit-center orientation to a national line-of-business profit-center orientation. As mentioned earlier, 13,000 employees in AT&T's corporate staff are being redeployed to the prospective postdivestiture division or subsidiary staffs. The relatively small number of employees who remain with AT&T's postdivestiture corporate staff will be organized around a policy/strategy/financial management framework appro-

---

[15] "Meeting Change with Change" (Speech presented by then President of AT&T Charles L. Brown before the Commercial Club, Chicago on November 21, 1978).

priate for the new market-based businesses. The new AT&T organization will, of course, reflect the separation of the detariffed portion of the business from the remaining portions (as required by Computer Inquiry II). It will also influence virtually every assumption, expectation, and belief system of AT&T's employees concerning the company and their positions within it.

3. Articulate the Value System Explicitly

It is critically important to communicate to all employees in specific terms precisely what the corporate value system is, especially in periods of change. At AT&T a carefully recast document, "A Statement of Policy," sets forth the corporation's evolving goals. From the day divestiture was announced, the principal officers have voiced clear messages of corporate positions and expectations. When asked how he wanted the business to be viewed in five years, Chairman Brown replied, "I really want the business to be regarded as one that adapted itself to what the public expected of it, was not a prisoner of embedded thinking, was alert to opportunities, and was able to take its place in a different setting with the same high regard for ethical conduct in a well-managed business that it has always had."[16]

These goals—to adapt appropriately, to think and act creatively, to maximize opportunities, to continue as a highly ethical, well-managed, powerful business—will shape the behavioral norms and ways of doing business at AT&T in the future. The articulation of these goals by the chairman is an important first step toward their achievement, and it will have a powerful influence on the corporation's culture.

4. Gear Training to Support Cultural Values

Another mechanism for effecting change in the corporate culture is management training that is explicitly geared to modify behavior in support of new corporate values. The Bell Advanced Management Program, a developmental experience for high performance fourth and fifth level managers of the business, exemplifies such training. Its components include business strategy formulation and implementation, financial challenges, strategic marketing, and the management of change. It seeks to prepare participants to create and implement strategies that will keep the company at the leading edge of change, and to anticipate and respond to strategic issues of the future in a rapidly changing business environment. It emphasizes entrepreneurship. Another example is AT&T's Corporate Policy Seminars, in which the top 2,000 subsidiary managers are brought in for policy presentations and discussions.

5. Revise Recruiting Aims and Methods

Professor Wickham Skinner of the Harvard Business School wrote that "acquiring and developing the right talents for the business as it changes strategy, technology, and products requires more shrewd, wise, long-range planning than any other corporate endeavor."[17] He might have added that

---

[16] "The Premium Now Is on Leadership," *Bell Telephone Magazine,* no. 1, 1983.
[17] W. Skinner, "Big Hat, No Cattle," *Harvard Business Review,* September–October 1981.

recruitment of such talent is a powerful, if indirect, means of influencing the corporate culture. In addition, potential problems of "culture clash" can be avoided by making certain that the individual value systems, personalities, and educational backgrounds of younger managers coming aboard are in harmony with the corporation's aims.

AT&T has a long history of recruiting and developing managers for a regulated milieu. This process tended to produce what Michael Maccoby, author of *The Gamesman,* described as "company men"—that is, employees who are dedicated to the business, who equate their personal success with the corporation's long-term development, and who have exceptional managerial skills.[18] Although much of this should be preserved, an added dimension is required for the competitive marketplace: the propensity to play a higher risk, higher reward game. Indeed, a share of Maccoby's prototype "Gamesman" may be in order for future years—perhaps to be found among the numerous managers recruited from outside the Bell System to staff sales and marketing jobs.

6. Modify the Symbols

Anthropologist Emile Durkheim proclaimed that shared symbols are necessary for cultural cohesion.[19] By the same token, modification of symbols is a necessary component of change.

At AT&T, for example, the loss of the Bell name and logo is a serious one. However, this does afford an opportunity to reinforce Mr. Brown's message, both internally and externally, that "Ma Bell doesn't live here anymore." By continuing to use AT&T as a trade name, the corporation capitalizes on its long-standing reputation throughout the world. By replacing the familiar logo (Bell within a circle) with a globe symbolically girdled by electronic communications, AT&T has a new symbol which "suggests new dimensions—of our business and our future."

Of course, not all symbols change. For example, another long-standing symbol, a 1917-vintage, 16-foot bronze statue personifying the Spirit of Communications, has been taken from the top of the old headquarters building, refurbished, and placed in the lobby of the new headquarters building. This statue, affectionately known to generations of AT&T people as "Golden Boy," will continue to stand for excellence in providing service (now around the world) in the years that follow divestiture. As Angus McDonald and other time-honored symbols begin to slip into corporate folklore, "Golden Boy" will continue to be a shared symbol, serving as a bridge between the past and the future.

Transition

With divestiture, AT&T will experience a metamorphosis that would challenge the most boastful caterpillar. The organizational, technological, and operational complexities to be faced are literally without parallel. Yet,

---

[18] M. Maccoby, *The Gamesman* (New York: Simon & Schuster, 1976).
[19] A. L. Wilkins, "Exchange" (Brigham Young University School of Management, Fall 1981).

more than one informed observer maintains that changing the corporate culture is still the most difficult task facing management.

The fact that corporate culture cannot be quantified makes it no less real and no less important as an ingredient in a corporation's fortunes than return on investment, market share percentage, hurdle rates, or debt ratios. AT&T Chairman Brown summed up both the objective and the importance of changing the corporate culture: "If we are able to adapt our marvelous culture to a different environment—and if we remember that the business in the 80s cannot be run by memory—we can set the course for the next century."[20]

---

[20] "The Premium Now."

What this article is about: The real stumbling block to innovation in large organizations is not lack of creativity but unsureness about priorities. The Chairman and CEO of 3M presents his recipe for innovation within his company.

4-8 The care and flourishing of entrepreneurs at 3M*

Lewis W. Lehr

Lewis W. Lehr is chairman and CEO of Minnesota Mining and Manufacturing Co.

The development of entrepreneurs boils down to a principle that is fairly simple. Human beings are endowed with the urge to create—to bring into being something that has never existed before. That drive to create is stronger in some than in others. But to some degree, it exists in just about everyone. It follows, then, that developing entrepreneurs simply means respecting that dimension of human nature and honoring it within the context of a profitmaking enterprise. To me, this means not simply encouraging innovation as an end in itself. It means encouraging the conversion of innovation into profitmaking businesses.

How can we do that? We can start with the notion that entrepreneurs are not hothouse flowers. They don't need to be coddled and protected in a special environment. To tell the truth, innovators are more like weeds. They pop up in all kinds of unexpected places, sometimes where they're least welcome. Given a little nourishment, and left to themselves, they'll flourish. It all comes back to a respect for people and their natural urge to create.

In our experience, that respect tends to take four highly specific forms:

1. The opportunity to create.
2. Rewards.
3. The chance to fail.
4. A clear challenge.

Of these, the most basic is opportunity. The real mother of invention may not be necessity. It is opportunity. Opportunity can take all kinds of forms.

---

* Reprinted from *Directors and Boards*. Winter 1986, pp. 18–20.

As just one example: At 3M we guarantee, as far as we can, that our people will have some time to pursue their own pet projects. We have an informal understanding that our technical people can spend up to 15 percent of their time in the laboratories on projects of their own choosing. Not everyone makes use of this option, but the opportunity is there and our people know it.

People know when an organization is hungry for new ideas. I'm thinking of a scientist in our health care group, Dr. Bill Isaacson. Bill had an idea that he couldn't get out of his mind—an idea for a contact lens that would wear longer, be more comfortable, and be safer for users over the long term than existing lenses. For more than five years, Bill championed his idea for gas-permeable, extended-wear, contact lens technology. He found experts in all kinds of fields to help out. He studied potential markets and selling methods that were new to him and new to 3M. And he pounded on doors to sell 3M management on his idea and to recruit the resources he needed. Then he put together a team of 3M professionals to develop his contact lens.

One group of 3M scientists and engineers developed new lens materials and new tests for evaluating the materials. Another group provided technology to reduce manufacturing costs. Still another group developed a computerized testing system for on-line inspection of the lenses.

It is a tradition at 3M that all of our technologies are available to anyone in the company who can use them. Bill Isaacson often said that he had 6,000 3M technical people on his staff and only four or five people on his payroll. What could be better than that?

Elements of Opportunity

Certainly Bill's drive and organization of supporting forces within the company is a true example of "intrapreneuring," or building a business within a company. Bill's experience illustrates what I believe are the three key elements of opportunity:

- First, there has to be an invitation to new ideas and it should be a spoken invitation. That is, one has to make it perfectly clear that new ideas are welcome and valued.
- Second, once a good idea emerges, there has to be support from management. And it has to be visible support, there for all to see.
- Third, there have to be resources available to help the innovator—intellectual, technical, and financial resources.

These needn't be too easy to get hold of, but they have to be there when they are needed. Together they add up to genuine opportunity. Offer them to innovators and they're off to the races.

Opportunity gets the innovator started. But somewhere along the line there should be a proper reward. And that is not always easy. Most entrepreneurs I know are start-up people. They operate by hook or by crook. They get things off the ground by the hook of market potential and the crook of appropriated resources. They'd rather be free than be rich. To them a win is better than a corner office. When forced to read procedure manuals, they become functionally illiterate. Give a choice between budget management and staff meetings, they choose the laboratory.

The worst thing we could do with people like that is to base their rewards on how well they fit into some preconceived management mold. They may need a separate career path, a series of stages which are equivalent in pay and perks to the positions of supervisor or manager. Rewards have to be tied directly to successful innovation as an alternative to an ability to manage others; some entrepreneurs don't want to manage.

Earned Freedom

Beyond that, there is a concept that one writer calls "earned freedom." Successful innovators are given progressively more freedom to work on whatever interests them. IBM's Corporate Fellows, for example, are free to roam the company for a period of time, working on what interests them most. At 3M, we're beginning to experiment with a new twist on this theme. In addition to our two existing career tracks—one for managers, the other for people outstanding in their disciplines—we're adding a third track. We call it the Venture Career Track, and it's for men and women with outstanding track records as entrepreneurs inside 3M.

Here's the way it works. In most companies you can judge the status and guess the pay of a manager by the size of the operation that he or she manages. The bigger the operation, the bigger the paycheck. Our new venture managers and directors will be promoted and rewarded for continuing to work with smaller projects, riskier projects—the kind they love the best. They won't lose out by continuing to take risks, by avoiding the safer paths.

If innovators like to think of a reward waiting for them at the end of a project, they really have to be concerned with what happens if they fail. The fact is, most innovators are going to fail, at least once in their careers and probably a lot more often than that. At 3M about 60 percent of our formal new-product programs eventually fall along the wayside. We use a saying: "You have to kiss a lot of frogs to find a prince."

What happens after a project fails affects much more than the people involved. If they are crucified, and find their careers in ruins, everyone else in the company hears the message loud and clear. They know they have a choice. They can play it safe, wait out their time, and receive a promotion after a while. Or they can buck the odds, try something new, and have a good chance of finding themselves back at the bottom of the ladder when they fall.

Positive Risk-Taking

People aren't stupid. They understand the odds. A while ago, *Time* magazine took a look at Western Europe's problems in keeping up with the U.S. and Japan in the high-technology race. One executive at a French computer firm put his finger on a basic problem. He said, "There is not a positive attitude toward risk taking. If you take a risk and fail, you are finished." In an atmosphere like that, after a while even the most avid innovator will give up or get out.

Frankly, I prefer the philosophy of the legendary ex-coach at UCLA, John Wooden, who said: "The team that makes the most mistakes usually wins the game." There is some truth in that. It is a good philosophy for just about any company. And some days it is a very comforting thought to carry around with you. Of course, what it really means is . . . if one doesn't make at least some mistakes, there is no progress.

Opportunity, reward, tolerance for failure. Taken together, they constitute management's commitment to a climate of innovation. They are the unmistakable signs that management honors and respects the creative drive present in just about all of us.

But as necessary as these elements are, they are not enough. They provide the starting point for innovation; they do not set the direction. In my view, the real stumbling block to innovation in large organizations is not lack of creativity. It is unsureness about priorities. I doubt there is a company anywhere these days which does not profess to be concerned about innovation. The subject works its way into employee publications, executive speeches, company slogans.

That's all fine. But what happens when that judgment day rolls around each year and managers are forced to defend their results? Does the manager who has spent money backing a few risky projects suffer in comparison with a manager who has milked his cash cow for one more year? If so, then managers and their people will be able to read the company's real priorities very clearly.

At 3M, we try to meet this problem head-on by setting a clear innovation target for our divisions. Basically, our divisions are expected to generate 25 percent of their sales each year from products new in the last five years. Of course, not every division hits its target every year. But our managers are judged, not only on their ability to make existing product lines grow, but also on their knack for bringing innovative new products to market.

Built-In Incentive

And they know it. So they have a built-in incentive to keep their R&D strong and to encourage all kinds of bright ideas from their people. So, to the other elements of a climate for innovation—opportunity, reward, and tolerance for failure—I'd have to add one more: challenge. A clear, unmistakable challenge to come up with new ideas, new technologies, new businesses. A challenge whose results can be measured.

That's my recipe for innovation. I wish we at 3M had the process down to a tidy formula, but we don't. Nobody does. We're still learning and we always will be—learning to walk the fine line between being supportive of new ideas and being selective in the projects we take through to completion, and certainly learning how to keep good ideas from becoming lost in a large organization.

What this article is about: This article presents a current account of how a cross section of managers and executives deal with values in the workplace. Some tentative conclusions are offered as to the central goals of today's managers.

4-9 Values and the American manager: An update*

Barry Z. Posner and Warren H. Schmidt

Barry Z. Posner is associate professor of management at the Leavey School of Business and Administration, University of Santa Clara, California. Warren H. Schmidt is professor of management at the Graduate School of Public Administration, University of Southern California, Los Angeles.

The values of American managers—particularly those of top executives—usually get attention when a corporate scandal hits the headlines. News of a faulty product, pollution of the environment, bribery, or some other gross misuse of corporate power causes people to ask, ''What kind of people are running our companies, anyway?'' On those occasions we become aware of the influence personal values have on managers and how those values are expressed in company policies and actions.

Values and ethics are difficult subjects to investigate with precision; nonetheless, some significant information and patterns emerge from the studies that have been made. For example, a 1980 *Fortune* article, headlined ''How Lawless are Big Companies?'' concluded that ''a surprising number of them have been involved in blatant illegalities.'' Of the 1,043 major corporations in their study, 117 (11 percent) had been involved in wrongdoing.[1] A 1977 *Harvard Business Review* article asked, ''Is the Ethics of Business Changing?'' Business executives were reported to be more cynical about the ethical conduct of their peers than they were 15 years ago.[2]

* Reprinted from *California Management Review* 26, no. 3 (Spring 1984), pp. 202–16. The authors gratefully acknowledge the helpful comments and suggestions of William W. May, Director, Program in Business Ethics, University of Southern California.

[1] Irwin Ross, ''How Lawless are Big Companies?'' *Fortune*, December 1980, pp. 57–63.

[2] Steve Brenner and Earl Mollander, ''Is the Ethics of Business Changing?'' *Harvard Business Review*, January/February 1977.

These studies, and others like them, reinforce the importance of continual vigilence on the part of executives and scholars alike in focusing attention on values and ethical behavior. As John Gardner has noted, ''Our problem is not to find better values but to be faithful to those we profess.''

Values and the American Manager: An Update

One place to begin is to ask questions such as: What are the values of American managers? What are the goals, people, and personal traits held in esteem? What principles guide managerial behavior? When faced with ethical dilemmas, how do managers respond?

These were among the issues we set out to explore when we polled 6,000 executives and managers in a survey sponsored by the American Management Association. While many of the questions have been asked in the past, none have been studied within the last five years. In addition, seldom had investigations of these issues differentiated the responses of top executives from those in the middle and lower managerial ranks. Furthermore, the influx of women into the managerial ranks in the last decade, made comparisons by gender possible for the first time. Figure 1 profiles the sample of managers responding to the questionnaire.

As we report our findings we are keenly aware that responses to a questionnaire may not be the same as how people actually behave. In fact, questionnaire responses are likely to be more positive (and idealistic) than the behavioral responses which occur when managers are under pressure and confronted with conflicting information and competing loyalties. There is little reason, however, to expect this bias to systematically affect managers differently according to their hierarchical level or their gender. Readers are therefore encouraged to think about the issues investigated in this study as they apply to each of us personally, and to propose possible interpretations different from our own.

Priorities among Organizational Goals

To be successful, an organization must pay attention to many different dimensions: productivity, profits, morale, growth, and so on. Some of management's toughest dilemmas occur in trying to strike a balance among these. Should current profits take priority over growth? Should efficiency be weighed more heavily than morale? In making these choices, the manager's individual values become particularly influential.

To find out how American managers assign priority to their organizational goals, we asked our respondents to rate a representative selection of typical goals (see Figure 2). We chose goals that previous researchers have demonstrated to be most directly related to managerial behavior.[3] Respondents were asked to rate each goal on a seven-point scale with a ''1'' indicating ''of little

---

[3] See, for example, George England, ''The Personal Values of American Managers,'' *Academy of Management Journal* 10 (1967), pp. 53–68; Barry Posner and Michael Munson, ''The Factorial Validity of England's Personal Values Questionnaire for Corporate Recruiters, Business Students, and Business Faculty,'' *Educational and Psychological Measurement* 41 (1981), pp. 1243–54.

Figure 1
Demographics of survey respondents (Percentages)

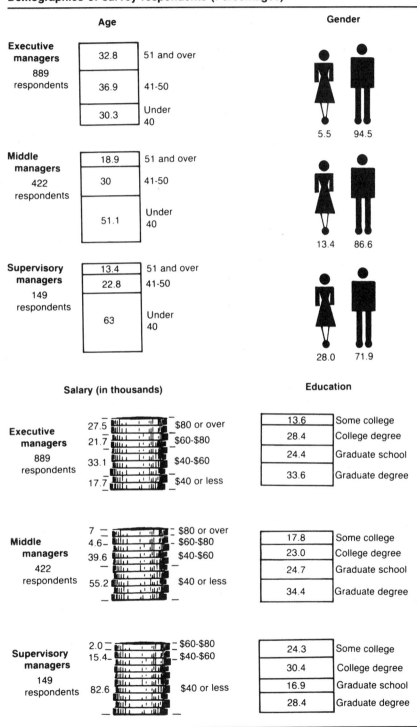

Figure 2
The importance of various organizational goals

Organizational Goals	Total Sample	Supervisory Managers	Middle Managers	Executive Managers
Organizational effectiveness	6.24	6.13	6.22	6.26
High productivity	6.11	5.97	6.02	6.16
Organizational leadership	6.09	5.90	6.12	6.11
High morale	6.02	6.03	6.04	6.01
Organizational reputation	5.98	5.76	5.93	6.04
Organizational efficiency	5.95	5.98	5.96	5.93
Profit maximization	5.22	4.53	4.98	5.44
Organizational growth	5.14	4.96	5.05	5.20
Organizational stability	5.12	5.14	5.07	5.13
Organizational value to community	4.87	4.82	4.92	4.82
Service to the public	4.80	4.99	4.92	4.68

NOTE: MANOVA F (Wilks Lambda) = 2.54, $p < .001$.

or no importance to me" and "7" indicating "very important to me." Because many of the goals were rated at the high end of the scale, our analysis focused on rank order rather than absolute rating.

The goal judged to be most important regardless of the manager's position in the hierarchy, age, gender, or educational level, is organizational effectiveness. This term may well serve as a catch-all for many other goals; nevertheless, it's the phrase that is most appealing to managers in our study.

A clustering of next most important goals include high productivity, organizational leadership, high morale, organizational reputation, and organizational efficiency. These are likely to be the goals that managers attempt to influence by their actions and/or use to evaluate whether they will contribute toward increasing the organization's effectiveness.

The cluster of goals which were rated as third in importance includes profit maximization, organizational growth, and organizational stability. At the bottom of the list were value of the organization to the community and public service.

The greatest difference between managers at different levels occurred over the importance of profit maximization. Executives ranked it seventh, middle managers ranked it ninth, and supervisory managers ranked it at the bottom—eleventh. This goal apparently takes on different meanings at different levels of the organization.

However, what is more striking is the similarity in ranking of organizational goals across managers at different levels in their organizations and across hundreds of different organizations. This seems to suggest a "managerial psyche." There is a strong sense of agreement among managers about the purpose and role of organizations.

Priorities among Organizational Stakeholders

While clarity about organizational goals is important, it is only one side of the coin. The other side concerns the issue of "whom do we serve" in executing these goals. For example, does the corporation aspire to high productivity in order to increase its return to stockholders, or to decrease its

Figure 3
The importance of various organizational stakeholders

	Supervisory Managers	Middle Managers	Executive Managers
Customers	5.57	6.10	6.40
Myself	6.28	6.29	6.28
Subordinates	6.06	6.30	6.14
Employees	5.93	6.11	6.01
Boss(es)	5.72	5.92	5.82
Co-workers	5.87	5.82	5.81
Colleagues	5.66	5.78	5.75
Managers	5.26	5.56	5.75
Technical employees	5.21	5.32	5.40
White collar employees	4.96	5.25	5.40
Owners	4.07	4.51	5.30
Craftsmen	4.14	4.75	5.01
General public	4.38	4.49	4.52
Stockholders	3.35	3.79	4.51
Elected public officials	3.81	3.54	3.79
Government bureaucrats	3.09	2.05	2.90

NOTE: MANOVA F (Wilks Lambda) = 1.81, p< .004.

sales price to various constituents? Managers often feel bombarded with conflicting claims, requests, and demands from different groups inside and outside the organization. Harlan Cleveland has written in his book, *The Future Executive,* that managers are being pushed more and more to be accountable to a growing number of constituencies.[4]

Some of management's most critical trade-offs are between the demands of different groups who each have a stake in some aspect of the organization's efforts. When such a "moment of truth" arrives, the manager faces the question, "who is really more important?" We asked our respondents precisely that question by having them rate on a seven-point scale the importance of 16 different organizational stakeholders. The list came from previously published research and included commonly recognized important stakeholders in organizations.[5] The list included: Customers, myself, subordinates, employees, boss(es), co-workers, colleagues, managers, technical employees, white collar employees, owners, craftsmen, general public, stockholders, elected public officials, and government bureaucrats.

Multivariate analysis of variance (MANOVA) results indicated that managers at different hierarchical levels tended to weight the importance of these stakeholders differently ($F = 1.81$, $p < .004$). However, as shown in Figure 3, the order of importance is quite similar. Customers top the list for executives, while it is ranked fourth for middle level managers and falls to seventh place for supervisors. Groups such as employees, subordinates, co-workers, and bosses are all rated as important and worthy of attention in pursuing the corporation's objectives.

Several comparisons of managers' evaluations of stakeholders (see Figure 3) seem worthy of comment. The relatively high rating of "myself" by all

[4] Harlan Cleveland, *The Future Executive* (New York: Harper & Row, 1972).
[5] England, "Personal Values"; Posner and Munson, "Factorial Validity."

three levels of management seemed both less than humble and quite candid. Furthermore, its high ranking did not diminish when the data were re-analyzed by such factors as gender, age, educational level, salary, or years of experience. These results failed to confirm the stereotype of the younger and better educated generation of professionals as being any more (or less) narcissistic (''me generation'') than other ''generations'' of managers in today's corporations. Perhaps it is more than just stylish to pay attention to one's self interests; it may be a realistic part of the managerial orientation. Others might argue, alternatively, ''that concern for myself'' has always been quite significant as a motivating factor for managerial behaviors. The difference may be that years ago it wasn't ''proper'' to admit it.

It was also interesting to note that the ''general public'' ($\bar{x} = 4.51$) was rated signficantly more important than ''stockholders'' ($\bar{x} = 4.18$). The stereotype of managers as running the nation's corporations for the primary benefit of their stockholders does not seem to be borne out by this data. As noted earlier in our discussion of organizational goals, managerial respondents seem to believe that running an effective organization that pays attention to its people (employees, subordinates, bosses, co-workers) will deliver value to the customer (and profits to its investors). This viewpoint is consistent with the lessons from America's best-run organizations.[6]

The low rating (in relative and absolute terms) for both elected public officials and government bureaucrats may also signal some difficulty. Many of today's complex problems require that managers from the private and public sectors work together closely. This suggests that there is a need for more effort to increase understandings between those on both sides of the public-private line. Our own recent studies of full-time managers who were pursuing M.B.A. or M.P.A. degrees indicates that greater mutual understanding can be particularly useful since there are surprisingly few significant differences between managers practicing in the private and public sector.[7]

Finally, the only real differences between male and female managers were found on items relating to the relative importance of managers and bosses. Female respondents rated both ''bosses'' and ''managers'' as significantly more important than did their male counterparts. As we have shown elsewhere[8] the organization (managers and bosses, in this case) seems to exert greater pressure on female managers than it does for the male managers in our sample.

Managers' Relationships with Others

Managers work with and through other people. Much of their effectiveness depends on the quality of their relationships with subordinates, peers, and

---

[6] Thomas Peters and Robert Waterman, *In Search of Excellence: Lessons from America's Best-Run Companies* (New York: Harper & Row, 1982).

[7] Barry Posner and Warren Schmidt, ''What Kind of People Enter the Public and Private Sectors? An Updated Comparison of Perceptions, Stereotypes, and Values,'' *Human Resource Management* 21, (February–March 1982), pp. 35–43.

[8] Warren Schmidt and Barry Posner, *Managerial Values in Perspective* (New York: AMACOM, 1983).

superiors in the organization. Some of these relationships seem to work smoothly, while others are tense and troublesome.

Many factors contribute to the development of an effective, enjoyable, working relationship with others. Generally, we look for certain qualities— or personal traits which we value—in a subordinate, a peer, or a boss. When we find these qualities, we feel fortunate. We also come to know that some kinds of people are more important than others in influencing our success.

We asked several open-ended questions to get at the issue of what managers value in their associates at work. For example: "What values (personal traits and characteristics) do you look for and admire in your superiors?" Similar questions were asked with respect to one's colleagues and subordinates. More than 225 different values, traits, and characteristics were identified. Subsequent content analysis by several independent judges resulted in the following 15 categories (in alphabetical order):

- Broad-mindedness (open-minded, flexible, receptive).
- Competence (capable, productive, efficient, thorough).
- Cooperativeness (friendly, team player, available, responsive).
- Dependability (reliable, conscientious, predictable).
- Determination (industrious, hard-working, motivated).
- Fairness (objective, consistent, democratic).
- Imagination (creative, innovative, curious).
- Integrity (truthful, trustworthy, has character, has convictions).
- Intelligence (bright, thoughtful, logical).
- Leadership (inspiring, decisive, provides direction).
- Loyalty (has a commitment to me, the company, or policies).
- Maturity (experienced, wise, well-grounded, has depth).
- Straightforwardness (direct, candid, forthright).
- Sensitivity (appreciative, concerned, aware, respectful).
- Supportiveness (understanding, empathic, helpful).

According to the executives and managers in our survey (see Figure 4), superiors (leaders) in the decade ahead will need to possess *competence* and *integrity,* as well as the ability to provide leadership and be supportive of subordinates. This assessment echoes some recent management literature. Michael Maccoby wrote about the "gamesman" as the prototype of the successful executive of the 1960s and 1970s. This innovative and daring person thrived on adventure and competition, was eager to get ahead at any cost, was willing to pay any price, and (coolly detached from emotions and sentiments) exploited people ruthlessly. In his latest book, *The Leader,* Maccoby writes that, "in the 80s, the gamesman's style no longer works."[9] At the core of the new model of corporate leadership is a new emphasis on

---

[9] Michael Maccoby, *The Leader* (New York: Simon & Schuster, 1981); Michael Maccoby, *The Gamesman* (New York: Simon & Schuster, 1976).

Figure 4
Qualities most admired in peers, superiors, and subordinates

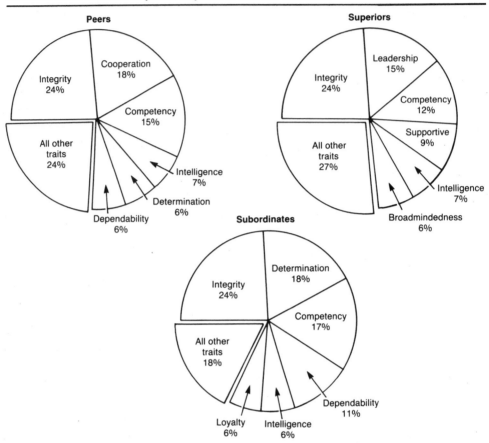

self-development and the development of others, reorganizing of work so that it contributes to people's sense of self-worth, pulling people together to achieve win-win objectives, and being responsive and responsible to people-oriented needs in an era of limited economic growth and accelerating technological change.

What managers value in their peers, in addition to integrity and competence is *cooperativeness* and *intelligence*. (The latter is, of course, related to competence.) Cooperativeness is ranked second only to integrity—underscoring their high interdependence in modern organizations. When we have no formal or hierarchical power over others, we have to rely more heavily on their sense of cooperation, their availability, and their responsiveness to another's concerns.

Recent studies of managerial behavior indicate that managers spend more time communicating and interacting with their peers (colleagues at the same organizational level) than they do with superiors or subordinates. For teamwork to exist in an organization, the spirit of cooperation clearly needs to prevail over the spur of competition.

Figure 5
Question: "I find that sometimes I must compromise my personal principles to conform to my organization's expectations." (Percentages)

	Strongly Disagree	Disagree	Agree	Strongly Agree
Supervisory managers	15.5	31.8	37.1	4.1
Middle managers	26.5	37.7	22.8	3.6
Executive managers	37.8	35.1	17.2	2.8

According to our survey, what comes to mind when managers think about qualities valued in subordinates are *determination* and *dependability*. Managers look for someone they can count on; someone who will stay with a job until it's finished and will deliver on promises. In the judgment of our respondents, these two qualities outrank even intelligence and loyalty. Integrity and competence still rank quite high as desirable characteristics in subordinates.

The results presented in Figure 4 apply equally to executives, middle managers, and supervisory managers. These are the qualities most admired at every level of the organization, irrespective of gender or position in the hierarchy. The striking consistency in the results, while reassuring, is not particularly surprising. The two qualities cited most often in all three categories—*integrity* and *competence*—are perhaps the qualities most basic to doing a good job, regardless of the level of the person who exhibits them. These are the essential characteristics of effective leadership. In the language of sociology, such a person has referent and expert power. These kinds of power influence people's attitudes as well as their behaviors. *Cooperation* is as important to the supervisor as to the executive, and *leadership* is valued by those at the top as much as by those at the bottom of the organization chart.

Pressures on Managers

It has been noted that managers view ethical decisions through the prism of their own personal values.[10] However, the distinction between personal and organizational values often becomes blurred, especially the longer one stays with a particular organization and/or advances up the hierarchical ladder. Managers were asked whether or not they sometimes had to compromise their personal principles to conform to organizational expectations (see Figure 5). Predictably, top executives reported this to be an infrequent occurrence (20 percent). Pressures to conform or compromise were felt more strongly by middle managers (27 percent) and even more strongly at the supervisory manager's level (41 percent).

All managers, regardless of hierarchical level, however, believed that pressure to conform to organizational standards (Figure 6) was strong (73 percent) as opposed to weak (27 percent). The majority felt that this pressure was relatively constant (45 percent). Less than 1 person in 20 felt that

[10] Frederick Sturdivant and James Ginter, "Corporate Social Reponsiveness: Management Attitudes and Economic Performance," *California Management Review* 19 (1977), pp. 30–39.

Figure 6
Question: "I believe that pressure to conform to organizational standards is . . ." (Percentages)

		Supervisory Managers	Middle Managers	Executive Managers	Male Managers	Female Managers
A.	Relatively weak and	(28.4)	(26.2)	(26.2)	(40.3)	(22.6)
	staying the same	15.5	11.2	11.9	20.9	7.0
	Becoming weaker	3.4	3.3	3.9		4.7
	Becoming stronger	9.5	11.7	10.3	18.6	10.9
B.	Relatively strong and	(71.7)	(73.7)	(74.0)	(59.7)	(77.4)
	staying the same	45.3	42.1	42.1	21.7	48.4
	Becoming weaker	9.5	12.7	15.3	17.1	7.0
	Becoming stronger	16.9	18.9	16.6	20.9	21.9

pressures to conform to organizational standards were weak and getting weaker.

It is of some significance to note that female managers felt that pressures to conform were relatively stronger than did their male counterparts. Seventy-seven percent of the female managers (compared with less than 60 percent of the male managers) expressed this view. Moreover, more than twice as many male managers as female managers believed that these relatively strong pressures were now becoming weaker (17.1 percent versus 7.0 percent). Coupled with other comparisons (not reported here) a picture of female executives begins to take shape. It suggests that female managers feel under more pressure to conform to organizational demands in order to be successful than do their male counterparts. For instance, female managers were 40 percent more likely than male managers to report that work created stress in their personal lives. They also felt under significantly more obligation to attend job-related functions when they conflicted with home-related activities than did their male counterparts.[11]

Influences on Unethical Behavior

More than 20 years ago Raymond Baumhart surveyed over 1,500 *Harvard Business Review* readers about the factors that influenced an executive to make unethical decisions.[12] He found "the behavior of a man's superiors in the company" to be cited as the primary influence. This finding was replicated a few years ago in another survey of *HBR* readers: "The behavior of one's superiors is the primary guidepost for unethical behavior."[13] Our data continues to support this finding, regardless of a person's position or level in the organization (see Figure 7). "What is the boss doing?" remains the significant bellwether for subordinates about what is expected and accepted, and about how behavior will be evaluated or interpreted by those above them in the organization. Both male and female managers were similarly inclined in these patterns.

The importance of ethical standards by the boss is underscored by observ-

[11] Schmidt and Posner, *Managerial Values.*
[12] Raymond Baumhart, "How Ethical are Businessmen?" *Harvard Business Review,* July/ August 1961.
[13] Brenner and Mollander, "Is the Ethics."

Figure 7
**Question: "Listed below are factors that many believe influence unethical
behavior. Rank them in order of their influence or contribution to
unethical behaviors or actions by managers."***

	Current Study (N = 1443)	1977 Study† (N = 1227)	1961 Study‡ (N = 1531)
Behavior of superiors	2.17	2.15	1.9
Behavior of one's peers in the organization	3.30	3.37	3.1
The ethical practices of one's industry or profession	3.57	3.34	2.6
Society's moral climate	3.79	4.22	—§
Formal organizational policy (or lack thereof)	3.84	3.27	3.3
Personal financial need	4.09	4.46	4.1

* The ranking is calculated on a scale of 1 (most influential) to 6 (least influential).
† From Brenner and Mollander, *Harvard Business Review*.
‡ From Baumhart, *Harvard Business Review*.
§ This item was not included in the 1961 study.

ing the strength of their influence (pressure to conform) on subordinate actions. When asked: "Would you resign if your boss insisted that you carry out some action that you strongly felt was unethical?" nearly one in every four middle managers and one in every three supervisory managers reported that they were either "not sure" or that they probably *would not*. This finding points out that subordinate managers are indeed vulnerable and susceptible to the influences of their superior, even when they feel the request is definitely unethical.

Counsel for Ethical Dilemmas

In today's turbulent times, being able to talk with others about ethical concerns associated with the workplace provides perspective and comfort. Recent studies, for instance, note that levels of moral reasoning and judgment are likely to be higher when managers get together and discuss ethical issues than when these choices have to be made in solitude.[14] Whom do managers consult with for ethical guidance and support?

We presented our respondents with a list of people one might consult with when "confronted with an ethical dilemma in performing their job." The choices were: No one (I work it out myself), spouse, legal staff, friend at work, friend outside the organization, my boss (superior), a clergyman (minister, priest, rabbi), colleagues (other people at my level), and other. We asked for both their first and second choices (see Figure 8).

The responses indicate that when faced with an ethical dilemma, managers typically consult with their boss (25 percent). This is especially true for supervisory and middle level managers, and somewhat less true for executives. Of course, top executives are likely to feel that they are "*the* boss" and

[14] Mary Lippitt Nichols and Victoria Day, "A Comparison of Moral Reasoning of Groups and Individuals in the 'Defining Issues Test'," *Academy of Management Journal* 24, No. 1 (1982), pp. 201–8; Barry Posner, "Individual's Moral Judgement and Its Impact on Group Processes" (Paper presented at the national meetings of the Academy of Management, Dallas, 1983.

Figure 8
Question: "When you are confronted with an ethical dilemma in performing your job, whom do you usually consult?" (Percentages)

	Supervisory Managers	Middle Managers	Executive Managers	Male Managers	Female Managers
Boss (superior)	30.0	28.8	22.9	25.2	28.8
Spouse	21.2	23.2	24.5	27.0	18.8
Colleagues (other people at my level)	19.4	18.4	19.7	20.1	18.2
No one (work it out myself)	3.7	8.3	12.2	11.3	10.1
Friend (at work)	10.1	9.7	6.1	8.8	7.7
Friend (outside work)	12.0	5.3	5.5	3.1	12.5
Legal Staff	2.8	5.0	8.1	3.8	6.2
Clergyman	.9	1.2	1.1	.6	2.5

NOTE: Respondents were asked to rank order the two most important. The percentages shown reflect adding together the first and second choices.

less likely to feel that there is another "boss" for them to consult with. A second important source of guidance turned out to be the manager's spouse (24 percent). In fact, this was the first choice of executives. Another significant top choice of managers is the advice and counsel of colleagues (19 percent). This pattern was approximately the same for male and female managers.

It seems interesting that "colleagues" were reported to be an important source of counsel while "friend," either at work or outside the organization, was selected less often as the source of advice. Perhaps this is because we expect more objectivity from our colleagues than we do our friends. Or, perhaps we feel that our friends, even at work, are not familiar enough with our dilemmas to offer realistic advice. We may be less likely to reveal to our friends the ethical dilemmas we face for fear of seeming to be incompetent or indecisive. It should be noted that female managers discussed ethical dilemmas with friends outside of work far more than did their male counterparts (12.5 percent as compared to 3.1 percent). This probably arises because the number of female colleagues (friends) *within* any one organization is unlikely to be very large, thus forcing women to look outside of the organization to friends for help.

"Working it out by myself" was a response often selected by top executives. This may reflect a sense of not having a boss to talk things over with, or their general feeling that wrestling with tough choices is part of their job. Middle managers, and particularly supervisory managers, were less likely to select this alternative. A similar pattern of responses along hierarchical lines was evident for managers in their consultations with the legal staff.

It might be argued that the nature of the ethical dilemmas associated with performing a job varies dramatically at different levels in the organization. It is probably *more* true to say that these dilemmas vary by degree but not by kind. After all, the issues of honesty and dealing fairly with people, the trade-offs between loyalty to the organization and responsibility to the general public, or the dilemma of representing the interests of subordinates when they conflict with the desires of superiors, are as real at the supervisory levels as they are in the executive suite.

Managerial Values: Some Tentative Conclusions

- Being (or becoming) an *effective* organization is the central goal for most managers. Being productive and efficient, having high morale, providing leadership, and maintaining a positive reputation may be the means to this end.

- Profit maximization and stockholders, contrary to popular opinion and stereotypes, are not the central focus of managers. In the relative scheme of important goals and stakeholders, attention to the public at large, or government, is also not very substantial.

- American managers have not, in general, lost sight of the importance of the customer. Top executives well recognize that attention to the customer is likely to ensure healthy (and effective) organizations.

- Integrity is the personal characteristic or quality rated most highly by managers at all levels. Subordinates want their bosses to demonstrate integrity. Bosses, in turn, admire subordinates with integrity. And when we look to our colleagues the characteristic of integrity is also paramount. While at times it may seem difficult to be truthful, or to stick to one's convictions, doing so is likely to be more than its own reward. The essence of "charismatic" leadership is managers with integrity. Most of us follow more readily one whose values are clear, consistent, principled, and fair. These are, as well, the characteristics that managers look for and admire in those who work with, and for, them.

- Managers perceive that pressures to conform to organizational standards are strong (and very few see these pressures diminishing). And, accordingly, the vast majority of managers believe that unethical behavior is largely dependent on the organizational climate—especially the action's of one's immediate boss and peers.

- Spouses play a significant role in helping their managerial mates think about ethical dilemmas. Their importance, however, seems to be largely an invisible phenomenon and probably warrants more direct examination. Perhaps spouses should be included when business leaders study issues of business ethics?

- Few managers attempt to wrestle with ethical dilemmas all by themselves, alone and without the advice and counsel of others. This is important because research evidence suggests that levels of moral reasoning are likely to be higher in group decisions versus individual deliberations. Organizations, like individuals, need the perspective of others (e.g., outside board members) to ensure that broader perspectives are applied to problems.

These are some of our tentative conclusions to the question "what have we learned about managers and their values?" It is apparent that the topic is complex and the data is not always entirely consistent. However, this is a subject where investigation and dialogue help to illuminate hidden and neglected assumptions while raising and clarifying our consciousness in the process.

What this article is about: This article provides a step-by-step guide outlining the actions that can be taken before, during, and after the strategy review session in order to ensure the success of an organization's strategic planning.

4–10 How to strengthen your strategy review process*

Ram Charan

Ram Charan is an independent management consultant based in Dallas, Texas.

Thank God it's over; now let's get back to work. This is my third strategy review. Same damn outcome. Nothing resolved. Every year we get together, fill in the forms—some of which don't even fit my business (and the planning instruction manual gets thicker by the year), make a 2½-hour slide presentation. We never get to the strategic issues. The discussion gets bogged down in nitpicking and number crunching, then we simply run out of time. Nobody really cares what's in the strategic plans. We must put on a good show, appear to be innovative, and go through the ritual. What really counts is the one-year operating budget.

> —*A divisional manager of an $8 billion in sales diversified multinational company*

We've had the strategic planning process in our company for almost five years, but we seem to find most divisional five-year plans all format and no substance. . . . Most show the hockey stick effect—down the first two years, promising superb performance over the next three years—regardless of whether it's boom or recession. . . . Year in, year out, the plans we get are unrealistic.

> —*A chief executive officer of a $15 billion non-U.S. multinational company*

Strategic planning has come of age. Most companies have it. Their planning processes may be in different phases of evolution,[1] but almost all

---

[1] Frederick W. Gluck, Stephen P. Kaufman, and A. Steven Walleck, "Strategic Management for Competitive Advantage," *Harvard Business Review*, July–August 1980, p. 155.

have a "review process," almost always conducted annually. Yet observations over the last several years clearly indicate that far too often the strategic review process is ineffective. Neither those who are being reviewed nor those who are doing the reviewing are happy. A lot of costly effort is put into preparation for the strategy review meeting. But cost aside, it is the mental frustration from such ineffective annual rituals that diverts managerial energy from other productive effort. A divisional general manager from a $4 billion company laments:

There are just too many people sitting around the table. Sometimes I wonder whether they even understand my business. Some of them never say a word. They certainly don't know my plan until I present it in the boardroom. Then the planners, the bright young people who "can analyze but can't do" lead the discussion of the plan. It is utterly frustrating. It's a waste of time for so many people. . . . Meetings in this company always start late—sometimes three to four hours late. Some of us have to fly in from over 1,000 miles away only to find the meeting is being postponed or being canceled altogether. . . . Very unproductive indeed.

Despite the intimate involvement of the chief executive in the strategy review, why is the process so often ineffective? The answer to this question is crucial, for the strategy review is really the most critical element in determining the success of the planning process and the implementation of its outcome. It sets the direction for the company; what is presented by a reviewee next year will depend upon what happens in the review meeting this year. The quality of the review process sets the tone and shapes management culture. The review can raise valuable questions: How can the substance of the plan be improved, what are the strategic issues, and how are they going to be managed? What actions are to be taken? What is different from what was proposed last year, and why? Should the review even take place every year for every division in a slavish manner?

The strategy review has enormous potential for contributing to the effectiveness of a business as a whole. But it involves, in many cases, looking at the review process in a fresh light, as a vital and flexible process rather than merely an annual rite. Some companies have broken with the tradition of the "annual review" and have maintained consistently high performance. Strategic issues become incorporated into the operating plan and quarterly operating reviews. In the process, actual review time is cut in half. A divisional general manager in one such company says: "Morale is high. Our strategic planning is now continuous. I am not sure we have to go through the traditional planning cycle every year. Why not every two years, formally? After all, one has to evaluate the cost of changing a strategy annually."

Perhaps this particular system cannot work in every company, but what are some basic elements of such a successful review process? This article will provide a framework for analytically examining the cycle of the strategic planning process, and the review process in particular. It will analyze the components of the strategy review process and develop suggestions for the chief executive, the corporate planning department, and the reviewee.

This analysis is based on longitudinal observations over the last eight years of several U.S. and foreign companies, ranging from $100 million to $25 billion in sales. Most of these companies are diversified multinationals, with several organizational hierarchies, where incentives are strongly tied to short-term performance. (See Figure 1.)

The Many Purposes of the Strategy Review

On first reflection, the purpose of a strategic review is obvious: to evaluate a business strategy for its validity and reality, testing it against the corporate goals, resource availability, and general strategic framework (assuming, of course, that top management has already developed its directions in these terms). On further reflection, some other common purposes of the strategy review are:

To ensure that the divisional general manager knows that the CEO knows that the general manager knows the business.

To evaluate the trade-offs general managers make in a changing environment—their risk-taking attitudes, their emphasis on long-term versus short-term goals, and the realism of their perception of the changes in cost and competitive patterns, particularly in an inflationary environment.

There are several other purposes, not usually explicitly articulated, and frequently unnoticed, which are at play nevertheless:

To forge a contract between top management and divisional management, whereby corporate management becomes committed to a certain resource allocation and the divisional general manager to delivering certain results. Subsequent reviews, whether annual or quarterly, provide for monitoring and follow-up of this agreement.

Figure 1
Closing the loop: The vital role of the strategy review process

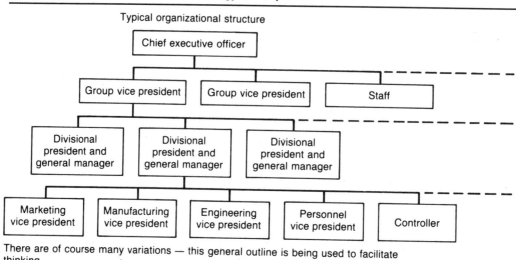

There are of course many variations — this general outline is being used to facilitate thinking.

To negotiate and integrate strategic issues among interdependent divisions—especially critical in organizations which operate in some form of matrix structure.

To broaden the scope of knowledge of all participants, including the chief executive. As one CEO put it: "The review forum could be the best device for education in realistic strategic thinking, business school seminars on the topic notwithstanding."

To provide a forum, sometimes hidden, but nonetheless real, where not only reviewers, but reviewees as well, can (and usually do) evaluate fellow executives' intellectual mettle, motivation, and attitudes.

The accomplishment of the above objectives depends not only on what happens during the review itself but on what takes place throughout the year—preparation of strategic plans, prereview analysis, preparation for the review session, postreview follow-up, and linkage of strategic priorities with the annual operating budget. (See Figure 2.) It is necessary to examine the various components of the strategic planning process to see how they can contribute most effectively to successful review and implementation.

Figure 2
Closing the loop: The vital role of the strategy review process

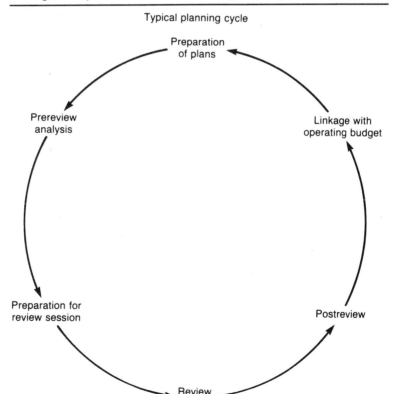

Typical planning cycle

Preparation of plans

Prereview analysis

Linkage with operating budget

Preparation for review session

Postreview

Review session

Preparing the Plans

The content of a strategic plan, length, techniques, and format notwith-standing, sets the basis for the quality of the review. The "planning exercise" in many companies involves a frustrating attempt to fill in stan-dardized forms designed by consulting firms or planners who may have never run a business. The plan must address the substance of the business, as only those who are running it know it.

Business have been built—and are being built—by asking a set of very fundamental questions; after all, a business is a business, regardless of its complexity. Although the questions are very basic, the answers must be specific, not lost in techniques and jargon, and reduced to a clarity and simplicity that decision-makers who may not be intimately familiar with the details of a particular business can comprehend. One such set of questions, tested on business strategies worldwide over the last 10 years, is as follows[2]:

Where are we now? Where are we taking the business?

How are we going to position our business vis-à-vis the competition and the marketplace as a whole?

How are we going to get there? What risk/reward consequences are we willing to take?

What critical operating actions are to be taken this year, by when and by whom, in order to implement the chosen strategy?

What are the attractive strategic alternatives for us? For our critical (not necessarily largest) competitors?

What major environmental assumptions (no more than six) will have an impact on our business? In the form of an integrated scenario, how will they affect *(a)* markets and market segments, *(b)* competition and industry structure, *(c)* fundamental cost structure in the business, and, if relevant *(d)* the structure and source of supply of key raw materials.

These questions have been tested on a wide range of some 300 businesses across the globe and are applicable to any business and any level—divi-sional, group, or corporate. The precise format and substance will vary from business to business and level to level, as will the relative importance of the questions—although questions 3 and 4 are very crucial questions, without which the exercise is shallow. Question 3 requires the strategist to define for a given strategic shift what changes in functional policies are required—for example, shifting policies between make and buy or between using manufac-turer's representatives and using a direct sales force. Question 4, the bottom line in strategic planning, is the derivative of question 3; here one spells out what critical actions need to be taken this year to implement the necessary changes in functional policies. The answer to question 4 determines the actions to be taken, assigns responsibility, provides for accountability, and forces the strategist to make an explicit trade-off between operating priorities

---

[2] For a more complete development of these six key questions, please see box "Framework for Strategic Thinking."

and the short-term actions required by chosen strategic priorities. Without this focus, short-term operating goals can continually postpone the critical short-term actions necessary for the implementation of a strategic plan. The purpose of five-year planning is not to cast in concrete what one will do five years hence. The purpose is to determine, after having thought through the possibilities, what to do this year which will maximize the chances of one's getting where one wants to be five years hence, considering the risks and reward consequences one is willing to take.

How many pages should it take to answer these six questions, regardless of business or level (leaving the data base aside)? Corporate-level management of one $15 billion company has answered the questions in six pages of text, with three pages of statistical exhibits. Another company has a rule that no strategy document will be read if it exceeds 20 pages (10 pages of text and 10 pages of exhibits, 4 of which are standardized). Thinking the strategic issues through, distilling them clearly, and developing realistic concrete actions are the central requirements of strategic thinking. The format, the forms, the tonnage of data, and the techniques may be helpful, but only as a supplement to incisive strategic thinking. The corporate planning instruction manual must demand substance and clarity from the divisions preparing their plans, while remaining flexible with regard to format.

To ensure successful implementation, the plan must have the commitment of those who will be implementing it. It must be prepared with the total involvement of the various divisional functional managers. Observations clearly show that plans made solely by the divisional general manager and/or the divisional staff planner are less realistic and have a smaller chance of being implemented effectively.

Prereview Analysis

Once the plan is completed, the corporate planning department can play a critical role in ensuring that the review will be conducted to its maximum potential. A great deal of sweat and pain goes into the preparation of divisional strategic plans, and reviewees, whether they say so or not, are quite disheartened when superficial treatment is given to their plan in a review. The corporate planning department can contribute immensely to the review process by analyzing and evaluating ahead of time the substance of the proposed plan and developing, in conjunction with the divisional general manager and any other relevant sources, the set of strategic issues that will form the central themes of the actual strategy review. These efforts should culminate in a one-page critique of the plan.

In evaluating a divisional strategic plan, the purpose is not to judge the document itself, but where it proposes to take the business, and why, and how. In critiquing the plan, the corporate planner checks for internal consistency and realism of goals and suggested actions, and tests the plan against the overall corporate framework of goals, available resources, and the interrelationships with other organizational units. The planning department has the opportunity during this analysis to discover what critical information is lacking in the document, get the required data from the division, and thus prevent the lack of information from causing bottlenecks during the review itself. If the review is to be constructive, it should not get hung up on minutiae.

The One-Page Critique

The one-page critique essentially requires the synthesis of the maximum five or six strategic issues which will be the focus of the review meeting (bearing in mind the time that will be allotted—usually between two and six hours). To be effective in their critique, more planners need to understand some critical elements of the business under review. ''We'll approve the goals and policies and let the division work out how to put them into effect'' has been a catchphrase for far too long. The divisional general manager has already thought through the strategic issues and how they will be resolved and implemented. Strategy formulation and implementation must be appraised simultaneously. Some actions required by the strategy could easily involve highly sensitive areas (e.g., changes in people and work force). The corporate planner should understand these implications. A few visits to the division prior to the strategy review might be very useful in providing the necessary information, as well as being effective on a human dimension.

One must bear in mind that a proposed strategic plan is very much a function of who is proposing it—their experiences, values, biases, and, sometimes, what they perceive the key reviewer (i.e., the CEO) wants. It is the role of the corporate planner to ensure intellectual honesty and not compromise on the five or six chosen issues as the central focus of the review meeting. The corporate planner decides on those that may require validation from outside or inside sources—other corporate divisions, such as research and development—eliminates minor issues, and makes necessary modifications but no compromises on the central issues.

It should be noted that although the role being proposed for the planning department is a strong one, it is still advisory in nature, a staff function rather than a line function. The degree of involvement will vary from company to company, but the planning department and the divisions must work together; the planning department should do all it can to help divisional general managers improve performance. For no matter how good the plan or the planning department, what really counts in the long run is performance. Seeking out knowledge about the divisions' business, maintaining intellectual honesty, and knowing the divisional people are all essential to the corporate planning department in creating a useful one-page critique for the review meeting. Divisional managers, while tending to remain silent, clearly judge the quality and value added of the planning department by activities such as divisional plan critiques. Even when they disagree with the planner's analysis, they do respect incisiveness and practicality.

Preparation for the Strategy Review Session

The Planning Department   Planning for the review session requires the planning department to critique the plan, plot the agenda, and determine (with the concurrence of the CEO and with the knowledge of the divisional general manager) who should attend the meeting and what is expected of them. The planning department should clarify with the CEO the final sequencing and time allotment for the agenda of agreed-upon strategic issues and how the meeting should commence and close. The planner openly discusses the proposed agenda with the divisional general manager and the list of other attendees, including the divisional staff. Full communication between the division and the corporate planning department is important—unnecessary surprises in the meeting are counterproductive and block communication between the division and the planning department in the long run.

One logistical point in planning for a review meeting, or any meeting, is frequently overlooked—breaks need to be prescheduled at appropriate points. Concentration of the group is important, and frequent comings and goings and telephone interruptions disrupt this concentration.

Finally, in preparing for the review session, the planner must plot time allocation not only to provide sufficient time for each issue, regardless of whether it is slated as first or last, but also to allow for a closure. A good number of strategy reviews simply never have a definitive closure; a disproportionate amount of time is lost on the first issue, and then the group runs out of time. Without an ending statement of what has been agreed upon, approved, tabled, and scheduled for further discussion and a determination of when the further discussion will be, the effectiveness of a meeting is left hanging.

The Attendees Preparation should be required from all attendees as well. The slide-show strategy review, a current practice of many companies, usually requires no prior preparation, and this has serious limitations. As the participants have no chance for preanalysis of the proposed material, the presentation tends to drag on and get sidetracked as attendees interrupt for clarification (with not only time, but coherence of thought, getting lost). Further, oral presentations can only be made linearly. The presenter is conditioning the sequence of thought processes. The attendees lack the opportunity to look back and forth, evaluate the total plan, reflect, and synthesize key issues before asking their questions.

Clearly, it seems that more productive feedback will result when all participants are prepared. One company requires every attendee (except, of course, the divisional staff under review) to submit to the CEO a one-page critique, with the three to five strategic issues thought crucial to the division's business. (The reviewers receive the plan document several days prior to the meeting.) The chief executive of this company enthusiastically supports this practice. It not only improves the quality and effectiveness of the review itself but also helps in training specialists and line and staff managers in strategic thinking. Each executive has to read, digest, and analyze strategic materials to identify key issues—these skills are bound to be transferred to his normal job. The executives also have an opportunity to broaden their perspectives by learning what other managers thought the key issues were. This process creates an environment in which one can be "brutally honest" and force the hidden agendas out into the open—ideas of those mentioned earlier who "never say a word" necessarily do emerge. Finally, this active participation encourages the thoughtful integration of strategic actions among interdependent divisions.

Another company uses a combination of the above two active/passive approaches. This extremely successful high-technology company believes that its engineer-managers find it painful to write coherent English prose and are more at home with "one-liners" on slides. The reviewers, therefore, go in "cold" to a slide presentation, watch, listen, and ask questions. Then they return a week or two later, and the actual review is conducted. The finally approved two-to-six page plans and critical action priorities are required in proper prose form.

The Chief Executive   Finally, to be successful, any meeting requires preparation from its chairman. This holds true for the strategy review—one hour of thorough preparation by the chief executive is worth several hundred man-hours of effort by all other attendees. The CEO, too, must prepare his five or six strategic issues for discussion, as well as his opening remarks and his sequencing of issues. One CEO allocates an hour prior to the review session to meet with the planner and go over the one-page critiques received from the other reviewers. He then writes down the four to six strategic issues to focus on. He is prepared; he leads rather than reacts.

Conduct of the Review Session Itself

If all participants in a review meeting arrive prepared, the conduct of the review requires merely the orchestration of effective communication on central issues and determination of the disposition of those issues. Every CEO has his own style, but certain universals emerge which seem to improve the productivity of the review session. These may appear very basic but, like all basics, are very important and surprisingly easy to forget.

Set a standard of punctuality. Tardiness cuts down not only on time and productivity but also on the inclination of the group as a whole to do disciplined listening and thinking.

Set the tone. Demand constructive thinking from reviewees and reviewers alike.

Keep the discussion focused on the central issues. Probe for actionable items, push for realism, and question buzzwords (e.g., get "My strategy is to be the dominant competitor at the lowest cost with internally generated funds" translated into quantifiable terms and concrete actions).

Keep an eye on the time, stick to the time allocation, summarize each issue, and move on to the next.

Ensure that the attendees are listening to one another, that the environment is conducive to the group's debating both sides of an issue.

As stated before, and it merits reiteration, the review session needs a closure, a summary in which the status of issues and actions is clearly spelled out. In one company, the CEO ends by first reviewing all one-page critiques prepared by other reviewers earlier. He checks that no major issues have been omitted from the discussion and in the process has the chance to compliment individuals showing unusual insight. He then asks each participant individually if, in his judgment, all issues have been covered. The divisional general manager is then asked to summarize what was approved, what is to be done, by when and by whom. (Initially, in this company, it was a shock when one divisional general manager recited at the end of the review exactly what he had proposed originally, disregarding the six hours of discussion. Still the process was responsible for raising valuable questions: Is this manager simply inflexible? Or perhaps just lacking the information needed to make convincing a basically sound plan? Should the CEO have been more sensitive during the meeting and have realized that the general manager was not following the tone of the discussion?)

Notes on the summary are taken by the CEO, the planner, the divisional staff, and managers from interdependent divisions. The CEO clarifies the summary, noting what interdivisional issues should be worked on jointly and discussed in subsequent reviews. More than likely, there will be issues still pending resolution; as far as possible, the status of these should be spelled out as well. The review thus ends with a tangible output and basis for action.

Behind Closed Doors

If certain issues cannot be discussed in the larger group (as is often the case), a smaller meeting immediately following the review should be an integral part of the review process. The divisional general manager, the chief corporate human resources officer, and the group vice president meet with the CEO to review in detail the implications the chosen strategy has for human resources. The CEO can approve which key concrete actions are to be taken, and a page of the agreed-upon items is prepared by the divisional general manager, the human resources officer, and the group vice president. Such a page is an important reference in reviewing progress as the year rolls out.

Linking Strategic Plans and Operating Budgets

The two one-page outputs—one from the review session and one from the smaller meeting—are refined by the divisional general manager into one page. After approval by the CEO and the group vice president, this becomes the first page of the annual operating plan (or budget). During the approval phase of the annual operating plan, essentially the same review process, this page serves as an effective link between strategic planning and operating realities. The monthly or quarterly operating review will now provide the CEO with an ample opportunity to probe and monitor a division's progress on agreed-upon strategic operating priorities. The corporate departments involved—corporate planning, human resources—compile all divisional and departmental outputs and synthesize them to draw out corporate issues and actions requiring monitoring and/or implementation. The issues that still require further work can be taken up at the time the annual operating plans are being approved.

The loop is closed; strategic thinking and operating actions are now moving in tandem, rather than linearly. The two are, after all, not discrete activities. In companies where this linkage has been implemented, it has been of great help to the corporate staff and the chief executive in keeping abreast of the divisions' business. If any agreed-upon item is not being

Framework for strategic thinking

1. *Where are we now? Where are we taking the business?*

Define the answer to the second part of this question in terms of:

a. Qualitative shifts in the character of the business.
b. Internally consistent financial measures, such as return on equity, cash flow, capital structure, market share, growth rates for revenue and earnings per share, and the like.

2. *How are we going to position our business vis-à-vis the competition and the marketplace as a whole?*

Explicitly articulate your view of what the industry structure, nature of competition, and market segmentation are now and what they will be several years hence, based on available knowledge. What implications does this view have for your business? How will the position of your business relative to the competition change over the plan period? Market segmentation is a particularly critical area to think through in this question.

Many plans are found wanting on this point. It requires not only an analysis of the present competition but some educated guesswork regarding the formation of new coalitions among existing competitors (e.g., American Express and Shearson Loeb Rhoades) or the emergence of new, nontraditional competitors. And "positioning" is often mistaken for market share. Positioning is defined in relation to the overall market segmentation and, while relative to the competition—as is market share—takes into account such factors as relative quality, relative price, relative control of channels, relative cost of production, and the like. Decisions now with regard to positioning can affect market share in the future.

3. *How are we going to get there?*

Implementation of the answers to questions 1 and 2 normally requires some policy changes affecting one or more functional areas: marketing, manufacturing, R&D, product mix, product development, financial policy, personnel, organizational structure, and organizational culture. What will these changes be?

Trade-offs and issues of resource allocation among functional areas must be clearly resolved at this stage. Far too often, divisions do not think these issues through, and they then get resolved incrementally, undermining the very aim of strategic thinking—to synthesize basic issues and develop a coherent blueprint from which to proceed.

4. *What critical operating actions are to be taken this year, by when and by whom, in order to implement the chosen strategy?*

This question translates the policies outlined in question 3 into reality. A strategic plan which contains no concrete actions to be taken in the first one-year operating period is probably not thought through and runs serious risks of being unrealistic at its core. Without these critical operating actions, the rest of the plan cannot be implemented. They usually number around 10 or 12, but in any case, the summary of these actions should fit on one page.

If it had been decided in question 3 that the marketing effort would be shifted totally during the plan period, from a system of manufacturer's representatives to direct selling, what will have to be done in the first year to ensure the realization of this goal? The total shift cannot be made successfully in one year—what is the crucial first step, without which the rest of the plan will not move? For example, what kind of people will have to be hired the first year?

Almost all critical actions involve task assignment and changes in resources allocation, people, or task force. The strategic actions may not (and usually do not) contribute to operating profits the first year. It is for this reason that the explicit trade-offs made here are critical, for without this focus strategic priorities are too often pushed aside by short-term operating goals.

5. *What are the attractive strategic alternatives for us? For our critical competitors?*

Identify critical competitors, existing and potential, and their attractive strategic alternatives. Any competitor has a theoretically infinite number of alternatives, but in reality the attractive and plausible alternatives are indeed limited—by resources, people in power, and past history.

Most strategic plans have a "Strengths and Weaknesses" section. This type of assessment is often viewed simply as an exercise of plugging lists into the appropriate places, with an overbalance of strengths shown for the division in question and an overbalance of weaknesses for the competition.

"Strengths" and "weaknesses," however, are not absolute. They are relative—to the competition and to market opportunities and threats. One must go beyond a simple description of facts to incisive and judgmental inferences about the future. To be sure, one cannot always predict exactly what a competitor will do, but no competitor with more than 500 employees can implement a strategic shift fully without sending periodic signals to competitors, customers, suppliers, and distributors. Thoughtful answers to this question can better prepare a manager to detect shifts in a competitor's strategy. By detecting a competitive shift early enough, one is in a position oneself to shape the rules of the game.

6. *What major (no more than six) environmental assumptions—political, economic, technological, global, social, etc.—will have an impact on our business in the future? In the form of an integrated scenario, how will they affect:* (a) *markets and market segments,* (b) *competition and industry structure,* (c) *fundamental cost struc-*

> *tures in the business, and* (d) *if relevant, the structure and source of supply of key raw materials?*
>
> These environmental assumptions should be trends that are very fundamental and very durable, ones that will continue to affect your business significantly for some time to come. If a high inflation rate persists, how can you make a profit given that inflation?
>
> No one has facts about the future, and though management may seek help from economists, sociologists, futurologists, and the like, management itself must do the disciplined, integrated thinking in deducing the evolving patterns of markets, competition, and costs. The purpose is not to forecast events right on the nose; it is to test a number of strategic alternatives vis-à-vis the one for our key competitors and deduce which environmental assumption is the key. How can we monitor it, or more, how can we influence it?
>
> The questions posed above can be used in any sequence desired. The questions do not in any way emphasize one technology or another, but constitute a framework to structure strategic thinking in a precise fashion. The emphasis is on the quality and specificity of thought, on distilling the data and ideas into a clear and useful plan.

implemented, why not? What should be done? The linkage eliminates a lot of unnecessary pain, but, further, it encourages involvement and understanding of the division's business on the part of the corporate staff.

If, then, strategy and operations are integrated functions and are reviewed simultaneously, it is natural to raise a question touched on earlier: Is an annual strategy review necessary? A divisional general manager must always be trying to anticipate what is coming which will have an effect on the business; he may have to change the strategy tomorrow or not for several years. Yet the strategy must be durable, for there is a tangible cost in shifting it every year. In some companies, a full-fledged strategic plan is developed every two years, and specific qualitative issues are tackled in alternate years; for example, focus on the analysis of competition this year, because it was weak in last year's discussion.

This is not a solution for everyone, however, and one must be careful in initiating such a change. Two conditions should be met before it is possible to reconsider the yearly review. The first, as one chief executive expresses it, is that "the managers have become 'well blooded' in the process and think and manage in an action-oriented framework." The second is that the composition of the management team involved in planning maintains a very high degree of stability from year to year. If the membership of the planning team changes dramatically from year to year, the annual review has an irreplaceable value in fostering a broader perspective among the newcomers and in developing shared perceptions and commonly understood strategic actions.

Some Concluding Observations

In our turbulent business environment, the importance of strategic management is beyond debate. Corporations must have durable strategies which permit active, flexible responses to shifting environmental opportunities and threats. Successful strategic management requires that no plan can be properly evaluated or approved until the "nuts-and-bolts" implementation implications have been thought through. The review process has enormous potential for the integration of strategy and operating realities, both in the way the process itself is carried out and in linking its outputs to the annual operating plans. Most companies have mechanisms in place which allow for the establishment of this integration.

Short-term operating performance so often pushes aside long-term priorities, and we can no longer afford shortsightedness. The type of review and monitoring process described encourages managers to make viable trade-offs between short- and long-term goals. This could be strengthened further by instituting compensation criteria which reflect demands of the chosen strategies and reward prudent risk takers building for the long term by taking appropriate short-term actions.

It will be necessary to look at the implications the strengthened review process has for the corporate staff. Will the corporate planning department require new people? Where will they be gotten? How long should they stay in the same planning function? The involvement of the human resources department has been mentioned. Should, in fact, the chief corporate human resources officer be able to understand and actively contribute to strategy evaluation and implementation? Managers at all levels may have to become "well blooded" in the strategic management process.

Finally, we must remember, above all, that the purpose of planning is not the elegance of the process or the techniques. The purpose is to improve performance. Planning exercises must culminate in implementable decisions and actions which can be monitored and rewarded. If the planning process in your company does not meet these criteria, the probability is high that you need to reexamine the total process. This article provides one framework that should be useful in doing so.

The key is in doing. Thinking is necessary, but insufficient in itself. It is well known that the Japanese excel in doing more than in the elegance of their techniques and process, and their success is beyond question. The realism imposed by doing does influence the choice of strategies and the quality of creative thinking. This is the challenge that American managers must face.